The Global 1989

1989 signifies the collapse of Soviet communism and the end of the Cold War, a moment generally recognised as a triumph for liberal democracy and when capitalism became global. *The Global 1989* challenges these ideas. An international group of prominent scholars investigate the mixed, paradoxical and even contradictory outcomes engendered by these events, unravelling the intricacies of this important moment in world history. Although the political, economic and cultural orders generated have, for the most part, been an improvement on what was in place before, this has not always been clear-cut: 1989 has many meanings, many effects and multiple trajectories. This volume leads the way in defining how 1989 can be assessed both in terms of its world historical impact and in terms of its contribution to the shape of contemporary world politics.

GEORGE LAWSON is Lecturer in International Relations at the London School of Economics and Political Science.

CHRIS ARMBRUSTER is the founder and Executive Director of the Research Network 1989. He also tracks the evolution of digital scholarly communication for the Max Planck Society at the Max Planck Digital Library.

MICHAEL COX is Chair in International Relations at the London School of Economics and Political Science and Co-Director of 'Ideas', a centre for diplomacy and strategy at the LSE.

The Global 1989

Continuity and Change in World Politics

Edited by

George Lawson
London School of Economics

Chris Armbruster
Max Planck Society

Michael Cox
London School of Economics

CAMBRIDGE
UNIVERSITY PRESS

CAMBRIDGE
UNIVERSITY PRESS

Shaftesbury Road, Cambridge CB2 8EA, United Kingdom

One Liberty Plaza, 20th Floor, New York, NY 10006, USA

477 Williamstown Road, Port Melbourne, VIC 3207, Australia

314–321, 3rd Floor, Plot 3, Splendor Forum, Jasola District Centre, New Delhi – 110025, India

103 Penang Road, #05–06/07, Visioncrest Commercial, Singapore 238467

Cambridge University Press is part of Cambridge University Press & Assessment, a department of the University of Cambridge.

We share the University's mission to contribute to society through the pursuit of education, learning and research at the highest international levels of excellence.

www.cambridge.org
Information on this title: www.cambridge.org/9780521147910

First published 2010

A catalogue record for this publication is available from the British Library

Library of Congress Cataloging-in-Publication data
The global 1989 : continuity and change in world politics / edited by
    George Lawson, Chris Armbruster, Michael Cox.
        p. cm.
    Includes bibliographical references and index.
    ISBN 978-0-521-76124-6 (hardback) – ISBN 978-0-521-14791-0 (pbk.)
    1. Nineteen eighty-nine, A.D.   2. World politics–1985–1995.
    I. Lawson, George, 1972–   II. Armbruster, Chris, 1969–
    III. Cox, Michael, 1947–   IV. Title.
    E860.G646 2010
    909.82′8–dc22
    2010024612

ISBN   978-0-521-76124-6   Hardback
ISBN   978-0-521-14791-0   Paperback

For Fred Halliday (1946–2010)

Inspirational friend; debunker of myths

Contents

Figures

Tables

Contributors

CHRIS ARMBRUSTER was born in the American sector of Berlin. He is
the Executive Director of Research Network 1989 – a global network
dedicated to exploring the causes and consequences of 1989. In the
process of researching the history of the Soviet empire and the revolutions of 1989, Chris spent time at UJ Kraków, ELTE Budapest,
Uniwersytet Wrocławski, Novosibirsk State University and the EUI
(Florence). Chris also works for the Max Planck Society, exploring
changes in scholarly communication, research evaluation and scientific publishing.

MICHAEL COX is Professor of International Relations at LSE and
Co-Director of IDEAS – LSE's Centre for the study of Strategy and
Diplomacy. He previously taught at Queen's University, Belfast and
The Department of International Politics, Aberystwyth. Professor
Cox is the author, editor and co-editor of several books includ-
ing: *Superpowers at the Crossroads* (1990); *US Foreign Policy After the
Cold War* (1995); *Rethinking the Soviet Collapse* (1998); *The Eighty
Years Crisis* (1998); *The Interregnum: World Politics, 1989–1999* (1999);
American Democracy Promotion (2000); *E. H. Carr: A Critical Appraisal*
(2000); *The Twenty Years Crisis* (2001); *Empires, Systems and States*
(2002); *How Might We Live?* (2002); and an eight-volume work – *The
International Relations of the Twentieth Century* (2007). He is currently
collecting his most significant writings into two compendiums: *The
Rise and Fall of the American Empire* and *The United States and World
Order*.

LAURE DELCOUR is Senior Fellow in charge of European
Neighbourhood Policy, Russia and NIS countries at the Institute of
International and Strategic Relations in Paris, and a member of the
Centre of European Studies of the French School of Administration
(ENA). A political scientist and historian by training, she wrote her
doctoral dissertation at the Institute of Political Studies (Sciences-Po)
on the European Union's policy in Russia (2000). She has written

and taught extensively on EU policies, including enlargement, the European Neighbourhood Policy and EU–Russia relations. Dr Delcour has recently published *Pioneer Europe? Testing European Foreign Policy in the Neighbourhood* (with Elsa Tulmets, 2008).

MARC DEVORE received his doctorate from the Massachusetts Institute of Technology and is now a post-doctoral fellow at the Centre for Security Economics and Technology at the University of St Gallen. His first major study – 'Armed Forces, States and Threats: Civil–Military Institutions and Military Power in Modern Democracies' – explores the impact of civil–military relations on the production of military power in modern democracies. Dr DeVore has been the recipient of a number of prestigious awards including Fulbright and Truman Scholarships, and fellowships from MIT, Harvard, Columbia and the French government. In 2002–3, Dr DeVore served as the National Security Advisor of the Central African Republic.

BARBARA J. FALK is Associate Professor of the Canadian Forces College and Royal Military College of Canada, and teaches at the Munk Centre for Global Studies of the University of Toronto. Her first book, *The Dilemmas of Dissidence: Citizen Intellectuals and Philosopher-Kings* (2003), examines the role of non-violent dissent in the fall of communism. She is currently writing a book comparing Cold War political trials across the East–West divide.

FRED HALLIDAY was, until his death in April 2010, ICREA research professor at IBEI, the Barcelona Institute for International Studies. From 1985 to 2008 he was Professor of International Relations at LSE. His books include: *The Making of the Second Cold War* (1983); *Revolution and World Politics* (1999); *Two Hours That Shook the World* (2001); *The Middle East in International Relations* (Cambridge University Press, 2005); and *100 Myths About the Middle East* (2001).

JOHN M. HOBSON is Professor of Politics and International Relations at the University of Sheffield. His main research interest lies in the critique of Eurocentrism and the reconstruction of a non-Eurocentric historical-sociological account of globalisation and inter-civilisational relations, past and present. His two most recent books are *The Eastern Origins of Western Civilisation* (Cambridge University Press, 2004) and *Everyday Politics of the World Economy* (Cambridge University Press, 2007) (co-edited with Leonard Seabrooke). Professor Hobson is currently finishing two books: one on J. A. Hobson entitled *The*

Struggle for the International Mind (co-edited with Colin Tyler) and the other entitled *The Eurocentric Origins of International Relations.*

GEORGE LAWSON is Lecturer in International Relations at LSE, having previously taught at Goldsmiths, University of London. He is convenor of the British International Studies Association's working group on historical sociology and International Relations (www.historical-sociology.org) and author of *Negotiated Revolutions: The Czech Republic, South Africa and Chile* (2005), as well as articles in *Review of International Studies, International Studies Review, International Political Sociology, Political Studies, Millennium* and *International Politics.*

WILLIAM OUTHWAITE studied at the Universities of Oxford and Sussex, where he taught for many years, and is now Professor of Sociology at Newcastle University. Recent publications include *The Future of Society* (2006), *European Society* (2008) and *Social Theory and Postcommunism* (with Larry Ray, 2005). Professor Outhwaite is currently working on social and political change in Europe since 1989, supported by a Leverhulme Major Research Fellowship.

SASKIA SASSEN is Robert S. Lynd Professor of Sociology at Columbia University and Centennial Visiting Professor at the London School of Economics. Professor Sassen's research focuses on globalisation, immigration, global cities, and changes within the liberal state that result from current transnational conditions. In her research, she has focused on the unexpected and counterintuitive as a way to cut through established 'truths'. Major publications include: *The Mobility of Labor and Capital* (Cambridge University Press, 1988); *The Global City* (second edition 2001); and *Territory, Authority, Rights: From Medieval to Global Assemblages* (2008).

RICHARD SAULL is Senior Lecturer in International Politics at Queen Mary, University of London. His research focuses on the international relations of revolutions, the theorisation of the Cold War and, more recently, the nature of US power. He has written two books on the Cold War, *Rethinking Theory and History in the Cold War* (2001) and *The Cold War and After* (2007) and is currently working on an international historical sociology of the far-right.

AVIEZER TUCKER has held research positions at the Central European University, Columbia University, New York University and the Australian National University, and has taught at Charles University, CEVRO University, Palacky University, New York University and Trinity College. He is the author of: *The Philosophy and Politics of*

Czech Dissidence: From Patočka to Havel (2000); *Our Knowledge of the Past: A Philosophy of Historiography* (Cambridge University Press, 2004); and *The Legacies of Totalitarianism: A Political Theory of Post-Totalitarianism* (forthcoming).

ARNE WESTAD is Professor of International History at LSE and Co-Director of LSE IDEAS. Among Professor Westad's books are: *The Global Cold War* (Cambridge University Press, 2005); *Decisive Encounters* (2003); *Brothers in Arms* (1999); and *Cold War and Revolution* (1993). Professor Westad is one of the editors of the journal *Cold War History* and co-editor of the three-volume *Cambridge History of the Cold War*.

Acknowledgements

The manuscript for this book was completed in the week often understood to mark the twentieth anniversary of the events of '1989 and all that': the fall of the Berlin Wall on 9 November 1989. For the most part, the anniversary was well observed: former activists – now often politicians, academics and, on occasion, businesspeople – explained how concerted struggle from below had brought communism to its knees; many former Soviet leaders – none more so than Gorbachev himself – argued that they had played the decisive role in sowing the seeds for the communist collapse from above; while Western policy makers were not shy in reminding viewers, listeners and readers the extent to which they, and the West more generally, had created the necessary conditions for the demise of the communist system. Of course, all of these accounts contain a kernel of truth. The events of 1989 were a conjuncture of both long-term trends and short-term triggers, caused by both internal and external processes, and enabled by the agency of both state actors and civil society activists.

This book, however, does more than ask why state socialism ended in Eastern and Central Europe. Rather, it seeks to move debate on: from a focus on causes to an examination of consequences, and from a concentration on Europe to a canvass which embraces the whole world. The principal aim of this book is to ask whether it is legitimate to talk about there being a 'global 1989' by examining the extent to which major historical processes of capitalist expansion, state formation and development were slowed down, hurried along, or left relatively unaffected by the events of 1989. In short, we explore the world historical importance of 1989, focusing on the continuities and changes, complexities and uncertainties which have taken place in world politics over the past two decades. Along the way, the most important impacts of 1989 – favourable and unfavourable, intended and unintended – come into view.

The main message of the book is that 1989 changed many things in world politics, but not everything, not always for the better and not always in the ways – or order – in which these changes were intended.

Lurking behind this assessment is a broader message that the world is much more complex than our theories of it. And, in turn, behind this point is a sense in which dates and snapshots often serve to occlude rather than enlighten debates about world historical development. We all need shorthands – 1989 included – in order to simplify complex events and assess processes of continuity and change. But we also need to be aware of how these shorthands often mask more interesting dynamics which lie beneath the surface. Working on this project has been a reminder of the capacity of history to surprise and, more generally, of the fascination which comes from looking critically at particular historical moments. Of course, this book should not be read as any kind of final word on the subject; it does not seek a definitive reckoning of the world historical significance of 1989. All dates – and all histories – are works in motion. Rather, this book should be seen as a way-station on an altogether more winding journey, one born from the sense of exploration and engagement which lie at the heart of the intellectual imagination.

Although the final revisions to the manuscript were completed in November 2009, the origins of the book go back much further. Discussions about the project began in 2007, leading to a workshop at the London School of Economics in mid 2008 when first drafts of most of the papers which appear in this book were presented. Our thanks to Research Network 1989, LSE IDEAS and the International Relations Department at LSE for helping to organise and fund this event. Chapters were subjected to major editorial revisions before submission of the first draft of the manuscript in early 2009. Our thanks to the CUP assessors for their close reading of the text and for the robust, constructive way in which they approached assessment of it. We must also thank several people who read all, or part, of the manuscript along the way and whose comments, queries and occasional denunciations feature in its pages, most notably Toby Dodge, Paul Kirby, Ned Lebow, Luca Tardelli and the participants of a panel on 'The Global 1989' at the 2009 ISA convention in New York. It feels moderately unfair that the book is both substantively different and notably better because of the input of these silent partners. But we can at least acknowledge how grateful we are for the ways in which the peer review process and broader sites of scholarly exchange have resulted in a much better book than we could have produced on our own.

GEORGE LAWSON, MICHAEL COX AND CHRIS ARMBRUSTER

Abbreviations

ACP	Africa, Caribbean and Pacific Group of States
ANC	Africa National Congress
CFSP	Common Foreign and Security Policy
CIA	Central Intelligence Agency
CoD	Concert of Democracies
COMECON	Council for Mutual Economic Assistance
COP	Common Operational Picture
CPA	Coalition Provisional Authority
CPSU	Communist Party of the Soviet Union
CP USA	Communist Party of the USA
CSSR	Czechoslovak Socialist Republic
DARPA	Defense Advanced Research Projects Agency
DPG	Defense Planning Guidance
DPRK	Democratic People's Republic of Korea
EU	European Union
EC/EEC	European Community/European Economic Community
ELN	Ejército de Liberación Nacional (National Liberation Army)
EMU	Economic and Monetary Union
ENP	European Neighbourhood Policy
EPLF	Eritrean People's Liberation Front
ESDP	European Security and Defence Policy
ESS	European Security Strategy
EUBAM	European Union Border Assistance Mission to Moldova and Ukraine
EVP	Eesti Vasakpartei (Estonian Left Party)
FARC	Fuerzas Armadas Revolucionarias de Colombia (Revolutionary Armed Forces of Colombia)
FDI	Foreign Direct Investment

FRETILIN	Frente Revolucionária de Timor-Leste Independente (Revolutionary Front for an Independent East Timor)
FRELIMO	Frente de Libertação de Moçambique (Liberation Front of Mozambique)
FSLN	Frente Sandinista de Liberación Nacional (Sandinista National Liberation Front)
GDP	Gross Domestic Product
GDR	German Democratic Republic
GNP	Gross National Product
GPS	Global Positioning System
GWOT	Global War on Terror
HIPCs	Highly Indebted Poor Countries
IAEA	International Atomic Energy Agency
IEDs	Improvised Explosive Devices
IFIs	International Financial Institutions
IMF	International Monetary Fund
INC	Iraqi National Congress
INFs	Intermediate-Range Nuclear Forces
JDAM	Joint Direct Attack Munition
KGB	Komitet gosudarstvennoy bezopasnosti (Committee for State Security)
MPLA	Movimento Popular de Libertação de Angola – Partido do Trabalho (Popular Movement for the Liberation of Angola – Party of Labour)
MRAP	Mine Resistant Ambush Protected
MTR	Military-Technical Revolution
NATO	North Atlantic Treaty Organization
NDP	National Defense Panel
NGO	Non-Governmental Organisation
NICs	Newly Industrialised Countries
NKVD	Narodnyy Komissariat Vnutrennikh Del (People's Commissariat for Internal Affairs)
NPT	(Nuclear) Non-Proliferation Treaty
OECD	Organisation for Economic Co-operation and Development
OSCE	Organization for Security and Co-operation in Europe
PDPA	People's Democratic Party of Afghanistan
PDRY	People's Democratic Republic of Yemen
PDS	Partito Democratico della Sinistra (Italian Democratic Party of the Left)
PGMs	Precision Guided Munitions

PNAC	Project for a New American Century
RENAMO	Resistência Nacional Moçambicana (Mozambican National Resistance)
RMA	Revolution in Military Affairs
RPGs	Rocket-Propelled Grenades
SAP	Structural Adjustment Programme
SED	Sozialistische Einheitspartei Deutschlands (Socialist Unity Party of Germany)
SNP	Scottish National Party
SPD	Sozialdemokratische Partei Deustschlands (German Social Democratic Party)
SSR	Soviet Socialist Republic
SWAPO	South West Africa People's Organisation
TPLF	Tigrayan People's Liberation Front
UAVs	Unmanned Aerial Vehicles
UCAVs	Unmanned Aerial Combat Vehicles
UN	United Nations
UNDP	United Nations Development Programme
WAAM	Wide Area Antiarmor Munitions
WMD	Weapons of Mass Destruction
WSF	World Social Forum
WTO	World Trade Organization

Introduction: the 'what', 'when' and 'where' of the global 1989

George Lawson

Laughter and forgetting

One of the central motifs of Milan Kundera's *The Book of Laughter and Forgetting* (1980) is the ways in which the present works to distort the past and, in particular, how ideologues seek to control the present by manipulating the past. To that end, Kundera tells the story of a photograph taken of two leading Czech communists, Vladimír Clementis and Klement Gottwald, celebrating the takeover of state power by communists in Czechoslovakia in 1948. The picture was later doctored to remove Clementis, following charges brought against him for 'deviationism' and 'bourgeois nationalism'. The erasure of Clementis from the photograph temporarily removed one of the leading architects of the Czech post-war state from the country's history. Clementis was denounced, put on trial and, eventually, executed. In some ways, of course, the very everydayness of this episode is its most disturbing aspect. The routinisation of coercion within totalitarian states – the use of murder and imprisonment, the control of populations via vast coercive apparatuses, the establishment of insidious networks of corruption – was the norm rather than the exception. As such, the events of 1989 and the disappearance of what Daniel Chirot (1996) calls 'tyrannies of certitude' from most parts of Central and Eastern Europe are acts well worth celebrating.

Alongside the pronounced celebrations which marked the passing of state socialism in 1989 lies a second widely held view – that 1989 serves the *ur*-demarcation point in contemporary world politics. Indeed, both academics and policy-makers tend to use 1989 and its surrogate frames (such as Cold War/post-Cold War) as the principal normative, analytical and empirical shorthands for delineating past and present. And as with the celebrations over 1989 and its associated events, such abbreviations are made for often sound reasons. Not only was 1989 a significant event for those people living in the immediate Soviet sphere of influence, it had important ramifications for those inhabiting (now often former) socialist states around the world. Elsewhere, too, the events of 1989 served to disrupt existing patterns: the European Union saw its centre of gravity shift, at least to some extent, from west to east; recent years have seen a rise (or return) of Asian powers which may, in turn, prefigure a shift in the metageography of international politics from the Atlantic to the Pacific; and in the West itself, and in particular its fulcrum – the transatlantic alliance – the loss of the Soviet 'other' has engendered an overriding sense of anomie. No longer quite clear what it is against, the transatlantic alliance seems equally unclear about what it is for. Alongside this topographical shake-up can be found important intellectual challenges: how to conceptualise the primary fact of the post-Cold War order – US power; how to employ suitable normative frames for capturing issues of sovereignty, intervention and responsibility in the contemporary world; and how to comprehend a complex security climate signified by novel notions of war, shifting meanings of combatant/non-combatant, and the changing character of terrorism both by and against states. In short, it is nigh-on impossible to imagine a world without 1989 – there are few issues which appear untouched by it.

This book does not seek to overturn these two core assumptions – they stand as the principal indicators of the influence of 1989 and its associated processes. But the book does seek to question three issues which lie behind, or perhaps lurk beneath, their easy acceptance. First, although the events of 1989 are, to be sure, acts worthy of celebration, they have also engendered some unintended, yet important, consequences, perhaps most notable amongst them exposure of the chronic weaknesses contained in a hyperventilated form of liberal capitalism. One of the core wagers of this volume is that the collapse of communism and the end of the Cold War have produced mixed, paradoxical, even contradictory outcomes. Although the political, economic and cultural orders generated after the fall of communism have, for the most part, been an improvement on what was in place before, this has not always been clear-cut. Substantively – as the contributions to this volume make clear – 1989 has bequeathed an ambivalent legacy.

Second, although 1989 can serve as a useful barometer between old and new, we should be careful about the general utility of this shorthand – there have been considerable continuities between the pre- and post-1989 eras. Four chapters in this book make this point forcefully. John M. Hobson (Chapter 1) argues that policies of post-Cold War intervention should be seen as the latest exemplars of an older suite of ideas rooted in nineteenth-century Western international thought. Aviezer Tucker (Chapter 7) highlights the impact of totalitarian legacies on Russian and Chinese development since 1989, looking at how the restoration of autocratic rule in these countries has produced a ruling class of post-totalitarian *nomenklatura* which seeks to strip the country's assets rather than engage in contractual politics. Richard Saull's discussion of the Middle East (Chapter 8) argues that, by removing the one-dimensional straitjacket associated with Eurocentric thinking and replacing it with a view that embraces the chronic unevenness, multiplicity and complexity of world politics, we begin to see the importance of *local* patterns of development on *global* politics. In Chapter 2, Saskia Sassen points to the ways in which post-Cold War capitalist expansion constitutes a return to long-established exploitative practices, albeit on novel scales. In this way, a complex picture emerges in terms of the temporality of 1989, one which embraces important continuities alongside, and to some extent instead of, simple notions of 'all change'.

Third, although the principal events and effects of 1989 took place in Europe, the volume looks beyond this immediate zone of impact in order to explore the many spaces of the 'global 1989'. Laure Delcour (Chapter 6) indicates the ways in which 1989 has brought into question core aspects of European integration, while William Outhwaite (Chapter 3) concentrates on the crisis of the European left invoked by the loss of socialism as an 'actual existing alternative' to market democracy. Michael Cox (Chapter 4) widens this lens to investigate how the post-Cold War era has weakened the Western alliance, perhaps fatally. Fred Halliday (Chapter 5) goes further still in exploring the diverse impact of 1989 on the thirty-plus former allies of the Soviet Union in the Third World. As with a need for subtle assessment of the multiple times of 1989, so there appears to be an equally pronounced need to understand the fracturing of space engendered by 1989 and its aftermath.

What have we learned from '1989 and all that'? Perhaps the wrong lessons, as Chris Armbruster (Chapter 9), Marc DeVore (Chapter 10) and Barbara J. Falk (Chapter 11) explore. Armbruster argues that the European experience of violence during the twentieth century engendered legacies that contributed significantly to the revolutions of 1989. In contrast, the revolutions of 1989 provided a model of large-scale transformation relatively unscarred by such violence. Marc DeVore traces how the revolution in military affairs led US hawks to believe (erroneously) that cutting-edge technologies could be used to reshape international order. Barbara J. Falk traces ten poorly conceived lessons which US policy-makers drew from the collapse of communism, lessons which were subsequently employed to legitimise the invasion of Iraq. These themes are picked up by Arne Westad in his concluding

chapter to the volume. As Westad notes, twenty years after the events
of 1989, it is possible to see as many continuities as there have been
changes to the basic marrow of world politics. His chapter joins the
others in replacing the 'cliché of 1989' with a more sober assessment of
the past two decades. What is clear is that we should neither laugh (in
triumphalism) about the events of 1989, nor forget (in an attempt to
control the past) the lessons of the post-1989 era. After all, as Kundera
notes (1980: 3), 'the struggle against power is the struggle of memory
against forgetting'. The remainder of this introduction substantiates
the importance of this struggle and lays out the general framing for the
volume as a whole, understood as investigation of the 'what' (substantive issues), 'when' (times) and 'where' (spaces) of 'the global 1989'.

The 'what' of 1989

In many ways, the events of 1989 stand as exemplars of what Nicholas
Taleb (2007) calls 'black swans': events which stand as 'outliers' from
prevailing frames of reference; generate a set of impacts beyond their
immediate field; and which are subsequently rationalised via pre-
existing tools of explanation. Certainly, all three of Taleb's categories
are fulfilled by 1989: the changes which took place in 1989, particularly
during the second half of the year, were as surprising to most observers
as they were to many participants; their impact has been extensive, if
uneven; and over the past twenty years, there have been no shortage of
attempts to explain, and sometimes to explain away, their occurrence
(e.g. Dahrendorf 1990; Garton Ash 1990; Habermas 1990; Bunce 1999;
Sakwa 1999; Tismaneanu 1999; Kumar 2001; Outhwaite and Ray
2005). One of the aims of Taleb's book is to illustrate how black swans,
for all the surprise they invoke, occur more frequently than we imagine.
And certainly, surprise is a constant feature of world history – take as an
illustration Lenin's (1968: 842) comment in January 1917 that 'we, the
old, may not live to see the decisive battles of the coming revolution'.
Before the year was up, of course, the Bolshevik Revolution had begun
the process not just of reshaping Russian politics and society, but also
broader strands of international relations. Along with the Bolshevik
Revolution, the events of 9/11 and the German invasion of Russia in
the Second World War, 1989 stands as an archetype of the continuing
capacity of human history, even events and processes of considerable
magnitude, to surprise.

Less surprising has been the cottage industry which has sprung
up around 1989 over the past twenty years. Some Kremlinologists

found that Soviet Studies could quite easily be translated into post-Soviet Studies. Many transitologists who had previously worked on the break-up of authoritarian regimes in Southern Europe and Latin America transplanted their models fairly straightforwardly to the canvas provided by events in Eastern and Central Europe. Political theorists and sociologists surveyed the possibilities and challenges of a global era (e.g. Held *et al.* 1999), International Relations scholars pondered the stability – or not – of a unipolar world (e.g. Wohlforth 1999; Brooks and Wohlforth 2008), while many economists saw 1989 as marking the final victory of Hayek over Keynes, often becoming directly involved in far-reaching privatisation and liberalisation programmes (e.g. Sachs 1994). Regardless of diverse orientation and intention, most of these accounts concentrated on three core issues: first, establishing the (usually endogenous) causes of the collapse of communism; second, assessment of the broader meanings of 1989, mostly in terms of its revolutionary quotient; and third, investigation of the consequences of 1989, particularly in Europe. This book goes beyond these studies by concentrating on the most important, yet often the most neglected, of these foci – the consequences of 1989 – and by exerting much of its efforts on examination of the world beyond Europe. As such, the book does not provide a history, revisionist or otherwise, of the events of 1989, nor does it seek to establish (again) why 1989 happened when and how it did. Rather, the volume is geared at unravelling the complexities of time, space and substance associated with the global 1989.

As John M. Hobson points out in Chapter 1, for both scholars and policy-makers, 1989 serves as an influential 'temporal othering' device, a shorthand used across the political spectrum. For liberals, 1989 marked the shift from 'bad Cold War' to 'good post-Cold War', liberating the world from an era of conservative order and intervention to a novel epoch in which international institutions, multilateral forms of governance, human rights and humanitarian intervention could bury 'backward' ideas such as sovereignty, power politics and *realpolitik*. For foreign policy realists, 1989 marked the reverse journey, from 'good Cold War' to 'bad post-Cold War' as bipolar stability was replaced by the instability of a unipolar and/or multipolar world, a crisis in global governance, and heightened levels of insecurity stemming from a range of security threats: a rising China, a restored Russia, a plethora of rogue and failed states, and the emergence of transnational terrorist networks such as al-Qaeda. John Mearsheimer (1990a) was not the only high-profile realist to argue that we would soon miss the sureties of the Cold War. And nor was Francis Fukuyama (1989) the only liberal to laud the unprecedented possibilities for prosperity and peace inaugurated by the demise of the Soviet Empire.[1]

For all their differences, both of these positions agreed that something substantial had taken place in 1989. The great debate about how to categorise the events of 1989 – as revolutions (rectifying (Habermas 1990) or otherwise), refolutions (Garton Ash 1990) or as part of a wave of liberal democratic transitions (Rustow 1990; Huntington 1991; Ackerman 1992) – tended to concentrate on three issues: the failure of revolutionaries to conjure novel utopian visions; the considerable continuities between old and new regimes; and their relative lack of violence. To start with the first of these, what many observers failed to note was the *liberal* utopia that underpinned 1989. Ideas of freedom, justice and equality may not have been new, but they were certainly utopian. As such, participants took these ideals seriously, whether this meant invoking shock therapy programmes in the interests of promoting radical economic freedom or establishing regimes which legitimised freedom of expression, even for former communists, neo-Nazis and other unsavoury types. Not all anti-communist activists proved to be cuddly – xenophobic nationalists and market fundamentalists were implicated just as much as liberal intellectuals in the fall of communism. Not only this, the experience of 1989's 'heartland states' over the past twenty years has served to illustrate the contradictions of revolutionary (in this case, liberal) utopianism in a way which will be familiar to students of past revolutions: the restrictions of political freedoms in order to provide security and order; the continued importance of state activism in the economic sphere in order to redistribute public goods, manage inequality and reduce other distortions of the market; and the requirement of a strong public sector which can curtail the abuses of uncivil society when it tends towards extremism and violence. Indeed, one of the ironies of 1989 has been exposure of the *limits* of unfettered political, economic and cultural liberalism. By ushering in an era of liberalism without critique, 1989 actually served to *renew* critiques of liberal utopianism, critiques which continue to gain strength both in the West and the wider world. These issues are tackled directly in this volume by John M. Hobson, William Outhwaite, Laure Delcour and Barbara J. Falk (Chapters 1, 3, 6 and 11, respectively).

A second question mark over the effects of 1989 focuses on the considerable continuities between old and new, whether seen in terms of

---

[1] Fukuyama would likely reject the depiction of himself as a liberal. However, for the purposes of this chapter, I am taking neo-conservatism to be an offshoot of a broader family of 'kinetic liberal interventionism'. On this, see Dodge (2009).

state personnel or broader social relations. In Chapter 7, Aviezer Tucker examines the 'privitisation of the *nomenklatura*' in post-communist Russia and China, arguing that the late-totalitarian elite managed to align its interests (maximising wealth and status) to its rights, successfully transferring power from the political sphere to the economic realm. Tucker's point is powerfully made. Although the newness of past revolutions is often exaggerated (Kumar 1987; Halliday 1999; Lawson 2005), there is something particularly old-fashioned about the 1989 variant. Rather than seeking to establish a new order, revolutionaries in 1989 rushed to embrace what they *imagined* the West to consist of: better politics (represented by pluralism and democracy), better culture (particularly in terms of music, fashion and food) and better economies (whether understood as Nordic or Anglo-Saxon variants of capitalism). Both old elites and activists approached the events from positions of mutual weakness – neither had the stomach for an extended conflict and neither had the capacity to win victory outright. As such, roundtables replaced guillotines. And roundtables provided plenty of scope for old regimes to transform themselves into new elites. Sunset clauses for the old guard, the restoration of 'recovering communists' in Russia, China and elsewhere (Jowitt 1992), and the emergence of so-called 'red barons' are common themes in those states which experienced negotiated transformations.

The third issue that clouds the revolutionary legacy of 1989 surrounds the limited use of violence. For many scholars and laypeople alike, the very essence of revolution lies in its violence. But such a view disguises a much more complex relationship between revolution and violence than is commonly understood. If violence and revolution are co-determinous, then of the 1989 revolutions, only the Romanian uprising would qualify as a revolution. Yet given the partial nature of social, political and economic change in Romania since 1989, it is difficult to see how it warrants the label revolution. Social change, in the form of great scientific breakthroughs or widescale parliamentary reform programmes, has no necessary link with violence. In fact, as Johan Galtung (1969) and others point out, violence in its structural forms such as repression, exploitation, marginalisation, sexism, racism and so forth is used to *suppress* rather than instigate change. Violence is a means of order – the stifling of change – as much as a signifier of upheaval. Often, revolutions have been relatively peaceful seizures of power; violence stems from battles *after* the initial takeover of state power, resulting from the need by these regimes to shore up their rule in the face of domestic and international attempts at counter-revolution, a cycle that can be observed in France (in particular in the Vendée) after 1791, Russia during its four-year civil war after 1917, and in Iran, by way of its war with Iraq and the brutal measures employed against the regime's 'un-Islamic' foes after 1980. Hannah Arendt (1963), in a survey of the connection between violence and revolution, found that violence only became associated with revolutionary change through the 'Terror' of the Jacobins during the French Revolution. The close link between revolution and violence is, therefore, a relatively modern connection. Violence has been neither a constant nor indispensable aspect of revolutions. And as such, the relative lack of violence in 1989 need not disqualify the transformations from being seen as revolutionary. Indeed, as Chris Armbruster makes clear in Chapter 9, the most significant legacy of 1989 may be the provision of a novel means of organising synchronous political and social change without recourse to high levels of overt violence.

Armbruster argues that it is best to see the events of 1989 as 'negotiated revolutions' (see also Lawson 2005). And certainly, the transformations succeeded in generating political, economic and social orders some way removed from their communist era predecessors: ideological monism gave way to open societies; the homogeneity of political life under communism was replaced by the pluralisation of political relations; and the stagnant formula of central planning made way for the uncertainty of market relations. However, it would be foolish to claim that everything has changed in post-1989 orders. In reality, some power relations proved to be so entrenched as to be unalterable, other measures have been blocked, and there are many things incoming elites neither wished nor attempted to change. No revolution can start from year zero and reinvent social structures from scratch. Rather, the story of revolutionary change, in 1989 as in other times, is bound up with compromise between social action and structural constraints, utopian ideals and the politics of the possible.

If 1989, therefore, can be understood as the relatively peaceful victory of a revolutionary form of liberal utopianism, one which in keeping with past revolutions has witnessed continuities as well as important ruptures, what have been its principal legacies? As William Outhwaite notes in Chapter 3, one of the unintended consequences of 1989 has been a depression of left-wing politics in the West. To some extent, as Outhwaite points out, the events of 1968 in Europe and the emergence of a virulent form of economic neoliberalism in the 1970s and 1980s began these processes in the generation before 1989, but they were certainly underlined, reinforced and emboldened by the events of 1989. Indeed, it is no exaggeration to say that it is no longer clear what it means to be 'left' after the fall of actual existing socialism. The attempt to construct a Third Way by the Blair and Clinton administrations, as well as by their continental imitators, proved to be short-lived experiments, while the new millennium saw the left fracture painfully and powerfully over international issues – something it appears to do in each generation. In the 1930s the split came over the Spanish Civil War and Stalinist purges; in the 1960s over the invasion of Czechoslovakia and the 1968 uprisings in Western Europe. In the 2000s, the war on terror split the left on familiar issues: internationalism and imperialism, sovereignty and solidarity, universal aspirations and particularist struggles. In more general terms, the left has turned away from issues of representation and redistribution in favour of those of recognition (Fraser 2008). This hollowing out of political and economic opposition in the West appears, at least in part, to have been met by renewed interest in issues abroad, whether this be campaigns for debt relief, the war on poverty, or the fostering of support for global civil society. These social movements are, of course, important. But as a substitute for a radically left-wing alternative to current conditions, they provide thin gruel indeed.

In this sense, as Fred Halliday argues in Chapter 5, if 1989 was a failure for socialism, particularly in Europe, it can also be seen as defeat for liberal capitalism. The dark side of capitalist accumulation, captured powerfully in Chapter 2 by Saskia Sassen, has been sharp increases in inequality and criminality – much of the world is poor and insecure. Most troublingly, it is clear that the 2008 financial crisis was not something external to the system, but a process which arose from a conjuncture of inefficiencies and perversities endemic to the system itself, most notably the shift towards a form of 'casino capitalism' (Strange 1986).[2] The latest failure of capitalism was also a failure of the economics discipline – the 'efficient market hypothesis', ideas of 'self-correction' and support for no-holds-barred deregulation became commonplace ideas within an economics profession that 'mistook beauty for truth' by employing a range of techniques which, although looking good on paper, turned out to bear little resemblance to how economies actually functioned (Krugman 2009). As Saskia Sassen notes, the 2008 crisis had its roots in fundamental shifts in ideas about, and practices of, the international political economy during the two decades preceding 1989. Indeed, the central ideas and ordering mechanisms of the contemporary international political economy (self-regulation, marketisation,

---

[2] Strange borrowed the idea of capitalism and, in particular, financial markets functioning as a casino (i.e. as a constant gamble based on ever riskier speculations) from perhaps the world's most influential economist during the early part of the twentieth century, John Maynard Keynes.

neoliberalism, privatisation, etc.) were already ascendant – and had taken institutional form – well before 1989, hence the immediacy of shock therapy policies in (and on) 1989 heartland states. In general, the idealisation of the market – by academics and policy-makers alike – acted as a blinker on real world events; markets turned out not to be perfect and rationality turned out not to be utilitarian, at least not much of the time. And the consequences of this utopian occlusion – on peoples, societies and markets around the world – proved to be painful in the extreme.

Given this, it could be argued that 1989 should be understood as a conjunctural rather than an epochal shift (Rosenberg 2005). In other words, 1989 did not mark the emergence and institutionalisation of a novel set of political, economic and social relations. Rather, it emerged primarily out of collapse and implosion – the disappearance, virtually without a shot, of the Soviet Union and, with it, the *final* strand of the Cold War order, much of which had already melted away. The shifts and reconfigurations of social, economic and political power relations associated with 1989, dramatic and extensive though they have been, are for the most part contained within existing forms of social, political and economic order rather than marking a fundamental epochal transformation in the nature of these configurations. Those states and other actors at the centre of 1989 sought not to generate novel institutional alliances or to remake international relations in their own image but to actively give away power, for example by joining international organisations, ranging from the European Union to International Financial Institutions (IFIs) such as the World Trade Organization. To put this in old language, the organic tendencies of the old have reasserted themselves, in a new context, and on a vaster scale. In more concrete terms, the failures of Western capitalism, political institutions and cultural mores since 1989 (Jentleson and Weber 2008; Khanna 2008; Zakaria 2008) have fostered new forms of opposition to Western order: political Islam, freed from its focus on the communist enemy (Gerges 2005); Latin American populism, no longer subject to Western concerns over 'extended deterrence'; and renewed forms of authoritarian rule in China and elsewhere, even if these now appear more as forms of political coercion than as alternative means of economic or ideological competition. In this sense, although the end of the Cold War has been felt mostly strongly in Europe, trends elsewhere have been both unanticipated and, on occasion, counter-cyclical. We have been here before, of course (e.g. Spengler 1926; Kennedy 1989). But this time, as Michael Cox and William Outhwaite both make clear, relative Western decline may be for real.

The 'when' of 1989

If the above analysis stands up to scrutiny, 1989 marked neither a distinct end nor a distinct beginning in world historical time. Indeed, in ascertaining the time – or times – of 1989, it is important to ask when 1989 started, not in the sense of the opening of the border between Hungary and Austria in September 1989 which was decisive in extending protests against communist rule, nor in the sense of the landslide victory won by Solidarity in the June 1989 elections in Poland (on the same day, so it happened, as the massacre in Tiananmen Square) which acted as an important stimulus for opposition movements throughout the region. This much we know. But part of any assessment of the impact of 1989 must consider which events it is to be judged *against*. For example, if we mark our temporal cards from 1945–89, then the events appear to herald the end – or at least the winding down – of the Cold War, whether we consider this as a single frame with multiple dimensions (Westad 2005) or as divisible into two discrete stages (Halliday 1984). If, following Eric Hobsbawm (1994), we prefer to see the twentieth century as somehow 'short' – sandwiched between the onset of World War One in 1914 and the events of 1989, we get a second, more bird's-eye, view on proceedings. And it is possible to go back still further: to 1848 and the Springtime of Nations, which, like 1989, also witnessed first-hand the mobilising force of nationalism, the apparently spontaneous eruption of protests in major European cities, the enduring power of ideas of freedom, equality and justice, and the (mostly peaceful) loss of nerve by the old guard; to 1789 as François Furet (1999) prefers, and what he considers to be the final burial of the modern revolutionary *geist* – or illusion – first witnessed in France; or perhaps to 1648 as some political theorists prefer, with 1989 marking the end of an era of state sovereignty first ushered in by the Peace of Westphalia. Beyond Europe, there are still other alternatives. As Richard Saull notes in Chapter 8, the Cold War in the Middle East operated with logics distinct from its European variant: the relationship between authoritarian states backed by the United States and revolutionary forms of state nationalism supported, at least in part, by the Soviet Union; the various punctuation marks (1948, 1967, 1973, 1987) provided by the Arab–Israeli conflict; the fluctuating role of petro-dollars in regional politics; and the mobilising power of strands of political Islam. In short, if 1989 stands as a point of historical reckoning, much is staked in terms of when observers choose to *start* counting as well as when they decide to stop doing so.

Many of the contributors to this book engage with the notion of 1989 as constituting some kind of 'rectifying', 'recuperating' or 'catching up' model of revolutionary change, an idea first associated with the German critical theorist Jürgen Habermas (1990) in the immediate aftermath of the revolutions. To some extent, Habermas has a point – 1989 did mark the end of a detour, albeit an exceptionally powerful one. State socialism matched liberal capitalism in offering a distinct take on what was considered to be the most authentic articulation of modernity: both were revolutionary creeds which sought to govern on this basis. In this sense, both liberal capitalism and state socialism can be seen as quintessentially modern. As such, it was no surprise to see ideas associated with the holy trinity of modern social theorists (Weber, Marx and Durkheim) appear both to explain 1989 and its consequences: from Weber, we saw the limits of the iron cage of bureaucratic rationality as captured not just by socialist state managers but also by their counterparts in the West and in international organisations; from Marx, we were reminded of the necessary inequities and exploitation inherent in the accumulative practices of industrial capitalism; and from Durkheim we could bear witness to the anomie of modern life – the lack of solidarist scripts that arise from the break-up of old forms of order (what the novelist Monica Ali calls 'the limits of autonomy'), intensely present in both the contemporary West and post-1989 states. All in all, the events of 1989 reinvigorated many old debates about what it meant to be both human (Latour 1993) and modern (Gray 2007). In short, 1989 reawakened commentators to many of the contradictory aspects of modernity of which great modern theorists were well aware and which social science is charged to study.

To some extent, therefore, dreams of a radical alternative to capitalism did fade after 1989. But, for two reasons, such dreams were never realistic. First, one of the great mistakes of Marx's theory (and, by association, those of neo-Marxists such as Immanuel Wallerstein) was its underestimation of capitalism's capacity for 'creative destruction' (Schumpeter 1942) – the capacity of capitalism to conjure new, dynamic forms of accumulation and profit. In this sense, what did for state socialism was the shift in Western economies to consumer-based, service-led economies, the emergence of computer-based technologies and the rise of financial innovations following the collapse of the Bretton Woods system in the early 1970s. Second, as Chris Armbruster notes in Chapter 9, state socialism contained chronic internal weaknesses. Stalinist purges, a militarised economy and the normalisation of revolutionary ideology into a self-perpetuating bureaucratic creed replete with its own ruling class – the *nomenklatura* – undermined the Soviet system from within. By 1968 or thereabouts, there were precious few communists – or at least Marxist–Leninists – left in the Eastern

Bloc. A Czech professor returning to Prague in 1970 after two years in the Netherlands complained that 'there were far too many communists over there. At least in Prague, I won't have to meet any'.[3] In this sense, what Isaac Deutscher (1960) described as 'the great contest' was anything but that, however it appeared to participants at the time. It was a contest which contained a predetermined victor, something captured evocatively by the post-War US ambassador to Moscow, George Kennan (1947), in the Long Telegram sent to his political masters at the onset of the Cold War. Gorbachev, 'new thinking' and other such *événements* were certainly significant in terms of the *timing* of Soviet collapse, but longer-term trends better explain how and why the system failed. We did not know precisely *when* communism would implode, but that it would at some point in time was not in question.

In this sense, therefore, 1989 was an end – an end that Francis Fukuyama (1989) was at least half-right to see as that between two rival ideologies: liberal capitalism and state socialism. But the twenty years since 1989 have ably demonstrated the ways in which political, military, economic and cultural forces find ways to reconfigure themselves along new lines. Capitalism may be the only game in town in terms of organising economies, but this comes at the cost of recurring crisis, something painfully illustrated by the global financial meltdown of 2008. But if there is no economic alternative to capitalism, this is not the case when it comes to political relations. In fact, it is not clear whether capitalism thrives best under authoritarian or democratic forms of governance. After all, some of the most rapid periods of growth – and the most unyielding forms of capitalism – have occurred in authoritarian states (Chang 2007): contemporary China or General Pinochet's Chile for example. As such, it is not just the European Union and the United States, but the 'soft dictatorships' (Kenney 2006) of China and Russia that offer powerful models for combining order and wealth creation in the contemporary world (Gat 2007; for an alternative view, see Deudney and Ikenberry 2009). Culturally, along with a certain flattening of language, style, music and food lies a mix and match of various hues and colours, creative heterogeneous fusions even amidst a certain homogeneity of aspiration. Barack Obama's Kenyan/Hawaiian origins are, in this sense, just the leading-edge of a much broader trend.

Alongside these uncertainties regarding economic, political and cultural relations lie contradictions in terms of the world's military relations, a process captured well by Marc DeVore in Chapter 10. On the

---

[3] A story told during a conversation with Profesor Jan Sokol at Charles University, Prague, 4 April 2001.

one hand, US military might provides it with full spectrum dominance on an unprecedented scale, something aided by organisations such as NATO, whose twenty-six members include ten post-communist states. On the other hand, this dominance is threatened by a certain democratisation in the means of violence – what can be seen as the 'other side of the revolution in military affairs'. Indeed, the widespread availability of Kalashnikovs and hand-held rocket launchers, alongside techniques of asymmetrical warfare such as suicide bombing, provide the means for small, determined groups to hold out against US force and, indeed, to counter it effectively, as demonstrated by the events of 9/11 and the unsuccessful invasions of Afghanistan and Iraq. DeVore traces this dynamic to the emergence of the revolution in military affairs in the final years of the Carter administration. DeVore chronicles a fight between traditional military elites convinced of the need for modernisation within existing structural command and control systems, and political elites dazzled by the possibilities of high-tech warfare. In the final analysis, DeVore concludes, the revolution in military affairs served as a utopian occlusion, blinding political leaders to the realities of military conflict which, regardless of stealth bombers, Unmanned Aerial Vehicles (UAVs), techniques of precision bombing and so on, remain gruesome fights to the finish.

Such lessons – one of the ten chronicled by Barbara J. Falk in Chapter 11 – stem from a delusion which appears to be shared by nigh-on the entire US political elite. As Falk notes, the fusion of overwhelming American power allied to powerful ideologies such as neo-conservatism has engendered a sense in which US power is not just good for the United States, but also a tool which can – and should – be used to reshape the world in its own image. Of course, this powerful cocktail of power and utopian ideals has not gone unchallenged. First, there is the challenge to US military hegemony noted by DeVore and others. Second, there is the political challenge to American primacy represented by alternatives models of governance: China, Russia and, to some extent, the European Union. Third, although much of the world is led by – or wants to be led by – American cultural trends, there is a certain unorthodox blend to this picture: Bollywood films, Chinese restaurants and other such global cultural formations are generating an increasingly complex, sometime hybridised, array of cultural forces. And economically, sovereign wealth funds, protectionist policies and forms of economic nationalism indicate a process of renationalisation, even as this sits alongside moves towards global, regional, transnational and local scapes (Mann 1997; Weiss 1998). In short, the most recent phase of capitalist accumulation is serving to fracture global space.

The 'where' of 1989

As Saskia Sassen notes in Chapter 2, the fracturing of spatial relations is not a new phenomenon, albeit one which is only now taking global shape. Indeed, as John M. Hobson (Chapter 1) and Richard Saull (Chapter 8) point out, the Cold War may only have *appeared* to delineate a certain singularity to world events because of a Eurocentric gaze on the conflict. After all, although the bipolar order was stable and relatively peaceful in Europe, this was not the case for many states and regions around the world where the post-1945 period was decidedly hot. In short, Europe was the central front of strategic and diplomatic calculations, but it was the Third World that generated the majority of the crises and nearly all of the casualties of the Cold War – over twenty million people all told. As Arne Westad (2005) puts it, both East and West imposed a 'regime of global intervention' which continued, at least to some extent, the exploitation of the colonial era. For the Soviets, this was premised on a general creed (albeit with Stalinist reservations) of revolutionary internationalism and a Leninist desire to attack capitalism via its weakest link. For the United States, responses to Third World uprisings were captured by NSC-68 (which followed the outbreak of the Korean War), détente (at least in part formulated as a result of post-colonial revolutions), and the acceleration of the Cold War under Ronald Reagan's administration in the early 1980s (undertaken, to some degree, because of the challenge posed by the Iranian and Nicaraguan revolutions and the invasion of Afghanistan by the Soviet Union). What James Mann (2009) calls 'the rebellion of Ronald Reagan' should, in this sense, be seen as a manifestation of a longer-term commitment by the United States to counter the Soviet challenge wherever it appeared.

To some extent, therefore, the Cold War could be understood as an inter-imperialist rivalry (the Soviet 'empire of justice' vs. the US 'empire of liberty'), as a contest between two revolutionary regimes, or, as noted above, as a confrontation between rival visions of modernity. But however it is described, as Fred Halliday points out, it was a conflict which, despite the chronic deficiencies which would eventually lead to its downfall, many participants thought the Soviets could win. Indeed, even in the early part of the 1980s, the correlation of forces looked somewhat favourable for the Soviets: Tanzania, Algeria and Nicaragua were showcases for leftist progressivism; there was a general, much lauded, drive towards 'Afrocommunism' and, in 1982, at the moment of the death of Soviet leader Leonid Brezhnev, the Soviet net stretched to thirty-one component states. This net included states run by Soviet clients (e.g. Cuba and Vietnam), states oriented towards socialism (e.g. Ethiopia and Nicaragua), two independent communist states (China and the Democratic People's Republic of Korea), a group of what the Soviets considered to be 'less advanced states of socialist orientation' (e.g. Algeria and Iraq), and several more marginal cases (e.g. Ghana and Suriname). Despite some of the more delusional aspects of these claims and regardless of structural Soviet weaknesses elsewhere, not least economically, there was good reason for the Reagan administration to develop a counter-offensive against what appeared as a picture of Soviet rude health.

However, as Halliday makes clear in Chapter 5, 'recognising the global *extent* of the Cold War is not equivalent to saying that it was *in the Third World* that the global conflict was decided any more than recording military conflict in the Middle East or the Pacific during the First and Second World Wars is equivalent to saying that it was these theatres that decided the outcome'. Indeed, as both Laure Delcour (Chapter 6) and William Outhwaite (Chapter 3) also discuss, the most obvious centre of gravity for discussion of 1989 is Europe. And here, as elsewhere, consequences have been mixed. Although the European Union has expanded, this has not been without cost, whether this be to decision-making capacities or a more general loss of nerve. The failure to ratify the proposed EU constitution and to deal effectively with important international processes in its near abroad (Georgia and Turkey in terms of foreign policy; the financial crisis in terms of economic policy) has left the Union curiously short of drive just as it appears to have maximised its basic capabilities. A certain sense of *Ostalgie* permeates European politics – and not just in the eastern half of the continent. Despite attempts at 'rethinking the left' for the 'new times' after the end of the Cold War, there has been a pronounced turn towards antipolitics, a search for forms of political authenticity in older notions of 'civil society' and 'moral economy' and an accommodation with prevailing patterns of stratification and authority rather than the conjuring of novel ideals and policy prescriptions (Kumar 2001; *European Journal of Social Theory* 2009).

To some extent, the desire of states to maintain control over their foreign and economic policies – despite claims to the contrary – stand as important markers of the post-1989 world. There has been a certain renationalisation of security functions (for example via new anti-terrorist legislation), economic policy (most credit crunch policy has either been state based or inter-state based) and identity politics (captured, for example, by the rise of anti-immigrant parties and movements). As with our understanding of time, therefore, 1989 appears to have brought us a complex spatial panorama in which we are both closer in terms of an acceleration of intersocietal integration, particularly in terms of economies, peoples and ideas, but also further apart in that this homogenisation has a doppelgänger in the form of a return to the local, whether visited in claims of local autonomy, ethnic identity or anti-immigration. Again, therefore, there is a fundamental contradiction in play: combined interactivity alongside uneven differentiation; universality and fragmentation; singularity and fracture.

Given this picture, it is difficult to establish any type of concrete hold on the multiple vectors which constitute contemporary global space. As Bob Jessop (2002, 2007) and others (e.g. Cerny 2006) argue, there is a new bargain emerging in terms of how states manage relations of regulation and accumulation, a process Jessop describes as a shift from Keynesian welfare states to Schumpterian workfare regimes. Part of this story, to be sure, is marked by a shift from national frames towards multinodal global, regional, transnational and local scales. We may not inhabit what Jürgen Habermas (2001) calls a 'postnational constellation', but there is a sense in which the fundamental relationships between states and markets, and between private and public spheres, are being recast – a message which forms a core part of Chapter 2, by Saskia Sassen. Of course, in and of itself, this is not a new phenomenon. Marx talked of capital's 'complex synthesis of multiple determinations' in the *Grundrisse* some 150 years ago, while the liberal notion of complex interdependence remains a useful depiction for much of the functioning of the international political economy, reminding us that the picture is, to a great extent, issue- and/or region-specific (e.g. Keohane and Nye 1973).

To some extent, therefore, as many contributors to this book note, there is a sense of *plus ça change*. Russia has, despite the emergence of previously submerged conflicts in Chechnya, Transnistria, Nagorno-Karabakh, Abkhazia and South Ossetia, largely held together. Former communist parties have continued to win votes, sometimes, but not always, following a change of name.[4] And for some states – China, North Korea, Cuba – the Cold War did not end, at least not in 1989/91. As such, claims of a 'new Cold War' look far-fetched (Buzan 2006).

---

[4] Interestingly, it was Western European rather than Eastern European communist parties which seemed most affected by the collapse of state socialism. The Italian communist party, for example, spent much of 1990 being called La Cosa (literally 'the thing') before settling on a new title – Partito Democratico Della Sinistra (the Democratic Party of the Left). In contrast, both the Czech and Hungarian communist parties continued to function as normal, more or less unapologetically. Indeed, today, of nineteen parties associated with the 'European Left' movement, eight are former communist parties.

There will, no doubt, be a certain rescaling of global political order in order to accommodate the many challenges to Western international order. And perhaps, over the *longue durée*, the last 300–400 years of Western domination will come to be seen as an exception as power returns once more to Asia. In the meantime, we will continue to cast around for apt frames for the contemporary conjuncture, whether this is understood as imperial (e.g. Hardt and Negri 2000; Ferguson 2008), a case of 'one superpower, many great powers' (Kagan 2008), or as Richard Haass (2008) prefers, 'nonpolar'.

Conclusions and openings

Yogi Berra, the famous American baseball player and pundit, once said that 'it is tough to make predictions, especially about the future'. 1989 is no exception to his maxim. Some twenty years after the fall, it is difficult to recall the sense of surprise and excitement which emerged from the removal of the Soviet empire, first in Eastern and Central Europe and, some two years later, from its own backyard. As the international media moved from city to city, and increasing numbers of Europeans came onto the streets in order to chase away the old order and to welcome in the new, there was a sense of the world shifting beneath people's feet. In some ways, the events of 1989 stand as epigraphs for a 'runaway world' (Giddens 2002) which precludes easy analysis. Perhaps world politics over the last twenty years has occupied some kind of 'liminal space' (Kumar 2001), serving as an 'interregnum' (Cox *et al.* 1999) or as 'abnormal times' (Fraser 2008). More likely, though, the Cold War only appears simple in retrospect. For those who lived through the period, the Cold War seemed anything but straightforward and the outcome of the conflict anything but certain, even during its final endgame. As such, this book does not seek to provide a *post-factum* flattening of the Cold War into a monochrome story with a predetermined outcome. Rather, the contributors seek to question how effectively the end of the Cold War works as a tool of 'temporal othering' between old and new, let alone as a normative framework depicting 'good' or 'bad'.

However imperfect any single frame may be for understanding the complexities of international politics between 1945 and 1989/91, it is clear that the system ended because of the defeat of one of the competitors by the other. And what followed was not the replacement of the Soviet Union by a single foe but by a multitude of contenders: authoritarian capitalists, virulent nationalists, Islamic terrorists and more. Given this picture, it is unsurprising that our concepts and frames have struggled to keep up. At the heart of understanding the global 1989 are striking contradictions: heightened interactivity alongside increased differentiation, simultaneous closeness and distance, the homogeneity of globalisation alongside the fracturing of public space. Such is both the blessing and curse of 1989: it has allowed us to leave behind some of the more obscuring, constraining blinkers of the pre-1989 era. But it has not yet offered us much in their place. We are in an era where we know what we are post (Cold War, Westphalian, imperial and so on), but have little sense of what is to come. In this sense, the post-Cold War era offers a profound lesson for academic enquiry as well as for policy-makers, reminding us of the need to ask good questions rather than look for easy answers, to use imagination rather than fulfil the requirements of 'normal science', and to work on developing sound judgements rather than following the latest fad. Our task in this book is to both problematise the place of 1989, but also to make sense of the major trends which have arisen over the past twenty years.

To that end, one of the central arguments in this book is that 1989 represents, at least for the most part, a triumph of *chronos* (sequential time) over *kairos* (qualitative temporal change) (Hutchings 2008). Although there have been, and there remain, claims to the exceptional in 1989, a fundamental rupture in world order does not appear to have taken place. Rather, much akin to the bionic man, the post-1989 era is quicker, stronger, faster – we have seen the acceleration of important reconfigurations in how we organise politics, economics and social life, but also the emergence of some curious contradictions: the linear time of the Cold War replaced by a fractured time of uneven development; the end and then, more recently, the return of history (Kagan 2008); the emergence of simultaneous time alongside a sense of temporal dislocation. For all its surprise, 1989 did not spring *de novo*, but had antecedents – 1789, 1848 and 1968 amongst them. And it has generated its own mimicries, from negotiations between Maoists and old regime loyalists in Nepal to second generation authoritarian transformations in Serbia and elsewhere. 1989 also faces competition from other dates which stand as way-stations to important trends in contemporary world politics, not least 1979, marker of both the Iranian revolution and the Soviet invasion of Afghanistan, events which, via many twists and turns, provided impetus to the development of radical political Islam *and* US neo-conservatism. The joining of these radical ideologies in armed conflict has engendered a new revolutionary conflict, one which will shape core aspects of world politics for many years to come. In this sense, it is not Viktor Yushchenko or Nelson Mandela, Hugo Chavez or Naomi Klein who best personify the present conjuncture, but Irving Kristol, Abu Musab al-Suri and their fellow travellers.

Given this, much as it is important to recognise the importance of 1989, one of the lessons of this book is that years and dates rarely act as sound guides to complex processes. In fact, rather like seeking to capture democracy only via elections, dates may serve to obscure more important, longer-term trends. In short, dates offer us punctuation marks to world history, but they should not be seen as the masters of world historical development. Our goal in this book is to draw together trends that, quite often, are seen only in parallel or as zero-sum: homogenisation and heterogeneity; modernity and jihad; Stalinist terror and Gorbachevian 'new thinking'. Each chapter in the book disrupts a prevailing wisdom and exposes 'uncomfortable truths' – in this sense, they represent high-water marks of academic enquiry and critical engagement. Of course, no book can – or should – close down a particular subject, and this is no exception. There are a range of topics not dealt with here: detailed survey of the normative landscape of the post-Cold War world, attention to the re-masculinisation of public space which has accompanied a relative decline in the position of women globally, and the emergence of the 'dark side of globalisation' as represented by people-trafficking, transnational criminal networks, the illicit drugs trade and so on (Halliday 2008). And there are many regions which have, at least in terms of extended discussion, slipped beneath our radar. What we offer, therefore, is not a definitive guide, but a series of openings about one of the iconic historical landmarks of our time. 'Out of the crooked timber of humanity', Kant wrote, 'no straight thing was ever made.' Our intention in this book is not to carve a straight line out of humanity's crooked timber. But we do aim to make sense of the complexities, contradictions and paradoxes of the post-1989 world. Ten years ago, a major study claimed that, following 1989, 'everything we know is up for grabs and what comes next is anyone's guess' (Verdery 1999: 83). This book seeks to provide the clarity afforded by an extra decade of hindsight.

Part I

What and when

1 Back to the future of nineteenth-century Western international thought?

John M. Hobson

The postmodern [European] state ... needs to get used to the idea of double standards. Among themselves, the postmodern states operate on the basis of laws and open co-operative security. But when dealing with more old-fashioned kinds of state outside the [Western] post-modern limits, Europeans need to revert to the rougher methods of an earlier era – force, preemptive attack, deception, whatever is necessary for those who still live in the nineteenth-century world of every state for itself. In the jungle, one must use the laws of the jungle.

Robert Cooper (2004: 61–2)

To suppose that the same international customs, and the same rules of international morality, can obtain between one civilized nation and another, and between civilized nations and barbarians, is a grave error ... In the first place, the rules of ordinary international morality imply reciprocity. But barbarians will not reciprocate. They cannot be depended on for observing any rules ... In the next place, nations which are still barbarous have not got beyond the period during which it is likely to be for their benefit that they should be conquered and held in subjection by foreigners.

John Stuart Mill (1859/1984: 118)

Some Americans have promoted multiculturalism at home; some have promoted universalism abroad; and some have done both ... A multicultural America is impossible because a non-Western America is not American. A multicultural world is unavoidable because global empire is impossible. The preservation of the United States and the West requires the renewal of Western identity.

Samuel Huntington (1996: 318)

We must preserve our Aryan nationality in the State, and admit to its membership only such non-Aryan race-elements as shall have become Aryanized in spirit and genius by contact with it, if we would build

I would like to thank the editors, and especially George Lawson, as well as the two anonymous reviewers, for their extremely helpful comments, though the usual rider applies.

the superstructure of the ideal American commonwealth [that should stand as an] example to the world.

John W. Burgess (1895: 407)

Introduction

The events of 11/9 were perceived by many observers in the West to be as dramatic and as world-changing as 9/11 would be to many observers just over a decade later. Visions of the Berlin Wall being smashed down on 9 November 1989 (11/9) were stamped into the Western imaginary in similar ways to the two infamous planes when they careered into the twin towers of the World Trade Center on 11 September 2001 (9/11). In each case, dramatic world events appeared to herald the dawn of a new era in which the old parameters of world politics were rapidly redefined, in turn requiring fresh thinking about international relations. The emergence of an 'all-change' idiom was expressed most powerfully in the elevation of globalisation as a new force in world politics, alongside the emergence of a liberal normative architecture based on human rights that was to reorder the world in the West's own image.

In this chapter, I argue that, far from comprising a 'new turn', post-1989 international thought has undertaken a *return* to many of the Eurocentric themes which dominated Western thought in the 'long' nineteenth century. My particular focus is on international thought, not least because this reflects, as well as acts as a performative vehicle for, the policies that the West undertakes vis-à-vis the non-Western world. Moreover, just as Edward Said (1978) used novels as an indicator of how Eurocentrism underpins Western thought, here I employ international thought as the litmus test for the degree to which Eurocentrism underpins Western thinking more generally. My aim is not to fit all contemporary Western international thought into the moulds that I delineate in this chapter, but to bring out the many parallels that mark much of Western international thought in the two periods.

My argument is that these *continuities* have been obscured by the tendency of Western thinkers to effect a 'temporal othering' of world politics before 1989 such that the pre-1989 scene is presented as the binary opposite of the post-1989 era. This occurs in two interrelated respects. First, political (neo)realists contrast the pre-1989 Cold War world of stability with the uncertainty of the post-1989 world (e.g. Mearsheimer 1990b; Waltz 1993). By contrast, liberals often associate the Cold War with stasis, which is then contrasted with a more progressive vision for the world after 1989 (e.g. Fukuyama 1989, 1992). Second, supposedly progressive and egalitarian values have come to the fore in the West since 1989 – universalist values associated with democracy and human rights – that were non-existent in the nineteenth-century imperialist phase of world politics and that were often sidelined by the superpower conflict during the Cold War. In this way, a binary temporal schema is constructed in which the nineteenth century is represented as more Eurocentric than it was so that the post-1989 era can be portrayed as less Eurocentric than it is (Young 1995). 'Decolonising 1989' reveals how Eurocentrism has returned, both defining a good deal of Western international thought in the contemporary world and, as a consequence, underpinning many Western foreign policies.

To substantiate these claims, I divide mainstream Western international thought over the past two centuries into two broad streams – what I shall call 'Western-idealism' and 'Western-realism' – and supplement this with a third overlapping variant that I call Western 'idealist-realism'.[1] The key point is that, in both periods, all such thinking is grounded in Eurocentrism insofar as it, either wittingly or unwittingly: places the West at the centre of the analysis while simultaneously consigning the East to a peripheral position; for the most part subscribes to a politics of Western neo-imperialism; and works normatively to defend or promote Western civilisation and Western norms. My principal concern is to reveal the Eurocentric lenses that underpin these approaches and, in the process, draw out the linkages between contemporary international thought and its nineteenth-century predecessor. More specifically, I show how, although Western-idealists and Western-realists seek to promote and defend Western civilisation, they do so in different ways. While the former sing the post-1989 world into existence with the anthem 'things can only get better for the West' and, by implication, for the world, Western-realists chant 'things can only get bitter for the West' and, by implication, for the world. Accordingly, Western-idealists assume that promoting Western civilisation and spreading Western norms is a progressive good, while Western-realists assume that defending Western civilisation against the Eastern threat is vital so as to maintain international order and 'civilisation'.

Both of these approaches display different 'temperaments'. The 'realist' variant is fuelled by a sense of Western civilisational *angst* and pessimism that promotes a sense of defensiveness, which paradoxically takes the form of an offensive-punitive international stance (on the basis that attack is often the best form of defence). Its pessimism gives birth to the

---

[1] Note that Western-realism should not be conflated with the theory of neorealism, as I explain later in this chapter.

idiom that 'things can only get bitter'. Conversely the idealist variant is oiled by a sometimes euphoric sense of Western triumphalism as well as a general sense of optimism that 'things can only get better'. In the middle lies 'idealist-realism', best represented by neo-conservatism. My labelling of this category as idealist-realism is reminiscent of the description of neo-conservatism as 'Wilsonian realism'. Paradoxically, such a label is more apt than would at first be recognised, since it turns out that Wilson's Eurocentrism yielded an imperialist politics (see Hobson 2009: ch. 6). Temperamentally, Western idealist-realism embraces a *conditional* optimism. Optimism can only prevail when the West, and especially the United States, engages in neo-imperial interventions in the East – hence 'things *could* get better'. But equally, should such intervention fail or should commitment to it wither, then neo-conservatives in particular revert to a realist sense of pessimism – hence 'things *could* get bitter'.[2] As this chapter explores, the category of Western idealist-realism is particularly interesting because it brings out the many shared overlaps between the 'realist' and 'idealist' wings of Western international thought.

The chapter proceeds in three main stages. I begin by providing a taxonomy of Eurocentrism. The second section examines how these metanarratives are embedded within Western-realism, while the third section does the same for Western-idealism. I choose not to allocate a separate section for Western idealist-realism, preferring to treat it within the second and third sections. And throughout the chapter, I examine the overlaps and continuities between post-1989 international thinking and its nineteenth-century predecessors.

Unpacking Orientalism/Eurocentrism

Following Edward Said (1978), post-colonialism suggests that Orientalism/Eurocentrism was fully consolidated in the 1750–1850 period, leading to an *imperialist consensus* across Western societies by the mid-nineteenth century. However, this umbrella concept is problematic because Said's monochromatic construction obscures a number of variants that comprise it. And, moreover, not all Eurocentric variants embrace imperialism. In essence, I argue that there are two forms of Eurocentrism/Orientalism that are particularly relevant here – paternalist (which is neo-imperialist) and punitive (which is part imperialist, part anti-imperialist) (see Table 1.1). Note too that Western idealist-realists draw on aspects of both these variants.

---

[2] Interesting in this context is Francis Fukuyama's recent disenchantment with neo-conservatism. Fukuyama's vision of 'realistic Wilsonianism' (Fukuyama 2006a) is situated within the idealist-realist category, but somewhat closer to the idealist wing.

Table 1.1 *Variants of Eurocentrism*

	Western-idealism	Western idealist-realism	Western-realism
Metanarrative	Paternalist Eurocentrism	Part paternalist Eurocentrism/ part punitive Eurocentrism	Punitive Eurocentrism
Temperament	Triumphalist and optimistic	Conditional optimism/ potential pessimism	Angst-ridden and pessimistic
Pro-imperialist nineteenth/ early twentieth centuries	Cobden, J. S. Mill, J. A. Hobson, Angell		Mahan, Mackinder, Giddings, Kidd, K. Pearson,
Neo-imperialist post-1989	Friedman, Wolf, Donnelly, Wheeler, Risse, Finnemore	Fukuyama, Kagan, W. Kristol, Krauthammer, Ignatieff, Ikenberry, Slaughter, Téson	Kaplan, Kennedy
Anti-imperialist nineteenth/ early twentieth centuries			Spencer, Sumner, Burgess, Jordan
post-1989			Huntington

Beginning with the left-hand side of Table 1.1, by the mid-nineteenth century 'Western-idealism', embodying a paternalist Eurocentrism, had become the dominant stream of Western international thought. This reflected the strong degree of triumphalism that the West basked in at the time (Pitts 2005); something that was illustrated in Britain's Great Exhibition, held in London in 1851. Three key points emerge here. First, a bipolar line of 'civilisational apartheid' was constructed that split apart East and West (or 'the West and the Rest') into two self-constituting autonomous entities. Second, the ethnology of difference between 'civilisation' (the West) and 'barbarism/savagery' (the East) was located in *institutional* factors, wherein Western rationality was contrasted with Eastern irrationality, thereby elevating the West over the Rest. It was this difference that formed the basis of the well-known logocentric formula in which the first term represented the superior

West, the second term the inferior East: democracy/Oriental despotism, science/mysticism, independent/dependent, individualism/collectivism and so on. Third, while the key bipolar divide was constructed between East and West, overlaid upon this conception was a tripartite *hierarchical metageography* in which the world was divided into three zones: civilisation (the First World of Europe), Yellow barbarism (the Second World of the 'Orient' and Middle East), and Black and Red savagery (the Third World of Africa, Australasia, pre-1492 America).

This metanarrative gave rise to an imperialist political stance. This derives from the premise that Eastern peoples *are* capable of progressing and becoming civilised but *only* if the rational institutions of civilisation are delivered to them by Westerners. In this imaginary, Eastern peoples are understood through a Peter Pan metaphor: namely that Eastern societies are immature and will never grow up *of their own accord*. Thus was born the idea of Western imperialism as a *civilising mission*; one that could deliver rational institutions to the East which would then kick-start their societies onto a developmental-maturation path that would culminate in their arrival at the developmental terminus of Western civilised society based on rationality, capitalism and liberal democracy. This Eurocentric imperialist vision was held by many leading liberals, including J. S. Mill, Richard Cobden, Norman Angell and J. A. Hobson (Hobson 2009: ch. 2; Hall and Hobson 2010). Importantly, as I explain in the next section, post-1989 Western-idealist thinking embraces a similar paternalist Eurocentrism.

By the end of the nineteenth century, a second generic approach emerged – what might be termed 'Western-realism' – which embodied a more *punitive* conception of Eurocentrism. This was a product of the rise of a sense of anxiety vis-à-vis the East among many Western thinkers. This angst was fuelled by a series of events which were thought to constitute a generic Eastern threat to the continuing hegemony of Western civilisation. One event often singled out here is the Japanese victory over Russia in 1905, an event which the scientific racist, Lothrop Stoddard, saw as 'an omen of evil import' such that 'the legend of white invincibility lay, a fallen idol, in the dust' (Stoddard 1920: 171, 12).

This brand of Eurocentrism embraced scientific racism, the ethnology of which located difference in biology and environment, though in its Lamarckian version, social factors were included as well (see Stocking 1982). It too embraced a tripartite hierarchy, though it was founded on a racial scale of civilisation: Whites followed by Yellows with Blacks at the bottom. Locating developmental prospects in terms of climate and genetics (and not infrequently 'Lamarckian' social behaviour) led *some* scientific racists to believe that development and civilisation were the monopoly of the white races and that difference between civilisations could not be transcended. For the most part, such thinkers embraced the social Darwinian conception of the struggle between races and the survival of the fittest wherein societies operated according to the laws of natural (racial) selection. Nevertheless, some racists, most notably Herbert Spencer and William Graham Sumner, believed that all societies and all races were capable of auto-developing, even though civilisation had been pioneered by the white races. Unlike paternalist Eurocentrism, scientific racism was internally divided on the question of imperialism, with some advocating and some rejecting it.

The pro-imperialist strand was found in the anti-laissez-faire liberal social Darwinists (e.g. Ward 1903/2002), as well as 'realist' social Darwinists and Eugenicists (who were stimulated in reaction to the laissez-faire version of social Darwinism). For these thinkers, imperialism was an important means of maintaining white supremacy. The extreme form was found in the Eugenicist strain, where the superior races had to be encouraged to have more children while the inferior races needed to be prevented from reproducing. Thus the English Eugenicist, Karl Pearson (1905), viewed imperialism as a vital resource in the struggle between races, constituting the means by which the inferior or 'vanishing' races had to submit to the superiority of the white race. More generally, social Darwinists, such as Benjamin Kidd (1898), saw imperialism as the means by which the superior white races would overcome the anarchy of the tropics so that their riches could be exploited and harnessed in order to advance Western industrialisation. While these thinkers shared a pro-imperialist stance with Western-idealist thinkers, nevertheless the notion of a civilising mission tended to be downplayed amongst Western-realists (though Paul Reinsch was a clear exception). For these punitive racists, colonialism was explicitly conceived as a means to advance white civilisation at the expense of the non-white races. And at the racists extreme, it was assumed that if the natives resisted Western intervention then genocide or extermination was justified.

As indicated in Table 1.1, some scientific racists *rejected* imperialism. This was a function of various arguments. Some argued against imperialism on the grounds that the natural laws of racial selection should not be tampered with and that colonialism would serve only to undermine civilisation within the coloniser society; and moreover, that because all races will naturally auto-develop into civilisation in the fullness of time so colonial intervention would serve only to disturb and undermine this process of non-European racial development (Spencer 1902; Sumner 1911). In contrast, others argued that external human intervention could not uplift the inferior races given that they were incapable of developing (e.g. Jordan 1901). Moreover, many scientific racists believed that the climate of the tropics would lead to an unacceptable degeneration of the white races, as would miscegenation/hybridity (i.e. blood-mixing). Thus commensurate international thought rejected colonialism and emphasised the need for strong immigration controls, all of which was based on the desire to maximise the distance between white and non-white races.

While contemporary Western-realists echo many of the themes that were first forwarded by the scientific racist analyses of the late nineteenth/early twentieth centuries, nevertheless, today *institutional* factors rather than climate/genetics/natural selection form the ethnology of difference. All in all, contemporary Western-realism and Western-idealism subscribe (for the most part) to a neo-imperialist politics, though some advance an anti-imperialism that derives from a defensive-Eurocentric metanarrative (as in Huntington 1996, 2004; see also Hobson 2009: ch. 11). The next two sections examine how these metanarratives play out within Western international thought.

'Things can only get bitter'

Figure 1.1 presents a summary of the two broad streams of international thought, as well as the overlapping interstitial category of idealist-realism, as they emerged in the post-Cold War era. This section shall consider the right-hand side while the following section considers the left-hand side. Note that I shall discuss the interstitial category in the relevant places in each of these two sections.

It is generally thought that the immediate response to the end of the Cold War and the defeat of 'quasi-Asiatic' Soviet despotism took the form of a euphoric wave of Western triumphalism, most closely associated with Francis Fukuyama's 'end of history thesis'. As he proclaimed: 'The triumph of the West, of the Western *idea*, is evident first of all in the total exhaustion of viable systematic alternatives to Western liberalism' (Fukuyama 1989: 3). While this certainly stole the headlines for a while it was, however, complemented by the simultaneous emergence of a pessimistic, angst-ridden vision, first relayed into the public imagination in a *National Review* article by Daniel Pipes entitled 'The Muslims are Coming! The Muslims are Coming!' (Pipes 1990).[3] This piece heralded a trend in which notable Western thinkers substituted the Muslims for the Soviets as the principal threat confronting Western civilisation in the immediate post-Cold War era, something that crystallised in Samuel Huntington's 1993 article, 'The Clash of

---

[3] Though to some extent Pipes questioned the alarmist perception of the Muslim threat that other 'Western-realists' voiced, and even disavowed the title given to his piece by the editors of the *National Review*.

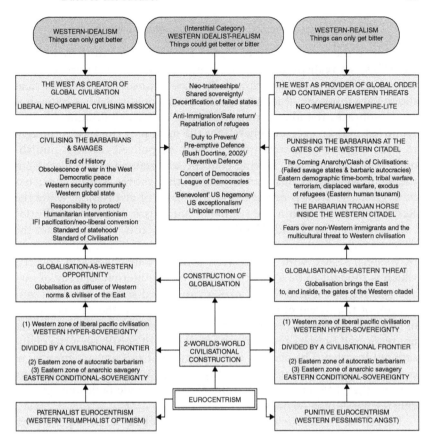

Figure 1.1 Post-1989 'international thought' as promoter and defender of Western civilisation

Civilizations?'. The key point here is that the immediate context of this response lay with an underlying punitive Eurocentrism that was nourished by a rapidly emergent sense of Western pessimistic angst following the fall of the Berlin Wall. It is this sense of anxious pessimism and fear that leads me to label this strand of thought 'Western-realism'. And Huntington's more recent words might be taken as a mantra of Western-realist thought for the post-Cold War era: 'this new world is a fearful world and Americans have no choice but to live *with* fear if not *in* fear' (Huntington 2004: 341). Particularly interesting here is that two of the founding fathers of these approaches – Fukuyama and Pipes – were both neo-conservatives, thereby testifying immediately to the overlaps between these two major approaches.

Constructing a tripartite Eurocentric global hierarchy

Starting in the bottom-right of Figure 1.1, we can see the base of post-1989 Western-realism comprising a punitive conception of Eurocentrism wherein difference resides principally in *institutional* factors rather than the racial ethnology of its nineteenth-century equivalent. Although it often embraces the idea of universalising Western civilisation (though Huntington is an exception here), for the most part the East is thought to issue a series of threats that can only be policed through punishment and containment. Having conceptually separated the West from the Rest, Western-realism overlays upon this a three-worlds construction. Here the West is privileged as the realm of civilisation, while the Rest are situated within the realms of barbarism (the Second World) and savagery (the Third World). Specifically, this view contrasts the Western zone of peace, which is founded on the civilised, pacific nature of Western states, with the Eastern zone of war, chaos and poverty, which is thought to be a function either of the internal anarchy of savage polities (the Third World of African 'failed states' in today's language), or the threat of barbaric autocratic polities (the Second World of Oriental despotism in nineteenth-century parlance). Ultimately, it is not territorial borders that define today's sites of conflict but the civilisational frontier. The clearest representation of this construction is, of course, provided by Samuel Huntington (1993, 1996), who likens the borders that differentiate East from West as tectonic fault-lines producing a zone of inter-civilisational conflict.

This three-worlds view also lies at the core of Robert Cooper's work (2002, 2004). In particular, Cooper differentiates European *postmodern states* – which have created a civilised zone of peace – from 'the Rest'. European states owe their peaceful relations to an 'honest' and civilised 'moral consciousness' that rejects war (or, more specifically, war between civilised states). The Second World comprises *modern states* (located principally in Asia) that engage in old-style relations involving Machiavellian principles of *raison d'état* and warfare. This approximates with the barbaric category, incorporating autocratic China and Middle-Eastern Islam (i.e., the Oriental despotisms of the nineteenth century). But it is the third category where Cooper's punitive Eurocentrism becomes most apparent. Cooper constructs a Third World of *premodern polities* populated by savage societies living in an anarchic state of nature torn apart by a Hobbesian war of all against all (i.e. 'failed states'). As an internal zone of anarchy emerges, it creates domestic chaos which spills out, or spews forth, a string of threats against the West including drug-trafficking, terrorism as well as ethnic/

tribal struggles that in turn project war, conflict and the refugee exodus beyond national boundaries. Interestingly, Cooper sees the world of postmodern states as referring primarily to the EU, placing the United States in an interstitial category, as does Robert Kagan, a point I come back to later in the chapter.

Eurocentric double standards and the bipolar/schizophrenic international

Crucial here is the Eurocentric double standard that emerges through the bipolar or schizophrenic construction of the international, wherein Western states treat each other differently to the way that they treat non-Western polities. Because Western states are deemed to be civilised, they are rewarded with dignity (i.e. sovereignty). Conversely, non-Western polities are deemed barbaric and therefore unworthy of dignity (i.e. sovereignty is withheld). This imperialist conception was an idiom of nineteenth-century Eurocentrism in all its imperialist guises (as I explain later). And in particular, nineteenth-century Western-realism asserted the right of Western states to colonise Eastern polities and societies in order to contain and punish the barbarians/savages. Significantly, the accompanying idiom of 'social efficiency' carried a great deal of weight. This idea stipulated that all societies had a duty to develop their lands productively. Should they fail, then Eurocentric Western thinkers believed that they had to make way for Western imperialists to do so for them. And in the extreme punitive Eurocentric vision, it was deemed legitimate to exterminate the recalcitrant natives who resisted this 'legitimate' Western incursion.

Some of these extreme measures are, of course, no longer valid: genocide is no longer advocated; since decolonisation, sovereignty has become enshrined as a right of all states; colonialism has been disavowed both legally and normatively, and scientific racism has been discarded. Nevertheless, contemporary punitive Eurocentrism has modified rather than abolished nineteenth-century positions. Thus contemporary punitive Eurocentrics argue that Eastern polities forfeit the right to sovereignty in those instances where such states are unable to bring order or democracy to their societies. Most obviously, non-Western polities are not recognised as sovereign if their instability poses a clear and present danger to Western states. Accordingly, such thinkers argue that Eastern polities/societies need to be punished through Western neo-imperial intervention. All in all, the imperial mantra of Western *hyper-sovereignty* and Eastern *conditional-sovereignty* has been reinstated following the 'exceptional period' of decolonisation. Notably, this hyper-sovereign conception is one that has been generally obscured both by the popular headlining argument that globalisation undermines the sovereignty of all states in general and by the idea of 'postmodern' European states which sacrifice aspects of their sovereignty within the EU more specifically.

Constructing globalisation-as-Eastern-threat

Moving up to the next level in Figure 1.1, Western-realism interprets globalisation as posing an Eastern threat to Western civilisation. Once again, such a conception was fundamental to nineteenth-century Western-realism. In the United States, the most notable geopolitical scholar was Alfred Thayer Mahan, who became famous for his thesis on the role of seapower in history, as well as for his seminal 1897 essay, 'A Twentieth-century Outlook' (Mahan 1890/1897). In Britain, Halford Mackinder led the way with his equally famous 1904 article, 'The Geographical Pivot of History'. Like most geopolitical scholars, Mahan and Mackinder were concerned with the emergence of global interdependence, or what they termed the 'closing of the world'. This was a central source of anxiety because it brought Eastern peoples onto the doorstep of the West via the revolution of transport and communications. For the geopoliticians, the resulting projection of the East out of so-called isolation was an omen for the West given their perception that the East was not merely hungry but keen to dethrone Western hegemony. As Mackinder put it:

> Every explosion of social forces, instead of being dissipated in a surrounding circuit of unknown space and barbaric chaos, will be sharply re-echoed from the far side of the globe, and weak elements in the political and economic organism of the world will be shattered in consequence. (Mackinder 1904: 422)

This barbaric chaos, then, was merely code for the rising Eastern racial challenge that global interdependence supposedly brought in its wake.

In the process, the question that motivated geopolitikers as well as other racist-realists was whether Western civilisation could maintain its position of hegemony in the face of the rising Eastern threat. As Mahan put it, '[w]e stand at the opening of a period when the question is to be settled decisively ... whether Eastern or Western civilization is to dominate throughout the earth and to control its future' (1897: 527). Moreover, one prominent American realist scientific racist, Franklin Giddings, argued that global interdependence 'has awakened a dormant sense of geography that will never again permit the American voter to look at his domestic problems with the old-time satisfaction in our secure isolation' (Giddings 1898: 596). If the economy and the white race were to be nourished, then colonising the inferior races – though difficult given the degenerative problem of the tropics – 'must be faced and overcome, if the civilized world is not to abandon all hope of continuing its economic conquest of the natural resources of the globe' (Giddings 1898: 600).

One important aspect of the 'Eastern-racial arrival' came in the form of non-white immigration, which took on particular significance in the United States. This phenomenon was constructed in terms of the barbaric peril or the 'yellow peril', while non-white immigration was likened to a 'racial invasion'. The arrival of Japanese and Chinese immigrants set off a clamour for strong immigration controls, leading to the 1882 Chinese Exclusion Act and culminating in the 1924 Immigration Act, which restricted quotas mainly in favour of white northern and western Europeans.

Echoing their nineteenth-century predecessors, contemporary punitive Eurocentrics display a deep-seated fear of a globalised world on the basis that this brings Eastern peoples onto the doorstep of the West, or into its heart via immigration. For many Western-realists, this threat is exacerbated by multiculturalism. And likewise, when coupled with the perception of a rising East, a sense of Western anxiety is fuelled. Thus Samuel Huntington argues that one reason for the clash of civilisations since 1989 is that:

[The] world is becoming a smaller place. Interactions between peoples of different civilizations are increasing; these increasing interactions intensify civilization consciousness and awareness of differences ... North African immigration to France generates hostility among Frenchmen ... Americans react far more negatively to Japanese investment than the larger investments from Canada and European countries. (Huntington 1993: 25–6; see also 2004: 14)

Huntington adds that, since 1989, the impact of globalisation has ushered in a profound identity crisis within the West (2004: 13).

In general, contemporary Western-realists point to technological mobility, especially through transnational weapons-movements, which enables non-Western – especially Islamic – terrorists to strike at the heart of the West. Moreover, the repressive policies of autocratic Second World rulers and the anarchy of Third World failed states threaten the West through wars, terrorism and refugee movements (which I discuss below). Thus, when Robert Cooper proclaims that the entire world is, potentially, our neighbour, he means that under globalisation the Eastern threat is now found at the gates of the Western citadel. Or as he put it in *The Breaking of Nations*, globalisation's ability to deliver terrorism and the dirty bomb 'could bring a nightmare in which states lose control of the means of violence and people lose control of their futures. Civilization and order rests on the control of violence: if it becomes uncontrollable there will be no order or civilization' (Cooper 2004: ix).

Western-realist literature perceives the Eastern threat in two conjoined ways: from without via terrorism and war, and from within via immigration and homegrown terrorism. Expressed in Eurocentric terms, this amounts to two idioms: 'barbarians at the gates of the Western citadel' and 'barbarians inside the Western citadel' (or 'the Barbarian Trojan Horse inside the Western citadel') (cf. Salter 2002). Here we move up one step in Figure 1.1 to the substance of these arguments, which I shall take in turn.

Barbarians at the gates of the Western citadel

The Western-realist sense of anxiety translates into a siege mentality in which the West is portrayed as a citadel that is under attack from the Eastern barbarians and savages who now stand barracking at the gates. Typifying this alarmist view is Robert Kaplan's 'The Coming Anarchy' (Kaplan 1994). Kaplan provides a snapshot of West Africa, a region he views as a microcosm of all that is wrong with the Third World. The result is a desperate picture of deprivation and depravity: of rampaging crime, disease, poverty, corruption, drug-trafficking, tribal conflict, ecological disaster, the explosion of population growth and an exodus of refugees that washes into the West like a human tsunami. Kaplan points to a 'criminal anarchy' in the context of failed and collapsed states that, in turn, poses a threat to the West. Interestingly, he draws explicit links to the Victorian era, insisting that West Africa 'is again becoming, as Graham Greene once observed "black" and "unexplored"'. He also deploys Malthusian logic in predicting a demographic doomsday scenario for the East. Invoking images of the 'teeming hordes' in what might be dubbed the coming 'Black Peril' that the West now faces, Kaplan argues that the breakdown of African societies 'will prompt mass migrations and, in turn, innate group conflicts ... will be the core foreign policy challenge from which most others will ultimately emanate'. Kaplan argues that '[w]e are entering a bifurcated world. Part of the globe [the West] is inhabited by Hegel's and Fukuyama's last man, healthy, well-fed, and pampered by technology. The other, larger, part [the East] is inhabited by Hobbes' first man, condemned to a life that is "poor, nasty, brutish and short".' As a result of this desperate condition, war between East and West is inevitable: 'there is a large

number of people on this planet, to whom the comfort and stability of a
middle-class life is utterly unknown [and therefore] find war and a bar-
racks existence a step up rather than a step down'. Kaplan concludes by
issuing a word of warning to Americans, echoing his realist predecessors Alfred Mahan, Franklin Giddings and Harry Powers. For in this
'age of cultural and racial clashes, when national defense is increasingly
local, Africa's distress will exert a destabilizing influence on the United
States … But Afrocentrists are right in one respect; we [Americans]
ignore this dying region at our own risk' (Kaplan 1994). And it turns
out, he argues, that the real threat to the West was not what was going
on between Europeans in Yugoslavia in the 1990s, but that which would
be spewed out by an inverted African black hole.

As noted above, one of the most important themes in the Western-
realist imaginary is the threat posed by Muslims. William Lind put it
thus: '[t]he implication of a Soviet collapse, of the disintegration of the
traditional Russian Empire, might be that Moslem armies would again
be sieging the gates of Vienna' (Lind, cited in Pipes 1990). This perception among Western-realists emerged quickly after 11/9, as Daniel Pipes
explains, although concerns over an emerging Muslim threat stem back
to the 1970s (Furedi 2007). There are two issues to consider here. First,
terrorism is equated with the Second-World barbarism of Islamic fundamentalism and the authoritarianism of Islamic states, which entwine
to produce a virulent form of anti-Westernism. Complementing this
is the equation of failed states (or savage polities) with terrorism. This
is based on the idea that the internal anarchy of failed states in the
black Third World breeds terrorists who subsequently seek to attack
the West. Since 9/11, this threat has been exacerbated by the perception
that failed states are thought to provide safe havens for global terrorist
networks (although see Hehir 2008). If the barbarians at the gates are a
cause for concern, no less important is the threat that they pose *within*
the Western citadel.

The barbarian Trojan Horse inside the Western citadel

At first sight, it might be thought that the American conservative critique of multiculturalism and political correctness, expressed in the
writings of William Lind, Samuel Huntington and others, following
on from Allan Bloom (1987), has little in common with international
thought. But in this discourse, the threat posed by immigration and
multiculturalism is the flip-side of the threat that the barbarians and
savages pose in the form of displaced warfare and terrorism. And, of
course, the link becomes tighter when we recognise that terrorists can

be homegrown (as with the 7/7 bombers in the UK). To this end, James Kurth argues that the 'real clash' is that between Western civilisation and multiculturalism within the West (Kurth 1994). Such an idea is fundamental to Samuel Huntington's famous 1996 book and is developed further in his more recent study (Huntington 2004).

In certain respects, it is the arguments concerning multiculturalism 'at home' where Huntington's Eurocentrism becomes most obvious. The roots of this threat are located implicitly within a Malthusian framework that couples the Eastern population explosion, which occurs as a function of a backward society, with the proliferation of the 'highly fertile' Eastern female. As noted earlier, for many Western-realists, the concern over a relative decline in superior white stock – superior in terms of health, literacy and education – is perhaps as great as the threat posed by terrorism. Such a concern has been usefully dubbed 'the return of the repressed' (Coker 1994: 29). And as Mark Salter points out:

The stereotype of barbarians who are more fertile and populous than 'civilized' individuals is one of the underlying assumptions of demographic arguments ... [And these] demographic arguments are mobilized in periods when the West feels threatened – even though the demographic data have remained largely the same since the turn of the twentieth century. (Salter 2002: 137)

It is within this context of Western anxiety that we encounter the idea of the 'teeming hordes', which is twinned with a revitalised 'Yellow Peril'; something which is applied in particular to Islamic immigration. And such an argument lies at the core of Huntington's thesis on the clash of civilisations:

The futures of the United States and of the West depend upon Americans reaffirming their commitment to Western civilization. Domestically this means rejecting the divisive siren calls of multiculturalism. Internationally it means rejecting the elusive and illusory calls to identify the United States with Asia ... [For when] Americans look for their cultural roots, they find them in Europe. (Huntington 1996: 307, 318)

Maintaining the ethnic and cultural purity of America is a vital factor in renewing America as the pinnacle of Western civilisation. Indeed the principal responsibility of the United States today is to police the Eurocentric line of civilisational apartheid in order to keep the contaminating influence of the East at bay. And from the seed planted in his most well-known book grew the subsequent text, *Who are We?*, in which Huntington launched a critique of Latin American immigration and its contaminating influence on the American Creed – referring to it as 'Hispanization' (Huntington 2004). Interestingly, such a

discourse returns us to the late-nineteenth-century American fear of
Western population decline in the face of rising non-Western immigration, where such immigrants were also seen as more fertile than Anglo-
Saxon stock (Teitelbaum and Winter 1985). In this context, Akira Iriye
(1997) makes an interesting comparison between Samuel Huntington
and Alfred Thayer Mahan. Nevertheless Huntington shares much more
in common with nineteenth-century scientific racists such as William
Graham Sumner (1911) and John W. Burgess (1895): a desire for strong
anti-immigration controls vis-à-vis non-whites; maintenance of the purity of Anglo-Saxon stock (Sumner) or Aryan-Teutonic stock (Burgess)
or the purity of Anglo-Saxon culture (Huntington). But above all, in
strong contrast to Mahan's pro-imperialist stance, Huntington shares
with Burgess and Sumner (as well as Jordan and Spencer) an anti-
imperialist politics.[4] In sum, for contemporary Western-realists, the
role of non-white immigration is viewed as an Eastern 'Trojan Horse',
which when combined with Western ideologies of multiculturalism and
political correctness, subverts the underlying structure of Western civilisation, bringing the citadel to its knees.

Western-realism and the resort to neo-imperialism

Huntington's defensive Eurocentrism excepted, it seems fair to say that
these idioms issue the call for Western neo-imperial or American 'hegemonic' interventionism in the East (e.g. Cooper 2002; Kaplan 2005);
an idea that also finds a strong place in Western idealist-realism, comprising various neo-conservatives (Krauthammer 1990/1991, 2004;
Kristol and Kagan 1996; Kagan 2004, 2008) and liberals (Rieff 1999;
Ignatieff 2003). These neo-imperialists sometimes deny a commitment
to imperialism, referring to the United States as a 'benevolent hegemon'
or, in Kagan's terms a 'Behemoth with a conscience'; concepts that in
turn rest on the idea of 'American exceptionalism'. This implies that
America's high degree of virtue means that other states do not feel
threatened since the US national interest *is* the universal interest (e.g.
Krauthammer 1990/1991, 2004). Significantly, though, the conflation
of the US national interest with the universal is a precise symptom of
Eurocentrism.

Crucial here is the point that such thinkers echo nineteenth-century
Western-realists such as Mahan, Mackinder, Giddings and Powers.
Although this imperial idea escalated after 9/11, it was already established

---

[4] However, as I explain elsewhere, Burgess turns out to have two theories of imperialism – pro- and anti-imperialist; see Hobson (2009: ch. 5).

after 11/9. Robert Cooper is a central figure in making this link with
nineteenth-century discourse. 'It is precisely because of the death of
imperialism that we are now seeing the emergence of the [Eastern
threats of the] pre-modern world ... If they become too dangerous, it is
possible to imagine a defensive imperialism ... perhaps even the need
for colonisation [which] is as great as it ever was in the nineteenth-
century' (Cooper 2002). Echoing Michael Ignatieff's argument about
'empire-lite', this imperialism is often portrayed in terms reminiscent
of the nineteenth-century concept of the civilising mission – 'one [that
must be] acceptable to a world of human rights and cosmopolitan values
... an imperialism which, like all imperialism, aims to bring order and
organisation but which rests today as the voluntary principle ... [based
on] the lightest of touches from the centre' (Cooper 2002). And if this
requires certain double standards on the part of the West, then so be it
(see his quote presented at the beginning of the chapter, p. 23).

In similar vein, Robert Kaplan (2005) likens US military engagements in the East to the waging of the war against the American-Indian
natives. Just as the European immigrants pacified unruly, uncivilised
space through wiping out native Indian communities and containing
them within reserves, so the extension of this principle into the Eastern
world is a necessary tool to protect Western civilisation today (though
genocide is no longer on the agenda). Moreover, in contrast to the more
benign conception of neo-imperialism articulated by Western-idealists,
Western-realists and idealist-realists emphasise the importance of military power to contain and punish the Eastern threat.

This explicit return to the discourse of nineteenth-century imperialism is a particular trope of Western idealist-realism. Thus the prominent neo-conservative, Robert Kagan (2004), argues that the nature of
the Eastern threat and Europe's retreat into a 'postmodern paradise'
means that the United States has no choice but to discipline and punish,
unilaterally if necessary, the savages in the East. In so doing he invokes
the nineteenth-century imperialist idiom of the bipolar international:

The problem is that the United States must sometimes play by the rules of a
Hobbesian world, even though in doing so it violates Europe's postmodern
norms. It must refuse to abide by certain international conventions that may
constrain its ability to fight effectively in Robert Cooper's jungle ... It must live
by a double standard. And it must sometimes act unilaterally ... only because,
given a weak Europe that has moved beyond power, the United States has no
choice *but* to act unilaterally. (Kagan 2004: 99)

Crucially, Kagan argues that, in the absence of US coercive-unilater-
alism Europe would no longer be able to live in paradise and, more
generally, that the very existence of civilisation would be threatened.

Thus rather than criticising the United States, as many Europeans have done, Kagan insists that it 'would be better ... if Europeans could move beyond fear and anger at the rogue colossus and remember, again, the vital necessity of having a strong, even predominant America – for the world and especially for Europe. It would seem to be an acceptable price to pay for [Europe's] paradise' (Kagan 2004: 101). Or, put differently, this would be an acceptable price to pay for the maintenance of civilisation.

Here it deserves reiterating that the nineteenth-century bipolar concept of the international, which inherently issues an imperialist rationale contained within the discourse of Western double standards, has returned in a neo-imperial form. Fukuyama's summary of Kristol's and Kagan's neo-conservative position exemplifies this point. For as he put it, they 'argued explicitly for regime change as a central component of their neo-Reaganite policy. They asserted that getting tyrannical regimes to play by civilized rules through agreements, international law, or norms was ultimately unworkable' (Fukuyama 2006a: 41–2). And interestingly, such a position shares much in common with the imperialist visions of John Stuart Mill and Richard Cobden that underpin Western-idealism, as we shall now see.

'Things can only get better'

As noted above, while Western realist-pessimism has become a loud voice since 1989, in the first instance it was the Western-idealist wing that struck the most immediate chord within the popular imagination. Nowhere was this clearer than in the timely publication of Francis Fukuyama's article, 'The End of History?', on the eve of 11/9 (Fukuyama 1989). The subsequent fall of the Berlin Wall unleashed a wave of euphoria that washed across Western societies. Not surprisingly, this sense of Western triumphalism found in Fukuyama's argument a ready-made vehicle for its theoretical expression, constituting the midwife in the birth of post-1989 Western idealism. It is, of course, true that Fukuyama expressed considerable worries about the end of history in the last paragraph of the article (1989: 18) and in the final part of his book (1992: 287–339). But the bulk of his message – and the part that has been picked up by other liberals since 1989 – is the optimistic and Western-celebratory posture. And while Fukuyama, much like Mill before him, held certain reservations about the final stage of history, he was, however, unequivocal that it was the best one (cf. Mill 1836/1977).

Beginning at the bottom left-hand side of Figure 1.1, contemporary Western-idealists filter the world through a paternalistic Eurocentrism, which in turn gives rise to a series of Western universalist ideas. In contrast to Western-realists, who embrace a sense of siege against perceived Eastern threats, the lowest common denominator of Western-idealism is a universalist/assimilationist Eurocentrism that seeks to promote Western norms around the world in order to civilise the barbarians. This genre promotes a 'soft' informal means of assimilation while Western idealist-realism adopts a 'hard' form. This formula – a triumphalist Western response to the end of the Cold War in the context of a 'benign' paternalistic Eurocentrism – propels us back to the future of the mid-nineteenth century, when the first wave of Western-idealism was in full flight, finding its expression in the various writings of Cobden and Mill (see Hobson 2009: ch. 2; Hall and Hobson 2010).

Constructing a tripartite Eurocentric global hierarchy

Moving up the left side of Figure 1.1, I note that this benign-paternalist version of Eurocentrism, much like its punitive counterpart, conceives a three-worlds view which contrasts a civilised Western zone of peace (the First World) with an Eastern realm of war that comprises the savage Third World (failed states) and the barbaric Second World (authoritarian/autocratic states). This much has been explained already. Nevertheless, while the Second World is represented by the likes of authoritarian Middle Eastern polities and Chinese autocracy, it is also true that there is an intra-Western dimension here, represented typically by authoritarian Russia. Accordingly, it is important to note that not all aspects of Western-idealism can be captured within the framework that I deploy here.

Western 'hyper-sovereignty' and Eastern 'conditional-sovereignty'

Having constructed a line of civilisational apartheid between East and West, Western-idealism returns us to the nineteenth-century schizophrenic conception of the international system. It is conventionally assumed that classical liberal Western-idealists stood for non-interventionism and peace. But it turns out that such a conception applied only to intra-Western relations. John Stuart Mill was typical in arguing for a schizophrenic/bipolar vision of the international (see quote at the beginning of the chapter, p. 23). In essence, while 'civilized states' should treat each other with dignity thereby entailing non-intervention (hence they were 'deserving' of sovereignty), barbarian peoples were deemed uncivilised and thus insufficiently advanced to warrant the same degree of respect – hence Eastern polities were undeserving of sovereignty. Moreover, because non-Western peoples were deemed to be immature, citizenship rights were seen as irrelevant. Accordingly, Mill argued in *On Liberty* that 'despotism is a legitimate mode of government in dealing with barbarians, provided the end be their improvement, and the [colonialist] means justified by actually affecting that end' (Mill 1859/1998: 14–15). This schizophrenic/bipolar conception of the international was one that was held generally by Western-idealists, including Cobden, Angell and Hobson, though it harked back to the likes of Vitoria, Grotius and Locke (Hobson 2009: chs. 2 and 10; Hall and Hobson 2010).

Likewise, post-1989 contemporary Western-idealists, as do the Western-realists, insist that Eastern polities should not be granted sovereignty in a once-and-for-all move. Western-idealism is ostensibly motivated by a desire to right the wrongs that Eastern peoples face within their own societies. Rather than seeking to *contain* Eastern societies (as in Western-realism), Western-idealists are more interested in *culturally converting* them along Western lines so that the injustices of the world can be overcome; a point that is shared with Western idealist-realism. Accordingly, not unlike their Western-realist 'counterparts', they argue that sovereignty in the Third World should have a 'conditional status'; that is, sovereignty should only be recognised when states treat their own populations fairly by respecting human rights contained within a democratic form of governance. But as we saw with respect to Western-realists, conditional sovereignty is a vital prerequisite or trigger for Western neo-imperial intervention, in the absence of which the abuse of millions of non-Western peoples continues unabated. Thus they share in the neo-imperial discourse of Western state *hyper-sovereignty*, which legitimises intervention in 'morally offensive' Eastern states on the basis of their 'conditional sovereignty'.

Constructing globalisation-as-Western opportunity

Moving up a level in Figure 1.1, I note that while Western-idealists pinpoint various threats ushered in by globalisation – ecological crisis and the flood of refugees from savage polities (i.e. failed states) – their central thrust revolves around constructing globalisation-as-Western opportunity. That is, globalisation enables the West to diffuse Western civilisational norms (economic, political, cultural and ethical) around the world in order to *culturally convert* all states along Western normative lines. In the economic sphere, the principal International Financial Institutions (IFIs) such as the World Bank and the World Trade Organization seek to civilise or culturally assimilate Eastern societies along Western neoliberal lines. And in general, Western-idealists perceive the task of capital mobility as performing a similar mission. In Thomas Friedman's well-known aphorism, globalisation forces non-Western polities to don a (Western neoliberal) 'golden straitjacket' (Friedman 1999; see also Wolf 2005). Indeed, modern Western-idealists adopt the arguments of Cobden and Mill, in turn echoing Kant, Smith and Ricardo, wherein global free trade acts as a 'civilising force', leading to the adoption of national 'self-help', 'specialisation' and 'comparative advantage' on the one hand, and incentivising Eastern peoples to intensively develop their economies through individualistic self-help and 'hard work' on the other. Moreover, the spread of liberal capitalism by the West promotes 'civilisational' norms of development, cooperation and ultimately peace.

Civilising the barbarians/savages

Moving up one level in Figure 1.1, we encounter a series of theories which advocate 'civilising the barbarians and savages'. Most prominent here is Francis Fukuyama's (1989, 1992) 'end of history' thesis which triumphantly pronounced Western market democracy as the final stage of human history; an argument that is echoed in Western idealist-realism. Fukuyama's Eurocentric approach is also echoed by 'democratic peace theory' (DPT). Here the civilised world of democratic states forms a zone of peace, while the barbaric world of authoritarian states forms a zone of war. DP theorists do not claim that liberal states are inherently pacific; merely that they do not go to war with each other. Thus they accept that liberal states go to war with authoritarian/autocratic states since the latter are inherently war-prone and cannot be trusted to act in a civilised or rational manner (Doyle 1983; Russett 1990; Owen 1994).

DPT constructs a dividing line between East and West, which acts as a frontier between civilisation and barbarism/savagery. Thus non-democratic states 'are viewed *prima-facie* as unreasonable, unpredictable and potentially dangerous. These are states either ruled by despots, or with unenlightened citizenries' (Owen 1994: 96); a formulation that returns us directly to the nineteenth-century theory of Oriental despotism. In its extreme form, as David Blaney (2001: 35) perceptively points out, 'nonliberal states are constructed as sites of legitimate intervention for liberal purposes and perhaps as objects of violent moral crusades – both paradigmatic forms of ... "liberal favoritism" in Owen's [term], democratic "xenophobia" in Russett's, and liberal bellicosity in mine'. In this conception we return to the bipolar imperialist conception of the international, wherein Western states are rewarded with civilisational status and hence hyper-sovereignty (the right to intervene in uncivilised states), while Eastern polities are demoted to the status of conditional-sovereignty (connoting the forfeiting of the right to self-determination). In sum, while advocates of DPT differ in tone on this point, the logical extension of DPT is the assimilation of non-liberal states into the universe of the civilised West (though it should be noted that some DPT advocates refrain from going this far – e.g. Doyle 1983). Failing that, the continuation of civilised Western democratic states and barbaric Eastern authoritarianisms serves as a means to define and reproduce the Western self against the Eastern other (cf. Tanji and Lawson 1997; Blaney 2001: 40–1), thereby unwittingly offering up the potential for 'perpetual war' with the Other.

Recently, this approach has been extended further within the Western idealist-realist camp, through the advocacy of a 'Concert of Democracies' (CoD). This entails a proactive Western posture vis-à-vis non-Western (as well as a few Western) non-democratic polities. In a seminal statement of this position, John Ikenberry and Anne-Marie Slaughter (2006) argue that current international institutions (especially the key IFIs and the UN) are no longer fit for purpose. While they call for reform of the UN, Ikenberry and Slaughter also suggest the need for a CoD that can ratify and institutionalise the democratic peace. If the UN cannot be sufficiently reformed, they suggest that the CoD trumps the UN and 'authorizes collective action [and the] use of force by super-majority vote' (Ikenberry and Slaughter 2006: 8). The new CoD approach incorporates interventionism in the non-Western world in order to extend the civilised democratic zone of peace, something which links closely with prominent neo-conservative thinkers, some of whom make a comparable case for a 'League of Democracies' (e.g. Kagan 2008: 97–105). It is notable that these ideas were supported by both candidates in the 2008 US presidential election. An additional strand of the CoD/League of Democracies thesis lies in the embracing of humanitarian interventionism (as well as the doctrine of pre-emption, to which I shall return shortly).

The concern with regime type overlaps with Western-idealism's humanitarian project, most notably coming together in the idea of the 'responsibility to protect'. This concept emerged most powerfully in the 2001 UN report on the subject, the upshot of which was the UN-mandated notion that Western states have a 'responsibility to protect' peoples living in countries where human rights abuses are taking place. Such a view rests on the assumption that abuses are carried out in Eastern states; either in autocracies (barbaric Oriental despotisms) or in failed states (savage polities living in an anarchic state of nature). The humanitarian interventionist argument finds its expression in liberalism (e.g. Donnelly 1998), solidarist English School work (e.g. Wheeler 2000) and constructivism (e.g. Keck and Sikkink 1998; Risse *et al.* 1999).

Focusing on the constructivist literature as an example, it is possible to detect two main Eurocentric aspects – one explicit and the other implicit. The explicit Eurocentric formulation takes the form of a triumphalist return to the civilising mission. As one critic aptly conveys this, the constructivist 'pro-interventionist attitude … is often focused on the diffusion of human rights norms from the international [the West] to the domestic level [within the East], and brimming with notions of their success in the betterment of the human condition' (Belloni 2007: 453). The second Eurocentric aspect emerges at an implicit level. Key here is the assumption that while 'progressive' humanitarian intervention was subverted by a racist discourse in the nineteenth century, today it takes a sincere and empathic form, free of racist and Eurocentric bias. One prominent constructivist scholar characterises the new socialising process as one 'by which non-white, non-Christian populations became "humanized" for the West' (Finnemore 2003: 157). This unwittingly serves to 'naturalise' humanitarianism, thereby obscuring some of the underlying continuities between contemporary intervention and its nineteenth-century imperial predecessor. Moreover, Finnemore claims that this new 'non-Eurocentric' humanitarian discourse has trumped warfare, whereas in the eighteenth century war was glorified and 'progressive' intervention shunned (2003: 135). But this could hold only if we confine our remit to *intra-Western* state relations, given that warfare between Western and Eastern states has been a commonplace since 1947. Interesting here is that certain Western idealist-realists explicitly recover this recessive Eurocentric imperial dimension in Finnemore's analysis of humanitarian intervention, proclaiming it as a fundamental component of US imperialism, albeit one of a liberal, benign conception: 'what is exceptional about American [humanitarian] messianism is that it is the last imperial ideology left standing in the world, the sole survivor of imperial claims to universal significance' (Ignatieff 2005: 16).

The desire to defend the West is also apparent in Western humanitarianism's anti-immigration stance. Belloni emphasises how European expansion/integration goes hand-in-hand with the creation of 'Fortress Europe', bolstering the civilisational frontier which keeps out refugees while simultaneously allowing for a 'weakening of legal principles and norms of refugee protection'. This is achieved through a twin strategy, comprising: a humanitarian agenda that is applied to those who remain within conflict zones – to wit, 'the over-riding principle ... should be to bring safety to the people, rather than people to safety' (Sakoko Ogata cited in Belloni 2007: 464); and second, the idea of 'safe return'. In contrast to the Cold War era when return was voluntary, refugees are now repatriated through encouragement or force (and often before peace in their home countries has been attained). Kishore Mahbubani (2004: 63) captures this idea powerfully, arguing that Western human rights activists see Third World citizens as akin to

> hungry and diseased passengers on a leaky, overcrowded boat that is about to drift into treacherous waters, in which many of them will perish. The captain of the boat is often harsh, sometimes fairly and sometimes not. On the river banks stand a group of affluent, well-fed and well-intentioned onlookers. As soon as those onlookers witness a passenger being flogged or imprisoned or even deprived of his right to speak, they board the ship to intervene, protecting the passengers from the captain. But those passengers remain hungry and diseased. As soon as they try to swim to the banks into the arms of their benefactors, they are firmly returned to the boat, their primary sufferings unabated.

Thus, within the Eurocentric discourse of Eastern 'failed states', humanitarianism functions as 'part of a control strategy designed to prevent the transmission of disorder and chaos from war-torn, poor and peripheral countries to the developed world' (Belloni 2007: 464).

Within the Western idealist-realist framework, the idea of humanitarian intervention has been extended into a proactive military 'preventionist' discourse – specifically the 'duty to prevent' (which returns us to the CoD approach). Slaughter and Feinstein (2004) developed the concept of the 'duty to prevent' as a direct corollary of 'the duty to protect' the human rights of peoples around the world. The duty to prevent refers to the problem of the proliferation of Weapons of Mass Destruction (WMD). Slaughter and Feinstein are particularly critical of the Non-Proliferation Treaty (NPT) which, they assert, is concerned only with the presence of WMD within a state rather than with a concern over that state's particular regime-form. As they put it, '[t]he problem with the [NPT's] approach is that its opening proposition is to treat North Korea as if it were Norway. This flaw has exposed the non-proliferation regime to abuse by determined and defiant regimes, especially those headed by dictatorial rulers' (2004: 143–4). Accordingly, they conclude, the non-proliferation campaign 'must be based ... on the recognition that leaders without internal checks on their power, or who are sponsors of terror, and who seek to acquire WMD are a unique threat' (2004: 145). In this discourse, Eastern autocracies are broadly akin to the 'barbaric' Oriental despotisms of the nineteenth century, which must be contained for the threat they pose. Indeed, Western states have a duty to prevent such dictatorships threatening the world, most obviously by undertaking interventionist measures. Thus prior to the acquisition of WMDs, Western states should apply a range of measures such as sanctions and, if necessary, military force;[5] an argument which explicitly overlaps with the neo-conservative pre-emptive defence argument that was enshrined within the 2002 Bush Doctrine.

Last, but not least, these Eurocentric themes are echoed in the literature on protectorates/international trusteeship/shared sovereignty. And, once again, on this point we find a convergence of Western-idealists and Western-realists (e.g. Herbst 2004; Fukuyama 2005; Krasner 2005; Sobjerg 2007). This involves a virtual return to the League of Nations Mandate System where Western powers 'come to the aid' of failed states and 'help' them govern their own jurisdictions. Such a form of direct interventionism, as in the B and C Mandates, is envisaged in terms of decades and 'quasi-permanence'. Pointedly, Jeffrey Herbst (2004) asks rhetorically why failed states which behave irresponsibly and repressively towards their own populations should be recognised as sovereign by the international community (read 'the West'). His response is to advocate a 'decertification process' for collapsed states or chronically failed states, whereby they are stripped of sovereignty altogether, thereby opening the East up to neo-imperial Western interventionism. Indeed such a discourse, William Bain points out, 'no matter how enlightened or well-intentioned, cannot escape by nature its imperial past because it belongs to a mode of conduct that is imperial' (Bain 2003: 75).

All in all, therefore, the liberal rise of humanitarian consciousness and with it the right and duty to intervene/protect/prevent returns us not only to the idea of the 'White man's burden' but also to the complementary nineteenth-century notion that states outside the West are undeserving of sovereignty. And as a corollary, only through a Western imperial civilising mission can they be brought into the civilised fold.

---

[5] One caveat is noteworthy here. While the stand against autocracy often takes a Eurocentric hue, it is not the case that all such states are located within the East. The unease over post-1991 Russian authoritarianism is a clear case in point, though it would be fair to say that the 'Oriental despotisms' of North Korea and Iran are viewed with particular suspicion as, of course, was Iraq.

Conclusion

One of the problems of international theory and, in particular, its hold over International Relations as a discipline is its *ahistorical presentism*, wherein the present is understood only through reference to the uniqueness of present conditions and concepts. When combined with the related problem of 'temporal othering', the past becomes seen as radically incommensurable with the present. In this way, seminal events such as 11/9 or 9/11 are viewed as ushering in new phases of world politics; phases that are deemed to be autonomous from previous eras. In this chapter, I have sought to overcome such presentism by deconstructing the binary constructions that are used to split apart the pre- and post-1989 eras of international thought, thereby revealing the many continuities between them. Specifically, nineteenth-century Western-idealism perceived the Other as culturally (and sometimes racially) inferior, requiring Western imperial tutelage to correct its deviancy either by assimilating the East to the West, or by containing the East to preserve Western civilisation. Thus, as in the nineteenth century, preserving distance from the Other through imperial containment underpins contemporary Western-realism, while Western expansion and the remaking of the world along Western lines defines contemporary Western-idealism.

Finally, it is worth reflecting on *why* post-1989 international thought has returned to many of these nineteenth-century themes. Between 1914 and 1989, the West underwent three debilitating civil wars – the First and Second World Wars and the Cold War. This dented the supremacy of the West in Eastern eyes, presenting the West as both divided and fallible. In addition, between about 1890 and 1975, the East resisted and finally overthrew Western imperialism, winning the status of sovereign-equal in the process. This challenged the central supposition of Eurocentrism: namely the 'subject status' of the West as the prime actor in global politics. Against this background, the dissolution of the Soviet Union was fortuitous insofar as it signalled the end of the third Western civil war, and furnished the West with the opportunity to unite and reassert itself as the prime actor of global politics. For Western-idealists, the end of the Soviet Union represented an opportunity for the West to consolidate itself and culturally convert the Other; for Western-realists, the Soviet demise prompted a Western identity crisis that needed to be solved by the construction of a new Other against which the West could consolidate its civilisational identity. In both imaginaries, the solution lies with the rolling back of the sovereignty of the Eastern state that had been won during decolonisation, while simultaneously rolling forward the sovereignty of the Western state. Ultimately, then, reinstating the nineteenth-century Eurocentric idea of the 'Western hyper-sovereign state versus the conditional-sovereignty of the Eastern state' means that the 'postcolonial interlude' can be happily relegated to an unfortunate footnote in the long 'normal' history of Western supremacy (see Furedi 1994: 103).

2   The return of primitive accumulation

Saskia Sassen

The return of primitive accumulation

1989 marks the rise of histories other than those of democracy and freedom. These are histories made in the wake of the shift to a unipolar world dominated by a sharp rise in US power. Alongside the emergence of the United States as the world's sole global power, 1989 also signals an unsettling and debordering of existing arrangements within the deep structures of capitalist economies. Here we find new modes of profit extraction in the most unlikely places, modes that have now become systemic to the extent of being hard-wired into the functioning of the capitalist system itself. Since 1989, countries in the Global South have become subject to a form of financial control – carried out by institutions like the International Monetary Fund (IMF) – which operates as a worldwide financial disciplinary regime. Survival here hinges on exporting and trafficking people because it is the one resource that many of these countries have. Indeed, the rise in people trafficking has become the last hope for survival not just for ordinary households in poor countries, but for a number of actors ranging from small entrepreneurs to governments.

Countries in the Global North have their own version of this parallel history. Prominent here is the growing informalisation of work, the sharp downgrading of the manufacturing sector, and the explosion of high-risk finance, all of which took off in the post-1989 period. Over the past twenty years, high-risk finance has launched a series of major micro- and macro-financial crises which have brought down several powerful economies, such as the manufacturing sector in South Korea, and eventually led to the subprime mortgage crisis of 2007. By 2009, some of the world's most powerful financial firms were bankrupt or partly nationalised – the overriding sense is of whole economies in deep crisis. In each of these crises, central banks poured taxpayers' money into rescuing the financial system. Under these conditions, finance functions as a mechanism for primitive accumulation, albeit of a different sort than classical economists envisaged some 200 years ago.

There are few resemblances between these post-1989 economic histories and the celebration of post-1989 peace and freedom in countries once part of the Soviet sphere of influence. Yet these economic histories emerge after 1989 in most of the world, including former Soviet-controlled countries. All of this points to a *systemic* feature of advanced capitalism, one that may have been held in check by the Cold War but which rises to its full capacity (for destruction) once freed from the constraints of bipolar restraint. The end of the Cold War pronounced the free market victorious and neoliberalism the best growth policy for countries. This was the setting that enabled finance to enter a new phase which legitimised the financialising of growing sectors of the economy. One of the ironies emerging from the growing complexity of finance was the possibility of implementing financial forms of primitive accumulation – the corporate global outsourcing of jobs can be seen as the latest version of an older story. In other words, among the effects of 1989 is to have enabled both the most complex financial system the world has ever seen and a vast expansion of primitive accumulation implemented through sophisticated organisational mechanisms.

In this chapter, I focus on this 'other' post-1989 history – the rise of financial power unleashed by the emergence of the United States as the sole global power. It is a history that somehow evades the, by now, ritualised 'post-1989' frame, a frame that is usually understood as a celebration of the post-1989 liberation of Central and Eastern European countries. In his exceptionally illuminating introduction, George Lawson problematises the putative 1989 old/new history divide. He examines the diverse contents, spaces and times of what is often forced under a univocal meaning of 1989, exploring how xenophobic nationalists and market fundamentalists were as involved in the fall of communism as liberal intellectuals and utopian liberals. Chris Armbruster (Chapter 9, this volume) also explores how the non-violent revolutions of 1989 actually helped to feed older European histories of violence that have now returned, notably narrow nationalisms and naked totalitarianisms. Indeed, the revolutions of 1989 served to weaken the influence of leftist political options, as Outhwaite (Chapter 3, this volume) describes.

In this chapter, I build on these contributions by demonstrating how older histories of economic violence re-emerged with renewed vigour in the 1980s and 1990s. In particular, I concentrate on three forms of contemporary primitive accumulation: first, the growing informalisation of types of low-profit activities in advanced economies, whereby informalisation can be seen as the low-cost equivalent of formal deregulation/liberalisation in major, high-profit economic sectors such as telecommunications and finance; second, the extraction of value from the Global South via neoliberal policy and debt services; and third, the (mis)use of residential subprime mortgages by banks to build investment instruments without becoming dependent on the ability of those households to pay their mortgages. The result was that millions of those households lost everything: their houses and whatever savings they may have had. The final part of the chapter explores the consequences of these innovations both for the international political economy and for our understanding of the events and processes associated with 'the global 1989'.

Advanced capitalism and its mechanisms for primitive accumulation

The end of the Cold War launched one of the most brutal economic phases of the modern era. Following a period of Keynesian-led relative redistribution, the United States became the frontier space for a radical reshuffling of capitalism. In the post-Cold War period, the United States presumed the title of leader of the free world. This has allowed it to pursue a dramatic 'open door' policy which sees the world as a giant market dominated by large corporate actors – a shift from one people to one market under God. But this vast project to a large extent played out in thick local settings, and these are often excluded from examinations of the post-1989 world. Important here is Saull's (Chapter 8, this volume) work showing how variable local histories also feed world politics and that this unevenness becomes legible once we go beyond a Eurocentric view of history.

Three mechanisms enabled new forms of primitive accumulation post-1989. First, there is the informalising and downgrading of a growing range of economic activities in the Global North after decades of extensively regulated economies, itself arising from workers' struggles throughout the twentieth century. The post-1989 period has seen a strong tendency towards a casualisation of employment relations worldwide, but most prominently in highly developed economies, especially the United States. The decline of labour unions in manufacturing, the growth of part-time and temporary jobs in all economic sectors, and the informalisation of work are all core features of this general trend, a development evident in cities as diverse as New York, Paris, London and Amsterdam. A common interpretation in the Global North holds that the growth of the informal economy is a result of the propensity of immigrants from Global South countries to adopt informal work practices. In my research, I find this claim to be incorrect. Both the informalisation and the more general downgrading of many economic activities are a structured outcome of trends in advanced economies – indeed, these trends extend into the political domain (Sassen 2008: chs. 6, 8 and 9).[1]

Second is the implementation of restructuring programmes in the Global South at the hands of the reinvented IMF and the newly minted World Trade Organization (WTO). These global regulators were but two of the best known footsoldiers in the makeover of the unipolar world that took off in the late 1980s. Countries in the Global South were subjected to an international debt-financing regime which put governments, firms and households under enormous constraints. In the case of developing economies, the IMF and WTO put undue pressure on them to implement a bundle of new policies aimed at furthering corporate globalisation. These include the forced adoption of structural adjustment programmes (SAPs), prominently including the opening up of their economies to foreign firms (World Bank 2005a); the elimination of multiple state subsidies to vulnerable or development-linked sectors, from public health to road construction (United Nations Development Programme [UNDP] 2005; 2008); and, almost inevitably, financial crises and the prevailing types of programmatic solutions put forth by the IMF (Reinhardt and Kaminsky 1999; Pyle and Ward 2003; see also Henderson 2005). In most of the countries involved – whether Mexico or Thailand or Kenya – these conditions have created enormous costs for certain sectors of the economy and for most of the people, and have not fundamentally reduced government debt. Among these costs are growth in unemployment, the closure of a

---

[1] A central hypothesis organising much of my research on the informal economy is that the processes of economic restructuring that have contributed to the decline of the manufacturing-dominated industrial complex of the post-war era and the rise of the new, service-dominated economic complex provide the general context within which we need to place informalisation if we are to go beyond a mere description of instances of informal work. The specific set of mediating processes that I have found to promote informalisation of work are: (1) increased earnings inequality and the associated restructuring of consumption in high-income strata and in very-low-income strata; and (2) inability among the providers of many of the goods and services that are part of the new consumption to compete for the necessary resources in urban contexts where leading sectors have sharply bid up the prices of commercial space, labour, auxiliary services, and other basic business inputs.

large number of firms in traditional sectors oriented towards the local or national market, the promotion of export-oriented cash crops that have increasingly replaced subsistence agriculture and food production for local or national markets, and finally, an ongoing and mostly heavy burden of government debt.

The third mechanism of primitive accumulation is the development of new types of investment instruments using mortgages oriented to low and modest income households. Finance has developed multiple ways of extracting profits over the last twenty years, including the securitization of bundles of thousands of small consumer debts, from credit card debt to auto loans. Subprime mortgages, embedded in complex financial instruments sold on the secondary financial market, serve as assets for the making of asset-backed securities and as a mechanism for the extraction of limited savings from modest-income households. These mortgages differ from traditional mortgages in two ways. First, the house itself functions as collateral only for those who own the instrument, which in a fast moving market of buying and selling may last for just two hours. Thus, when an investor has sold the instrument, what happens to the house itself and to the loan is irrelevant. The other is that the profit of the lender comes not from mortgage repayment, as in traditional banking, but from bundling up as many of these mortgages as possible as fast as possible and then selling off the package to an investor in the secondary financial market. The creditworthiness of the borrower is secondary at best – what matters are the number of mortgages issued and the speed with which the lender can secure the needed quantity of mortgages. Millions of these mortgages have been sold in the United States to people who had not thought of owning houses, who had not asked for a mortgage, and who were not in a position to afford mortgages, particularly not in a time of rapidly escalating interest rates. The result was that their savings were extracted via the mortgage instrument and millions lost both their savings and their house. And there are more losses to come as many of these mortgages shift into variable interest rates between 2009 and 2011. Both features of these mortgage instruments become alarming if their central target is the low- and moderate-income household market, which in a globalised financial market represents an enormous population. Ultimately these new types of mortgage-backed financial instruments can function as a vehicle for extracting even small savings from billions of modest-income households around the world (Sassen 2008). As such, if this mechanism of primitive accumulation began in the United States, it need not end there. The new mortgage business has no frontier.

The informalising of work in advanced economic sectors

The recent growth of informal economies in major global cities in North America, Western Europe and, to a lesser extent, Japan, raises a number of questions about what is – and what is not – part of today's advanced urban economies. As I have looked in depth at this mechanism for primitive accumulation elsewhere, I discuss it only briefly here (see Sassen 2001: ch. 9; 2007: ch. 4).

One problem in understanding the meaning of these informal economies in global cities is that analysts and policy-makers often group together informal and illegal activities. Both are simply classified as breaking the law. This obscures two important questions: first, why have these licit activities become informal considering that they are activities which can be done above ground, unlike illegal activities such as tax evasion or trading in prohibited drugs; second, why have they become informal only now after a century of successful efforts to regulate them in most developed countries, and certainly in Europe and in Japan? Typically, the emergence of informal economies is seen as the result of a failure of government regulation and as an import from the less developed world brought in by immigrants – immigrants replicating survival strategies prevalent in their home countries. Related to this view is the notion that backward sectors of the economy are kept backward, or even alive, because of the availability of a large supply of cheap immigrant workers. The assumption is that, if there is an informal economy in highly developed countries, the sources of this can be found in Third World immigration and in backward sectors of the economy. These two arguments – government failure and economic backwardness – sit alongside a third: that this phenomenon is peculiar to Northern cities with the correlate assumption that nothing has really changed in the long-standing informal economies of the Global South.

In my reading, each of these three notions is inadequate. Government failure cannot explain a simple fact: many governments had solved the issue of informal work by the mid-twentieth century. As such, for decades this has not been an issue, begging the question, why now? Equally, although immigrants, insofar as they tend to form communities, may be in a favourable position to seize opportunities represented by informalisation, these opportunities are not *caused* by immigrants. In fact, as I explore in the next section, these processes are a structural outcome of trends endemic to advanced capitalist economies. Further, if there is indeed a global infrastructure for running and servicing the global economy, then global cities of the South are undergoing, or will undergo, a comparable transformation, albeit with their own specificities. Indeed, conditions akin to those in the global cities of the North appear to be producing a new type of informal economy in global cities of the South premised on the same politico-economic restructuring processes that led to the emergence of a new urban economy in the late 1980s and onwards which, in turn, enabled the formation of new informal economies. The decline of the manufacturing-dominated industrial complex that characterised most of the twentieth century, and the rise of service-dominated economic complexes, provide the general context within which we need to place informalisation if we are to go beyond a mere description of instances of informal work.

In this sense, it is more appropriate to see new forms of informalisation as the low-cost equivalent of formal deregulation in finance, telecommunications and most other economic sectors in the name of flexibility and innovation. The difference is that, while formal deregulation is costly, and tax revenue as well as private capital goes into paying for it, informalisation is low-cost and largely carried out on the backs of the workers and firms themselves. This, in turn, explains the particularly strong presence of informal economies in global cities. And it contributes to a mostly overlooked development: the proliferation of an informal economy of creative professional work in these cities – artists, architects, designers, software developers. In the case of the new creative professional informal economy, these negative features are mostly absent – informalisation expands opportunities and networking possibilities. There are strong reasons why these artists and professionals operate at least partly informally – it allows them to function in the interstices of urban and organisational spaces often dominated by large corporate actors and to escape the corporatising of creative work. In this way, they contribute to a specific feature of the new urban economy: its innovativeness alongside a certain type of frontier spirit. This is a trend not just present in Northern global cities, but those of the South as well. As such, it is clear that today's informalisation is not something restricted to the Global North, or a result of government failure and/or immigration, but a process embedded in core features of advanced capitalism.

Extracting earnings and revenue from the Global South

The second form of primitive accumulation in the contemporary world that concerns me here is the extraction of value from the Global South and, in particular, the implementation of restructuring programmes at the hands of the IMF and the WTO. Debt and debt servicing problems have been a systemic feature of the developing world since the 1980s. They are also a systemic feature of new global circuits of accumulation. The effect on people, economies and governments is mediated through the particular features of this IMF negotiated debt rather than the fact of debt per se. Among these particular features are cuts in specific government programmes in order to pay off interest on the debt to mostly Global North lenders, both private and public. It is with this logic in mind that this section of the chapter examines various features of government debt in developing economies.[2]

Much research on poor countries documents the link between hyper-indebted governments and cuts in social programmes. These cuts tend to affect women and children in particular through cuts in education and healthcare, both investments necessary to ensuring a better future (for overviews of the data, see UNDP 2005, 2008; World Bank 2005b, 2006). There is by now a large literature in many different languages on this subject, including a vast number of limited-circulation items produced by various activist and support organisations. An older literature on women and debt also documents the disproportionate burden that these programmes put on women during the first generation of structural adjustment programmes (SAPs) in the 1980s in several developing countries in response to growing government debt (Moser 1989; Tinker 1990; Ward 1991; Beneria and Feldman 1992; Bradshaw *et al.* 1993; Bose and Acosta-Belen 1995). Unemployment of women themselves but also, more generally, of the men in their households has added to the pressure on women to find ways to ensure household survival (Elson 1995; Safa 1995; Rahman 1999; Standing 1999; Lucas 2005; Buechler 2007). Subsistence food production, informal work, emigration and prostitution have all become survival options for women and, by extension, often for their households.

Heavy government debt and high unemployment have brought with them the need for search-for-survival alternatives not only for ordinary people, but also for governments and enterprises. And a shrinking regular economy in a growing number of poor countries has brought with it a widened use of illegal profit-making by enterprises and organisations. Thus, we can say that, through their contribution to heavy debt burdens, SAPs have played an important role in the formation of

---

[2] This section is based on a larger research project (Sassen 2008) that seeks to show how the struggles by individuals, households, entrepreneurs and even governments are micro-level enactments of larger processes of economic restructuring in developing countries launched by the IMF and World Bank programmes, as well as in WTO law implementation during the 1990s and onwards.

counter-geographies of survival, of profit-making, and of government revenue enhancement. Furthermore, economic globalisation has provided an institutional infrastructure for cross-border flows and global markets, thereby facilitating the operation of these counter-geographies on a global scale. Once there is an institutional infrastructure for globalisation, processes that have operated for the most part at the national or regional level can scale up to the global level even when this is not necessary for their operation. This contrasts with processes that are by their very nature global, such as the network of financial centres underlying the formation of a global capital market.

Even before the economic crises of the mid-1990s, the debt of poor countries in the South had grown from US$507 billion in 1980 to US$1.4 trillion in 1992. Debt service payments alone had increased to $1.6 trillion, more than the actual debt. According to some estimates, from 1982 to 1998, indebted countries paid four times their original debts, and at the same time, their debt stocks went up by four times (Toussaint 1999). These countries had to use a significant share of their total revenues to service these debts. Thirty-three of the forty-one highly indebted poor countries (HIPCs) paid $3 in debt service payments to the North for every $1 in development assistance. For years, many of these countries paid between 20 and 25 per cent of their export earnings for interest on their debt (Ambrogi 1999). As of 2006, the poorest 49 countries had debts of $375 billion. If to these 49 poor countries we add the 'developing countries', we have a total of 144 countries with a debt of over $2.9 trillion and $573 billion paid to service debts in 2006 alone (Jubilee Debt Campaign UK, 2009).

The debt burden that built up in the 1980s, and especially the 1990s, has had substantial repercussions on state spending composition. This is well illustrated in the case of Zambia, Ghana and Uganda, three countries that global regulators (notably the World Bank and the IMF) see as cooperative, responsible and successful at implementing SAPs. A few examples of expenditure levels paint a far more troubling picture. At the height of these programmes, the mid 1990s, Zambia's government paid $1.3 billion in debt but only $37 million for primary education; Ghana's social expenses, at $75 million, represented 20 per cent of its debt service; and Uganda paid $9 per capita on its debt and only $1 for healthcare (Ismi 1998). In 1994 alone, these three countries remitted $2.7 billion to bankers in the North. Africa's payments reached $5 billion in 1998, which means that for every $1 in aid, African countries paid $1.40 in debt service in 1998. In many of the HIPCs, debt service ratios to gross national product (GNP) have long exceeded sustainable limits; many are far more extreme than what were considered unmanageable levels in the Latin American debt crisis of the 1980s (Oxfam 1999). Debt to GNP ratios were especially high in Africa, where they stood at 123% in the late 1990s, compared with 42% in Latin America and 28% in Asia. Generally, the IMF asks HIPCs to pay 20% to 25% of their export earnings towards debt service. By 2003, debt service as a share of exports only (not overall government revenue) ranged from extremely high levels for Zambia (29.6%) and Mauritania (27.7%) to significantly lowered levels compared with the 1990s for Uganda (down from 19.8% in 1995 to 7.1% in 2003) and Mozambique (down from 34.5% in 1995 to 6.9% in 2003). In contrast, in 1953, the Allies cancelled 80% of Germany's war debt and only insisted on 3% to 5% of export earnings debt service. Relatively favourable conditions were also applied to Central European countries in the 1990s.

These features of the contemporary conjuncture suggest that many of these countries cannot escape their indebtedness through strategies like SAPs. Generally, IMF debt management policies from the 1980s onwards can be shown to have worsened the situation for the unemployed and poor (Ward and Pyle 1995; Ismi 1998; Ambrogi 1999; Oxfam 1999; UNDP 2005, 2008). The 1997 financial crisis in the rich and dynamic countries of Southeast Asia shows us that accepting the types of loans offered, and indeed pushed, by private lenders can create unmanageable debt levels also among rich and high-growth economies, bringing bankruptcies and mass layoffs to a broad range of enterprises and sectors. Even a powerful economy like South Korea found itself forced into SAPs, with attendant growth in unemployment and poverty due to widespread bankruptcies of small and medium-sized firms catering to both national and export markets (Olds *et al.* 1999). The US$120 billion rescue package brought with it the introduction of SAP provisions, which reduce the autonomy of the governments. On top of that, most of the funds went to compensate the losses of foreign institutional investors rather than help address the poverty and unemployment resulting from the crisis.

It is in this context that alternative survival circuits emerge. The context can be specified as a systemic condition comprising a set of particular interactions including high unemployment, poverty, widespread bankruptcies and shrinking state resources (or allocation of resources). The central implication is that the feminisation of survival goes well beyond households; it extends to firms and governments. There are new profit-making and government revenue-making possibilities built on the backs of migrants, and women migrants in particular. As such, examining the question of immigrant remittances offers valuable insights into the broader subject of the formation of alternative political economies and how these unsettle older notions of an international division of labour.

The remittance business

Immigrants enter the macro level of development strategies through the remittances they send back home.[3] These represent a major source of foreign exchange reserves for the government in a good number of countries. Although the flows of remittances may be minor compared with the massive daily capital flows in global financial markets, they can matter enormously to developing or struggling economies. The World Bank (2006) estimates that remittances worldwide reached US$230 billion in 2005, up from US$70 billion in 1998; of this total amount, US$168 billion went to developing countries, up 73 per cent over 2001; in 2007, remittances reached US$318 billion, of which US$240 billion went to developing countries (*Migrant Remittances* 2008: 2). Immigration firms can also benefit. Thus, the Inter-American Development Bank (IADB) produced a series of detailed studies which show that, in 2003, immigrant remittances generated US$2 billion in handling fees for the financial and banking sector on the US$35 billion sent back home by Hispanics in the United States (see also Robinson 2004). The IADB also found that for Latin America and the Caribbean as a whole, these remittance flows exceeded the combined flows of all foreign direct investment and net official development assistance in 2003 (see, generally, Orozco *et al.* 2005; and the quarterly issues of *Migrant Remittances*).

To understand the significance of these figures, they should be related to the GDP and foreign currency reserves in the specific countries involved, rather than compared to the global flow of capital. For instance, in the Philippines, a key sender of migrants, in general, and for women in the entertainment industry in particular, remittances were the third largest source of foreign exchange over the past several years. In Bangladesh, another country with significant numbers of its workers in the Middle East, Japan, and several European countries, remittances represent about a third of foreign exchange. In Mexico, remittances have long been the second source of foreign currency, just below oil and ahead of tourism, and are larger than foreign direct investment (World Bank 2006), though early 2008 saw a decline in total inflows

---

[3] The basic source for remittances comes from the Central Bank of each receiving country. These figures exclude informal transfers. The scholarship on these subjects is vast. As such, it is not possible to reference fully each of the major propositions organising this discussion. For broader discussions of the literature, see Sassen 2001, 2006b, 2007.

Table 2.1 *Countries with highest remittance inflows as share of GDP,
2002–5 (US$ million)*

Country	2002	2003	2004 (estimate)	2005 (estimate)	Remittances as a share (%) of GDP (2004)
1. Tonga	66	66	66	66	**31.1**
2. Moldova	323	486	703	703	**27.1**
3. Lesotho	194	288	355	355	**25.8**
4. Haiti	676	811	876	919	**24.8**
5. Bosnia/ Herzegovina	1,526	1,745	1,824	1,824	**22.5**
6. Jordan	2,135	2,201	2,287	2,287	**20.4**
7. Jamaica	1,260	1,398	1,398	1,398	**17.4**
8. Serbia/Montenegro	2,089	2,661	4,129	4,650	**17.2**
9. El Salvador	1,954	2,122	2,564	2,564	**16.2**
10. Honduras	718	867	1,142	1,142	**15.5**
11. Philippines	7,381	10,767	11,634	13,379	**13.5**
12. Dominican Republic	2,194	2,325	2,471	2,493	**13.2**
13. Lebanon	2,500	2,700	2,700	2,700	**12.4**
14. Samoa	45	45	45	45	**12.4**
15. Tajikistan	79	146	252	252	**12.1**
16. Nicaragua	377	439	519	519	**11.9**
17. Albania	734	889	889	889	**11.7**
18. Nepal	678	785	785	785	**11.7**
19. Kiribati	7	7	7	7	**11.3**
20. Yemen, Rep.	1,294	1,270	1,283	1,315	**10.0**

Source: World Bank 2006.

(*Migrant Remittances* 2008: 1). (See also details about the money generated through illegal trafficking in Kyle and Koslowski 2001 and Naim 2006).

Remittances represent around one-quarter of GDP in several poor or struggling countries: Tonga (31.1%), Moldova (27.1%), Lesotho (25.8%), Haiti (24.8%), Bosnia and Herzogovina (22.5%) and Jordan (20.4%) (see Table 2.1).

However, if we rank countries by total value of remittances, the picture changes sharply. The top remittance recipient countries in 2004 include rich countries such as France, Spain, Germany and the United Kingdom. As Table 2.2 shows, the top recipients are India (US$21.7 billion), China ($21.3 billion), Mexico ($18.1 billion), France ($12.7 billion) and the Philippines ($11.6 billion).

Table 2.2 *Top 20 remittance-recipient countries, 2004 (US$ billions)*

	Billions of dollars
India	21.7
China	21.3
Mexico	18.1
France	12.7
Philippines	11.6
Spain	6.9
Belgium	6.8
Germany	6.5
United Kingdom	6.4
Morocco	4.2
Serbia	4.1
Pakistan	3.9
Brazil	3.6
Bangladesh	3.4
Egypt, Arab Rep.	3.3
Portugal	3.2
Vietnam	3.2
Colombia	3.2
United States	3
Nigeria	2.8

Source: World Bank 2008.

Trafficking as survival

The growing immiseration of governments and economies in the Global South launches a new phase of global migration and people trafficking, strategies which function both as survival mechanisms and profit-making activities. To some extent, these are older processes which used to be national or regional and today operate on global scales. The same infrastructure that facilitates cross-border flows of capital, information and trade is also making possible a range of cross-border flows not intended by the framers and designers of the current corporate globalisation of economies. Growing numbers of traffickers and smugglers are making money off the backs of men, women and children, and many governments are increasingly dependent on their remittances. A key aspect here is that, through their work and remittances, migrants enhance the government revenue of deeply indebted countries. The need for traffickers to help in the migration effort also offers new profit-making possibilities to 'entrepreneurs' who have seen other opportunities vanish as global firms and markets enter their countries, as well as aiding criminals able to operate their illegal trade globally. These survival circuits are often complex, involving multiple locations and types of actors, and constituting increasingly global chains of traders, traffickers and workers.

Spaces of globalisation

Globalisation has also produced sites that concentrate a growing demand for particular types of labour supplies. Strategic among these are global cities, with their sharp demand for top-level transnational professionals and for low-wage workers, often, women from the Global South. These are places that concentrate some of the key functions and resources for the management and coordination of global economic processes. The growth of these activities has, in turn, produced a sharp growth in the demand for highly paid professionals. Both the firms and the lifestyles of their professionals generate a demand for low-paid service workers. Thus, global cities are also sites for the incorporation of large numbers of low-paid immigrants into strategic economic sectors. This incorporation happens directly through the demand for mostly low-paid clerical and blue-collar service workers, such as janitors and repair workers. And it happens indirectly through the consumption practices of high-income professionals both at work and in their households, practices that generate a demand for low-wage workers in expensive restaurants and shops, as well as for maids and nannies at home. In this way, low-wage workers get incorporated into the leading sectors, but they do so under conditions that render them invisible, therewith undermining what had historically functioned as a source of workers' empowerment – being employed in growth sectors.

This mix of circuits for labour supply and demand is deeply imbricated with other dynamics of globalisation: the formation of global markets, the intensifying of transnational and trans-local networks, and the geographic redeployment of a growing range of economic and financial operations. The strengthening, and in some of these cases, the formation of new global labour circuits, is embedded in the global economic system and its associated development of various institutional supports for cross-border markets and money flows. These circuits are dynamic and changing in terms of their location. Some of these circuits are part of the shadow economy, but they use some of the institutional infrastructure of the regular economy. Most of these circuits are part of the formal economy and they service leading economic sectors and places worldwide. This mix of labour supply and demand circuits is dynamic and multi-locational.

Using modest-income households to develop investment instruments

The third form of contemporary primitive accumulation arises from financial developments that have produced sharp realignments in terms of income and inequality. Inequality in the profit-making capacities of different sectors of the economy and in the earnings capacities of different types of workers has long been a feature of advanced economies. But what we see happening today is taking place on an order of magnitude that distinguishes current developments from those of the post-war decades. The extent of inequality and the systems in which it is embedded, and through which these outcomes are produced, are engendering massive distortions in the operations of various markets, from investment to housing and labour. There are at least three processes that feed these outcomes. Although not necessarily mutually exclusive, it is helpful to distinguish them analytically: (1) the growing inequality in the profit-making capacities of different economic sectors and in the earnings capacities of different types of workers and households; (2) socio-economic polarisation tendencies resulting from the organisation of service industries and from the casualisation of employment relations; and (3) the production of urban marginality as a result of new structural processes of economic growth rather than decline.

Of all the highly developed countries, it is the United States where these deep structural trends are most legible. National level data for the United States show this growth in inequality. For instance, economic growth from 2001 to 2005 was high but very unequally distributed. Most of it went to the upper 10% and, especially, the upper 1% of households. The rest, that is 90% of households, saw a 4.2% *decline* in their market-based incomes (Mishel 2007). If we disaggregate that 90%, the size of the loss grows as we descend the income ladder. Since the beginning of the so-called economic recovery in 2001, the income share of the top 1% grew 3.6 percentage points to 21.8% in 2005, gaining $268 billion of total US household income. In contrast, that of the lower 50% of US households fell by 1.4 percentage points to 16% in 2005, amounting to a loss of $272 billion in income since 2001 (see Figure 2.1).

The invention of mortgages for modest-income households needs to be understood against this larger picture of growing inequality in earnings. Developing instruments to access the limited savings of

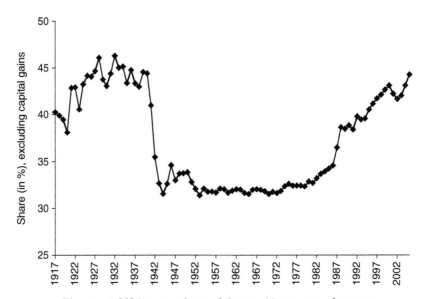

Figure 2.1 US income share of the top 10 per cent of earners,
1917–2005 (source: Mishel 2004)
*Income is defined as market income but excludes capital gains

modest-income households became a must in a setting where 80 per
cent of households own their house. What was left as a market was
the low-income population. Beyond its social and political role, housing has long been a critical economic sector in all developed societies.
There have historically been three ways in which it played this economic role: as part of the construction sector, as part of the real estate
market, and as part of the banking sector in the form of mortgages.
In all three sectors it has, at times, been a vector for innovations. For
instance, solar energy has largely been applied to housing rather than
offices or factories. Mass construction has used housing as a key chan-
nel to develop new organisational formats. Finally, one of the main
sources of income and innovation for traditional-style banking has been
mortgages. The thirty-year mortgage, now a worldwide standard, was
actually a major innovation for credit markets. Japan in the 1980s and
China today instituted respectively ninety- and seventy-year mortgages
to deal with a rapidly growing demand for housing finance in a situation where three generations were necessary to cover the cost of housing in a boom period – the 1980s in Japan and the 2000s in China.

Today, housing has become the instrument for several innovations.
The first is a novel financial instrument that lengthens the distance

between itself and the underlying asset (the house or apartment) to an extreme which is usually associated with high-risk finance. This is not the first time the financial sector has used housing to produce an instrument that lengthens the distance from the house itself. What makes this different, and in that sense an innovation, is the extent to which these mortgages function purely as a financial instrument in that they can be bought and promptly sold and, secondly, the fact that low- and moderate-income households are a major target for investors. This asymmetry between the world of investors (only some will be affected) and the world of home-owners (once they default, they will lose the house no matter which investor happens to own the instrument at the time), creates a massive distortion in the housing market and the housing finance market. Most investors can escape the negative consequences of home mortgage default because they buy these mortgages in order to sell them. But no home-owner can escape default on her own mortgage. Thus investors can relate in a positive way to even the so-called subprime mortgages (poor-quality instruments) and this, in itself, is bad for home-owners. We see here yet another sharp inequality in the current conditions.

Innovations in housing finance in advanced economies over the past two decades have changed the role of the housing sector in the economy at the local, national and global levels. This results partly from the growth of mortgage capital (expressed as a ratio to GDP) and the development of secondary mortgage markets (where financial instruments based on mortgages, rather than the houses themselves, get sold). Both of these, in turn, contribute to considerable spill-over effects to other economic sectors. At a time of massive concentration of financial resources in a limited number of super-firms, whoever owns a good share of the subprime mortgages when the mortgage default crisis hits gets stuck with massive losses. In an earlier period, ownership of mortgages was widely distributed among a range of banks and credit unions; hence losses were more distributed as well. The fact that large, powerful firms have also felt that they could get by with high-risk instruments has further raised their losses. As they say, the chickens have come home to roost. The greed of super-firms and their capacity to control these markets has made them vulnerable to their own power in a sort of boomerang effect.

It is important to emphasise that the viral infection of subprime mortgages originated in the United States but spread to other countries via the globalisation of financial markets. This spread was helped by the fact that non-national investors are, as a group, the single largest buyers of some of the weakest types of mortgage instruments, the so-called subprime mortgages. Together with banks, non-national mortgage buyers account for over one-third of all subprime mortgage holders. Foreign ownership strengthens the potential for spill-over effects well beyond the United States. A comparison of the value of all residential mortgage debt (from high- to low-quality mortgages) as a ratio of national GDP across developed countries shows sharp variations. The average for the period 2001–6 stood at around the equivalent of 20% of GDP for Italy and Austria; closer to 30% for France and Belgium; 40% for Japan, Finland, Canada and Spain; 50% for Sweden, Norway, Ireland and Germany; 70% for the United States, UK and Australia; and a whopping 90% for the Netherlands and Denmark.[4] To some extent, the variation in this value is a function of timing. For instance, the Netherlands has long had a high share of public housing ownership; thus when regulations were changed in the 1990s, there was a sudden sharp growth in the privatisation of housing, a process that should eventually stabilise. In the United States, the UK and Australia, the housing market has long been private and, importantly, the financial system is highly developed on a broad range of fronts. Thus the incidence of mortgages is both high and widespread in terms of the variety of financial circuits it encompasses.

There are other differences that can only be captured at the local level. In the case of the United States, race and locality can have a substantial impact. The following three tables show clearly that race and income level matter: African-Americans and low-income neighbourhoods show a disproportionately high incidence of subprime mortgages as of 2006. In Washington, DC, 70% of the purchase mortgages and 84% of the refinance mortgages made to African Americans in 2005 were subprime mortgages. Table 2.3 shows the extreme difference between Manhattan (one of the richest counties in the whole country) and other New York City boroughs: in 2006 less than 1% of subprime mortgages were sold to Manhattan home-buyers compared to 27.4% sold in the Bronx. This table also shows the sharp rate of growth in subprime mortgages in all boroughs, except Manhattan.

A further breakdown by neighbourhoods (community districts) in New York City shows that the worst-hit ten neighbourhoods were poor – and had between 34% and 47% of subprime mortgages among home buyers (Table 2.4).

---

[4] The IMF, which reports these measures, bases them on several sources: IMF national accounts data; European Mortgage Federation; Hypostat Statistical Tables; the US Federal Reserve; the OECD Analytical Database; Statistics Canada; and IMF staff calculations; see IMF 2005, 2006.

Table 2.3 *Rate of subprime lending (%) by borough, 2002–6*

	2002	2003	2004	2005	2006
Bronx	14.2	19.7	28.2	34.4	27.4
Brooklyn	9.2	13.9	18.4	26.1	23.6
Manhattan	1.3	1.8	0.6	1.1	0.8
Queens	7.7	12.6	17.8	28.2	24.4
Staten Island	7.2	11.1	13.9	19.9	17.1
NYC total	7.0	10.8	14.9	22.9	19.8

Source: Furman Center for Real Estate and Urban Policy, 2007.

Table 2.4 *Ten New York City community districts with the highest rates of subprime lending, 2006*

Sub borough area	Home purchase loans issued by subprime lender (%)
University Heights/Fordham	47.2
Jamaica	46.0
East Flatbush	44.0
Brownsville	43.8
Williamsbridge/Baychester	41.6
East New York/Starrett City	39.5
Bushwick	38.6
Morrisania/Belmont	37.2
Queens Village	34.6
Bedford Stuyvesant	34.2

Source: Furman Center for Real Estate and Urban Policy, 2007.

Finally, we see a similar pattern if we control for race (Table 2.5). Whites, who have a far higher average income than other groups in New York City, were much less likely to hold subprime mortgages than other groups, reaching 9.1% in 2006 compared with 13.6% of Asians, 28.6% of Hispanics and 40.7% of blacks. The table also shows the much lower growth rate in subprime lending from 2002 to 2006 of whites compared with other groups. It doubled from 4.6% to 9.1% for whites, but tripled for Asians and Hispanics, and quadrupled for blacks.

In brief, the case of New York City, a city with vast numbers of financial firms and resources, where finance is a subject of general debate in television news, shows that the aggressive tactics of financial actors fell disproportionately on poorer neighbourhoods. This should send an alarm bell ringing through developing economies that are now

Table 2.5 *Rate of conventional subprime lending (%) by race in New York City, 2002–6*

	2002	2003	2004	2005	2006
White	4.6	6.2	7.2	11.2	9.1
Black	13.4	20.5	35.2	47.1	40.7
Hispanic	11.9	18.1	27.6	39.3	28.6
Asian	4.2	6.2	9.4	18.3	13.6

Source: Furman Center for Real Estate and Urban Policy, 2007.

seeing very sharp growth rates in mortgage lending, a trend I turn to next.

Central to this story is the difference between the value of housing loans as a ratio to GDP and the growth rate of such loans. Thus, the former is very low in countries with young housing markets, such as India and China, where it stands at 10%.[5] In contrast, in more mature markets in Asia, this value can be much higher – standing at 60% in Singapore, and 40% in Hong Kong and Taiwan – but the growth rate is much lower. Between 1999 and 2006, the average annual growth of housing loans in India and China was extremely high, certainly above the growth of other types of loans. Both countries have rapidly growing housing markets and are, therefore, at the beginning of a new phase of economic development. While most other Asian countries have not experienced comparable growth rates to India and China in the mortgage market, they have seen a doubling in such loans during this period. If we consider the particular financial innovations of concern in this chapter – moderate- and low-income households' mortgages and subprime mortgages – then we can see how attractive the Indian and Chinese residential mortgage markets become with their millions of low-income households.

The next two figures provide comparative data on the incidence of residential loans to total loans in several highly developed and so-called emerging market countries. These two figures also help situate the residential mortgage market in the rapidly growing and diversifying financial world of loans. Developed countries with multiple financial circuits, such as the United States and the UK, clearly show that compared to other types of loans, mortgages are a relatively small share of all loans,

[5] In China, the total value of mortgage finance is higher than suggested by residential mortgage-lending data alone because loans to developers are not well-recorded and could be rather large.

even if most households have mortgages. It is important to note that the same low level of mortgage loans to total loans in economies marked by a small elite of superrich individuals has a different meaning from that in the United States and UK: hence, Russia's extremely low incidence of residential to total loans in the economy is an indication of a narrow mortgage market (mostly for the rich and very rich) and the fact that there are vast financial circuits centred on other resources.

While residential mortgage capital is growing, it needs to be situated in a larger financial landscape. Thus even though mortgage finance measured as a ratio to GDP is high in countries such as the United States and the UK, the total value of financial assets is far higher. The ratio of finance as a whole to US GDP is 450 per cent, as it is for the Netherlands. The other story, then, is the extent to which finance has found mechanisms for raising its revenue that have little direct connection to the material economy of countries. In this regard, the securitising of residential mortgages can be seen as a powerful instrument for the further financial deepening of economies. Finally, yet another way of understanding mortgage capital is its share in total loans. Figures 2.2 and 2.3 show this share for developed and emerging market economies. There is considerable variability within each group of countries. But the general fact is that there is much room for residential mortgage debt to grow in both. And some of this growth may well take the shape of subprime mortgages, with its attendant risks for modest-income households.

An important distinction is that between the ratio of residential mortgages to GDP shown in Figures 2.2 and 2.3, on the one hand, and the growth rate of residential mortgage finance on the other. Thus the former is very low in countries with young housing markets, such as India and China, where it stands at 10 per cent. In contrast, in more mature markets in Asia that value can be much higher, but the growth rate much lower. The average annual growth of housing loans between 1999 and 2006 in India and China was extremely high and above the growth of other types of loans; both countries have rapidly growing housing markets and they are at the merest beginning of a whole new phase in their economies. While most other Asian countries have not had the extremely high growth rates of India and China in the mortgage market, they nonetheless had a doubling in such loans from 1999 to 2006. In brief, understanding the weight of the residential mortgage market in the rapidly growing and diversifying world of lending, including household credit, gives us an indication of the growth potential of mortgage finance.

An important question raised by these developments is the extent to which developed and developing countries will follow this troublesome

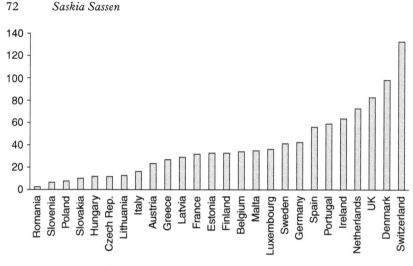

Figure 2.2 Ratio of residential mortgage debt to GDP, select countries, end 2006 (source: Miles and Pillonca 2007: 370)

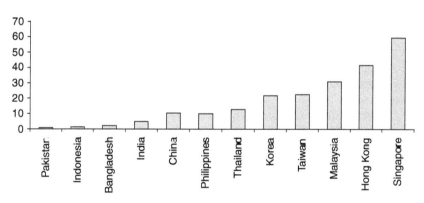

Figure 2.3 Ratio of residential mortgage debt to GDP: emerging Asia, 2007 (source: Warnock and Warnock 2008)

'development' path, which ultimately has become another way of extracting value from individuals, in this case through home mortgages that even very poor households are invited to buy, partly because once the sellers get the poor households to buy such a mortgage, they bundle them up and sell the package to an investor, thereby passing on the risk and removing an incentive to care whether the home-owner manages to hang on to the house. The data (e.g. Table 2.6) showing the growing share of loans those households are taking on as a share of disposable

Table 2.6 *Ratio of household credit to personal disposable income (%), 2006*

	2000	2001	2002	2003	2004	2005
Emerging markets						
Czech Republic	8.5	10.1	12.9	16.4	21.3	27.1
Hungary	11.2	14.4	20.9	29.5	33.9	39.3
Poland	10.1	10.3	10.9	12.6	14.5	18.2
India	4.7	5.4	6.4	7.4	9.7	...
Korea	33.0	43.9	57.3	62.6	64.5	68.9
Philippines	1.7	4.6	5.5	5.5	5.6	...
Taiwan	75.1	72.7	76.0	83.0	95.5	...
Thailand	26.0	25.6	28.6	34.3	36.4	...
Mature markets						
Australia	83.3	86.7	95.6	109.0	119.0	124.5
France	57.8	57.5	58.2	59.8	64.2	69.2
Germany	70.4	70.1	69.1	70.3	70.5	70.0
Italy	25.0	25.8	27.0	28.7	31.8	34.8
Japan	73.6	75.7	77.6	77.3	77.9	77.8
Spain	65.2	70.4	76.9	86.4	98.8	112.7
United States	104.0	105.1	110.8	118.2	126.0	132.7

Source: IMF 2006.

household income is an alarming trend in this regard. Finally, when we compare the ratio of housing mortgage debt to GDP in different regions of the world we can infer the potential for growth in those countries where it is still a minor share.

Home mortgages are today a sort of new frontier for using financial high-risk innovations to extract profit. This is most acute in the United States, but other countries are following rapidly. Just to mark the situation empirically, in the vast financial sector of the United States, the ratio of residential mortgage finance to US GDP is 70 per cent; it is important to note that the total financial value at play in the United States is almost five times (450 per cent) the value of its GDP. The power of finance is its capability to invent instruments and to invent ways of subjecting more and more sectors of an economy to those instruments. The subprime and moderate-income home mortgages are an acute example of this. In this new game, modest-income home-owners are the peons and housing mortgages are the vehicle for a new investment instrument and a new way of extracting the savings of moderate- and low-income households, a vast target in a globalised financial world.

Conclusion

The fall of the Soviet Union allowed proponents of free markets to proclaim that the market knows best. For these commentators, 1989 represented the 'ultimate triumph of Hayek over Keynes' (Introduction, this volume). But while the Adam Smith market – think of a village farmers' market – was a sorting and pricing mechanism that worked, today's markets dominated by large corporations and powerful financial firms are neither free nor do they approximate Smithian markets. We might say that, after 1989, state repression in the Soviet sphere has been replaced by corporate economic control with a concomitant capacity to eliminate competition. While focused on different modes of explanation, this chapter coincides with Tucker's (Chapter 7, this volume) examination of how the post-communist *nomenklatura* in Russia transferred its political rights to the economic sphere after 1989/1991. In each case – the Soviet Union and the post-Cold War neoliberal global economy – we can speak of the ascendance of single-rule systems. While such single-rule systems rarely achieve their full goals, they do succeed in reshaping vast stretches of the terrain they rule over.

Many of the critical components that are part of the post-1989 global economy were already present and under development in the early 1980s. As such, just as 1989 is the iconic representation of a political process that had been building for a long time, so the corporate globalising that took off in the late 1980s started many years earlier. Indeed, once we start looking, we can find numerous Trojan political and economic horses as in the case of structural adjustment programmes and forms of financial innovation. But 1989 did make a major difference, most notably in giving these innovations the run of the world via the legitimating aura of market triumphalism. The outcome was the formation of a new kind of global economy. This political economy contains three core dynamics. The first arises from the informalisation of particular types of low-profit activities in advanced economies. The second comes about, at least in part, from the interventions by the Global North in poor countries which extend back into those same Global North countries, but through alternative circuits (such as the trafficking of women), completing a loop that starts with decisions taken by the IMF and other international financial institutions. The third dynamic uses high-risk structured finance to develop new asset-backed securities based on mortgages (often forcefully) sold to modest-income households which are then bundled up and circulated in secondary financial circuits unconnected to the housing itself. These three dynamics have had the effect of generating mechanisms for primitive accumulation. Taken together, they indicate that one of the core features of the 'global 1989' has been the return of primitive accumulation on vast scale.

3   What is left after 1989?

William Outhwaite

1989 and the left

This chapter is concerned both with the left in a narrow political sense and with broader aspects of the socio-political context which has developed in Europe and elsewhere in the past two decades. I shall focus particularly on Europe, since it is the region I know best, and in situating a reflection on post-communist Europe in the context of Europe as a whole, my aim is to complement other contributions in this book, not least Barbara Falk's emphasis on the United States (Chapter 11), Fred Halliday's chapter on the post-socialist Third World (Chapter 5) and, most directly, Laure Delcour's chapter on the shift to a 'global Europe' (Chapter 6). I have not addressed the situation in Russia, since this is well covered in Aviezer Tucker's chapter (Chapter 7).[1]

Major turning points in European and, to some extent, world history of the recent past can be located in 1945, or 1968, or, more pessimistically, the mid-1970s as the prosperity of the West came under pronounced economic and environmental pressures. It was, however, the developments of '1989 and all that' which attracted the newly reinvented label of the 'End of History' (Fukuyama 1989) and encouraged some of the 'post'-conceptualisations which had emerged earlier.[2] The revolutions of 1989 also provided a particular challenge to social-scientific explanation. The tip of this iceberg was the element of surprise they provided for almost all observers (Outhwaite and Ray 2005: ch. 1).

---

[1] This is a first attempt at addressing the questions on which I am working from 2008 to 2011 in a project generously supported by the Leverhulme Foundation with a major research fellowship. I gratefully acknowledge this support, and that of my new colleagues at Newcastle in encouraging me to apply for the fellowship when I was not yet even on the payroll. My thanks also to Paul Blokker, the late Vladimir Fours, Aviezer Tucker and the editors for comments on an earlier draft.
[2] First among those is of course the 'postmodern', anticipated in the United States but now associated with Lyotard (1979); this had considerable appeal in parts of the post-communist region, partly because it was new and partly perhaps because it resonated with a reality in which so much had become fluid.

More substantial was the question they raised about causal processes in society: whatever our general preferences for structural explanation or for *histoire événementielle*, we must, I think, be impressed by the conjunction of long-term tendencies such as the economic slow-down and the ideological and cultural erosion of the state socialist dictatorships on the one hand, and Gorbachev's initiatives with all their intended and unintended consequences on the other. Something similar can be said for the post-communist transition decades (the plural is intentional): apparently open futures rapidly solidifying into relatively conventional political and economic structures, but with repeated shocks as developmental trajectories were abruptly interrupted, accelerated or redirected (Kitschelt 2003). The process of post-communist transition shows, in particular, the dangers of bypassing society and assuming that it was enough to 'fix' the economic and political-legal systems. In the analysis of post-communist transition, a particular conception of linear progress, and the imperatives allegedly resulting from this, is shown to dominate social and political discourse across the post-communist world and to pre-empt and occlude political choices (Kennedy 2002; Blokker 2005; Wydra 2007).

The 1989 revolutions were, of course, highly concentrated in time, confining themselves to the autumn and early winter of that year. As with 1968, however, it makes sense to speak of 'the 1989 years', with important pre-shocks in the preceding years, notably with Solidarity in Poland,[3] but also to be found in ecological movements and initiatives in the Baltic states (Strayer 1998: 153), Central Europe, Bulgaria and elsewhere. The aftershocks of 1989 are still continuing. As Okey (2004: vii) puts it, 'Just as the grand narrative of feudal absolutism's overthrow by bourgeois democracy in 1789 breaks up in the hands of modern historians, so in hindsight do ideas of a communist totalitarian model suddenly hitting the buffers in 1989.' Another historian, Padraic Kenney (2006: 114), makes the same point:

'1989' is in many cases an inaccurate shorthand; the real end to authoritarian rule would take another decade. The fall of second-generation authoritarian

---

[3] As the historian Robin Okey (2004: 30) notes, 'In a communist experience divided into two phases by the suppression of the Prague Spring, the Solidarity crisis [of 1980] falls halfway through the second phase, sharing some traits with 1968 but in others anticipating 1989.' In 1989 itself, 4 June, for which we remember the Tiananmen Square massacre in China, was also the day on which Solidarity won all the seats in the Polish senate and all but one of the seats available in the *Sejm* (Okey 2004: 69–70). Harald Wydra's superb book, *Communism and the Emergence of Democracy* (2007), shows the importance of the earlier movements of dissidence and resistance for shaping the democratic transitions of 1989 and after.

governments in 1997–2000 was at times no less dramatic than the events of 1989. Four cases – Slovakia, Romania, Croatia and Serbia – each show, paradoxically, how much harder it was for a democratic opposition to succeed when the repression of the communist era gave way to a soft dictatorship that offered a program of xenophobic nationalism and crony capitalism.

The collapse of the USSR in 1991 and the 'colour revolutions' which are still continuing[4] can, I think, be seen as 'catching-up revolutions' in Habermas' sense – perhaps more appropriately than when he coined the term (Habermas 1990).[5] The Chinese transition to capitalism under the continuing dictatorship of the Party should also, I think, be seen in this context.

This contextualisation of 1989 suggests a further expansion beyond the communist world. 1989 was, of course, primarily marked by the end of state socialism in its Stalinist and post-Stalinist sense. It also, however, provided a major boost to what we were just beginning to call globalisation and to the neoliberal ideologies and regimes which were already well established. More controversially, it might be seen as making an important contribution to the end of three processes: the long social democratic century which began in the second half of the nineteenth century; the age of affluence running from the late 1940s in Western Europe and North America and the 'European social model/welfare state'; Atlantic or 'Northern' hegemony in the world.[6] Before turning to these processes, however, I take stock (albeit somewhat selectively) of some of the major vectors of change – and continuity – in East and East-Central Europe over the past two decades.

---

[4] The removal of Milošević lacked a specific colour but was manifestly in the same vein. The colour spectrum may – or may not – be drawn upon in candidate states for a further rectifying revolution such as Belarus and North Korea. David Edgar (2009) comments interestingly that 'in retrospect, rather than being the last of the 20th-century revolutions, 1989 looks more like an anticipation of the colour/flower-coded revolutions of the 21st'.

[5] Catching up, in other words, with the post-Second World War capitalist democracies. As Fred Halliday points out in his chapter, Habermas' phrase was implicitly inverting Khrushchev's prediction that socialism would catch up with and overtake capitalism. Habermas, like François Furet, was struck by the absence of new ideas in 1989, though this is perhaps unfair to dissident thinkers who were indeed not *inventing* liberalism and democracy but were upholding them in difficult conditions (see Lawson 2005; Wydra 2007; Blokker 2005).

[6] The term 'trente glorieuses' was used by the economist Jean Fourastié (1907–90) to refer to the years of post-war affluence ending roughly with the oil price shock of 1973. For a useful recent discussion of the European social model in the context of politics after 1989 see Azmanova (2008); see also my discussion of the work of Frank Castles and others in Outhwaite (2008: ch. 3). On Atlantic hegemony, see in particular the work of Kees van der Pijl (1984).

From communism to post-communism

Examining the effects of '1989' in the post-communist region means beginning with what Ezra Vogel described as 'communist universals' (one-party state, planned economy, etc.).[7] Among these are, at least for the more developed parts of the post-communist world:

(1) a relatively peaceful transfer of power, sometimes involving a 'transition pact' or 'handshake'[8] between the old elites;

(2) a broad-spectrum political opposition movement, such as Solidarity in Poland, Civic Forum in Czechoslovakia or Sajudis in Lithuania,[9] which tends to break up soon after the takeover of state power along either familiar, or less familiar, lines of political division;

(3) an economic (and therefore social) 'transition shock', amounting to anything from two to five or more years of negative growth ('transition recession') and enterprise closures, unemployment, high suicide rates etc.;

(4) discrediting, sometimes followed by relatively rapid rehabilitation, of previously ruling communist parties, including purges; and, as in other spheres

(5) 'lustration' – the exposure of members of earlier elites and others (including members of the anti-communist opposition movements) found to have collaborated with the security police;

(6) finally, a pattern of politics characterised by a quite substantial degree of egalitarianism (or at least opposition to growing inequalities) but without forms of class-based politics still found in much of non-post-communist Europe.

These processes modulated differently[10] (or, in the Czechoslovak case, within different parts of the same state), but what is striking in hindsight

---

[7] See Chalmers Johnson (1970) and Tőkés (1997: 109).

[8] See Lawson (2005) on the modular dimensions of these 'negotiated revolutions'.

[9] Hungary, one of the countries where the opposition was strongest, is an exception to this pattern (Waller 1994: 94). These catch-all movements ironically illustrate the old joke that if another party were allowed to oppose the communist single party everyone would join it and there would again be only one party.

[10] Paul Blokker and Vladimir Fours have reminded me that these fit the Central European and Baltic states much better than other parts of the region. Rather than abandon these categories in favour of a different set for Southeastern Europe and the former Soviet Union, however, I am inclined to see them as tending to manifest themselves much more gradually, unevenly and in some cases hardly at all. Conversely, Tucker's elite continuity model fits Russia, as he notes, better than the rest of the bloc. Looking ahead, I would anticipate more 'colour'-type revolutions leading gradually towards something like the outcomes in East Central Europe and the Baltic republics.

is the degree of convergence. The bulk of formerly communist Europe is now in the European Union, with economies and political regimes at least sufficiently respectable to satisfy the accession criteria. As Jan Zielonka (2006: 79) writes:

When we look at democratic institutions across the enlarged EU there is no clear East-West divide, at least from the formal point of view. All new members are either parliamentary or semi-presidential republics ... They all have constitutions providing checks and balances between different branches of power. Citizens' basic rights and freedoms are guaranteed by law. True, laws on the media in the new member states are in constant flux, with government officials trying to manipulate television broadcasting in particular. However, in this sense the situation is not as bad as in some old EU member states such as Italy.[11]

The striking differences in initial conditions, such as the substantial private sector and opposition in Poland contrasting with virtually no private sector and an almost entirely underground opposition in Czechoslovakia, may have influenced the initial political shape of the transition, but they appear to have had little long-term effect. The same goes for the violent transition shock in Poland, contrasting with a more gradualist approach in the Czech and Slovak republics. As Kenney (2006: 25) writes:

Whether countries chose the Big Bang, or gradualism; won the foreign-investment lottery (Hungary's per capita FDI was eight times that of Poland) or employed vouchers, or nomenklaturization, or some combination of these, did not greatly affect their success. More important has been the level of social and economic development *before* the fall of communism.[12]

The fates of ex-ruling communist parties were more variable. Depending on the local and geopolitical context, but also on their own capacity to adapt, they survived or faded away only gradually in some parts of the bloc; elsewhere they were quarantined but often bounced back surprisingly quickly as in Hungary, Lithuania or Latvia (though not in nearby Estonia). Overall, what is striking is the peaceful nature of the transition and the relative acceptance of residually or formerly communist politicians and parties, in a context of rather strong suspicion of *all* political

---

[11] See also Merkel (2008). Zielonka (2006: 38–43) concedes that things are less rosy in the other post-communist countries.

[12] It is, of course, difficult, as George Lawson (2005) has pointed out, to distinguish long-term factors of this kind from the short-run effects of the way in which the revolutions took place. My conjecture, for what it's worth, is that even if the revolutions had been much longer, messier and bloodier than they were, these conditions would in the end have substantially shaped the outcome. Certainly, the example of the Baltic states supports this line of analysis.

or civic activity (Curry and Urban 2003; Grzymała-Busse 2003; Hough *et al.* 2006). In other words, what Ken Jowitt (1992) called 'the Leninist extinction' was not followed by the extinction of the Leninists (not that this is a particularly good description of the disillusioned careerists and technocrats who filled the ruling communist parties in the 1980s in any case). The only possible explanation seems to be that people objected to the *methods* used by the communists and the poor performance of the regimes rather than what one might call the *acquis communiste* of modernisation, urbanisation, educational expansion and so forth. As Robin Okey (2004: 30) stresses, 'the red thread running through the East European communist experience was not hostility to the regimes' developmental goals, but distrust of communists and their means'. Post-communist electorates might not fully trust the old parties, but they trusted them at least as far as they could vote for them, in justified anticipation that they could, if necessary, vote them out again. If what Jowitt has called the 'recovering communists' agreed to change their spots, they were permitted to take part in political debate alongside other political groupings. As such, their fate became subject to the same contingencies as other left or centre-left parties in the rest of Europe, a point I return to below (see also Naimark 1999: 325).

On the other hand, one of the factors shaping post-communist politics continues to be the past of the parties and their personnel. In Poland, for example, the division between former communists and oppositionists remains highly salient, and right-wing parties have repeatedly used scandals from the communist period to discredit their opponents. The varied approaches across the post-communist region to the issue of lustration reflect, in part, the balance of political forces as well as more universalistic considerations of political morality. Initially, except in Germany, where the Stasi had been a target from the beginning of the transition, with raids of their headquarters in several cities during the winter of 1989–90, the tendency had been to draw what Tadeusz Mazowiecki called a 'thick line' under the past. In Czechoslovakia, Václav Havel spent part of his 1990 New Year address arguing that there was no point in 'laying all the blame on those who ruled us before' (Kenney 2006: 82). The term lustration was introduced in Czechoslovakia much later, in 1991, at a time when the attempted coup in the USSR had aroused fears of a return of communism. Those shown to have collaborated with the secret police or to have had certain roles in the Party were banned from public service jobs for five years. In Poland, a similar law was not implemented until 1999, though without a ban on work except in those cases where it could be shown that suspects had lied about their past (David 2006).

A related issue is the relative lack of celebrations or memorials of the transition. In Germany, the opening of the Berlin Wall and the Day of German Unity are celebrated and a monument to 'freedom and unity' is planned. Elsewhere, however, what one finds is more often just the removal or replacement of monuments (of which of course there had been an over-abundance) and a certain amount of renaming of streets, as well as museums like the 'House of Terror' in Budapest or the Museum of Genocide in Vilnius. The tenth anniversary of 1989 passed without much notice, and the same appears to be true of the twentieth (present company excepted). Harald Wydra (2007: 204ff.) writes that, 'the very symbols of the revolutions of 1989 or 1991 have all but eroded'. This reflects more than just the absence, in for example Poland and Hungary, of crucial dates such as 9 November in the GDR or 17 November in Czechoslovakia (which *are* of course celebrated). It suggests a broader conclusion, that 'the share of dissidence in the destruction of communism was hardly recognised by domestic and international publics' (Wydra 2007: 209).

The exceptionally fraught relation to the past, however, remains a distinctive feature of post-communist political life,[13] and one which often still overrides the left–right division. What other distinctive features can one identify? Post-communist Europe remains the poorer half of the continent, though increasingly catching up as Western growth rates slow down. As Daniel Chirot (2002) has emphasised, these differences may not last:

> If Serbia had not been led into a disastrous political adventure ... it would have emerged from communism no more backward than Poland. The differences in degree of modernization between Romania or Bulgaria, and, say, Hungary or Poland, need not last more than one or two generations. Similarly, all of postcommunist Europe has the capacity to substantially catch up to Western European levels well before the end of this new century. After all, in 1960 Spain, Portugal, Greece, and Ireland were so backward that hardly anyone thought they might have reached near-Western levels of modernity by 2000.

The oft noted volatility of post-communist politics might be another distinctive feature, though Western politics seems also to be heading in this direction, as recent developments in Italy, France and now the UK illustrate. Some fragility or rootlessness is surely to be expected of relatively new political parties. Attila Ágh (1998) has commented on

---

[13] Almost all European states have a history as perpetrators, victims or, in the case of the neutral states, collaborators of fascism and Nazism. Post-communist states combine this with reflection on their communist past, in unstable and shifting compounds.

the over-parliamentarisation of post-communist politics, and Michály Bihari (cited by Tőkés 1997: 136) on the way in which the Hungarian party system has tended to float above real political life. But such processes can also be seen in Western 'postdemocracy' (Lawson 2005: 105). The other side of this coin is, of course, the role of civil society, which flourished dramatically in the late 1980s (especially in Poland and in a much more muted form elsewhere – for example in the churches in Germany) and fizzled out no less strikingly in the first post-communist years (Outhwaite and Ray 2005: ch. 7). Here as in other respects, the East replicates patterns in the West, where civil society politics developed in the '1968 years', but over a shorter time period.[14]

Nationalism, which Adam Michnik aptly called the terminal illness of communism, attracted a good deal of attention in the post-communist region in the early years, for reasons which were all too obvious in the former Soviet Union and Yugoslavia. Looking back after twenty years, however, one is struck by how much did *not* happen. The break-up of the USSR, Yugoslavia and Czechoslovakia all occurred in a quite casual way,[15] with only the long-expected demise of Yugoslavia going disastrously wrong (Vujačić 1996). We shall never know whether, as some people have suggested, a rapid offer of fast-track EU membership to Yugoslavia along with other post-communist states would have averted the tragedy, but this must come high on the list of missed opportunities. In the post-Soviet case, there was a time when fragmentation along national/regional lines seemed to threaten the whole of Russia, with some even anticipating the secession of cities like St Petersburg.[16] Whatever the long-term consequences of the break-up of the Union, which remains after all one of several possible sites for a third world war, Russia has held together with at least a semblance of democratic order. The break-up of Czechoslovakia may be a pity, but it was hardly driven by nationalism in any strong sense, and after the demise of Vladimir Mečiar's regime in Slovakia, the damage seems relatively slight. The rapid passage of Slovakia from pariah in the 1990s to EU member in 2004 illustrates the speed with which things can change in the region.

---

[14] On these effects of 1968, see Bhambra and Demir (2009), especially the chapters by Lynne Segal and Ken Plummer.

[15] Russia's relation to its empire, which Alexander Filippov (1992) brilliantly analysed in the 1990s, remains to be worked through. Lara Ryazanova-Clarke (2008) has suggested in conversation that the term 'empire' is currently looming much larger in Russian public discourse.

[16] When I asked a sociologist from St Petersburg about these rumours, he joked that even some *districts* of the city were showing interest in the possibility of breaking away from the rest.

For what it is worth, the surviving rogue state in post-communist Europe, Belarus, is anything but nationalist, having re-established, at least for the time being, a close union with Russia. Post-communist nationalism, therefore, remains dangerous primarily because it occurs in dangerous regions, notably those on the Russian periphery. But it is otherwise no more prominent than separatist nationalism in much of Western Europe.

What of the place of the region overall on the political spectrum? One of the surprises of 1989 was the relative lack of interest in 'third ways' between capitalism and socialism, and a distinct preference for more macho forms of capitalism over softer 'Nordic' ones. The Czech prime minister – and later president – Václav Klaus notoriously rejected the social market economy in favour of a market economy 'without adjectives', and the popularity of flat taxes in Estonia and elsewhere is a telling illustration of this general inclination. Yet Klaus' neoliberal bark was not matched by his bite and the region retains quite strong egalitarian traditions, no doubt reinforced by the sense that most people who have got very rich under post-communist conditions have probably done so in dubious ways. Survey evidence suggests a majority perception in East-Central Europe that there are 'strong' or 'very strong' conflicts between managers and workers and that income differentials are 'too great', and a relation between the perception of conflict and objective inequality as measured by Gini coefficient (Delhey 2001: 203–5). In other words, post-communist electorates remain more egalitarian in their attitudes than Western Europeans, to a degree more closely related than in the West to actual levels of inequality in their societies.

The traditional expression of egalitarian attitudes, in Europe and to some extent elsewhere, has been social democratic politics, but the scissor effect in the post-communist countries of the local demise of socialist/communist political and economic policies and the general reorientation of Western social democracy into third way or 'new' politics has perhaps hindered what would otherwise have been an organic development. The relative weakness of social democracy is the other side of the surprising resilience of many former ruling communist parties. It rapidly became clear that social democracy was not going to inherit the post-communist political terrain. In the first free elections in Hungary, Poland and the GDR, social democrats outpolled former communists in only the GDR, and there only marginally (22 per cent as against 16 per cent); elsewhere they barely achieved between half and a quarter of the (itself modest) communist share of the vote, as Coppieters and Deschouwer (1994: 8) noted. They concluded (1994: 15–16):

Social democracy may be considered to be marginalized in eastern Europe by the very logic of the transition process, whose ends and means fit more easily both into the liberal programme on market economy and into the nationalistic conception of a state-building process. Class solidarity and international solidarity are not perceived as appropriate means to carrying out the transition process towards a market economy. The defence of workers' rights in industries unable to survive under the new economic conditions is easily perceived as being 'conservative'. The east European social-democratic programme of reforms convinces voters less than does the liberal or the nationalist one.

The double paradox of the relative success of ex-communist parties and the relative lack of success of (other) social democratic parties in the region[17] reflects a more fundamental paradox: the sense in public opinion both that transition is inevitable and that it is deeply problematic. According to the regular New Europe Barometer surveys, in several post-communist countries, including Hungary, recorded approval of the communist regime was consistently higher than approval of the 'current' regime. On the question of the relative approval of the economic system, only the Czech Republic and Poland showed significantly higher support for the current system than the communist one; in Slovenia, opinion was evenly balanced. Seeing the glass as half-full rather than half-empty, one can say that the more successful countries prefer post-communism, and even the post-communist economy, to the communist one and that the Hungarian exception is explained by that country's relatively better political and economic state before 1989 than its neighbours' (Ekiert 2003: 96–7). The 2001 and 2004 surveys show a shift towards support for the post-communist status quo, though also an increase, except in the Czech Republic, in approval of the former communist political regimes. This is not the same as wanting to re-establish communism, which is very much a minority opinion (ranging in 2004 from 42% in Russia to a mere 7% in Estonia the means for EU members and applicants (Bulgaria, Romania and Croatia in 2004) being 15% and 23% respectively (Rose 2006: 25)). It does, however, show that 'Ostalgie' is by no means peculiar to eastern Germany.

The position of political forces in the post-communist region continues, therefore, to be shaped by the transition process itself, the types of regime resulting from this and the way in which it is evaluated. Influences of this kind are not unique to post-communist Europe: economic crisis and the collapse of communist parties may push you, depending where you live, towards Berlusconi, or the Front National, or Scottish nationalism. Nevertheless, this global impact of transition

---

[17] The Czech Republic, where the communist party was historically strong, is something of an exception.

suggests that post-communism remains more than an historical expression (Stenning and Hörschelman 2008).[18]

I have concentrated to date on the national state level, but a major part of any account of the post-communist decades must also explore the transnational impact of the EU. This theme has perhaps tended to fall between the two stools of a focus on the EU's enlargement on the one hand, and on the politics of individual states on the other; the excellent study by Vachudová (2005) is a welcome exception. In Vachudová's analysis, the EU's shift after the Copenhagen summit from 'passive leverage', which merely reinforced liberal tendencies in countries already on that path, to 'active leverage' which changed the balance of political forces in more marginal countries such as Slovakia and enabled political elites to groom them for eventual accession, was a crucial contribution. The EU, like the West as a whole, was slow to respond to the needs of post-1989 Europe, but its long-term impact has been massively beneficial overall. Unlike the situation in Western Europe, no post-communist state has rejected the option of membership and none seems likely to. Having reinforced differences between post-communist states in what has been aptly called the 'regatta' towards accession, the challenge for the Union is to develop common policies to reduce the dangerous inequalities which persist between member states. EU accession has often been taken as a marker for the end of post-communist transition, and with border-free travel, currencies pegged to, or already replaced by, the euro, it is easy to slip into this way of thinking. But we need also to bear in mind the persistence of the past, both in the theme of post-communism as a 'return' to capitalism, national independence and so on (Lagerspetz 1999) and in the viscosity of social structures which was so often overlooked in the early 1990s. And in this vein, I turn now to other aspects of the impact of 1989, in particular the three themes identified at the beginning of this chapter: social democracy, affluence and hegemony.

What is left?

First, Western social democrats, like those further to the non-communist left, could reasonably expect to pursue 'business as usual'. Whatever

---

[18] Despite its age, the four-volume series edited by Karen Dawisha and Bruce Parrott (1997) remains a valuable source on post-communist politics, both for its comprehensive coverage and because the contributors were asked to address a common range of questions listed in the appendix to each volume. Among more recent works I would highlight the edited collection by White *et al.* (2003) and the monographs by Vachudová (2005), Zielonka (2006), and Wydra (2007).

they understood by socialism as a long-term goal, it was not (except in the caricatures of their enemies) what has gone down the drain in Eastern Europe. On the other hand, even if one did not make, as the communists did, the 'opportunism' of social democracy a definitional property, it was clear that most Western parties were slowly but surely following the path taken in 1958 by the German SPD, even if in Britain, for example, it took Blair, in 1997, to baptise the mutation with the label 'New Labour'. In Germany, of course, the SPD had long been over-taken on the left by the Greens and Alternatives (except electorally), though the subsequent performance of the Greens since their participation in the SPD-led government became more unpredictable.

How much difference did 1989 make to this general trajectory? Probably not a lot. If, somewhat improbably but perhaps not impossibly, the Soviet Union was still ruling much of Europe today, no doubt in Chinese style, Western social democracy might well look much as it does now. At best, the demise of state socialism made it possible for reformers like Blair and Giddens to present the Third Way as a clearly desirable alternative to neo-Stalinism and neo-conservatism – the former dead in the water and the latter showing signs of desperation. The demise of Western social democracy has been so often predicted since the 1950s that it would be unwise to assume it now, however unpromising the current situation in almost all of Europe except the Iberian Peninsula. Electoral support for social democratic parties, as Anderson and Camiller (1994) show, was much the same in 1974–90 as in the 'glorious years' of 1945–73. On the other the hand, traditional 'labour movement' links between trade unions and socialist political parties, where they existed at all, have greatly weakened, as have unions themselves. Social democratic parties and their close competitors like the German Greens and now also the Left Party have long been divided between traditional themes of material security and more 'post-materialist' ones. Albena Azmanova (2008) has taken this further in suggesting that the contrast between material and cultural issues also links to conceptions of risk and opportunity, with some social democrats, for example, embracing the Europeanisation of politics and others reacting defensively against it. Increasing electoral volatility means that apparently substantial parties can be virtually wiped out, like the French socialists in 1993 and the Italian left in 2008. As the profile of traditional social democratic parties becomes less and less socialist, supporters may migrate to 'The Left' in Germany or the SNP in Scotland, both closer to traditional social democratic values than the SPD or Labour, that is if they do not switch, as many have done in France, Italy and Austria, to the extreme right.

In post-communist Europe, residually left parties have survived the initial image problems created by the 'soc'- prefix in the aftermath of 1989. It was the guiltless Italian communist party which dissolved itself (Magri 2008), not the deeply compromised Hungarian one, which felt the need merely to drop the word 'Workers' from Hungarian Socialist Workers' Party. Of the nineteen parties currently affiliated to the 'European left', eight include the word communist in their names, including the Hungarian Communist Workers' Party and the Party of Communists of the Republic of Moldova. There has been a shift from labels such as 'communist', 'socialist' or 'workers'' to the snappier 'left', as in Germany, where the antecedents of Die Linke were the Partei des demokratischen Sozialismus (PDS), the successor to the East German SED, and the West German Wahlalternative Arbeit und soziale Gerechtigkeit – a mouthful even by German standards. The name-change and merger, bringing together the former East German minister Gregor Gysi and the West German leftist Oskar Lafontaine, seems to have finally got the PDS out of its ghetto; meanwhile its namesake, the Italian Left Democratic Party (PDS again) dropped the 'Party' (the most neutral word in its name) to become Left Democrats, de facto rather centrist, like the Radicaux de Gauche in France. The Estonian Social Democratic Labour Party changed its name in 2004 to the Estonian Left Party (EVP).

Social democracy may persist, then, in both East and West, in the double form of left-centre or 'Third Way' formations, with a more radical variant attached or adjacent to them.[19] On the other hand, these formations seem increasingly hollow and hence vulnerable in a context of 'postdemocracy' (Crouch 2004) which favours more volatile and populist forms of politics. It may well be, as Darrow Schecter (2007) has argued, that the real action on the modern left is in social movements, regional, national and global, rather than in party politics. We have, of course, been saying this sort of thing since 1968, but, like weather such forecasts, such forecasts do occasionally come true, if not always at the time predicted. From this perspective, 1989 appears as an intermediate marker between 1968, the official birth year if there is one of new social movements, and the present, rather as 1968 appears as a way-station in the democratisation of communist Europe.

Second, it is tempting to see the 'thirty glorious years' of post-war affluence as also the golden years of social democracy, though one has to remember that, in France and Italy, socialist and communist parties

---

[19] Something like Eurocommunism, for example, lived comfortably enough as a minority strand inside the Labour Party in Britain.

had not yet entered government in the mid-1970s. The broader point remains true, however, that the fate of left parties is intimately linked to that of welfare states. The demise of the welfare state, like that of social democracy, has been greatly exaggerated, but the figures of constant or even rising expenditure mask a real decline in the quality of provision as expectations rise and the age structures of almost all European populations become more problematic. Even more importantly, the terms of the debate have been transformed. What was previously a matter for national politics is now increasingly shaped by the EU, which may choose to sustain or improve welfare and labour regimes or, in the name of mobility of labour and free competition, to erode standards achieved after long struggles in the wealthier member states. The EC/EU has traditionally steered clear of this messy area, but it is not clear that it can continue to do so, as what is inelegantly called 'social dumping' undermines what is left of the European social model. This is less a problem of individual member states, which can be kept roughly in line by minimum legal thresholds of social provision, safety regulations etc., as of the Europeanisation of commercial contracts. Domestic employers, partially tamed over decades of trade union struggles, are increasingly being supplanted by transnational gangmasters. Capitalism has arguably become more dangerous, both to itself and to democracy (Habermas 2009; Outhwaite 2009).[20]

My third conclusion is somewhat more contentious. The United States and its allies won the Cold War in the late 1980s, in the sense that their principal opponent declared peace and its former allies switched sides soon after 1989. Twelve of NATO's current twenty-eight members are post-communist countries, though not all these states existed or were in the Warsaw Pact in 1989; the Soviet *animatrice* of the Pact has of course itself ceased to exist. The new world order announced by President George H. W. Bush was clearly meant to be led by the United States, and Hardt and Negri's *Empire* was an ironical reflection of US hegemony. On the other hand, the long predicted economic collapse of the United States now seems to be taking place, albeit in fits and starts, while its moral reputation, such as it was, has been trashed by George W. Bush.[21] The EU, having failed to prevent the second Iraq war and

[20] There is an important issue here whether one sees the Anglo-American style of capitalism as discredited by 2008 or still empowered by the longer-term developments since 1989, as Saskia Sassen argues in Chapter 2, and now simply in a phase of temporary retrenchment (though perhaps heading for another fall).
[21] What novelist could have dreamed up a fantasy in which the United States, occupying a military base in a corner of Cuba while having threatened nuclear war in 1962 if Cuba installed some Soviet missiles on its own territory, would go on, four decades later, to establish a concentration camp there for kidnapped foreigners? Obama may

gone along with the occupation, also has a somewhat tarnished image and lacks the will to polish it up. Russia too, as the successor to the USSR, is subject to something of a double standard (Sakwa 2008) but does everything possible to live up to its bad reputation, most recently in Georgia, while China, which had benefited from a double standard in the other direction, is now also being seen in more realistic terms.

What is not in doubt, I think, is the long-term trend towards the marginalisation of Europe and North America in the economic and political life of the world.[22] In this context, the double unification of Europe, in the sense of both the overcoming of division and the gradual progress towards political union, becomes more and more a matter of local rather than global interest. This does not however make it any less important *within* Europe, and books like this which address the fundamental importance of 1989 are important in that they tackle *both* of these impacts.

1989 and its others

2008 saw the celebration of another anniversary, that of 1968, and it makes sense to look at that year and 1989 together. An excellent volume by Gerd-Rainer Horn and Padraic Kenney (2004) puts 1968 into an appropriate context. 1968 differs from 1989 and, for that matter, from 1945 in that they both brought about a specific outcome: the end of dictatorship and, for much of Europe, occupation, war and genocide. We may be nostalgic for the demonstrations or for the breaching of the Berlin Wall in the wonderful autumn of 1989 and, if we are old enough, for the celebrations of victory or liberation in 1945,[23] but these are in a sense ancillary to the main events: in 1968, the main action was the *événements*.

1989 is, of course, also linked in more direct ways to 1968. In Czechoslovakia and across the Soviet bloc as a whole, it marked a clear end to the period initiated by the 'Eastern' 1968 of reform in the spring,

---

be able to partially restore the image of the United States, but it remains the case that under the Bush administration it managed to destabilise world politics (via the invasion of Iraq) and the world economy (by pioneering dangerous financial operations which were imitated elsewhere with disastrous results).

[22] This long-standing theme has recently been addressed in a number of studies, for example Parag Khanna's *Second World* (2008).

[23] There is a significant Western bias in much of the reflection on 1945 and 1989: the triumphalist idea that 'we' got rid of fascism in 1945 and held back communism until it collapsed in 1989. This has to be balanced by a more self-critical account of the West's sustained preference for short-term stability over support for Eastern democratic movements, culminating in a miserably desultory response to the opportunities to contribute to the reconstruction of much of Europe after 1989.

followed by repression in August and 'normalisation' thereafter. The failure of 1968 in that part of the world, along with the failures of opposition in 1953 in East Germany and 1956 in Hungary, at least achieved a further unmasking of state socialism as a viable alternative to capitalism. For leftists in the West, 1989 was the demise of a real, if unattractive, alternative to capitalism. This could be seen either positively, as the removal of a distraction to the pursuit of socialism in the West, or, more pessimistically, as a sign of its unviability. The rather Western-centred response of Jürgen Habermas in his notion of a 'catching-up' or 'rectifying' revolution has to be seen in this context. To the extent that 1968 was a *communist* movement, the events of 1989 might be seen as its end, or at least its indefinite deferral (Elliott 2008). On the other hand, if 1989 was the end of *scientific* socialism – meaning that socialism now had to be presented, if at all, as an attractive aspiration (in Engels' dismissive contrast, a utopia), what Alain Touraine perceptively characterised as the 'utopian communism' of 1968 is in some ways closer to the equally democratic and anti-authoritarian spirit of 1989.

But is 'celebration' the right way to capture either 1989 or 1968? We must again ask *why* there is so little official celebration, at least up to the present, of the 1989 anniversaries in the various countries of the bloc. The Baltic states and Germany are an exception, but they have national independence (and in the German case also reunification) to celebrate, and everyone does that. We can still ask whether there should be *general* celebrations to mark the events of 1989. The Stalinist paradigm was played out and the Mexican or, as it was known in Poland, South Korean alternative, combining authoritarian politics with economic liberalisation and now of course represented by China, did not present themselves. The casualties, except in Yugoslavia and part of the periphery of the Soviet Union, were social, consisting in suicide and other forms of premature death rather than the result of military violence. Although the new world order did not come about, nor did the scenario of nationalist and sub-national fragmentation widely anticipated for Russia and elsewhere. However, as Larry Ray and I have argued (Outhwaite and Ray 2005), 1989 was in at least one way a bad time for the revolutions: the neoliberal heyday meant that economic policies were quite unnecessarily destructive and the prospect of a second Marshall Plan for post-communist Europe rapidly faded. There was, however, quite a lot of talk of such a thing; Janine Wedel (1998: 29–30) writes that, although the United States had ruled out a Marshall-type action by May 1990, it was only in 1993 that Witold Trzeciakowski, who had been aid coordinator in Poland in 1989–90, realised that it was not going to happen. Whereas 90 per cent of Marshall Aid after the Second World War was in grant form, this was the case for only 10 per cent of aid to post-communist Europe up to 1992. In brief, therefore, the economic decline was unnecessarily harsh, and contributed to the limitations of already weakened socialist organisations such as trade unions and women's movements, and of the oppositional and critical civil society which had attracted such optimistic hopes.

When did 1989 end? Has it done so even today? Okey (2004: 174) suggests that 'The East European transition from communism will not be over until the region is successfully integrated with the European Union'. Note that he says integrated *with*, not *into*. Many of the most interesting and important issues for the future concern the relation between these two prepositions, in particular as they are played out in Ukraine, Moldova, Belarus and Russia itself. The accession of Ukraine looked a more realistic prospect before the brief, but nasty, war between Russia and Georgia in August 2008. On the other hand, as Georg Vobruba (2005) has emphasised, the European 'dynamic' is essentially one of expansion and inclusion. Wherever the EU border lies, the state on the inside has an interest in encouraging the accession of its outside neighbour, to avoid economic competition, border difficulties and so forth (Vobruba 2005: 27). This explains, for instance, current Polish policy with regard to Ukrainian accession, or that of Greece in relation to Turkey, despite the continuing tension over Cyprus. At some point, however, the EU's stated aim of stabilising its periphery has to be 'decoupled' from the prospect of full membership (Vobruba 2005: 75). In many ways it would make sense to draw the line at the border of Russia, which is geographically huge, has an Asian as well as European presence and the sort of delusions of grandeur which France and the UK have more or less got over. Whether Russia can be persuaded to go along with this is, of course, another matter.

As with 1968, it is more appropriate to think of '*les années 89*', not just because the transition in the Soviet Union, which initiated the unravelling of the bloc which Stalin had built, took a couple of years longer, but because the processes are still continuing there and elsewhere. As an acute Ukrainian commentator, Mykola Riabchuk (2008) has pointed out, citing James Sherr, there is a striking parallel with the 1848 revolutions, which removed some regimes but left other liberalising transformations only half-finished.[24] At some point, no doubt, we

---

[24] Sherr was referring specifically to Ukraine's Orange Revolution, but the point has a more general application.

shall stop referring to post-communist or post-socialist Europe, just as we no longer refer in contemporary terms to post-Nazi Germany or post-Francoist Spain, but it will take some time (See Stenning and Hörschelman 2008). Then, at last, 1989 will take its appropriate place in the sequence of Europe's revolutionary dates.

Part II

Where

4   Transatlantic relations in the shadow of the Cold War

Michael Cox

Introduction

The relationship between the United States and Europe constitutes one of the most intimate in modern history. Indeed, if the United States, in Irving Howe's view (1979: 243) began life as a European project propelled forward by European settlers, European technology, European markets and largely European ideas, Europe's great crisis between 1914 and 1945 brought about a major role reversal that left the western powers on the continent less masters in their own house and more servants of an all-powerful, liberal, hegemon situated 3,000 miles away across the Atlantic. There was no inevitability about all this. Nor were the states of Europe (Germany least of all before 1945) particularly willing to accept something like a new American century. Still, there was no escaping the fact about who was increasingly shaping international relations and who was not. In fact, long before the end of the Second World War, one could already detect a geopolitical shift taking place. As Trotsky (1984) observed in the 1920s, the most important consequence of the First World War (aside from the Russian revolution itself) was not just to make Europe ripe for revolution – true in theory, if not in practice – but to tilt the balance of power away from the old world towards the new. As in many things, Trotsky was a man ahead of his time, and it was to take another war to complete the process he envisaged. But complete it most certainly was by 1945, and as the dust began to settle and a divided and much weakened Europe began to take shape, one thing became increasingly clear: the continent that had been the driver of world events since the late sixteenth century had been moved to the margins of history.

The relationship between the United States and its European allies after 1947 was in formal terms at least an equal one voluntarily entered into by sovereign states. In effect it was to be shaped by three realities: necessity, inequality and dependency. This was not something that brought much joy to the hearts of Europeans, even less so to powerful

communist parties in France and Italy. Even some of the United States'
more willing European allies occasionally complained when it acted
in ways which they felt ran counter to their own interests. But as John
Ikenberry (2001) has pointed out, a grand bargain was struck after 1947
that proved strong because it was based on two principles rather than
just one: the principle of trust between each other and the principle
of fear of the 'other'. Indeed, one of the most obvious measures of the
strength of the relationship was that even though the two parties dis-
agreed over many big issues – decolonisation in the 1950s, the Vietnam
War in the 1960s, US economic policy in the 1970s, and US Cold War
strategy under Reagan in the 1980s – they remained close. No doubt a
community based on shared values alone would not have been as resili-
ent. By the same measure, a classic alliance founded upon threat alone
would not have been so durable. But durable it most certainly proved,
in no small part (rather ironically) because of the USSR itself, whose
often incompetent efforts designed to weaken the West only ended up
having the opposite effect. Indeed, the more the Soviet Union tried to
undermine the US presence in Europe, the more the Europeans felt
they needed to keep the Americans 'in'. Equally, the more the Soviets
tried to divide the transatlantic alliance – a central plank of Moscow's
so-called 'peace offensive' – the more the two bonded together fearing,
with some justification, that if they ever allowed their disagreements to
break out openly, the only beneficiary would be their menacing neighbour to the East (Lundestad 2008).

The Cold War, therefore, developed its own kind of logic based
upon a set of certainties about who 'we' were and how the 'other'
would behave. Imagine, thus, the initial confusion caused when the
'other' took upon itself a series of changes in its foreign policy which,
to paraphrase Mikhail Gorbachev, were designed to remove it from
the West's enemy list. Imagine the even greater consternation when
the Soviet Union decided to pull out of Central Europe altogether. For
some American ideologues of course, the collapse of state socialism
represented the ultimate victory of Western liberal values over those of
Eastern collectivism. But those Western leaders who had to deal with
the fallout of these events on the ground were by no means as enthu-
siastic as certain op-ed writers back in Washington. In London, for
instance, Prime Minister Thatcher (if not the Foreign Office) railed
against the dangers of a resurgent Germany and feared for the future
of a Europe without the USSR. In Germany, the social democratic left
worried about the failure of socialism in East Germany and its impact
on their own political chances in any new German set-up. Meanwhile,
in France, François Mitterrand was hardly delighted by the prospect

of communist collapse (and by implication German unification) (Bozo 2007). Indeed, in discussions with the British, and later with Gorbachev himself, the French President made it clear that Germany did 'not have the right to upset the political realities of Europe'.[1] Even the Americans were clear that, while they were more willing than some of their more nervous European allies to move with the tide of history, they did not want this tide to sweep away everything which had been constructed during the Cold War (Cox and Hurst 2002). President Bush even went on record supporting the USSR, insisting that although 1989 was to be welcomed insofar as it supported the cause of freedom in Europe, the same set of events should not undermine the stability and integrity of the Soviet Union itself.

The passing of the Cold War in Europe, therefore, posed a series of questions to which there were then no easy policy responses and whose long-term consequences could only be guessed at. Twenty years on, 1989 continues to be debated, most obviously the minutiae of the events themselves, their deeper causes, why the experts failed to predict them, and, less frequently, why the great upheavals that led to a new order in Europe were not quite so welcome in the West as many now seem to believe. Much ink has also been spilled contemplating the survival skills of the transatlantic relationship post-1989, with realists on one side annually announcing the demise of the alliance in the absence of a clearly defined threat, and liberals on the other insisting that the rela-tionship was bound to hold together because both sides formed part of a larger security community united by shared economies, ideas and insti-tutions. Certainly, for an international relationship that on the surface looked so staid, the transatlantic relationship has caused quite a fevered debate. Indeed, it is perhaps an indication of the relationship's ongoing importance – and the sensitivities that continue to surround it – that when one influential American conservative (Robert Kagan) argued in the year before the invasion of Iraq that there was little that could be done to unite those all-powerful American Hobbesians from Mars and those peace-loving Kantian Europeans from Venus, this occasioned one of the great debates in the twenty-year period following the collapse of the old European order (Cox 2003).

The purpose of this chapter is not to go into all these issues in detail. Even less will it discuss how NATO has been transformed, the extraor-dinary degree of economic interdependence that has grown up between the new Europe and the United States since 1989, or why Europeans

---

[1] Quoted in a 'Letter from Mr Powell (No.10) to Mr Wall'. *Documents on British Policy Overseas. VII German Unification, 1989–90* (2009: 16).

still look to the United States for their security (Mearsheimer 2009). Rather, it will explore the historical legacy of the Cold War and the lessons drawn from that 'clash of secularisms' in order to assess how these have helped to shape American views of their struggle against jihadism. In other words, it will look at the connections between a great power and its alliances defined through conflict in an age of bipolarity and its policies defined towards the same allies in an age of unipolarity.

The chapter is divided into two main parts. Part one examines the parallels drawn between the new 'war on terror' and the old Cold War. As I show, the Bush administration raided the archives of the Cold War with the express intention of casting its own policies within a long American tradition of resisting totalitarianism. But as I point out in the second section, these efforts have been less than successful. Not only have they not convinced Americans themselves (which is one of the reasons President Obama has dropped the term), it has not convinced America's European allies either. If anything, the war on terror (unlike the Cold War) has done more to divide the West than to unite it. This was self-evidently true under President Bush. But it also remains true even under the for-the-moment highly popular President Obama. Furthermore, although Obama has done a great deal to restore the United States' 'soft power' position in Europe, even during a time of profound economic uncertainty, he still finds it difficult to create anything like a transatlantic security consensus. No doubt some kind of transatlantic bargain will hold; there is too much at stake for it to fail. Still, as the clash with radical Islamism intensifies – as it is now doing in Afghanistan, Pakistan and, indeed, the very heart of Europe itself – this is likely to increase rather than decrease tensions across the Atlantic. Twenty years on, it would seem that the West has still not fully recovered, and almost certainly never will, from the passing of the old order in 1989.[2]

The 'war on terror' as a 'new' Cold War?

If 1989 represented formal closure on one era, then so too – in many American eyes – did the attacks on the United States on 11 September 2001; and as the dust began to clear from the streets of downtown Manhattan a raft of born-again, mainly conservative, pundits emerged from under the rubble to declare the bloody end to a decade of post-Cold War drift and lethargy. Each crisis in history produces its own particular version of the immediate past; and so it did once more in the

---

[2] For an overview of these issues, see Cox and Stokes (2008).

days and months immediately following the 2001 attacks. Indeed, in the same way that the crisis generated by the onset of the Cold War in the late 1940s led policy-makers to return to the 1930s in order to point to the moral and strategic dead-end that was appeasement, now, more than a half a century later, policy-makers in the Bush administration did something not too dissimilar in relationship to the 1990s. Now, of course, the point of reference was not Neville Chamberlain – although his name (and that of Churchill) was mentioned more than once by certain Bush hard-liners – but republican hate-figure Bill Clinton. Clinton's crime, however, was not so much a failure to recognise that totalitarian states and movements are aggressive by nature, but rather his limited understanding of the way the world actually worked. Liberal in outlook and opposed almost constitutionally to the idea that force was sometimes necessary to advance the cause of freedom, Clinton appeared to believe that the United States could sustain peace through political example, the spread of markets, and the consolidation of international institutions. How dangerously wrong this particular approach to the world turned out to be, at least according to his critics. Still, every crisis (as they say) is also an opportunity; and if nothing else, the crisis caused by 9/11 did at least bring about a rapid wake-up call. Consequently, US policy-makers now stood – as their predecessors had done before them in 1947 – confronting an implacable ideological enemy determined to undermine the West and the American way of life. As one senior member of the Bush foreign policy team was reportedly said to declare a few days after the attack, the United States in 2001 (like the United States a half century earlier) was once again 'present at the creation' of a new international order.[3]

There has been a vast literature describing the response by the Bush administration to the attack on the Twin Towers and the Pentagon. Interestingly, though possibly unsurprisingly, a good deal of this has concentrated less on the US decision to go to war against the Taliban in Afghanistan (significantly without NATO by its side at first) and far more on the war of choice that led in the end to the deceptively speedy overthrow of the Ba'ath regime in Iraq in spring 2003.[4] This literature has in the main been critical not just of the decision itself, but of

---

[3] The official in question was Dr Condoleezza Rice.

[4] See in particular Bob Woodward's four best-selling books on the Bush administration, why it decided to liberate Iraq and how then it became defined – some would argue undermined – by that decision. *Bush at War* (2002) describes the path to war with Afghanistan following 9/11. The other three volumes deal with Iraq both directly and indirectly: *Plan of Attack* (2004); *State of Denial: Bush at War* (2006); and *The War Within: A Secret White House History* (2008).

the many apparently novel theories – the most novel of all being neo-conservatism – that lent support to the war. What is often left out in this discussion is how much the Bush administration, faced with what it regarded as a quite novel historical conjuncture, constantly returned to the past in order to make sense of what it was doing after 2001. Given the oft-repeated Bush mantra – repeated most famously perhaps by Vice-President Cheney and Secretary of Defense Rumsfeld – that strategies like deterrence and containment were now irrelevant, this was really quite extraordinary. Indeed, for a menace which they daily claimed was radically new, it was odd how many lessons from apparently bygone eras were repeated by policy-makers and public intellectuals alike.[5] No doubt because it was the first attack on the American homeland since the beginning of the nineteenth century, something (though not much) was made of the war between Britain and America when the former had the temerity to burn down the White House (Cox 2002). Much more, of course, was made of Pearl Harbor, a 'surprise attack' if ever there was one, carrying the important message that when ruthless men do unspeakable things to the United States, they had better beware the consequences.[6] But it was the Cold War that was compelled to do the heaviest lifting of all, so much so that in a relatively short space of time a number of pundits began to talk of the 'war on terror' as representing something akin to a new Cold War: some because it was the conflict they remembered best (Lieven 2001), a few because most of Bush's key advisers were Cold War warriors themselves (Mann 2004), and a good number because national security was now back at the top of the policy agenda in much the same way as it had been between 1947 and 1989 (Lieven and Hulsman 2006). For all these reasons, and no doubt a few more, it was not at all unreasonable for writers to think of this new and uncertain present in terms of a known past.

Within the Bush team, however, the purpose of such analogical thinking was less to reflect seriously about the past and more to establish frameworks within which it could legitimise policy decisions. In the process, it did what all administrations since the end of the Second World War had done: derive the lessons it wanted to draw and ignore those that complicated the telling of a particular tale. That said, the tale it narrated had its own appeal, not least because it began with the end of the Cold War itself. Here the Bush administration was uncompromising, if not exactly subtle. The defeat of Soviet communism, it

[5] For the use of analogy in the run up to the war in Iraq, see Record (2007).
[6] 'The Pearl Harbor of the 21st century took place today', Bush noted in his diary on the night of 9/11. Cited in Woodward (2002: 37).

repeated, represented a massive victory for freedom that had left the United States in a position of unrivalled primacy. This development, though, had the unfortunate consequence of leaving the United States without a purpose. As one well-known American historian close to the White House pointed out, the United States had won the Cold War but, as a result, had become a nation lacking a grand strategy (Gaddis 2002). Now, at a stroke, the vacuum had been filled by the challenge posed by political Islam. This was the almost perfect antidote to Western sloth and what some around Bush viewed as a United States grown decadent and flabby in an era personified by Clinton and exemplified by a foreign policy that wandered aimlessly between policy options that rarely touched upon the United States' vital interests. Some were even more explicit. Without a clear and present danger similar to that which had existed before 1989, the United States was more likely to decline than to lead. Indeed, in the view of these critics, the end of the Cold War had been marked by a serious 'threat deficit'; and no amount of clever talk about promoting democracy and spreading the virtues of liberal economics could hide the fact that the United States had lost the capacity to define the international agenda. It may have had most, if not all, available power capabilities, as writers like Charles Krauthammer (1990/1991) suggested. And it had no serious rivals worthy of the name (Ikenberry 2002). But there was very little the United States seemed to be able to do with all this spare capacity. To all intents and purposes, the United States had turned into a superpower – perhaps even an empire – without a mission. And now, because of 9/11, the United States appeared to have discovered one (Cox 1995).

If 9/11 provided a solution to what some regarded as the United States' strategic vacuum, the Cold War offered the Bush White House a ready-made supply of easy arguments about what to do next (Buzan 2006). Naturally, Bush himself was highly selective in terms of what he chose to learn and from whom. However, the fact he felt compelled to learn anything at all says a lot about the power of the past and the hold it had on a president of even his limited intellectual powers (Shapiro 2007). Unsurprisingly, the Cold War president whom Bush clearly tried to learn the most from was Ronald Reagan – republican hero, enemy of the original evil empire (no coincidence of course that Bush himself later talked of an 'axis of evil') and ultimate reason (at least according to many on the American right) as to why the Soviet Union was finally consigned into the proverbial dustbin of history. Reagan seemed to be the perfect role model. Like Bush, he believed in power and establishing clear positions of strength. He entered office after what was regarded as a period of foreign policy drift (Reagan often talked of the 1970s as a 'decade of neglect'). There were, moreover, many around Reagan who were anything but 'realist' in international outlook. Finally, Reagan (like Bush) saw the United States being opposed by a dangerous global threat which, if not checked, could threaten nuclear Armageddon. Naturally, there were differences. Thus when Reagan assumed office he did so with a fairly clear idea of what he wanted to do abroad. Bush, on the other hand, did not acquire such an outlook until after the attacks of 9/11. Reagan was heir to an ongoing Cold War, not facing what many around Bush felt was something quite novel.

Bush, however, was not deterred by what he regarded as cosmetic differences. In Reagan, he not only saw someone willing to challenge the status quo by employing US military power, but a leader of rare courage unafraid of discussing international affairs in ethical terms. Indeed, as Bush noted when praising one particularly influential book that drew parallels between Reagan's successful struggle against the Russians and Bush's ongoing war against terrorism, Reagan conducted his affairs abroad in a distinctly no-nonsense American way, and as a result brought about regime change in the USSR in much the same way as Bush himself was to do in those states which had hitherto sheltered the West's enemies.[7] The so-called Bush Doctrine may have appeared radical in terms of the US foreign policy tradition. But as Bush and others pointed out, with its focus on transformation rather than order, and its attempt to frame US policies in terms of more general universal principles, there was something very Ronald Reagan (and by extension something very Cold War) about the war on terror (Leffler 2003).

If Reagan served as an important point of reference for Bush, so too in a more general sense did one very important part of the wider US foreign policy tradition: that which saw a direct connection between US security and the promotion of democracy. Here again the United States' larger role in the world after 1947 served to inspire and guide those whose job it was to conduct the new war on terror. Of course, critics might argue that the United States was driven in the early part of the Cold War, as it was later motivated in the post-Cold War era, by less exalted goals: preserving the balance of power, maintaining stability and securing US access to key commodities and markets. But as a number of realists like Morgenthau and Kennan discovered during the Cold War (and others of a similar persuasion discovered when Bush was in office), US foreign policy was not merely driven by realist calculations of interest but rather (though to what degree remains open) by a desire to change the world in its own image. Thus when Bush talked in grand,

---

[7] The book in question is Sharansky and Denmer (2005).

if not always eloquent, terms of defeating al-Qaeda by sowing the seeds of liberty in the Middle East, this was not mere rhetoric. Rather, Bush was drawing on a Cold War vocabulary that saw the United States' 'fundamental purpose' – to paraphrase NSC-68 – as not just containing its enemies, but eliminating them altogether. And there was no better way of doing this than by holding firm to its liberal principles (Dodge 2009).

Selling the 'Islamic threat'

The post-Cold War world, therefore, saw the emergence of what on the face of it looked like a new sense of US purpose defined around an irreconcilable enemy. Admittedly, this new enemy was fundamentally different from communism in terms of its ideology. Nevertheless, there were similarities. It was totalitarian in nature – just like communism. It was implacably opposed to the West – just like communism. And most critically, it sought (or so it was claimed) something akin to world domination – just like communism. There was every reason, therefore, for Western powers to unite. Indeed, when a day after 9/11, NATO invoked Article 5, insisting that the attack on the United States had been an attack on all members of the Alliance, it looked to all intents and purposes as if the West had never been so united. Even publics on both sides of the Atlantic appeared to be coming closer together. Certainly, if opinion polls at the time were to be believed, it looked very much as if the transatlantic relationship was being reborn in the shadow of the Twin Towers with Europeans and Americans now taking very much the same view (a decidedly hostile one) about Muslims in general,[8] and the 'Islamic' threat in particular.[9] They also appeared to display a very similar (and high) degree of hostility towards those who either supported, or even showed the slightest degree of sympathy with, the activities of jihadists (Hoese and Oppermann 2007). On both official and public measures, the transatlantic relationship looked to be alive and well – again.

But even in the midst of all this hand-shaking solidarity, cracks began to appear. The decision to go to war against Iraq was one very obvious example of, and reason for, this. But the drift had already begun to take place before 2003 and was precipitated less because of what the

---

[8] 'Fifty six per cent of Americans and Europeans do not feel that the values of Islam are compatible with the values of democracy' (*Transatlantic Trends Survey* 2006: 4).

[9] 'Large numbers of Americans and Europeans agree on the importance of global threats with the largest increase over the year in those who see Islamic fundamentalism as an "extremely important" threat' (*Transatlantic Trends Survey* 2006: 4, 7–8).

United States had decided to do about Saddam Hussein – though the implications of this for the transatlantic relationship were near catastrophic – and more about what was meant precisely by the notion of a 'war on terror'. This idea immediately provoked something of backlash, and the first to take the idea to task was the seasoned British writer, Sir Michael Howard (2002), one of the doyens of Western strategic thought. As Howard pointed out in an influential critique, the idea of a 'war on terror' was a dubious one which not only lent legitimacy to al-Qaeda, but also presupposed an extended conflict that could continue ad infinitum. Not only that, the notion itself, he continued, was strategically incoherent. No state or group of states could declare war on a method, and nor should it try to do so. As time passed, such critics grew in confidence to such an extent that some Americans (and at times Bush himself) began to experiment with other ideas, and at one point even replaced the notion of a global war against terror (GWOT) with the apparently less offensive idea of a 'long war'.[10] At one level, such rhetorical framing mattered very little. However it did point to (at best) a lack of strategic clarity and (at worst) to a lack of confidence in what the United States and its allies were supposed to be uniting against. It also compared rather unfavourably with the common sense of purpose which had existed during the Cold War. As we knew then (and realise even more now), there was a great deal of debate in the West about the Soviet threat (Cox 1992). Indeed, no less a figure than George Kennan raised a series of fundamental questions about the Cold War that challenged Western policies to the core. But in the final analysis, once governments had decided that there was a threat of some kind, they neither questioned nor seriously challenged the idea. Once a consensus, always a consensus it seemed, at least until Gorbachev began to change the rules of the game after 1985.

This in turn raises a second – more theoretical – issue about whether or not it is possible to sustain an alliance against (or around) something as nebulous as 'terror'. Here the comparison with the way alliances have been forged in the past, and the way this new alliance might be constructed, bears serious comparison. As different writers have shown, alliances may be formed for many different reasons, one having to do with the existence of a serious asymmetry in the balance of power and another – according to Stephen Walt (1987) – with the existence of threats. Even constructivists who stress shared values in alliance

---

[10] See 'Abizaid Credited with Popularizing the Term "Long War"', *Washington Post*, 3 February 2006. President Bush also sought to place the enemy in the camp of fascism, hence his brief use of the term 'Islamo-Fascism' to describe jihadists of all shapes and sizes.

formation still accept that it is easier to sustain such formations when there is a clear and present danger around which to unite (e.g. Risse-Kappen 1995). The key issue, therefore, is not whether threats exist or perform a specific role but rather how *credible* any particular threat happens to be. There may be many different answers to this question. But even members of opposing theoretical schools would find it difficult to disagree with what realists have to say on this issue: namely, that it is difficult to construct, maintain and legitimise a threat over the long-term unless the threat in question has serious capabilities, which under modern conditions means that it must be a state of some form. Hence, the USSR could be viewed as a threat, not simply because it had an opposing ideology and was not a democracy (though both things helped in helping sell the threat) but because it had successfully industrialised after 1929, occupied a large swathe of territory, had huge resources, and happened to have the largest army in Europe (at least after the Second World War). Take all of this away, then it is unlikely that a Soviet Union with minimal capabilities and a weak state – however aggressive its ideology and repressive its polity – would have produced the same level of concern as it did in the West (Cox 2007).

Viewed within this framework, it becomes perfectly easy to understand why the war against Islamic-inspired terrorism has not been anywhere near as successful in forging a new sense of purpose across the Atlantic. As Barry Buzan (2006: 112) has observed, 'while serious, the terrorist threat' simply lacks the 'depth of the Soviet/communist one'. There are several good reasons why. One has to do with threat perception and how to sustain this when the threat in question only acts very sporadically. No doubt ordinary people in the West accept that there is something 'out there' seeking to do them harm. The problem is that if this threat does not materialise in an attack, opinion can rapidly change. Indeed, one of the features of the period since 9/11 is that threat perceptions have risen and fallen with considerable speed. Hence, even if immediately after the London bombings of 2005, British opinion was decidedly hawkish, it soon began to return to 'normal' (*Transatlantic Trends Survey* 2006: 4). Meanwhile in other countries in Europe where no such attacks occurred (with the exception of Spain), views tended to range from the complacent to the war-weary. Even in the United States, public opinion has not been consistent, something that poses a problem which security services have tried to resolve by repeating the refrain that just because there have been no terrorist outrages since 2001, this does not mean they are not being planned. Prevention of terrorist attacks may be a mark of success for Western security services, but to the public, they only appear to indicate that the threat posed is relatively minimal.

To complicate matters even further, there was (until Obama's election) a growing belief on one side of the Atlantic at least, that the Bush administration was merely using or manipulating tensions created by the security situation to further its own political ambitions. The fact that the war on terror helped to get the Republicans re-elected in 2004 (though not in 2008) hardly helped generate consistent, across-the-board support for US goals, especially in Europe (Jenkins 2007). Nor did scandals such as Abu Ghraib and Guantanamo Bay. On the contrary, not only did such acts do enormous damage to America's reputation around the world, they also markedly affected how Europeans began to see the United States. Indeed, instead of the 'war on terror' (involving what many regarded as highly dubious methods) bringing the two continents closer together, it was evident that the opposite was taking place. Certainly, by the end of Bush's first term, relations between the two had rarely been so bad with anti-Americanism spreading like wild-fire on one side of the Atlantic, and exasperated outbursts on the other about the inconsistency and weakness of those so-called allies in Europe who, with the exception of the British (who were not really European anyway), had little stomach for a fight and very little understanding of the dangers that confronted the West (Wilkinson 2005: 17–18, 24–5).

This brings us to the question of Islam itself – the problematic ideological source of 'jihad'. Here again, the global war on terror involving the wider Atlantic community faced (and probably still faces) significant, perhaps insurmountable, obstacles in generating a clear point of reference around which to unite. There are at least three reasons why. First, radical Islam, unlike communism, has only limited ideological appeal. It is not, in other words, a universal threat. Consequently it is less likely to have the same uniting and mobilising capacity as communism. Second, the overwhelming majority of Muslims (unlike the overwhelming majority of communists during the Cold War) do not seek the overthrow of the various states under which they live. Indeed, as opinion polls in the West have shown, while ordinary Muslims may not approve of Western interventions in the Middle East, only a very small majority are prepared to translate that criticism into militant action. Third, though Islam may be defined by some in the West as 'the problem', policy-makers themselves realise that if jihad is to be successfully contained, the West has to seek some understanding with those states that are Islamic in character. Indeed, the United States has been forced by the logic of its 'war' to reinforce its alliances with at least two countries – Pakistan and Saudi Arabia – whose elites have either displayed some 'sympathy' with the terrorists or have been willing to use them for their own political purposes (on the former, see Zahab and Roy 2004; on the latter, Wright 2006). It could, of course, be argued that the Cold War was not without its complexities. After all, China after 1978 supported American 'imperialists' against the USSR, orthodox communists appeared to regard dissident members of the communist movement as more dangerous than the international bourgeoisie, and the Soviet elite occasionally did make deals with its capitalist enemies. But even these gyrations cannot compare to the complex, debilitating manoeuvrings now involved in fighting the war on terror.

In sum, the current conflict is taking place in a world that is, in many ways, much more complex than the somewhat simpler world left behind in 1989. As Fred Halliday (1984) reminded us some time ago, the great success of the Cold War in mobilising support and forging accord between potentially fractious and competitive states was not because the USSR was more powerful than the United States. Rather it was because the United States as leader of the West was able to construct the world in such a way that other critical issues were seen either as secondary or were folded into the larger framing of East–West competition. This nesting of issues has not been so easily achieved over recent years. Here again, opinion polls tell an interesting story. That people in Europe and the United States are together concerned about terrorism is clear. But it is not the only – or even the most important thing – they are concerned about. If anything, what polls reveal is a hotchpotch of concerns ranging from a rising China to climate change and what many see as the gravest danger of all: the global financial crisis. Indeed, since the Wall Street crisis of 2008 and the election of a very different kind of US president (one who has never used the term 'war on terror'), the debate in the United States and Europe has shifted dramatically away from national security towards economics. And as one of the more innovative US think-tanks (New America Foundation 2008) recently pointed out, 'no matter what the issues were yesterday', it was becoming clearer by the day 'that the economy' was becoming 'the biggest political issue' in the United States. In and of itself, this did not pose any existential threat to the transatlantic relationship. However, it did pose a problem of sorts, in large part because, as economic stress intensified on one side of the Atlantic, publics were likely to become less concerned about what was happening to allies on the other.

Conclusion

In this chapter, I have asked a deceptively easy question: whether or not the Atlantic community as forged during the Cold War could be recreated, restored or revived by the oldest strategic device of all, namely of having a shared enemy (or in Schmittian terms, an 'other' standing both inside and outside the gates of the polis) posing a fundamental threat to its continued existence? As I have argued, while the new international conjuncture has changed the world in important ways, it is most unlikely to recreate some 'golden age' (if such an age ever existed) of transatlantic unity. This vision, I have implied, died in 1989. This does not mean that shared economic interests, similar values and overlapping membership of international institutions do not matter. Nor is it to ignore those areas where there has been concrete cooperation (especially at the intelligence and financial levels) in the wider struggle against terrorism. But as I have tried to demonstrate, the idea of the West has not been rekindled around the idea of an Islamic threat. Nor is this likely to happen any time soon (Garton Ash 2004: 234).

Critics of this view could, and often do, respond by pointing to NATO's new role in Afghanistan. The more subtle amongst them could also point (and again do) to the fact that both the United States and the European Union tend to sing from the same political hymn sheet about the need to act against global terrorism. Indeed, the well-publicised EU document dealing with 'grand strategy' published in March 2003 mentions the threat of terrorism on numerous occasions. But neither of these points hit home. First, while it is true that NATO has been given a new lease of life by Afghanistan, its experience there has exposed some deep fissures within the organisation. Indeed, this expanded mission – inconceivable only a short while ago[11] – has not only revealed sharp differences between Americans and Europeans on the ground,[12] but also exposed important clefts within Europe too. The same is true in the broader sphere of security. Here differences in outlook persist between a militarily preponderant United States and a rather ill-equipped Europe. As a result, the two continue to look at the world through different strategic eyes. Hence, whereas Americans continue to view problems and their resolution largely in 'hard power' terms, Europeans invariably perceive them in altogether 'softer' ways. In fact, the world order

[11] 'Afghanistan today provides the "why" for NATO's continuing transformation. Few would have predicted, even five years ago, that 26 Allies and 11 Partners would support more than 30,000 troops 3,000 miles from alliance territory in making a long-term commitment to the peace and stability of that country.' Speech by Victoria Nuland (US Permanent Representative to NATO), 23 October 2006, Brussels. See Nuland (2006).

[12] Though we are told (rather unconvincingly) that the 'ISAF Commander meets with his US counterpart for Operation Enduring Freedom every week to coordinate activities ... great effort', it concluded, 'was being made to ensure maximum synergy between the two operations'. See *NATO Briefing: Afghanistan* (2005: 6).

described in the European Security Strategy (ESS) of 2003 seemed to owe more to liberal theories of international politics than to a US doctrine of exceptional power. The ESS also appeared to reject altogether the US notion of unipolarity, insisting that in an interdependent world, there could be no unilateral solution to particular issue-areas.[13]

So where does this leave the Atlantic relationship? The answer will depend on a host of fairly concrete factors, including in no particular order: the changing structure of the Euro-Atlantic economy (now under significant stress); developments in Russia (another issue that is likely to divide rather than unite Europeans and Americans); and whether or not Turkey is admitted into the European Union (something Europeans oppose more than Americans). But of one thing we can be sure: Western unity will not arise via something as ill-defined as an 'Islamic threat'. This might not spell the 'death of the West' as such. However, in the absence of some common purpose, and confronting as it does all the tensions that are bound to arise as a result of the world economic crisis, it is not unreasonable to suggest that the West is likely to become an increasingly fractious space. Admittedly, the election of a new US president who seems to feel as much, if not more, at home with Europeans as he does with many of his own citizens (a significant minority of whom do not regard him as being properly American) has changed the atmospherics to a degree. The transatlantic relationship is certainly in better shape now than it has been for some time. But whether this can outlast his presidency remains an open question.

---

[13] For a useful guide to the *European Security Strategy* and its similarity (or otherwise) with the US National Security Strategy Document, see Shepherd *et al.* (2006: 71–109).

5   Third World socialism: 1989 and after

Fred Halliday

Conjunctures and multiple outcomes

The events of 1989, and their immediate antecedents and consequences, qualify, on any general criteria, as one of the most striking,
and unanticipated, international conjunctures of modern history, comparable in the coincidence and interlocking of events with such classic
earlier moments as 1648, 1789, 1848, and the ends of the First and
Second World Wars. In all of these cases a set of interlocking processes – military, political, economic, ideological – seemed to come in
unison to crisis point. The result was both the shattering of established
forms of state power, combined with the emergence of new forms of political and social opposition and an ensuing, and often remarkably rapid,
recomposition of a new intra- and inter-state order. In such cases, the
conjuncture marked both crisis and re-creation, both the culmination
and denouement of an earlier set of changes, and the initiation of a new,
different order. In all of these cases, the consequences were felt widely
across the world, even if, faced with major changes within powerful
states, be they France in 1789 or the USSR in 1989–91, states and societies reacted in markedly different ways: an interconnected set of societies and states is not a homogeneous, integrated, totality.

The analytic challenge facing the student of such conjunctures
comprises at least three different elements: first, the establishment of a
historical record, recognising global context and national specificity of
the events of this and adjacent years; second, specification of the international and transnational vectors of the conjuncture (such as environment, international war, economic crisis and ideological upheaval) from
those which were more specifically national, random or coincidental;
and finally, a delineation of the overall international, regional *and* global changes which the conjuncture brought about. At the same time,
there also needs to be recognition of the degree to which systemic crisis
had contradictory effects, and of how far, even while some countries
were swept up in the changes around them, others remained strikingly

112

immune or, more paradoxically still, reacted in a manner contrary to the externally prevailing trends.

1989 embodies all three of these analytic challenges. While it would be an exaggeration to say that 1989 affected every country in the world, it certainly transformed world politics as a whole, and had a direct impact on at least a quarter of the states in the world. The list of these would normally start with the over thirty states that in the years prior to 1989 were, in some form or another, ruled by communist, pro-Soviet or other forms of authoritarian and self-styled 'socialist' regimes. At the same time, the collapse of Soviet power had, in a range of (perhaps over a dozen) other countries, the contrary effect of undermining the power, or claim to the legitimacy of emergency rule, of right-wing regimes, in both Southern Africa and Latin America, that had, with varying degrees of plausibility, justified their authoritarian system by reference to the threat of 'international' communism. Three other direct consequences of 1989 may also be noted: the removal of legitimacy from pro-Soviet regimes that ruled parts, in both cases the weaker parts, of divided countries (Germany and Yemen both united under pro-Western regimes in 1990); the fragmentation, along lines of the hitherto inoperable 'federal' system within each state, of multi-ethnic communist regimes, peacefully in the USSR and Czechoslovakia, violently in Yugoslavia and Ethiopia; and the alarming of former Soviet allies, who subsequently acted much more rashly on the international and/or domestic stage – most obviously Saddam Hussein with his invasion in August 1990 of Kuwait, less overtly Fidel Castro via his move to suppress dissent within the Cuban army through show trials of prominent army officers.

When we turn to the other analytic challenges of conjunctures – that of distinguishing international from local factors and drawing up a differentiated balance sheet – 1989 is equally difficult to assess. Much has been written on the broader issue of *why* the Soviet Union collapsed, and why, in Europe, it did so both suddenly and peacefully (e.g. Blackburn 1991; Halliday 1991; Bisley 2004). Suffice it to register that, as in other comparable world historical conjunctures, there were a multiplicity of causes for the collapse of Soviet rule. For all their prominence during the Cold War, and in 'realist' analysis of it, military and security dimensions played a relatively limited role in the end of the Cold War. More important in the context of this chapter is the question of the role of the 'Third World', broadly conceived, in the Soviet collapse. For some, before and after 1989, this Third World dimension with its associated economic burdens, not least those arising from the war in Afghanistan, was the dominant, if not sole or determinant, factor that explains Soviet collapse. For others, the disappearance of Soviet communism was, above all, a result of the conflict in Europe itself, be this, for some, political and economic competition between the Soviet and Western blocs, for others, the burdens and risks of the nuclear arms race.

On this matter, moreover, the third broad analytic question, that of the *consequences* of the crisis, provides a striking, if insufficiently noted, perspective: for, while the Cold War was indeed an international – and in some ways global – context (Westad 2005), and while the collapse of Soviet power had global causes and consequences, the actual consequences for Third World allies, and, more broadly, for Third World socialist and left-oriented authoritarian regimes, were much less uniform. In some cases, such as the flourishing of new forms of authoritarian capitalism in East Asia, they were markedly unexpected. There is, indeed, an argument to be made that, for all the global character of the Cold War, the end of the nuclear arms race and of the Soviet–American rivalry in 1989–91, in its political and ideological dimensions the collapse of Soviet communism was, to a considerable extent, a predominantly European affair. Earlier conjunctural crises, such as the ends of the Napoleonic wars, and of the First and Second World Wars, had shattered global systems of political control: the Spanish empire in Latin America in the first place, the Romanov and Ottoman empires in the second, and the European colonial system in Asia and Africa in the third, closely followed by the Chinese revolution in 1949. Arguably, a swathe of states running from Afghanistan to Ethiopia excepted, the collapse of the USSR, revolutionary as it was in strategic and ideological terms, had more limited political impact on, and sometimes counter-cyclical consequences for, the countries of Asia, Africa and Latin America.

World revolution and the colonial world

The Cold War, the third, longest and final chapter in what Eric Hobsbawm (1994) has termed 'the short twentieth century', was, more than the two previous international conflicts, the First and Second World Wars, certainly a global process, spanning Europe, west and east, East and South-East Asia, the Middle East, and extending to Afghanistan, Central Asia, much of Africa, north and south, and Latin America. If Australia itself was immune, the archipelago to its north, in, as it were, its 'front yard', comprising Indonesia and East Timor, most certainly was not. Only North America, major protagonist of the Cold War, and target of any possible nuclear conflagration, remained immune to this pattern of revolution, combat and counter-revolution, even though it too, in the early and late 1960s, was the site of large-scale popular mobilisations in the civil rights and anti-war movements. At the same time, and as the North American case shows, the Cold War, much more than the First World War but in parallel with the Second World War, was a conflict involving multiple levels of rivalry: it was military, at both the inter-state and social levels; political, in terms of competition for state power within countries; diplomatic, in terms of relations and alliances between states; ideological; and, in considerable measure, economic and aspirational.

This combination of temporal and geographic spread, across four decades and five continents, with multiple, intersecting but also autonomous, areas of competition, poses a series of fascinating questions as to how to analyse the course, outcome and legacy of this geopolitical chapter. In terms of crises and historic events, the conflict in Europe, determinant in the outbreak of the Cold War in the 1940s, with the crises over Berlin and the Greek civil war, was, in military and political terms over by the late 1950s. Henceforth it was the Third World that was to be the site of Cold War incident and alarm: the wars in Indochina and Southern Africa, the Cuba missile crisis of 1962, the Arab–Israeli wars and then, in the period from 1974 to 1980, a spate of no fewer than fourteen anti-imperialist revolutions, most affiliated in some way or other with the USSR, served to shift attention from Europe, now apparently stabilised, to Asia, Africa and Latin America (Halliday 1984).

Throughout the forty years of Cold War, there was consequently widespread debate and speculation, as much in the West as in the communist camp, about the role of the Third World in the overall global contest, and, in particular on the relationship, the articulation in military, political and ideological terms, between the confrontation on the 'central', European front, fixed at the end of the Second World War, and stabilised with the balance of nuclear terror, and that in the unstable, unfixed, countries of Asia, Africa and Latin America. No history of the Cold War, and the rise and fall of the alarms, strategic breakthroughs, diplomatic processes and, not least, bursts of ideological aspiration associated with it, can afford to ignore either the balance of power in Europe, with its implications for the nuclear arms race and the consolidation of rival blocs (NATO, Warsaw Pact) on the one hand, or the set of wars, some of them long in duration and bloody in consequence, that punctuated the Third World from the late 1940s until the 1980s and, indeed, as in Angola, Congo, Colombia, Palestine, Afghanistan, local wars with a strong Cold War component, well into the 1990s and beyond. If Europe always remained central to conventional nuclear

and Great Power diplomatic calculations, it was the Third World that
generated the majority of the military and political crises of the Cold
War, and where nearly all the casualties, over twenty million dead in
all, of the conflicts of this period were found. This is evident above all
from the account of Arne Westad (2005), which argues that the Great
Powers, East and West, imposing what he terms a 'regime of global
intervention', continued to act in the Third World very much as had the
colonial powers before them.

At the time, and in retrospect it is striking how far on both sides of
the Cold War global divide this issue – the articulation of metropolitan advanced economic conflict with the Third World – matched by
stasis in one, and by fluidity and unpredictability in the other, generated widespread differences of opinion which, even now, with the
benefit of hindsight, allow of no easy resolution. First, there was the
question of relative importance, and of the intersection of metropolitan
and Third World conflicts. Thus on the Western side a figure such as
George Kennan, author of the theory of containment, could argue that
the United States should in large measure ignore the Third World, and
that revolutions in poor countries were bound to end in failure, and
would act as a burden on the Soviet Union. At the same time, a writer
on strategic rivalry, Allan Lynch, could argue that, with the stabilisation of the situation in Berlin in 1961, and the signing of the Nuclear
Test Ban Treaty in 1963 along with other nuclear negotiations that followed, the Cold War, defined above all by the European 'central' front,
had in effect ended (Lynch 1992). On the other hand, from the late
1940s onwards, there were those in Washington, and in Europe, who
saw the rise of revolutionary regimes, some nationalist, some socialist,
a few, as in Vietnam, communist, as a direct threat to the West, part of
'encircling movements' and other Soviet, later Chinese, 'adventurism'
that in the end would threaten the core states of the West. For these
Western strategists the Cold War was 'a global struggle'. The communist victory in China in 1949 and the outbreak of the Korean War in
1950, the Cuban revolution of 1959, the Vietnam War of the 1960s and
early 1970s, and the spate of 1970s revolutions, among them Ethiopia,
Afghanistan, Iran, Nicaragua, served to promote consternation in
Washington: if it was the outbreak of the Korean War in June 1950 that
led to the formulation of the first US Cold War doctrine as embodied in
NSC-68, it was the revolutions of the 1970s that ended détente, precipitated the election of Ronald Reagan in 1980, and prompted the Second
Cold War (Halliday 1984).

On the communist side, a similar uncertainty and diversity of views
could be noted. If classical Marxism had shown little interest in, or hope

from, the colonial world, Marx famously welcoming the US attack on Mexico and the British occupation of Egypt, his Bolshevik successors were more open-minded. While the hope of the Russian revolutionaries remained that of a revolution in the advanced capitalist world, first Germany, then Britain and France, later Spain, the outbreak of nationalist movements after the First World War also led the Communist International to support anti-imperialism in Asia, Africa and Latin America. In a famous slogan of the early 1920s, attributed to Trotsky, it was said that 'the road to Paris lies through Peking and Calcutta'. In what history would later turn into an ironic lesson, Trotsky, no doubt impressed by the anti-British stance of Afghan King Amanullah, added 'Kabul' to this list (Deutscher 1954: 457). Lenin saw revolution as occurring where global capitalism had its 'weakest link' and Trotsky's theory of 'uneven and combined development', where the 'uneven' was defined above all in socio-economic terms, gave broad theoretical backing to the political insight that imperialism, starting with the British, could be undermined from the colonial world. These conceptions of revolution, taking the world as a unit, but placing emphasis on the Third World, were to be replicated in later revolutionary movements: in that of the Chinese revolution, which saw the Third World as a set of rural areas encircling the cities of the north, and in Cuban conceptions of guerrilla war in Vietnam and Latin America as being part of a 'tricontinental' battle. Both the Chinese and Cuban, as well as other (Vietnamese, Algerian, Angolan) revolutions introduced a further political and, by implication at least, theoretical innovation, whereby the hitherto neglected or, by Marx himself, despised social class, the peasantry, were now seen as revolutionary agents, sometimes even superior to the timid and corrupted working class.

On the other hand, there were many within the communist movement who doubted, or after initial enthusiasm came to doubt, such a global perspective. Stalin, for one, showed limited interest in the Third World, especially after the defeat of the Chinese communist insurrection in 1927. Stalin did support, and more strongly in military terms than was clear at the time, the Chinese revolution of 1949, but even here he sensed limits, and was wary of Mao's independence of, when not rivalry with, Moscow. When the first Arab–Israeli war broke out in 1948, Stalin supported the Zionist movement, regarding it as an anti-imperialist force resisting Arab feudalism and its British backers. When a nationalist movement was elected in Iran in 1951, on the USSR's borders, Stalin held back and his supporters in Iran tarnished Mohammed Mosaddeq, the nationalist leader and premier, as a US stooge. Only in the middle and late 1960s, with the rise of Arab socialism in Egypt, and of a broad Afro-Asian Solidarity Movement, later to overlap with the separate Non-Aligned Movement, did the USSR, under Khrushchev, come to support Third World liberation and nationalist movements. Moscow maintained this commitment for about two decades, increasingly finding itself in competition not only with the United States but also, from the early 1960s, with China. For Moscow, such engagement with the Third World, at a level of military, political and economic commitment far lower than that of the West, provided several advantages, not least that of global prestige, but also of military bases. In each of the main dimensions of the Cold War, the USSR, cautious and with limited resources, nonetheless sought engagement with the Third World.

Soviet allies in the Third World

Soviet theory accommodated this commitment in two general analytic frameworks. One was that of the 'Correlation of Forces', a conception of a global rivalry comprehended in military, political, economic and ideological terms, and in which, over time, the advantage shifted to the communist world (Light 1989). In some ways analogous to the Western concept of 'Balance of Power', it differed in having an underlying, historically progressive, dynamic. The other analytic distinction was that of the different categories of Third World states and allies. Roughly, Moscow distinguished between those countries ruled by what it recognised to be pro-Soviet communist parties, analogous to those of Eastern Europe, from those which, while in some ways socialist and anti-imperialist, and with the potential of becoming fully socialist, remained at an earlier stage, this being variously denoted as 'non-capitalist', 'national-democratic' or, in much later formulation, 'states of socialist orientation'. Yet another category comprised those states which, while fully communist in internal organisation, were independent of, when not hostile to, the USSR (Hough 1986).

The high point of Soviet commitment to, and alliance formation with, the Third World came in the late 1970s and early 1980s, precisely the accumulation of power that so alarmed Washington and which led, or perhaps deluded, the Soviet leadership into thinking the world was going in the direction of 'developed socialism' as they coyly categorised the Soviet system. A tally of such states drawn up in November 1982 (Halliday 1989: 99), at the moment of the death of Soviet leader Leonid Brezhnev, reveals that, in total, the Soviet net stretched to thirty-one component states:

(1) *Six Core Communist Party-Ruled States*: Afghanistan[1], Cambodia, Cuba, Laos, Mongolia, Vietnam.

(2) *Five Leading States of Socialist Orientation*: Angola, Ethiopia, Mozambique, Nicaragua, People's Democratic Republic of Yemen.

(3) *Two Independent Communist Party-Ruled States*: China, Democratic People's Republic of Korea.

(4) *Fourteen Less Advanced States of Socialist Orientation*: Algeria, Benin, Burma, Cape Verde, Congo-Brazzaville, Guinea, Guinea-Bissau, Iraq, Libya, Madagascar, São Tomé, Syria, Tanzania, Zimbabwe.

(5) *Four Marginal States of Socialist Orientation*: Burkina Faso, Ghana, Seychelles, Surinam.

This picture of an inexorable advance of socialism in the Third World, and, by implication, on the world scale as a whole, whether in its Soviet, Chinese or Cuban variants was, however, open to question. Leaving aside the high quotient of revolutionary utopianism and nationalist exaggeration involved in both the image and understanding of these states, events in several of these countries and broader world trends did not necessary favour the rise of socialism. First, from the early 1960s, Moscow had lost its most important ally and the most populous country in the world – China. In addition to dividing communism ideologically in a split that was never overcome, this significantly weakened the political, diplomatic and, as Indo-China was to show, military potential of the Soviet bloc. That other states followed, Albania and Romania in Europe, North Korea in Asia, only compounded the problem of fissures within the core communist movement. In a culmination of this process, a movement representing an ultra-fanatical offshoot of Maoism, that of the Khmer Rouge in Cambodia, came to power in 1975 and, after massacring a significant part of its own people, ended up going to war with another socialist state, Vietnam, in late 1978.

Second, the gamut of countries comprised in the 'half' or 'developing' socialist category were vulnerable to distortion and deviation of many kinds. Even in 1982, when 'developed socialism' was supposed to be prevailing on a worldwide scale, the number of incipiently 'socialist' or revolutionary regimes that had already been overthrown was significant. Some, such as the Dominican Republic, Ghana and Indonesia

---

[1] Although Afghanistan was officially not classified by Soviet writers as a 'socialist' state, this was deceptive as, to all intents and purposes, it was considered by Moscow to be a core, communist party-ruled ally, hence the high levels of military and economic support that it received.

in 1965, Chile in 1973, later Grenada in 1983, were ousted in military coups or invasion by the United States. Others, after affecting support for Soviet conceptions of socialism and foreign policy, began to lessen their commitment to the USSR and hedge their bets, even while not switching sides: Syria, Iraq, Libya, Algeria in the first category; Egypt above all in the second. The 'loss' of Egypt in the early Sadat presidential period, between 1972 and 1976, when Egypt had been the most important Soviet ally and showcase in the non-communist Third World, was not only a major strategic blow, removing Moscow's only naval bases in the Mediterranean, but even more so an ideological blow. It was even said of the USSR that, in the late 1970s, it suffered from an 'Egypt Syndrome', parallel to the 'Vietnam Syndrome' of the United States – a reluctance to engage in Third World adventures or to devote prestige and resources to it. One or two initially 'socialist-oriented' states did appear to be moving towards full socialism, such as South Yemen and Ethiopia, but the majority did not.

Third, the USSR found itself, in attempting to form alliances in the Third World, and in a situation of strategic and political conflict and fluidity, drawn into crises. This led to a more active role and a commitment to provide resources: Cuba, the outpost on the doorstep of the United States, absorbed major amounts of economic assistance; Ethiopia threw itself, with a militarised nationalism compounded by revolutionary ardour, into a series of offensives to try to crush the guerrillas in Eritrea; Egypt and Syria lurched into wars with Israel in which they then expected the USSR to rescue them; and above all, the Afghan communists, in the People's Democratic Party of Afghanistan, a group founded only in 1965, probably the last communist party established anywhere in the world, proceeded, when they came to power in April 1978, to impose arbitrary reforms on much of the people, thereby provoking a rural uprising from which only the Soviet military intervention of December 1979 could rescue it.

Finally, in terms of its own core ideological justification, that of the ability of socialism to fulfil the tasks of modernity more effectively than capitalism, these tasks including national independence, industrialisation, education, democratic development, the promotion of social welfare, the claim that Third World *socialist* states were more successful than capitalist ones began to wear thin. For some decades after the Chinese and Cuban revolutions, and with the examples of a range of other 'progressive' countries like Tanzania, Algeria and later Nicaragua to draw on, it could be claimed that, for all that these regimes were authoritarian and, so it was said, arresting democratic development, they were notably more successful at mobilising national resources in a planned and self-reliant way, at meeting basic health and educational needs, and at defending the independence of their countries. Well into the 1980s, Western academic literature drew attention to the achievements and effectiveness of these socialist states (White *et al.* 1983; Fagen *et al.* 1986). However, the rise in East Asia of the Newly Industrialised Countries (NICs) such as Taiwan, South Korea, Hong Kong and Singapore undermined the ideological and political case for Third World socialism and, indeed, had a demoralising impact within the Soviet Union itself.

By the 1980s it was evident to both Third World revolutionaries and Soviet theorists of 'socialist orientation' alike that the inexorable march of socialism through the Third World, let alone its extension to Europe and North America, had been halted and, to some extent, reversed (Hough 1986). At the same time, the United States, caught off guard by the Iranian and Nicaraguan revolutions of 1979, and still wounded by Vietnam, began to formulate a policy of counter-offensive – the 'Reagan Doctrine'. Taking seriously the role of the Third World in the Cold War, and seeking revenge for Vietnam, the United States began to promote anti-communist guerrillas in a range of countries with the aim of weakening, discrediting, overstretching and, where possible, overthrowing Soviet allies in the Third World. Thus in Nicaragua, Angola and above all Afghanistan, the CIA set to work backing opposition guerrilla movements, while in Cambodia, now ruled by a pro-Vietnamese regime, the United States at least permitted Chinese support for the Khmer Rouge resistance. The result was that, by the end of the 1980s, communist and socialist Third World countries were in large measure on the defensive. While still animated by an official goal of socialist transformation, and still in some degree backed by the USSR, they were not in the vanguard of world revolution. The pressures placed on them, both internal and from the United States, further constrained their room for manoeuvre.

The Soviet collapse and the Third World

Against this background, it becomes possible to assess the role of 1989 in the Soviet collapse and, at the same time, the consequences of 1989 for socialist countries and for socialism in general in the Third World. Throughout the 1980s, it appeared as if a major, if not 'the' major arena of competition between the US and Soviet camps was in the Third World: the wars in Nicaragua and El Salvador were considered by the Reagan administration to be necessary defences of the United States' immediate neighbourhood, its 'back yard'. The war in Angola was part of the international fight against Cuban influence, while that in Afghanistan provided the means to weaken the USSR itself and pay back Moscow for Vietnam. On the Soviet side, the decade began with a commitment to sustaining the core communist regimes in the Third World, as well as some newfound authoritarian allies in Africa, notably the 'Afrocommunist' regimes of Ethiopia, Mozambique and Angola (Ottaway and Ottaway 1981), above all with defence of the People's Democratic Party of Afghanistan (PDPA) regime in Afghanistan. Soviet ideologue Mikhail Suslov even went so far as to express the belief that, just as the communist state of Mongolia had acted as a 'beacon' of socialism in Asia after 1917, so would a socialist Afghanistan inspire the Middle East and Muslim world in the 1980s. But by the mid-1980s, and in particular with the accession of Gorbachev to power as Communist Party of the Soviet Union (CPSU) Secretary-General in March 1985, such ideological visions appeared antediluvian: socialism in the Third World was not working and the costs – economic, military and diplomatic – to the USSR, above all of the war in Afghanistan, which Gorbachev in 1987 termed a 'bleeding wound', were too high.

At first, the instinct of the new Soviet leadership was to increase military pressure, backing or launching new offensives in Angola, Ethiopia and Afghanistan. But while in Angola the Popular Movement for the Liberation of Angola – Party of Labour (MPLA) gained some ground, the offensives of Ethiopia and Afghanistan failed. Instead, by 1987, Gorbachev was pursuing a new course, calling for 'New Thinking' in international affairs based on negotiation, compromise and Soviet–US agreements. Part of this involved promoting what he termed 'national reconciliation', the signing of peace agreements and the holding of elections in hitherto war-torn states, but other less overt changes of policy were also involved. One was ideological: just as he had by around 1987 come to abandon the idea that the model of socialism within the USSR itself could be improved or 'accelerated', so Gorbachev, and his close advisers, turned abruptly away from commitments to socialism or 'socialist orientation' in the Third World. Whether this was because of the costs to the USSR such states occasioned, whether it was a result of the evidently greater success of the NICs, whether it was more a general weariness, born of experience inside the Soviet Union, that Gorbachev and others transposed to the Third World, we may never know. Beyond general invocations of the need for peace and negotiation, Gorbachev showed little interest in, or sympathy for, the Third World: he never visited Afghanistan and looked uncomfortable on the few visits he did make to Soviet Third World allies, such as that to Cuba in 1989.

If the declared aims of Gorbachev's 'New Thinking' in regard to the Third World were, in broad terms, two: the end of conflict and 'national reconciliation' on the one hand; and a lessening, when not dissolution, of the aspiration to Third World 'socialism' and 'socialist orientation' on the other, then a retrospective balance sheet, two decades later, reveals a mixed record. The outcomes range from cases where the collapse of the USSR had a major and direct impact, to consequences where the impact was muted, to cases where the collapse of the USSR provoked changes that were, at best, paradoxical, and certainly not what Gorbachev, his advisers or his US interlocutors would have anticipated or desired. The lesson from this is not only that major events have unintended consequences, but also that, within analysis of the overall international scope and impact of a world historical conjuncture, the ability of states and social movements to react in an alternative, counter-cyclical, manner, should never be underestimated.

In broad terms, the impact of 1989 on the Third World can be seen in terms of four processes. The first was the impact of Gorbachev's policy of 'national reconciliation', a policy that related not just to Afghanistan, but to a range of countries where Soviet allies were involved in civil wars or major conflicts, among them: Korea, Cambodia, Palestine, Yemen, Ethiopia, Angola, Mozambique, Namibia, South Africa, Nicaragua and El Salvador. Although at first the United States was sceptical about the new Soviet approach, from 1987 onwards a series of negotiations, some public, others more discreet, were held on 'regional issues'. The outcome was a spate of compromise agreements, some of them directly the result of a change in Soviet policy, some consequences of the collapse of Soviet power, some more broadly influenced by the relaxation of international tensions accompanying the end of the Cold War. These agreements included: the first direct talks between the Democratic People's Republic of Korea (DPRK) and South Korea; a UN-sponsored peace settlement in Cambodia; independence and access to power of South West Africa People's Organisation (SWAPO) guerrillas in Namibia; a negotiated transition to majority rule and an Africa National Congress (ANC) government in South Africa; a peace settlement in Mozambique between the Liberation Front of Mozambique (FRELIMO) and the Mozambican National Resistance (RENAMO) guerrillas; a negotiation process in Angola that lasted until renewed fighting in 1992; a negotiated agreement on Soviet withdrawal from Afghanistan; negotiated and, initially, peaceful reunification of North and South Yemen; an end to the Iran–Iraq war; negotiations at Madrid and Oslo on a Palestinian–Israeli peace settlement; independence for Eritrea; transition to democracy in Chile; peace settlements in Nicaragua, El Salvador and Guatemala.

For sure, the change in Soviet policy was only one part of the explanation for these changes, but significant it was. That some of these agreements, notably Afghanistan and Palestine, later unravelled, while others, such as Angola, failed until many years later to be concluded, did not detract from the impact of the new atmosphere in international relations. Here too, for sure, autonomy and counter-cyclical trends were evident: some conflicts, notably Cyprus, Ireland, Western Sahara and Colombia, remained resolutely set apart from any new trend towards international détente, while other conflicts, in particularly the Iraqi invasion of Kuwait in August 1990 erupted. And as became clear in the 1990s, the very fragmentation of some formerly communist states into new independent or aspiring states in the former Soviet Union, former Yugoslavia and the Horn of Africa, introduced a new set of regional and local conflicts that more than offset the peace dividend of the late 1980s.

The second broad consequence of the changes in Moscow was the withdrawal of Soviet military, political and economic support from Third World allies. Of the six core pro-Soviet 'communist' states in 1982, one, Mongolia, abandoned the communist political system altogether and became a multi-party state. A second, Afghanistan, was overthrown by force: the PDPA regime in Kabul, starved of funds and military support, fell to the Islamist guerrillas in April 1992. Three others – Vietnam, Laos, Cambodia – retained political control of the communist party, the latter two affecting multi-party elections and opening their countries to foreign investment and market forces on a rough imitation of the Chinese model. For its part, Cuba opened to what foreign capital it could obtain against the US embargo, but maintained tight social controls and one-party rule and, after surviving the privations of the 'Special Period' of the 1990s, began in the early 2000s to grow again. Speculation that the Cuban regime would fall in the late 1980s or early 1990s like those of Eastern Europe proved unfounded, but the Cuban state evidently took these predictions seriously, and, in particular, sought to offset any attempt by the United States, now covertly assisted by Moscow, to use the Cuban armed forces to stage a Romanian-style coup from within. Hence, as a precaution, the show-trials of prominent and popular Cuban army officers in 1987.

Of the two independent Third World communist states, one, China, turned to the market economy, while retaining communist political control, with far-reaching global consequences, while North Korea, more than any other state in the world, maintained a rigid communist command and control system, with only minor investment from outside, most notably South Korea. Of the more advanced states of socialist orientation, two, the People's Democratic Republic of Yemen (PDRY) and Ethiopia, were in effect destroyed by force: the extant military and political structures of the PDRY, preserved within the original confederal inter-Yemeni unity of May 1990, were crushed in the civil war of May–July 1994; the military regime of Haile-Mariam Mengistu, ushered in by the revolution of 1974, fell to a combined assault of Tigrean and Eritrean rebels in 1991. Two more advanced 'states of socialist orientation', Mozambique and Nicaragua, were forced by continued military harassment into compromises with their right-wing opponents that all but destroyed the political and social legacy of the revolutionary period. As for Angola, a brief period of peace to 1992 was followed by ten years of war until the death of anti-communist guerrilla leader Jonas Savimbi in 2002; the first multi-party elections were only held in 2008. The fate of the remaining 'states of socialist orientation' varied widely: some, such as Somalia and Guinea-Bissau, collapsed into lawlessness, or, in the case of Iraq, were destroyed by invasion; in others, such as Tanzania, Ghana, Madagascar, Burkina Faso and Benin the socialist legacy evaporated; in others, such as Syria, Libya, Algeria and Burma, what were once pro-Soviet military dictatorships continued in place, sometimes as in Algeria and Burma with a pretence at elections but shorn of any 'progressive' embellishments. Whatever their particular trajectories, these surviving authoritarian states, run by coercive oligarchies, were no foretaste of socialism, being rather 'states of socialist disorientation' whose rulers retained one priority more clear than ever before – control over the state and of the economy associated with it.

These two more or less direct sets of consequences of 1989, in regard to negotiated outcomes of war, and changes within communist and socialist states, were, however, accompanied by two consequences that were less expected. One was the impact of 1989 on the right in the Third World. Part of this can be seen in a crisis of state power and legitimacy akin in some ways to that experienced by communist states. Losing their ideological justification for a continued monopoly of power, authoritarian regimes in a range of countries agreed to free elections and a return to democracy, in Chile after two decades, in South Africa after four. In other cases, such as Namibia, El Salvador and Guatemala, right-wing autocrats were pressed by Washington to negotiate with their opponents, often socialist and communist groupings themselves open to compromise in the new international climate.

Yet while this more accommodating response from the right could be noted across a regime of state responses, this was far from the case when it came to opposition groups formed in the Cold War and who, as much as other actors, had now lost their main enemy and, with it, their strategic orientation. It is as if, freed of the political and ideological constraints of the Cold War, and with no radical rival on the left, right-wing radicalism, similar in some degree to European fascism of the period after the First World War, and, like fascism, appropriating much of the vocabulary and organisational practice of the communist movement, the militant right could now enjoy a new freedom of action and of rhetoric, whether this be Islamist in the Middle East or Hindu chauvinist in India. The most striking examples of such groups were, of course, those of Islamic fundamentalism, some defined by political activity such as the Muslim Brotherhood, some armed guerrillas, such as al-Qaeda. Hitherto the main enemy had been defined as socialism as embodied in a number of Arab states, and, beyond this, atheistic communism and the USSR. A stock in trade of Islamist rhetoric, from state and non-state groups alike, was to blame the Russian revolution and communism on 'the Jews'. Not insignificantly as far as militant Islamism was concerned, 1989 was also the year in which a second Islamic Republic, after that of Iran a decade earlier, was formed, this time by a military coup initially allied to the Muslim Brotherhood, in Sudan, the most populous country in Africa. It was Sudan that, for five years from 1991 to 1996, provided a home and base to Osama bin Laden. A decade of sustained but, in the end, fruitless attempts to export Islamic revolution to Saudi Arabia, Egypt, Tunisia, Algeria and other states followed in a distorted reproduction by a right-wing, and consciously anti-communist, regime of the policies that left-wing revolutionary states had pursued in the decades before.

The fourth component of the Third World response to 1989 was that of the socialist, communist and, more generally, 'anti-imperialist' left in these countries. To some degree, the formerly communist and socialist left in the Third World followed the pattern of communist parties in Europe, and, accommodating to the new ideological and political realities, moved towards more reformist policies: this was particularly true in Latin America, but it also applied to parts of Africa and South Asia. Indeed, in the case of some Latin American countries, there emerged a powerful new reformist socialism which led, a decade later, to the presidencies of Lula in Brazil, the first head of state in the world to be an industrial worker, Michele Bachelet in Chile, and Leonel Fernández in the Dominican Republic. At the same time, other, less conformist and conjuncturally determined, trends could be observed. In some countries, radical populist regimes, articulating a virtually unchanged vision of social reform and anti-imperialism, were the order of the day: Hugo

Chávez, elected President of Venezuela in 1998, Evo Morales elected in Bolivia and Rafael Correa in Ecuador in 2006 were the standard-bearers of this radicalism, which found some common cause, both political and economic, with already existing revolutionary regimes in Cuba and Iran, and with the rump of the Sandinistas, led by Daniel Ortega, who were returned to power in Nicaragua in 2008. The Kirchners, espousing a newly militant, if eternally inchoate, post-Peronist discourse, straddled the gap, or at least sought to do so, in Argentina.

More militant, and apparently unruffled by world history, were guerrilla groups in some other countries that continued their armed struggle if, in keeping with globalisation, also combining this with trade in drugs and other illegal or illegally acquired commodities: in Nepal, the Maoists signed an agreement that led to their leader, known simply as Prachanda, becoming president in 2008; in Eritrea, the Eritrean People's Liberation Front (EPLF) came to power following the defeat of the Ethiopian military and the triumph of the Tigrayan People's Liberation Front (TPLF) in 1991–3; in Colombia, the Revolutionary Armed Forces of Colombia (FARC) and the National Liberation Army (ELN) controlled large swathes of the country and a not insignificant part of the drugs trade. In East Timor, the Revolutionary Front for an Independent East Timor (FRETILIN), which had fought so heroically against the Indonesian occupation for two decades, took power in 1999 after a change of policy, itself facilitated by the end of the Cold War, in Indonesia, only to collapse some years later into factionalism. In Peru, on the other hand, the Maoist guerrillas of Sendero Luminoso, who in the late 1980s had controlled much of the countryside, were over time defeated, their leaders imprisoned and humiliated, and their utopian and violent project almost completely crushed.

This varied picture of communist, socialist and radical politics in the years after 1989 would not be complete, however, without introducing a further important development, that of a new internationalist movement that, from the late 1990s, emerged in the Third World, Europe and the United States. This movement, variously termed 'anti-globalisation' or 'global justice movement' had its origins in the annual World Social Forum (WSF) meetings at Porto Alegre in Brazil, a deliberate counter to the meetings of the World Economic Forum in Davos, Switzerland. If the early 1990s had seen the left, internationally and ideologically on the defensive, the organisation of mass demonstrations against the meeting of the World Trade Organization in Seattle in 1999 and the annual WSF meetings provided a new impetus to this process, one articulated by journals such as *Le Monde Diplomatique*, in the spread of interest in 'civil society' and NGO groups, and in the articulation of a broad critique of US foreign policy by writers such as Noam Chomsky and of Western capitalism more generally by ecologists, socialists, feminists and others.

In some ways the WSF and its affiliates was a beneficiary of the collapse of Soviet communism since, even though states such as Cuba and Venezuela sought to influence it. The WSF appeared to be opposed to all that was authoritarian and violent in the revolutionary past. But at the same time, the very activist origins of the WSF, and the sense of virtuous ideological distance from the experiences of earlier decades of struggle, acted as a sort of mask, a denial of the degree to which ideas, and often practices, inherited from the communist past remained present. Alongside this was a failure, at once both political and moral, to address the negative lessons which that past, conveniently separated by the quietist decade of the 1990s, embodied. The survival and rebirth of a global left in the Third World and developed countries alike contained, and was perhaps made possible by, a pervasive failure of intellectual and moral engagement with the socialist past, an amnesiac radicalism in the manner of Rip Van Winkle which burst into the open in the late 1990s, appropriating the idealism and utopianism of the left for a set of recycled, and historically discredited, policies and practices (Halliday 2003). Of the many contradictions contained in this movement, none was perhaps more evident than the embrace by the WSF, one of whose core values was feminism, of leaders such as Chávez, themselves allies of the virulently misogynist and feminicidic regime in Tehran. In all of this, of course, the supposedly 'new' global protest movement acquired in 2001 an important, if unwitting, ally, in the form of George W. Bush, whose crass response to 9/11 and subsequent invasion of Iraq provided exactly the kind of illusory justification for its programme that the new world left required.

Nuclear weapons and Third World conflict

Having established a record of what happened to socialist regimes and movements in the Third World after 1989, it is possible to return to broader analytic questions, not least an examination of the role of the Third World in the collapse of the USSR and of Soviet communism more generally. That from the early 1980s Third World socialism was on the defensive, and was far from representing the vanguard of global revolution that had been imagined in earlier decades, was evident. As Arne Westad (2005) has so powerfully shown in his commanding study of the issue, the Cold War was a global struggle, with both sides compelled, by ideological and political reasons as much as, or more than, by military and economic factors, to intervene around the world throughout these four decades. Yet recognising the global *extent* of the Cold War, its universal remit as it were, is not equivalent to saying that it was *in the Third World* that the global conflict was decided any more than recording military conflict in the Middle East or the Pacific during the First and Second World Wars is equivalent to saying that it was these theatres that decided the outcome. Germany was defeated by the USSR in Eastern Europe; Japan by two nuclear bombs, its armies in China and Indo-China still intact.

Whatever else, the overall record of conflict in the Third World during the forty years of Cold War does not support the thesis, latent in all Marxist and post-Marxist theories of imperialism, as much as in Western alarm about communism gaining ground in the Third World, that somehow events in these countries fundamentally affected the power of Western states. In this sense at least, Kennan and Stalin got it right; Lenin, Trotsky, Mao and Guevara got it wrong. What is more plausible, if sometimes overstated, is the opposite case, namely that it was Third World and the commitments it entailed which held back, and to some degree undermined, communism. Perhaps the overall 'burden' that Third World allies, Afghanistan excepted, placed on the USSR was exaggerated. Since no expert, Soviet or Western, has been able to put real prices on Soviet figures and to cost in any persuasive manner Soviet aid and trade with these allies, we will never be sure (for one attempt to evaluate this trade and aid, see Cassen 1985). In broad terms, the conventional estimate of the mid-1980s appears plausible – that Soviet bloc aid accounted for approximately 8–10 per cent of all state aid to the Third World.

Much has been made of the impact on the USSR of the war in Afghanistan, in which Soviet forces were involved from 1979 to 1989, and from which the USSR was forced, after a UN-brokered agreement with the United States and Pakistan in April 1988, to withdraw. In strictly military terms, this war, albeit next to the Soviet frontier, was not a major defeat for the USSR: its troops levels at most were 120,000, a fifth of the US level in Vietnam; its casualties likewise, at around 15,500 killed, were a quarter of those of the United States. At no point did the war in Afghanistan have any visible impact on adjacent Soviet Central Asian states. Moreover, the pro-Soviet regime of the PDPA, which the 1979 intervention was designed to protect, survived both the Soviet pullout in August 1989 and the subsequent mujahidin offensives. What it did *not* survive was the removal of Soviet military and economic aid following the failed August 1991 coup in Moscow, partly as a result of pressure by the United States on the new Yeltsin government to abandon the Kabul regime. It was August 1991 that sealed the fate of the PDPA: financial strangulation after August 1991 led to military and ethnic mutiny in early 1992, and, in April 1992, to the collapse of the Afghan state and army.

Where Afghanistan, and other commitments, did extract a toll, which the West was eager to exploit, was in the diplomatic and strategic field. What was most evident to Soviet leaders was the cost in diplomatic and bilateral relations of Third World commitments, in particular the way in which apparent advances or risk-taking by Moscow in the Third World impacted on the nuclear arms race and on nuclear arms negotiations. Here, in the link between Third World conflict and nuclear weapons, lies one of the guiding threads both of the Cold War and of the conjuncture of the late 1980s: for, while the purely monetary or budgetary impact of sustaining the arms race on the USSR may have been exaggerated as a factor explaining Soviet collapse (again, we have nothing but informed broad brush qualitative intuitions to guide us), we do know, from US–Soviet negotiations and from US and Soviet policy at the time, that both Moscow and Washington perceived there to be an immediate link between the Third World and policy in the nuclear domain.

Most particularly, one of the main reasons that impelled Gorbachev to announce, and carry out, the Soviet withdrawal from Afghanistan in 1987–8 was his belief that failure to do so would prejudice an agreement on Intermediate-Range Nuclear Forces (INFs) – US installed cruise and Pershing missiles, Soviet SS-20s – in Europe. It was the threat from the US INFs, not Afghanistan, which preoccupied the Soviet leadership at the time. Equally, it was evident in 1986–7 that the increased Soviet military activity in Angola was impacting negatively on US policy. Here, more than in the unity of the world economy or an integrated global political and social totality, lies one of the central conjunctural themes of the whole Cold War. From the Korean War of 1950–3 and the 'Cuban missile' crisis of October 1962 onwards, both sides perceived their Third World policies, and their standing, as affecting directly their policies on nuclear weapons. Failure in the former was followed by increased expenditure and development of weaponry in the other. Conversely, when the Cold War began to wind down in the latter half of the 1980s, one of the preconditions for a reduction in the nuclear arms race was a lessening of Third World conflicts and, in particular, of Soviet military and political backing to its allies.

Thus in looking for international links, 'conjunctural' and consequential, it is as much here, in the perceived policy intersection of the Third World with nuclear weapons, that the unity of the Cold War and its denouement may be seen (for one examination of the political logic of 'extended deterrence' see Mike Davis 1982). Such a link had long been evident to both US and Soviet thinkers, to the former as 'extended deterrence', the pursuit of nuclear superiority and flexibility so as to better control the Third World and protect allies, to the latter as part of the 'correlation of forces' supposedly moving in Moscow's direction. Much was made during the Cold War, especially by critics of the nuclear arms race, of the 'irrational', even bureaucratically determined 'exterminist', character of the nuclear arms race, as it appeared to serve no political or strategic purpose and seemed to lie beyond human and political calculation. Those who argued in favour of nuclear weapons tended to focus on the military, competitive dimensions and on the need for continued technological and engineering change. However, a survey of the two dozen or so cases when the United States, and the one when the USSR, put their nuclear forces on alert, and issued general warnings, shows that nearly all were related to crisis in the Third World (Halliday 1984). This connection was, moreover, explicit in the reaction of each side to major strategic setbacks in the Third World: the Russians to the Cuba crisis of 1962 when they were forced to withdraw their missiles; the Americans to the spate of pro-Soviet and radical revolutions in the Third World from 1974 to 1980. This linkage between strategic nuclear capability and political conflict in the Third World was, therefore, arguably a more potent factor in explaining the progress and end of the Cold War than the supposed threat by revolutions in Vietnam or Cuba to the stability of the advanced capitalist countries, or of the arming by Reagan of anti-communist rebels in Nicaragua and Afghanistan.

The failings of capitalism

A focus on the USSR and on the fate of socialist states in the Third World does not, however, exhaust the set of questions posed by 1989 and its consequences. For, if socialism and the communist system 'failed', in the European world collapsed, and delivered the variable consequences in the Third World outlined above, there is also a need to look at the fate of its capitalist rival. One can indeed argue that, in many respects, capitalism outside Europe and North America also 'failed' in the aftermath of 1989: first, while market relations spread to former communist states, especially in East Asia, this was not in many countries and, especially outside Latin America, accompanied by the spread of liberal and democratic values supposedly linked in Western history and theory to the market; second, because in many former communist countries and in a swathe of former socialist and pro-Western states alike, the end of the Cold War, and accompanying changes associated with globalisation, led to the degeneration of state and society, the spread of crime, corruption, illegality of many kinds, some of this within established but enduring states such as Russia or Serbia, at others in conflict zones and newly created independent states of the post-communist world (Kirby 2006; Glenny 2008). Within the European Union itself, Bulgaria and Romania became by-words for corruption. Russia and its junior allies were riven with illegal and arbitrary conduct which contained enormous, if ill-defined, international ramifications.

In the twilight zones of the former communist world – Bosnia, Kosovo, Transnistria, Nagorno-Karabakh, South Ossetia, Abkhazia and others – crime of many sorts flourished, not on the margins of, or separate from, Russia and other established states but as integrated parts of the post-communist mafia-run system. In two formerly communist Muslim countries, Afghanistan and South Yemen, grotesque forms of social regression, violence against women and corruption prevailed, as they did in combat-plagued Iraq, and, even more so, in Somalia. Meanwhile in West Africa, the formerly vanguard socialist state of Guinea-Bissau, the country that produced the outstanding revolutionary leader Amilcar Cabral, fell from 1980 increasingly under the control of corrupt military leaders, with the result that in 2008 it had become the main transit state for Colombian drugs en route to Europe (Ferrett and Vulliamy 2008). In Southern Africa itself, the corruption and dictatorship of Mugabe left little to the imagination, as did that of Mozambique, while the ANC, long adrift of the moral authority conveyed on it by its former leader Nelson Mandela, and creaking under the weight of political and personal factionalism, became increasingly a vehicle for personal advancement, clique-building and corruption. In Nicaragua, meanwhile, the Sandinistas, the great hope for a non-authoritarian and morally superior revolutionary socialism of the 1980s, fell into disunion, losing leading figures such as Ernesto Cardenal and Sergio Ramirez after they denounced the *piñata* (from *piña*, a pineapple, hence a bag of sweets or presents hung up at a fairground and beaten till the contents fall out) – the robbery of state property, houses and wealth at the end of the Sandinista National Liberation Front (FSLN) rule in 1990 under the supreme practitioner of these arts, Daniel Ortega. In other words, one of the main legacies of the collapse of communism was the disappearance not only of social provision and a rough commitment to social equality, but of the basic order-providing state. Any balance sheet of the 'failure' of communism must, therefore, be matched by acknowledgement of the 'failure' of its replacement.

This issue, of the change in the character of states and the collapse of state control and authority, lies at the heart of the most fundamental question of all, namely what the whole communist and socialist experiment was about, and what 1989 can tell us about this history. In essence, the revolutionary socialism of the twentieth century espoused a political and ideological goal, that of overtaking and replacing capitalism, which it could never have achieved. The image of a communist world superseding, outflanking or undermining the advanced capitalist West was, from the beginning, a chimera. Yet it was sustained, with great commitment and sacrifice, by the enormous desire of people around the world to rid themselves of an oppressive and iniquitous system. This global movement was sustained by the fortunes of war, above all in the Second World War and subsequent Third World revolutions, and by the failure of the West to incorporate much of the non-Western world into the political and economic prosperity that it enjoyed. As for the developed capitalist world itself, and herein lay the deepest of several major flaws in the theories of Karl Marx, it was not incubating another social order, or laying the bases for a transition to socialism and communism, but continuously innovating, destroying and rebuilding itself, and, in its central zones, with a skill at innovation and capacity for growth that socialism could never match. This was the conclusion to which Jürgen Habermas was drawn with his observation, a revision of a slogan of Khrushchev's, that the revolutions of 1989 in Europe could be seen as 'revolutions of recuperation' (Habermas 1991).[2]

The communist experiment, therefore, in the 'developed socialist' USSR and Eastern Europe, in China and in the various categories of Third World state was, in this sense, a product of the contradictions within capitalist modernity, but not a strategic or historically progressive alternative to it. Rather it was an attempt at revolt within states that were not among the most developed and in which military power without, and coercion within, substituted for the economic and political resources that capitalism could, on most occasions, deploy. In other words, it was a chapter, lasting in the end no more than one human lifetime, of revolt and exceptionalism, in particular of authoritarian statehood and economic development. It achieved a remarkable amount but was, in the end, doomed to failure. In most cases, be they Russia, China, Vietnam or what one may subsequently call 'states of socialist *disorientation*' across Asia and Africa, and, in the case of Nicaragua, Central

---

[2] The term Habermas used, *nachholende Revolutionen*, literally 'catching up with revolutions', in this case with capitalism, was an implicit play on the famous boast by Soviet leader Nikita Khrushchev in the late 1950s that socialism would 'catch up with and overtake' (in Russian *dognat i peregnat*) capitalism.

America, it was the formerly communist elites, or sections of them, who realised this most clearly and, in effect, jumped socio-economic ship. In all of this, the socialist Third World states and the socialist movement in the Third World played a less central role than many, friend and foe, had attributed to it. Economic and social separation, variously termed 'de-linking', 'self-reliance' and 'autarky', were unsustainable goals: these states remained as much part of the global structures of power as did the USSR and its clients in Eastern Europe.

Here, of course, lies the final lesson of 1989: that, in the end, the USSR, and more broadly the post-1917 revolutionary experiment, were neither reinforced nor defeated in Asia, Africa or Latin America, not in Dien Bien Phu, Soweto or the Bay of Pigs, nor by the land reforms, mass literacy campaigns, emancipation of women and effective government of Third World socialist states. The course of the Cold War, and the ebb and flow of strategic conflict, was indeed greatly affected by events in the Third World: but the overall outcome was not. The global contest was decided by the outcome of competition with socialism's main rival, developed capitalism, both in the United States and, of great demonstrative and paradigmatic importance for the Soviet bloc, in Western Europe. What Isaac Deutscher had, in his famous lectures of the early 1980s entitled 'The Great Contest', was in the end decided, as Deutscher's argument at the time implied, by competition between the more advanced components of each bloc. Here Kennan and those others who insisted throughout the Cold War that Europe, and the West in general, remained the 'central' front, in political and socio-economic as much as in military terms, were right. Moreover, as a student of capitalist development and of its expansive and innovative capabilities, Marx, for all his misguided philosophy of history, would have understood this too. Turning back on itself Gramsci's famous observation, that 1917 was 'a revolt against *Das Kapital*', we may, therefore, conclude with Jürgen Habermas that 1989 was a revolt in its favour. Where Habermas' analysis was flawed, or at least of limited application outside Central and Eastern Europe, was that the former socialist states did *not* catch up, and, if they were doing so, as in the case of China, this was certainly not by embracing Western European economic and political practices. This, the enduring brutal inequality and constantly changing global interaction of capitalism, and the continued crises, internal and external, of its component states, was, of course, the underlying cause of the whole history of revolution in the twentieth century. It will, no doubt, albeit in different form, be the cause of much conflict, upheaval and recomposition in the twenty-first century to come.

6   Towards a global Europe?

Laure Delcour

1989 and the European integration process

While 1989 is widely acknowledged as a watershed in international relations, it is also regarded as the most major upheaval in the course of European integration since its onset in the 1950s. A glimpse at the chronology of the European integration process makes it obvious that 1989 paved the way for the building of a political union as well as for enlargement to new members. Only three years after the collapse of the communist system, the European Community transformed into a European Union with new and extended competences, including a Common Foreign and Security Policy. In the early 1990s, the European Commission designed a method to enlarge the Union further, opening a wide-ranging process which culminated in the accession of ten new member states in 2004 and two additional members in 2007. The consequences of 1989 for the European integration process were, therefore, far-reaching.

At the same time, 1989 did not happen in a vacuum for the European Community (EC). In the span of thirty years, it had successfully established peaceful relations among its member states. And it had equally successfully sustained cooperation projects which had boosted growth in Western Europe. Even though the European Community had no relations with the Eastern bloc,[1] by the mid-1980s it had gained a sense of attractiveness by way of its integration projects which, arguably, influenced the events which took place in Central and Eastern Europe during the final acts of the Cold War.

Interactions between the events of 1989 and European integration, therefore, highlight clashing temporalities but interwoven logics: in

---

[1] Understood here as the economic counterpart of the EC, i.e. the Council for Mutual Economic Assistance (COMECON). The EC had limited relations with some communist countries, especially Romania, that were included in the Generalised System of Preferences in 1974 and that signed an agreement with the Community on industrial products in 1980.

1989, the European Community had to cope with political upheavals in the eastern part of the continent at the time that it was giving a new impetus to its own integration process. Such a temporal dialectic shaped the subsequent architecture of the continent. However, in the wake of 1989, a linear and univocal interpretation of the events' signification for Europe prevailed among western European policy-makers. This interpretation almost exclusively focuses on the European Community's attractiveness for former communist countries (the 'return to Europe' argument) and on the transformations it has induced in the eastern part of the continent. It implicitly considers European integration as the third component of the 'transition' package, together with democratisation and the development of a market economy. Joining the EU is presented as a necessary path to follow, the direction of which is unquestionable and ineluctable. In other words, the relationship between 1989 and the EU has commonly been considered as a one-way process, with communism being finally 'dissolved' into EU integration. Such an interpretation downplays – or even overlooks – important elements of interaction, in particular the implications of 1989 on the EU itself.

These features are also widely reflected in academic discourses. Indeed, changes in the former eastern bloc and the EU after 1989 have mainly been analysed as parallel dynamics. On the one hand, the processes through which the EU has changed Central and Eastern European countries in the 1990s have been extensively studied. Literature on the enlargement process has mobilised scholars from a number of countries and disciplines, including economics, sociology, political science and International Relations. More recently, the way that the EU has exerted influence over former Soviet countries through its neighbourhood policy has triggered the interest of scholars. Even though most of them point to the limited influence of the EU on the Western New Independent States when compared to Central European candidate countries (Cremona and Hillion 2006; Kelley 2006), the foundations of the argument remain the same, based as they are on the central assumption of the EU's transformative power and, specifically, how this impacts on former communist countries. Quite apart from this literature has been the emergence of an alternative focus on the European integration process. A number of publications have been dedicated to the changing nature of the European Union, either in terms of the evolution of its decision-making system (Wallace *et al.* 2005), its new policies, or its 'actorhood' in international relations (Knodt and Princen 2003; Smith 2003, 2005; Hill and Smith 2005). Over the past few years, European studies has become a core curriculum in top universities either in the EU or elsewhere, e.g. in the

United States or in Russia (Belot and Georgakakis 2004). Thus, scholars have grasped both the multiple evolutions of the EU after 1990 *and* its increasing importance as a political, economic and international entity. At the same time, no systematic effort has been made to detect possible connections between changes in European integration processes and the events of 1989.

My argument in this chapter is that much research on the former eastern bloc and the European integration process leaves crucial questions open and important crossroads unexplored. Specifically, we need to interrogate several questions surrounding the significance of 1989 for European construction:

(1) To what extent and how did the EU contribute to 1989?
(2) What is the global impact of 1989 for the EU integration process?
(3) To what extent does this impact shed light on the history of European construction before 1989?
(4) To what extent is the impact of 1989 incorporated in the current integration process?

By concentrating on EU-initiated changes *on* Central and Eastern Europe, analysts have de facto minimised, or omitted, the implications of 1989 *on* the development of the EU. These implications, expected to be easily managed and positive, especially in terms of continental reunification, have turned out to be durable, deep and, most importantly, ambivalent.

This chapter, therefore, questions the unambiguous character of prevailing interpretations about the relationship between 1989 and European integration. The principal aim of this contribution is to shed light on the complex, multifaceted relationship between the collapse of communist rule and EU enlargement, processes which call for re-assessment of how 1989 impacted on Europe and the ways in which the European Union has influenced 1989 and 'managed' the subsequent period. The first section analyses the assumptions underlying the European Community's responses to the collapse of communism. I then challenge four key assumptions relating to the impact of 1989 on European development: first, that the collapse of the communist regime has enabled the unification of the continent under the auspices of the European Community/Union; second, that 1989 ushered in a revival of the European integration project, mainly through an extension of the EC/EU's competences to the political sphere; third, that the 'return to Europe' of Central and Eastern European countries which materialised with the EU's enlargement process has made possible the definition of sustainable borders for the European Union; and finally, that 1989 has consecrated the EU's 'civilian power' and turned the EU into a fully fledged international actor.

The return to Europe?

The first commonly accepted argument concerning the relationship between 1989 and Europe relates to the assessment of 1989's consequences on the continent's architecture. It claims that the collapse of communism has enabled the reunification of Europe[2] through the return of former communist countries to their natural geopolitical location and to the sphere of influence they historically belong to. The 'return to Europe' argument is grounded on two underlying assumptions which have shaped the immediate interpretations of 1989 and the subsequent reordering of the continent: the 'parenthesis assumption' and the 'winner-takes-it-all' assumption.

The parenthesis assumption

The parenthesis assumption begins with a simple fact – the overthrow of communist regimes put an end to the division of Europe which arose after the Second World War. Nevertheless, while the end of the Yalta system was widely celebrated, there were few attempts to grasp the meaning and possible consequences of such a lengthy separation of the continent's basic architecture. Since the division of Europe was deemed to be artificial (the product of a specific historical context), its reunification seemed natural. From this perspective, 1989 triggered feelings of enthusiasm which overshadowed debates about how to interpret communism and how post-communist states could be institutionalised as part of the transformation process. Scenes like Rostropovich's concert near the Berlin Wall in November 1989 were used to create symbols of the reunified Europe and to forge a sense of 'new common present', while alternative histories, particularly those associated with divisions, were occluded. In Central and Eastern Europe, initial steps in nation- and state-building coincided with a reappraisal of history. However, this process often induced a rejection of the communist past and of the corresponding period of Soviet domination without any comprehensive attempt to grasp their meaning, at least in the years immediately after 1989. In Western Europe, if one excepts the analysis of economic

[2] The use of the word 'reunification' instead of 'unification' is in line with the 'parenthesis assumption', i.e. it implies that the two parts of Europe have not significantly changed for four decades.

discrepancies and political steps required for transformation, 1989 did not trigger sustained reflection by policy-makers on deeply rooted, structural differences between the two parts of the continent.

Accordingly, the four-decade break-up of Europe into two antagonistic blocks was seen as a parenthesis to be closed. Communist party rule, Soviet domination, centralised economies and welfare regimes were expected to be easily overcome and quickly forgotten. The vanishing communist legacy was considered to be straightforward for Central Europe in 1989, but especially so after the collapse of the Soviet Union in 1991. Interestingly, the 'parenthesis assumption' was made explicit in eastern policy-makers' discourse. For instance, as early as 1992, Russian leaders (in particular President Yeltsin and Minister of Foreign Affairs Kozyrev) called for the return of Russia to the 'community of civilized states'. It seemed as if seven decades of communist rule were to be considered as an abnormal period in Russian history (just like the Tatar invasions of the thirteenth century) and that this interregnum was to be followed by a rapprochement with Europe as part of the normal course of Russian history.

The winner-takes-it-all assumption

The second assumption – 'winner takes it all' – saw the reunification of the continent as the result of a zero-sum game, i.e. as a consecration of Western values and the defeat of state socialism. This interpretation was moulded around German reunification, which was carried out via the absorption of the German Democratic Republic by the German Federal Republic rather than through the merger of the two countries. The dissolution of communism into western market democracy then forged the accession strategy designed by the European Union for Central and Eastern Europe countries, which consisted of a series of criteria required for fulfilment in order to adopt western standards and join the elite club. The 'winner-takes-it-all' assumption was expressed simply by Chancellor Kohl, 'Our ideas are spreading across the whole European continent' (quoted in Delors 1992), and by Jacques Delors (1992: 134), then President of the European Commission, 'It is not the East that drifted towards the West, but the West that attracted the East ... The Community's structures and framework pave the way for organizing tomorrow's Europe.'

Among EC policy-makers, the transformation of Central and Eastern European countries was seen as a process of 'catching-up'. Against this background, the principal task of western European elites was to guide former communist states along the path of market democracy and to provide them with a suitable institutional framework for their return to Europe. With the main objective of reuniting the continent based upon western values not in doubt, debate centred on *how* to accomplish this process. As highlighted by Jacques Delors and others, the European Economic Community (EEC) quickly emerged as the natural institutional receptacle for the return to Europe. Yet such a role was far from obvious for an organisation which had, to date, focused almost exclusively on economic issues, hence its deserved reputation as an economic giant and a political dwarf.

Two factors help to explain why the EEC took on such an important role in reshaping post-Cold War Europe. First, other institutions or alternative modes of organisation were not considered to be suitable. At a time when the Soviet threat seemed to be eliminated, political and economic issues rather than military or security challenges were considered paramount. Therefore, NATO was not a viable option for bringing the two parts of Europe together. The Organization for Security and Co-operation in Europe (OSCE), as a pan-European organisation covering a wide range of issues, could have played such a role, but it lacked effective decision-making mechanisms and power beyond consultative competences. Potential alternatives suggesting new modes of socialisation between East and West, such as Mikhail Gorbachev's 'Common European Home', remained empty shells. By 1989, the prevailing feeling was one of historical unity to be translated into a project which the Soviet Union could no longer inspire.

The EEC thus emerged as a default option, but it was also considered as the best possible vector for the continent's 'reunification' process for reasons related to its own history. By contrast to the USSR, the EC was pictured as a flourishing example of integration. Even though it did not play a major role in the overthrow of communist regimes, the EC thus appeared to Central European countries as an 'antidote' to Soviet integration (la Serre *et al.* 1994: 111). Both its successful record and, paradoxically, its failures were considered as assets. Created in 1957, the EEC had built upon the record of the European Community of Coal and Steel by reconciling former enemies such as France and Germany and promoting sustainable peace in the western part of the continent. The Customs Union and the first Community policies attracted new members, including the initially reluctant United Kingdom, which applied for membership as early as the 1960s. At the same time, the integration process remained limited to the economic sphere, with a few attempts at intergovernmental cooperation in political areas (e.g. the European Political Cooperation for foreign policy in the early 1970s). Paradoxically, these limits turned out to be positive in the context of

1989. The EC's lack of a military dimension – due to the initial failure of the European Defence Community in 1954 – made it appear as a 'neutral' institution in comparison to military alliances like NATO. The idea of a 'special historical responsibility' of the Community vis-à-vis other parts of the continent emerged on this basis.

United or divided Europe?

Following the 'return to Europe' assumption, in the wake of 1989 the continent was to be united under the auspices of the European Community. Thus, 1989 was supposed to cement Europe while at the same time allowing the continent to move away from the reliance on US power that had protected it during the Cold War. From this point of view, the fifth and sixth EU enlargements (1 May 2004 and 1 January 2007) are considered to be major milestones symbolising the end of Europe's reunification process. Nevertheless, the interpretation of 1989 as a gateway to a united Europe has been challenged by both events and perceptions during the enlargement process and following the accession of Central and Eastern European countries. Many of the ongoing debates within the European Union reflect divergences between 'old' and 'new' member states and thus seem to reproduce an East/West rift.

An asymmetrical Europe

This rift finds its roots in the EU enlargement process itself, which, in line with the 'parenthesis' and 'winner-takes-it-all' assumptions turned out to be highly asymmetrical. As an institution praised for its record in developing stable economic and political environments, the EC was first entrusted with the responsibility of managing western aid to Poland and Hungary even before the communist regimes collapsed in July 1989. The overthrow of communist rule in Eastern Europe further required the prompt design of a far-reaching EC political strategy.

Three interconnected elements are salient in terms of the vision of enlargement developed by the EC for Eastern Europe. First, even though the idea of enlargement was discussed in the early 1990s, the EC developed a gradualist strategy divided into several stages and milestones. It began with association agreements (also significantly called 'Europe agreements') signed with Central European countries and the three Baltic states in the early 1990s. The next step was the recognition of a 'European vocation' for these countries at the Essen Council in 1993 and the definition of the Copenhagen accession criteria the same year.

Accession negotiations started in 1998 with a first wave of applicants joining in 2004 and a second wave in 2007. The second salient aspect is the use of conditionality as the core element in the methodology of the enlargement process. Accession to the EU was made conditional on the fulfilment of the Copenhagen criteria, which were specifically designed for Central and Eastern Europe applicants.[3] Progress from one step to the next was subject to the fulfilment by applicants of a number of conditions. The third element was the control kept by the European Union, more specifically the European Commission, over the process. Through designing benchmarks and monitoring the progress of applicants,[4] the Commission played the role of a gatekeeper in charge of granting each country access to the next stage.

The many-steps approach was thus meant to enhance EU control over access to each stage. The accession strategy triggered widespread disenchantment in Central and Eastern European countries as early as the mid-1990s. It was criticised by applicants for being overly onerous and one-sided. When compared to previous enlargements, the developments of the European integration process at the end of the 1980s and early 1990s had seen a major increase in the volume of *acquis* to be met. Moreover, conditions set by the EU under previous enlargements were made harder for Central and Eastern European applicants who had to adopt the full *acquis* before acceding. Finally, the EU consistently added new conditions during the accession process, for instance in the framework of the Accession Partnership. While the EC had thus far mainly relied upon imitation mechanisms with adaptations to the local context to reach its external policy objectives,[5] the social logic behind the enlargement process was largely one of assimilation via internalisation of the European model. Such logic was tightly connected to the

---

[3] Before the 1990s, the European Community had not formalised accession criteria. Being a democracy was the only criterion, as shown by the late accession of Greece, Spain and Portugal, which joined the Community only after the overthrow of dictatorships. However, the huge discrepancies with former communist regimes prompted the EC to officialise and detail three overt accession criteria: political (stability of institutions guaranteeing democracy, the rule of law, human rights, and respect for and protection of minorities); economic (existence of a functioning market economy and the capacity to cope with competitive pressures and market forces within the Union); and acceptance of the Community *acquis* (ability to take on the obligations of membership, including adherence to the aims of political, economic and monetary union).

[4] Especially through the screening method which entailed checking the progress of applicants in approximating their legislation to the EU's *acquis communautaire*.

[5] For instance, such an imitation logic can be found in the promotion of regional integration in EC assistance programmes and policies for ACP (Africa-Caribbean-Pacific) countries.

oversimplified interpretation of 1989 as a consecration of the Western European model.

A clash of interpretations

While EC management of 1989 was effective in bringing Central and Eastern European countries into the Union, it failed to unite the continent or, in other words, to fulfil the task it had been assigned to following the overthrow of communist regimes. Over the past few years, a number of events have reflected divergences between 'old' and 'new' member states. Such tensions are unprecedented – they did not occur following previous accession rounds to the EC/EU. Indeed, the adjectives 'old' and 'new' were never used before 2004 to distinguish among member states. They suggest deeply rooted differences going beyond the technicalities of the accession process and relating to the interpretation of the events of 1989 itself.

Divergences between 'old' and 'new' member states can be found both over foreign policy and in other institutional areas. While the so-called axis of European integration, Germany and France, refused to take part in the US-launched 2003 intervention in Iraq, several new member states, principally Poland, sent troops to support the US-led initiative. This division resurfaced at the end of 2007 when Poland and Lithuania blocked the opening of negotiations for a new agreement between the EU and Russia. Poland and the Baltic states also adopted a firmer stance than 'old' Europe during the conflict in Georgia in August 2008. At the same time, Poland took a hard stance during negotiations for a Constitutional treaty and over the Lisbon Treaty, requiring the inclusion of a formula on the Christian roots of Europe in the Constitution.

How can such differences be explained? A first analysis suggests that Central and Eastern European countries are now enjoying the privilege of being fully fledged members of the Union. After years of efforts to comply with EC conditions, they are maximising their institutional rights as EU member states. However, this interpretation does not account for the content of divergences between 'new' and 'old' member states. A second set of explanations focuses on the coexistence of divergent memories within the EU, as highlighted by the harder stance of eastern EU members vis-à-vis Russia, a stance which can be understood principally through the memory of Soviet occupation. A third analysis questions the very concept of a single or united Europe and highlights a clash of interpretations regarding European integration. It argues that the six founding member states and subsequent applicants shared a similar, or at least compatible, vision of the project. Their positions suggest a novel conception of the European Union, one interlaced with Central European historical experience and shaped by two main factors: first, the lack of a tradition of multi-level governance involving shared competences and the combination of intergovernmental and supranational approaches, as is the case within the European Union; second, the suspicion of supranational integration as a legacy of Soviet domination. Central and Eastern European countries' conception of the European Union is therefore shaped primarily by their experience and by their attachment to the national sovereignty they recovered after 1989. This interpretation is more comprehensive so far as it connects member states' history and traditions to their positions regarding the European integration process. However, two points need to be added to this analysis. First, to what extent do the new eastern member states constitute a bloc opposed to, or different from, old member states? The monolithic character of such a bloc needs to be questioned. Recent events have highlighted uneven progress and developments among the new members (e.g. Slovenia and Slovakia adopting the euro while the others keep their own currencies), but also different positions on various issues (e.g. Slovakia criticising Georgia's attack on the breakaway region of South Ossetia whereas Poland and the Baltic states asked for EU sanctions against Russia). Second, how far will new member states' specificity be maintained over time? Functionalist theories argue that the process of EU integration makes different conceptions and traditions of member states compatible, if not convergent. While it is too early to verify this hypothesis for new member states, other examples such as the UK suggest that this is not always the case. In other words, the EU integration process would not suffice per se to bridge the gaps between national legacies. Rather, its role is more effective in this respect when it is combined with concrete advantages for member states and acceding countries, such as economic growth (as illustrated by the examples of Greece or Spain).

The main lesson to be drawn from these differences between 'old' and 'new' EU member states invalidates the dominant interpretation of 1989. It indicates that the communist past cannot be simply erased or dissolved by the EU accession process. Current tensions within the EU also reflect shortcomings in the enlargement methodology as far as little attention was paid – and no time dedicated to – grasping the *meaning* of four decades of division. On the whole, as Aviezer Tucker points out in Chapter 7 (this volume), the persistence of legacies inherited from this period downplays the prevailing interpretation of 1989 as being a sharp rupture in which authoritarian regimes became functioning democracies overnight.

Revival or breakdown of the European integration project?

1989 is usually considered as a turning point in the course of European integration, inasmuch as it is naturally associated with the impetus given to that process in the 1990s. In other words, in the European imagination, the 'what for' question received a new answer after the overthrow of communist regimes – the construction of a political union. However, a thorough examination of the dynamics at stake shows that the picture is much more blurred. Other factors have played a role in boosting the European project in the 1990s. Moreover, the impact of 1989 on European construction can be assessed as ambivalent, at least as far as enlargement slackened the rhythm of integration.

A new grand design for Europe?

There is a widespread understanding that 1989 was instrumental in insufflating a new breath to the European construction. But this is, at least, partially misleading in that it overlooks major developments before this period. Before 1989, EC institutions (in particular the European Commission) initiated wide-ranging projects to invigorate the integration process after a period of Euro-sclerosis. These focused on the economic sphere, e.g. the completion of the Internal Market (decided by the Single European Act in 1986) and the ambitious launching of an Economic and Monetary Union (EMU, planned by the 'Delors packages' in 1988). These projects were both bold and far-reaching. First, whereas the Treaty of Rome only provided for the creation of a 'common market', eliminating obstacles to trade within the Community, the Internal Market went further, entailing the harmonisation of national norms and legislation in order to enhance competitiveness. Second, the Treaty of Rome contained neither demands regarding macroeconomic policy nor plans for monetary cooperation. At the same time, although unforeseen by the initial Treaty, both the Internal Market and EMU were in line with previous integration efforts. The choice was made to revitalise the European Community through deepening integration in areas where it had all started thirty years before – trade and economics. Moreover, the Community continued to rely upon the integration (Monnet) method used since the creation of the Coal and Steel

Community, entailing cooperation to be extended to new sectors over time.

The collapse of the communist system gave further impetus to the revival of the EC, while at the same time shifting integration to the political area and calling for a change in methods of integration. In the wake of 1989, it was commonly agreed that a qualitative jump was required in order to respond to upheavals in the eastern part of the continent:

History accelerates. We must accelerate too ... I have always been a proponent of a small steps policy, as shown by the current framework to give a new impetus to the European integration process. But I am moving away from it now because time is short ... We need a qualitative jump both for our conception of the Community and for our external action modalities. (Delors 1992)

Both the content and methods of integration which had prevailed previously were thus considered to be inadequate to tackle challenges stemming from the overthrow of communist regimes. Where the EC had concentrated on economic issues, the challenges of 1989 were primarily political. Moreover, the small steps that the Monnet method employed were insufficient in that the spill-over effects it triggered were limited to the economic sphere. Therefore, European construction had to be altered. The feeling of responsibility vis-à-vis the former communist bloc led major EC leaders, Helmut Kohl and François Mitterrand, to propose a second intergovernmental conference on the political union, in parallel to that planned on economic issues. As a result, new EC competences and new pillars of EC action (in particular the Common Foreign and Security Policy, Justice and Home Affairs) were enshrined in the Treaty of Maastricht. This was a major breakthrough in the history of European integration. In paving the way for political integration, 1989 is also indirectly the source of subsequent developments in this area, not least in terms of the creation of a Security and Defence Policy at the end of the 1990s, as well as in progress on developing common policies on asylum and migration-related issues. In short, the collapse of communism in Central and Eastern Europe made unavoidable an inflection in the course of integration towards areas which, due to member states' reluctances, were previously unexplored and highly sensitive.

The end of European integration?

At the same time, the development of the European integration project in the aftermath of 1989 displays obvious limits. These stem only indirectly from the overthrow of communist regimes and rather reflect shortcomings in the EU's management of the post-1989 era.

Alternative methods used during the 1990s and since the beginning of the century have focused on intergovernmentalism. However, they have yielded little so far. First, *intergovernmental negotiations* used to modify the Treaties have not introduced the institutional changes which would have allowed an efficient functioning of the EU-27. All the intergovernmental conferences organised since the early 1990s have reflected tough negotiations and deep differences between EU actors. Major institutional modifications were postponed by the Amsterdam intergovernmental conference in the mid-1990s and, due to divergent interests among member states, the solutions proposed by the subsequent Nice conference in the early 2000s were rickety in the extreme. Second, the *open method of coordination* – an innovative method adapted from the enlargement process – displays important limits. To allow further progress of cooperation in areas which do not fall within EC competences, the open method of coordination relies upon soft law mechanisms (benchmarking, monitoring) and peer pressure (naming and shaming) with a view to stimulating member states into harmonising their positions. However, its record has been mixed in the principal area (employment) where it has been applied so far.

Difficulties experienced in achieving convergence between national positions and policies are also correlated to the increased number of EU members induced by enlargement to Central and Eastern Europe countries. Because national preferences are more miscellaneous and because the content of integration is now wider than before 1989, agreements on the agenda of European construction are significantly more difficult to reach. As a consequence, parallel schemes of integration have been initiated since the 1990s, and different speeds and rhythms of cooperation coexist within the EU-27. For the first time in the history of European integration, opt-out provisions were included in the Maastricht Treaty. In contrast to these provisions, mechanisms to develop further integration for those member states willing to do so in specific areas were formally introduced in the Amsterdam Treaty in the form of enhanced cooperation.

The picture of the EU-27 therefore looks like a mosaic of rules and procedures. Even though they do not strictly correspond to the procedure of enhanced cooperation, the European Monetary Union, as well as the Schengen area, illustrates the possibility for an 'avant-garde' to move forward and work closely together. They have turned out to be effective tools to progress on the way of integration in specific areas. Nevertheless, there is no evidence that forerunners will eventually be caught up by laggards. Rather than a multi-speed Europe, one may witness the development of a 'Europe à la carte' in which each member state picks up the activities it wants to implement and the rules it is ready to obey. This would constitute a profound alteration of the initial integration project as designed by Schuman and Monnet in the early 1950s. And it is in this context that the recent major crises in European construction should be analysed. Repeated negative votes on European affairs in various member states highlight incertitude on the EU's current identity. For instance, the rejection of the Constitutional Treaty in France and the Netherlands in 2005 reflected much more than a mere refusal of the political document issued by the Convention. Negative votes in two of the EC's founding members expressed one of three possibilities: disappointment with the lack of EC action in certain areas (such as the social sphere); criticism vis-à-vis a Union perceived as becoming overweening in areas traditionally the preserve of member states; or dissatisfaction with an enlargement process which had been only superficially explained to European citizens. In other words, through making the EU more diverse and more fragmented, through shifting the integration project from its initial philosophy, 1989 has indirectly contributed to blockages in European construction.

Clarifying borders or blurring boundaries?

Whereas 1989 has generated a new pace and direction in European integration, it has also been instrumental in changing its contours. In European construction, the 'where' question has thus been dramatically altered by the overthrow of the communist regimes.

A revolution in geography

From the 'where' point of view, 1989 is a breakthrough as far as it shattered the geographical framework in which the European Community was created. The first attempts towards European integration were carried out in the late 1940s, in the aftermath of the Second World War. However, even though the European integration process finds its roots in the Second World War and in the rejection of future wars on the continent, it is also deeply embedded in the Cold War. The growing tensions between eastern and western blocs indirectly triggered economic cooperation projects among western European countries, which served as a basis for the future EEC. For instance, major EEC founding fathers actively participated in the Organisation for European Economic Co-operation which was meant to dispatch US assistance provided via the Marshall Plan. The European Community was thus formally created at a time when the Cold War provided apparently natural and durable geographical limits. The 'Iron Curtain' constituted an obvious, yet implicit, boundary of the newly born organisation.

Within this overarching metageography, EC borders did not remain rigid. They evolved over time as the Community welcomed new members: the UK, Ireland and Denmark in 1973; Greece in 1981; Spain and Portugal in 1986. However, 'enlargement policy' – an expression to be used cautiously since it was neither formalised nor translated into official accession criteria – was tightly connected to the Cold War. In other words, in the early period of the European integration process, adherence to the western bloc (together with NATO membership) was seen, at least implicitly, as an essential criterion for EC membership. This is perfectly illustrated by the case of Turkey, which was considered as an important ally during the Cold War context and thus expected to join the Community once it was ready to do so. The Association Agreement (known as the Ankara Agreement) signed in 1963, aimed at bringing Turkey into a Customs Union with the EEC and, thereby, a step closer to full membership, provided that, 'the EEC's support to the efforts undertaken by the people of Turkey to improve the standards of living will facilitate Turkey's accession to the Community'.[6]

Against this background, the events of 1989 raised, for the first time in the Community's history, the issue of the final borders of EU integration. Through paving the way for the unification of Europe, the overthrow of communist regimes not only changed the EC's boundaries; it also seemed to open unprecedented avenues for defining the EU's new identity and thus its final borders.

Post-1989: a missed opportunity

1989 is arguably a missed opportunity in this respect. The events in Central and Eastern Europe called for a firm answer to the 'where' question, i.e. rethinking the geographical framework which had shaped European construction in its first thirty years. However, while the EU carefully designed an accession strategy in the early 1990s which included political and economic criteria, it left wide open crucial questions regarding its future shape. What should be the EU's frontiers and who should be allowed to apply for EU membership? On the basis of which criteria should such a decision be made?

---

[6] Preamble, Agreement establishing an Association between the EEC and Turkey, in *Official Journal of the European Communities*, 24 December 1973, No. C 113/2.

The example of application criteria illustrates the absence of EU efforts to define the boundary between itself and its near abroad. While accession criteria reflect the political and economic model of the Union, application criteria are meant to mirror the EU's self-perception regarding its final boundaries. The rejection of Morocco's application in 1987 was a first step towards clarification of this issue. However, application criteria were not specified further in the 1990s. And the corresponding article of the EC Treaty has not been modified since 1957. It provides that 'any European country which respects the principles set out in article 6 (1) may apply to become a member of the Union'.[7] Before 1989, the reference to the EU's principles was sufficient to exclude Central and Eastern Europe as well as the former Soviet Union. After 1989, the coincidence of application criteria and geopolitical context disappeared. Combined with the absence of additional application criteria, the EU's choice – enlarging rather than deepening – was interpreted as an open-door policy.

Whereas in-depth debate on the definitive boundaries of European integration eluded policy-makers after 1989, this had few implications until the early part of the new century. The progress and finalisation of accession negotiations moved attention towards the external consequences of enlargement, in other words on ways to manage the EU's future borders. The fifth and sixth waves of enlargement would bring the EU much closer to open or frozen conflicts such as the Palestinian–Israeli conflict, the conflicts in Transnistria and those in the Caucasus. It also put the EU in contact with poorer and fragile states, characterised by a strong degree of corruption, institutional weakness and limited ability to undertake reforms. The European Neighbourhood Policy (ENP) was designed as a comprehensive answer to these challenges. The ENP was inspired by the desire to create a buffer zone around the enlarged Union, composed of stable countries protecting the EU against possible threats. However, it calls upon ambivalent logics and policy tools. On the one hand, the ENP relies on the EU's power of attraction to bring partner countries closer to the Union in key areas such as the Internal Market, transport, infrastructure, education and research. Its objective is to bring neighbours closer to the EU through legal approximation in order to avoid the development of new iron curtains in Europe. On the other hand, the ENP includes a coercive dimension in line with concerns expressed in the European Security Strategy, which as early as 2003 emphasised the need to ensure security

---

[7] Article 49, Treaty on European Union, http://eur-lex.europa.eu/en/treaties/dat/12002M/htm/C_2002325EN.000501.html.

beyond EU borders: 'Our traditional concept of self-defence – up to and including the Cold War – was based on the threat of invasion. With the new threats, the first line of defence will often be abroad' (Solana 2003: 7).

Tools such as visa facilitation and readmission agreements illustrate the externalisation of EC security policy towards neighbouring countries. Readmission agreements set out clear obligations and procedures for the authorities of partner countries as to when and how to repatriate people who are illegally residing in the EU. As a result, partner countries – for instance Russia or Ukraine – bear the financial and administrative burden for taking back illegal immigrants from the EU border to their homeland. At the same time, due to the entry of new member states into the Schengen area in 2007, the border between the EU and its neighbours has been harder, creating a 'Paper Wall' across Europe. As a consequence, neighbouring countries are both excluded from – and included in – the European integration process.

While ambivalent dynamics of inclusion/exclusion blur the boundaries of EU integration (Lavenex 2004), no answer has been provided to the issue of the EU's final borders. Strong expectations of countries like Ukraine shed light on the inadequacy of application criteria, not least because it is difficult to query Kiev's European character. Moreover, through relying upon approximation of neighbours' legislation with parts of the *acquis*, the ENP also creates applicants for the EU before it is ready to engage in new enlargement processes (Cremona and Hillion 2006). The EU's 'absorption capacity' – a condition formalised by the European Council in 2006 to limit further enlargements – cannot substitute for a definition of the EU's final borders. However, this entails defining the Union's identity and its *finalité*, something which the diversity of the enlarged EU precludes. This analysis also invalidates the argument that the definition of the EU's borders prior to 1989 would have blocked the enlargement process – recent developments highlight a reluctance both to define borders and enlarge further. The debate opened in 1989 regarding the 'where' question is far from being closed.

Beyond 'civilian power'?

The impact of 1989 is also dual when it comes to the 'how' question, i.e. the ways in which the EU exerts influence worldwide and interacts with other stakeholders. On the one hand, the collapse of communism has consecrated the EC's modes of influence and has boosted the EC's attractiveness. On the other hand, upheavals in

Central and Eastern Europe in the aftermath of 1989 have shown the
limits of the EC's soft power and introduced novel modes of political
influence.

The collapse of the communist system did not only significantly
strengthen the European Community's role in Europe. After 1989,
the EC turned into a global actor. In the past, the Community had
relied upon the military capabilities of the United States, so much so
that it had often been mocked for its lack of international influence
as illustrated by Henry Kissinger's famous words, 'If I want to call
Europe, who do I call?'. 1989 paved the way for the emergence of institutional arrangements which bridged that gap. The Common Foreign
and Security Policy (CFSP) introduced by the Maastricht Treaty enabled the EU to go beyond foreign policy declarations and to implement
joint actions, something developed further in the Amsterdam Treaty.
Moreover, the position of High Representative for CFSP was created
to embody the EU's foreign policy and to increase consistency; units
dedicated to external relations developed both within the Commission
and the Council. Beyond this institutional framework, evidence of the
EU's new international assertiveness can be found in the extension of
its network of programmes and agreements worldwide after 1989. In
the 1960s, the EC had started to develop relations with former colonies
(e.g. Africa-Caribbean-Pacific countries) and countries within the
Western bloc (e.g. the United States, Turkey, Canada). Over time, these
relations were gradually extended to Mediterranean, Asian and South
American countries. But the EC had not established official links with
the USSR or its satellite countries before 1989. After this time, the EU's
external action became global for the first time.

The overthrow of communism thus consecrated the specific modes
of influence developed by the European Community and framed by
its own history, particularly the lack of military capabilities after the
rejection of the European Defence Community in 1954. As early as
the 1970s, the EC had been called a 'civilian power',[8] i.e. an entity
exerting influence through attraction rather than coercion. This also
referred to the predominant role played by trade and assistance in EC
external action. 1989 augmented the EU's attractiveness. More specifically, the use of conditionality which had been initiated in the 1980s
became a cornerstone of the enlargement process, enabling the EU to
export its norms, standards and values (Sjursen 2006). The European
Neighbourhood Policy provides an illustration of the EU's 'normative
power' (Manners 2002): closer cooperation with Eastern and Southern

[8] The expression was first used over thirty years ago by François Duchêne (1973).

neighbours (including their participation to specific EU programmes and policies) is made conditional upon the progress of partner countries in respect of 'shared values' and approximation to EC *acquis*. Even though (unlike candidate countries) full alignment is not required from neighbours, the neighbourhood policy highlights an asymmetrical process – taking into account the policy framework, partner countries have few possibilities to resist the EU's attempt to model its environment in its own image.

At the same time, in the aftermath of 1989, the EU was confronted with the limits of its 'civilian power', in particular its incapacity to contain conflicts on the European continent or its periphery. Wars in the Balkans in the early 1990s exposed both differences within member states and the EU's lack of influence in terms of conflict management. The institution which had been praised for its success in promoting peace between former enemies proved unable to prevent genocide and wars at its borders, or even to contribute effectively to their settlement. The Kosovo conflict in 1999 confirmed these shortcomings while showcasing the primacy of NATO. These events led to the development of a military dimension in the European construction, first with the Petersberg tasks adopted in the early 1990s, then with the design of a European Common Security and Defence Policy (ESDP) at the end of the 1990s. The deployments of European troops under the ESDP in the Balkans and elsewhere reflect a watershed in the EU's conception of external influence; 1989 has been one of the most important factors in this process. The rise of security issues on the EU's agenda and the use of military capabilities are considered to undermine the EU's specificity as an international actor (Smith 2005). However, either the EU's Security Strategy or field operations highlight a specific understanding of security issues, with a preference for conflict prevention/crisis management, as shown by the European Union Border Assistance Mission to Moldova and Ukraine (EUBAM).

As far as the EU's international actorhood is concerned, 1989 has once again resulted in ambivalent processes, with the increasing assertion of the EU's normative power and, at the same time, a re-examination of its influence. The overall picture is mixed, reflected in recent events such as the conflict in Ossetia – also a long-term consequence of 1989. On the one hand, the EU is sufficiently attractive to appear as the only possible mediator between Russia and Georgia, and to act effectively in this position since a ceasefire was quickly reached. At the same time, the EU is strongly constrained by Russia's military superiority in the field. Subsequent events in Georgia demonstrate clearly that the EU has few possibilities to influence an actor (Russia) which is determined to act aggressively, which relies on coercion to defend its interests, and which only accepts the European model on a selective basis.

Conclusion

A closer look at the consequences of the overthrow of communism on the European Union highlights both *compressed and stretched temporalities* as a result of clashing rhythms between Eastern and Western Europe at the end of the 1980s. First, the events of 1989 coincided with a wide-ranging reform process launched in the European Community via the Single European Act in 1986. These reforms were meant to improve the decision-making process in order to deepen economic integration between member states. In this way, they gave a new impetus to the European project which contributed to increasing the attractiveness of the EC and which allowed the Community to appear as a beacon for guiding Central and Eastern European towards market democracy. However, at the end of the 1980s, the EC became increasingly involved in navel-gazing debates about its own integration. It was, therefore, unprepared for new external responsibilities. In spite of this, the EC proved able to provide at least some answers to the upheavals in the eastern part of the continent, both by providing assistance programmes and subsequently through the design of an enlargement methodology.

At the same time, while the EC succeeded in managing compressed temporalities in 1989, it failed to take into account the possible consequences of the upheavals both on itself and its projects. Nor did it manage to answer crucial questions about its own construction. Before 1989, these questions had either been irrelevant (e.g. the issue of final boundaries) or they had been elided in order to avoid divergences between member states (e.g. regarding the final goal of European integration). In other words, the pre-1989 European project, whatever its successes, was limited as far as it was framed – and constrained – by the international context, namely the Cold War. The questions raised as a consequence of 1989 were overshadowed, at least for a while, by the enormity of enlargement. As a result, the direct and indirect implications of 1989 for the European Union have become visible only over the last few years, stretching the temporality of 1989. In the new millennium, and especially since 2004, the EU has been faced with challenges stemming from its management of 1989. While bringing the enlargement process to an end, the accession of then Central and Eastern European countries in 2004 and 2007, together with high expectations from former Soviet Republics, confronted the Union with crucial questions, in particular the *finalité* and the ultimate boundaries of its integration process.

Analysis of the impact of 1989 on European integration also sheds light on the *interwoven logics, yet clashing interpretations* stemming from the EC's management of 1989. First, in a situation characterised by urgency, but also by limited competence, the option taken by the European Community in 1989 and during the early 1990s entailed including Central and Eastern European countries in the European project (mainly through enlargement) *and* pursuing the process launched in the 1980s to deepen integration between member states. The social logic and method used for enlargement (assimilation, adoption of EU *acquis* prior to accession) are meant to enable candidate countries to fully participate, once they have acceded, in a project of European integration which continues to develop in parallel to the enlargement process. At the same time, the European Community has overlooked the changes which the accession of Central and Eastern European countries brings to European integration. Such a shortcoming is linked to the two assumptions which guided its management of 1989: the parenthesis and winner-takes-it-all assumptions. The strong belief in development, stages and linearity led the EC to reduce candidate countries to a 'transitional' status, seeing them as en route to democracy, a market economy and, thereby, the EU itself. These assumptions overshadowed the legacies of pre-communist and communist pasts, the divergences of interpretations between 'East' and 'West' on EU integration, and the backlash that 2004 would bring on the EU as a consequence of its neglect. The result of this neglect is a European project now at a standstill.

Through challenging the four assumptions which lie at the core of prevailing interpretations about 1989 and Europe, this chapter has shed light on four ambivalent processes. First, the continent is now formally united under the EU's banner, yet tensions and divisions remain vivid as a consequence of the EC's management of 1989 and the lack of reflection (in both parts of Europe) on the *meaning* of these four decades of division. Second, 1989 ushered in a revival of European integration through paving the way for a political Union. At the same time, through making the EU more diverse and more fragmented, and through shifting the integration project from its initial philosophy, 1989 has made European construction more fragile. Third, the overthrow of communist regimes has enabled the EC to define its own borders, which had previously been limited by the international context. Yet a prerequisite for doing so requires clarification of the EU's *finalité*, a task that has been carefully avoided since 1958. Finally, 1989 has consecrated the

EU's 'civilian power' and turned the EU into a global actor. Yet as far as foreign policy is concerned, decision-making is cumbersome and the EU lacks basic instruments and capacities which would enable it to become a fully-fledged international actor. Interestingly, in taking these four assumptions for granted, the EU is increasingly challenged by the country that acts as a successor to the USSR, Russia – a country which at the beginning of the 1990s was supposed to move closer to the EU even as the transatlantic link was supposed to gradually distend. Over the past few years, Moscow's aggressive stances and its willingness to stand outside the dominant model of development embodied by the EU have defied both conventional interpretations of the communist/post-communist periods endorsed by the Union and the consequences of 1989 on the European integration project. In other words, Russia disavows the parenthesis and winner-takes-it-all assumptions, but also the lessons that have been drawn by the EU after 1989.

The picture of the impact of 1989 on Europe is therefore much more fuzzy than indicated both by current interpretations and official EU discourse. As far as the European integration process is concerned, 1989 has raised more questions than it has provided answers and, as a result, the consequences of 1989 on EU construction are far from being settled. In short, 1989 is not over in Europe.

7   Restoration and convergence: Russia and China since 1989

Aviezer Tucker

Authoritarian and totalitarian legacies

Conventional political wisdom considers 1989 to be the year when communist China and the Soviet bloc parted ways: China continued on its course, while the Soviet bloc converged with the post-authoritarian Latin American and Southern European paths in transitioning to democracy. Consequently, as George Lawson mentions in his introduction to this volume, the early transition theories recycled Latin American models for Eastern Europe. In this chapter I challenge this conventional wisdom. I argue that the differences between authoritarian and totalitarian regimes and societies are pivotal for understanding the *different* paths they followed in the post-totalitarian and post-authoritarian eras. These path dependencies explain why, twenty years after 1989, there is increasing convergence between Chinese and Russian politics and patterns of social stratification. The apparent divergence in 1989 was not as sharp as it appeared at the time. Post-totalitarian Russia and China emerged from a process of the adjustment of the rights of the late-totalitarian elite – the *nomenklatura* – to its interests. The apparent differences between the bumpy road of Russia and the smooth track of China in the decade after 1989 resulted from the spontaneous nature of this process in Russia, whereas in China this adjustment was planned and enounced publicly. Understanding the global post-totalitarian 1989 requires understanding the evolution of the totalitarian ruling class from that of political revolutionaries to that of the property owners.

Totalitarianism is distinct from authoritarianism in establishing a monopoly of a single elite in *all* social institutions. The revolutionary totalitarian elite establishes itself as the single elite in society by eliminating all existing, potential or possible alternative elites. Without such elimination, there is no *total* control of society by a single hierarchically united elite, the hallmark of totalitarianism. Unlike authoritarian elites, totalitarian elites must eliminate not just all competing *political* elites, but all actual and potential alternative elites: economic, military,

religious, local, artistic, educational, etc. To achieve this end, roughly
10 per cent of the population must lose all social status, power and
rights, either by being killed, imprisoned or exiled. Higher percentages
of totalitarian mortality result from the death of the weakest members
of society in hunger as a result of the expropriation of their means of
subsistence in the collectivisation of agriculture in the Soviet Union and
China. Once the elimination of all actual or potential alternative elites
is achieved, factions within the totalitarian elite turn on each other.

In totalitarian revolutions, a revolutionary elite gain control of the
Ministry of the Interior and, through it, control of the secret police,
the militia and the ordinary police. The secret police then undertakes the radical revolution, seizes, consolidates and protects power.
Thereafter, the elite fight among themselves to secure and protect
power in the absence of a political mechanism that allows for peaceful competition. The surviving totalitarian elite suffer from insecurity,
purges, arrests and revenge against both themselves and their families.
During their revolutionary stage, therefore, totalitarian regimes do not
have a stable elite and do not develop a *ruling class* – rather, a temporary
group of thugs emerges and takes over power (Arendt 1973). At the end
of its revolutionary stage (the end of the Stalinist purges after 1953 in
Eastern Europe and the end of the Cultural Revolution in China), the
surviving elite reaches a tacit pact to lower the stakes, rein in the secret
police and rule collectively. By then, there are no alternative actual or
even potential elites. As such, the single surviving totalitarian elite can
become stable enough to become a class unto itself. To secure their rule,
this new elite class must choose docile bureaucrats as their deputies and
eventual successors. In late-totalitarianism, a bureaucratic elite gradually replaces the professional revolutionaries, or as Hall (1995: 82)
put it, *technocracy* replaced *ideocracy*. The kind of elite that survives the
revolutionary stage knows not to create enemies by drawing attention
to itself. It is too grey and anonymous to generate a personality cult.
It accumulates power not so much by the ruthless and arbitrary use of
violence as through networking, lobbying, creating alliances, conspir-
ing and appearing loyal.

This new elite, like any upper class that wishes to maintain itself,
requires private property or its functional equivalent to secure its
own future. This was predicted well in advance of the emergence of
an actual-existing totalitarian elite, for example by Robert Michels
(1962: 348) who foresaw the emergence of a bureaucratic hierarchy
under socialism, and its transformation into a ruling class when parents
attempt to pass on their status to the next generation. However Michels,
like those who held similar ideas, including most tragically Czechoslovak

president Edvard Beneš, did not foresee how long this process would take. They expected it to follow the revolution. But the first revolutionary totalitarian generation was too fanatic, too sadistic, too impersonal, and too briefly in power to form a coherent ruling class. Such a class only emerged with the second and third post-revolutionary generations as a result of their selection of bureaucratic successors. Although younger bureaucrats with a taste for wealth and class gradually replace the old revolutionaries, the old guard do not always sympathise with, and collaborate in, their mission of personal enrichment. Consequently, the bureaucrats are involved in a struggle for liberation against the old revolutionaries and the institutional rules they constructed – in other words, a struggle to adjust their institutionalised rights to their interests.

Communist societies call their elites the *nomenklatura*. Formally, the *nomenklatura* was composed of officeholders whose appointments had to be approved by the highest party hierarchy, the Central Committee of the Communist Party or even the Politburo (White and Kryshtanovskaya 1998: 128). In the Soviet Union, *nomenklatura* career trajectory tended to start in the communist youth movement (the *Komsomol*) from where the chosen elite member moved to the Communist Party and roles in the Soviet state as economic manager, diplomat and official. The cohesiveness and unity of the totalitarian elite was encouraged by this process as members of the elite were supervised by different people and encountered different people during the course of their careers. Only members of the elite with an economic career trajectory had a single specialisation moving from one economic position to the next. The children of the *nomenklatura* remained a part of this informal ruling class. Since as upper-class children they benefited from higher education and entered professions, they became the vanguard of the transformation of the *nomenklatura* class into an upper class in the traditional sense, a class with its own interests that were strikingly similar to those of the bourgeoisie in non-totalitarian countries: personal security, freedom to enjoy one's wealth, property rights and higher (if not high) culture.

The degree of autonomy and the diffusion of power within the Soviet *nomenklatura* elite in the late-totalitarian 1970s and 1980s is disputed (Higley *et al.* 2003: 16–20). Yet, clearly the tug of war between centre and periphery, revolutionary thugs and bureaucratic thieves, resulted in the liberation movement of the *nomenklatura* that R. V. Barylski called elite self-emancipation (Bunce 1999).

As the end of the old regime was approaching, the *nomenklatura* split into two groups: unreformed communists, who remained dogmatic, and pragmatists, who wanted to get rich off the transition. The pragmatists tended to include enterprise managers, young communist officials, and all kinds of operators. Although they facilitated the collapse of communism, they did not desire a normal market economy; they wanted full freedom for themselves but overwhelming regulations for others. They bought commodities at home for a fraction of their world-market prices and sold them abroad, thanks to export privileges. They insisted on massive state credit to themselves at highly negative real interest rates. To make these outrageous practices politically palatable, the pragmatists presented their program as a set of socially conscious gradual reforms. For a variety of reasons, many Westerners played along. When these parasites won, the outcome was a rent-seeking society. (Åslund 2002: 217)

I am not sure the 'parasites' always bothered to present their theft in social-democratic terms; certainly the rhetoric of privatisation and capitalism was just as effective for the same goal – the appropriation of the state. Still, otherwise Åslund describes correctly the post-totalitarian reality.

The end of totalitarianism is the end of monolithic social hierarchy dominated by a single, united elite. However, the emergence of new and alternative elites is a process that takes at least a generation because of the elimination of all indigenous pre-totalitarian elites during the revolutionary totalitarian stage and the strict control of upper mobility by the totalitarian elite thereafter. Beyond politics and sometimes the media, the late-totalitarian elite remains in control of everything else: the economy, the state bureaucracy, the security services, the legal system, and the education system merely by default, because after totalitarianism there are no alternative elites to replace them.

There are two main theories about post-totalitarian elites: elite adaptation and elite competition. *Elite adaptation* is a theory of continuity – the late-totalitarian elite remains in place and becomes the post-totalitarian elite. The *elite competition* thesis suggests that, during late-totalitarianism, the elite divides between an older class of political administrators and a younger acquisitive class in positions of economic management (Lane and Ross 1999). Hughes and John (2003: 131) suggest that both theories are true in the sense that the new post-totalitarian elites were recruited from both groups: 'for the Russian elites the major concern is self-preservation, political flexibility and pragmatism, combined with *enrichissez vous* practices'. As such, these two theories offer complementary perspectives on the same phenomenon. From without, i.e. from the perspective of ordinary citizens of post-totalitarian countries, the more things change in society and politics, the more they remain the same. They were barred from the elite before and the same elite seem to continue to run their countries. However, from within, i.e. from the perspective of members of the elite, there is a perception

Table 7.1 *Totalitarian and authoritarian legacies*

Totalitarian legacies	Authoritarian legacies
Elite homogeneity and continuity	Elite heterogeneity
Lack of elite interest in power as an end in itself	Elite maintains interest in political power as an end in itself
Transformation of political power to economic wealth: the privatisation of the state by the elite	The economy is not fully controlled (and never was) by the authoritarian elite
Feeble civil society	Vigorous civil society
High levels of corruption	Initially high levels of corruption
Subservient judiciary and weak rule of law	Independent judiciary
Control and manipulation of mass media	Free media
End to ideology as a mobilisation tool	Ideologies continue to mobilise voters
Low levels of retribution and reparation	Eventually high levels of transitional justice
Members of the former secret police continue to be powerful	Continued special role and power for the military and military veterans

of competition over scarce resources between competing groups. Some cliques are more successful than others. In this context of limited competition, the late-totalitarian elite remains outwardly united, as in the Northern European post-communist states. In the absence of such competition, elite in-fighting is common, as in Russia.

Consequently, 'unlike in Argentina in 1982–83, Uruguay in 1984, or Chile in 1988–89, ruling Communist elites in Eastern Europe had little reason to fear that newly ascendant political forces would undertake vengeful actions' (Gonzáles Enriquez 1998: 278). In authoritarian regimes there are alternative, though non-political, elites that can replace the existing elites at the helm of the state and the judicial system and then act to implement measures that come to terms with perpetrators and compensate victims. When the state's control of civil society and of legal and educational institutions is not *total*, there are some democratically oriented lawyers and judges, as well as other professionals and civil leaders, who can manage and operate the institutions of government. Table 7.1 indicates the key differences, therefore, between totalitarian and authoritarian societies.

The self-liberation of the *nomenklatura*

All of the above are manifestations of one deep process: *the adjustment of the rights of the late-totalitarian elite to its interests.* Post-totalitarianism is *the nomenklatura's self-liberation.*

The late-totalitarian elite inherited from its revolutionary predecessors rights to censor, imprison, torture, execute and control minute aspects of the lives of their subjects. The elite could decide whether subjects were to be free or jailed, which kind of employment they would have and whether they would be promoted, what level of education they and their children could enjoy, where they could live and how big would be their home, what quality of medical treatment they would receive when in need, whether they be given an exit visa and so on. But the elite also assumed some duties. According to the late-communist social contract, the elite had to assure formal full employment, low economic growth, and a low minimal welfare by Western standards, in return for political acquiescence and non-resistance. Much of this distribution of rights and duties in late-totalitarianism was inherited from revolutionary totalitarianism. With the exception of the late-communist social contract, this distribution of rights and duties reflected the interests of the first revolutionary totalitarian elite, people who were more interested in power than wealth and valued more highly the domination of the lives of their subjects than the accumulation of wealth and its transfer to their children. These extensive rights were of little use to people who perceived their interests as enrichment and the passing of this wealth to their families. This social distribution of rights and duties was highly dissatisfying for the second-generation bureaucratic totalitarian elite.

The late-totalitarian elite also inherited from the revolutionary elite duties against its interests. Ritualistic duties such as marching on May Day must have been very exciting for first-generation revolutionaries, but for second-generation bureaucrats they are no more than a time-wasting nuisance. The duty to hide from each other their wealth, avoid engaging in conspicuous consumption and the restrictions on passing hidden wealth to their descendants were painful. Since members of the *nomenklatura* are in charge of enforcing their duties on each other, they can spontaneously relax their mutual controls through neglect and let a thousand corruptions bloom. They therefore initiate a process which adjusts rights to interests. On the one hand, they gradually cease to exercise their rights to control the minute aspects of their subjects' lives. On the other hand, they attempt to gain for themselves de facto property rights.

Throughout the 1980s, parts of the *nomenklatura* all over the communist world, especially those with actual control over goods and services, began the process of spontaneous privatisation and involvement in the second economy. In Poland, for example (Łoś and Zybertowicz 2000: 73):

In the 1970s, managing the country became for the Party elite synonymous with owning it, that is, having unhampered use of its wealth and institutions. In the 1980s, the Party introduced pseudo-market reforms that enabled a formal legitimization of the *nomenklatura*'s informal property rights of the earlier period. The new pro-entrepreneurial, pro-market rhetoric facilitated a conversion of the long-standing *nomenklatura* practices of illegal appropriation of state resources, corruption and organized crime into officially hailed schemes of privatization that turned the party apparatchiks into entrepreneurchiks.

The economy failed partly because members of the *nomenklatura* acted increasingly as economic right holders. To reduce costs/duties, the Soviet *nomenklatura* gave up on East Europe and ended the Cold War. They also assumed the economic rights they wanted: to own, consume conspicuously, and bequest to their children. In transition, the East European *nomenklatura* lost some of its political rights that were not in its direct interest, but augmented its economic rights that were in its interest, both by spontaneously appropriating the properties it had managed prior to the end of totalitarianism, and by separating assets from liabilities, rights from duties, possessing the first and transferring the second to the state. As such, 'the main reasons why the late communist elite, or its more dynamic networks, relinquished their political monopoly without resistance were less a lack of ideological self-legitimation than the process of their conversion into capitalists, which suited their long term interests better than did the economically bankrupt and internationally shunned communist system' (Łoś and Zybertowicz 2000: 107). In the Soviet Union and Eastern Europe, unlike China, the adjustment of rights to interests was spontaneous – it did not follow deliberation or a collective decision of the *nomenklatura* to adapt its rights to its interests. The adjustment of rights to interests happened as the aggregate of individual and uncoordinated actions.

Continuity or revolution?

Many observers (e.g. Bozóki 2003) note the significance of elites and elite strategies in post-totalitarian politics. In post-totalitarian countries, some negotiations took place in countries where alternative elites of dissidents or professionals were tolerated during the late totalitarian era. The obvious, indeed blatant, economic success of the *nomenklatura* and its virtual immunity from being held to account for its years of oppression have led to a flurry of accusations directed at dissidents who participated in negotiations with the *nomenklatura* over the transfer of political power, of cutting a secret deal granting immunity and economic assets to the *nomenklatura* in return for being handed official office. Łoś and Zybertowicz (2000: 109) acknowledge that they have no way of verifying whether an agreement along the lines of political power for Poland's Solidarity in exchange for the economy to the communists 'was explicitly negotiated and achieved, [but] it can be argued that the whole process of systemic transition unfolded as if such an agreement were in force'. However, even more *nomenklatura* success and immunity have also been present in countries like Russia and Ukraine where there were no alternative elites and no negotiations over the transfer of political power. The differences between post-totalitarian states where there were negotiations and those where there were no alternative elites are rather between the replacement of the political elite and its continuity. Post-totalitarian continuity of economic, social and bureaucratic elites is universal.

Beyme (1996: 4) argues that the absence of alternative elites and ideologies excludes the changes that took place in 1989–91 from being considered revolutionary. As Shevtsova (2002) stresses, *perestroika* was too brief to allow for the emergence of alternative elites. The Soviet *nomenklatura* was pressured neither by alternative elites, nor from people below it in the hierarchy. It appeared willing to play by democratic rules, but was under no constraint to do so. It continued to rely on personal networks rather than institutions and attempted to subordinate society. Post-totalitarian power remains with the bureaucracy, the former *nomenklatura* and secret police, who co-opted representatives of the main new political and social groups. In the Southern European post-communist countries like Romania there is high correlation between economic, political and social status. Informal networks, or clans, in Russian, are the basic units of the post-totalitarian elite just as they were of the late-totalitarian one (Hughes and John 2003: 134–5). As Chris Armbruster notes in Chapter 9 (this volume), the necessary collapse of the system of control founded on Stalinist terror led to *re-traditionalisation*, when old systems of patronage and informal exchange outside the formal totalitarian hierarchy reasserted themselves. Though the late- to post-totalitarian elite is interested in wealth, its members have few skills for effectively competing for it in a genuinely free market. They have political skills and abilities, experience in lobbying and corrupting, and social capital to operate networks in the government bureaucracy to protect monopolies and receive subsidies. This affects the character not just of the post-totalitarian economic and bureaucratic elite, but the very nature of the economic and state institutional systems they construct and manage.

Most, though not all, members of the late-totalitarian elite have maintained their positions in the post-totalitarian elite. Everywhere there is more continuity in the economic elite than in the political elite, although there is a difference of degree between East-Central Europe and the former Soviet Union where there is a greater degree of elite retention. This is particularly obvious in the political realm, where most Russian politicians were members of the Communist elite, while in East-Central Europe there are genuine alternative political elites that win elections. In 1993, in Poland and Hungary, about a quarter of the late-totalitarian elite became businessmen, around 20% were managers and professionals and about 15% were directors in the state sector. Only about 5% went into politics and about a quarter retired, early or according to their age. In comparison, in Russia, a quarter of the late totalitarian *nomenklatura* were managers in the state sector in addition to a quarter in politics. Only 2, 4 and 8% respectively, of the Russian, Hungarian and Polish *nomenklatura* experienced any downward mobility by 1993 (Wasilewski 1998). Russian estimates of late Soviet elite continuity are half to two thirds in business and 80–5% in local politics and in administrative elites (Gel'man and Tarusina 2003: 196). The late-totalitarian elite that prospered after totalitarianism prepared or anticipated the fall of communism if not its form and timing by 'nest-feathering', transforming itself into a class of 'businessmen', cashing in on patronage networks to position themselves favourably in the privatisation process. Others benefited from the weak state to become a mafia, or became reformed social democrats in Bulgaria, Hungary, Lithuania, Poland and Slovakia (Higley *et al.* 2002).

One interesting move is the *double* conversion of political elites during the Gorbachev era into economic elites and then back into politics. This is the accepted view among Russian scholars who talk of *nomenklatura* capitalism, *nomenklatura* democracy and *nomenklatura* organised crime. About three-fifths of the business elite, half of the deputies, about 75% of the administrative elite, and more than 80% of the regional elite in Yeltsin's Russia were former *nomenklatura*. Many of the non-*nomenklatura* post-totalitarian members of the Russian elite were members of the '*prenomenklatura*,' deputies of *nomenklatura* members, who effectively received their promotion into the *nomenklatura* after the end of totalitarianism, thus demonstrating the survival and continuity not just of the elite, but also of the class hierarchy it was based on. Only 16 per cent of the Russian elite have never held *nomenklatura* or *prenomenklatura* positions. The collapse of the Soviet Union seems to have accelerated promotions. Consequently, the elite are younger by an average of eight years. Under Brezhnev there was correlation between age and status – in short, a gerontocracy. Under Gorbachev, age distributions became more even while under Yeltsin there was a reversal amounting to a revolution of the younger *nomenklatura* (White and Kryshtanovskaya 1998: 135).

The continuities from the late- to the post-totalitarian era are hardly surprising. They fit the general pattern of elite retention and replacement that Dogan and Higley (1998) observed across historical contexts and periods: the higher the hierarchical level of the examined social class, the higher the rate of replacement. By sector, there is more replacement among the political elite than among other elites such as the bureaucracy, the business elite or the clergy. There is more replacement at the political centre, the capital, than in the provinces. The longevity of the regime determines whether there are readily available alternative elites. Change of elites can only happen when there is a reservoir of counterelites, notably absent in post-communist societies (Dogan and Higley 1998: 21–3). These variables explain the variations between the former Soviet Union and the rest of former communist Europe by the longevity of the regime there, though the differences need not be exaggerated. In Poland (Łoś and Zybertowicz 2000: 111)

the post-1989 transformation was a conversion of political assets into economic ones ... The bulk of the *nomenklatura* class succeeded in retaining its dominant position by exerting control over the spontaneous and formal privatization processes, capital formation, and creation of new economic and financial institutions. A smaller but still significant segment of the former political *nomenklatura* (approximately one-quarter) managed to hold on to their senior decision-making posts in various domains of public life during the succession of Solidarity-led governments in the 1989–1993 period. The ex-communist elite access to political power rapidly expanded, however, in the wake of their electoral victories of 1993 and 1995, resulting in a near-monopoly of power at all levels of public and economic administration that lasted until the September 1997 general elections. In short, they appear to have initially traded their political capital for economic capital and then used the latter to regain political power.

Similar processes can be detected in other post-communist countries where the immediate post-1989 governments were not communists, e.g. Hungary.

Elite continuity is typical of post-totalitarian societies, even ones that passed directly from revolutionary totalitarianism to post-totalitarianism without going through late-totalitarianism courtesy of a foreign intervention, such as West Germany. This is because totalitarian regimes eliminate any actual or potential competitive elite and strictly control all the channels (educational, bureaucratic etc.) through which new elites may emerge. After just twelve years of totalitarianism in Germany, denazification was impossible because there were no non-Nazi elites to take over from the Nazi or collaborationist members of the elite. The Western powers therefore were forced to either rule directly, an expensive option, or allow former Nazi bureaucratic elites to hold on to power. Thorough change, i.e. actual elite replacement, took place only in West German politics and the media, just as in post-communist post-totalitarianism (Hoffmann-Lange 1998a, 1998b).

The continuity in social stratification and the absence of violence lead me to conclude that there was no social revolution in 1989–91. As George Lawson notes in his introduction, the only the country where the end of communism was accompanied by violence, Romania, actually displayed some of the highest rates of elite continuity in Eastern Europe; during the 1990s the Romanian political elite continued to be communist. Though Armbruster exaggerates the extent of revolutionary change in the post-communist universe, he is right that in the global geopolitical realm there indeed was a revolution, a radical discontinuity with the past, a new order and a new hierarchy. However, this global 1989 revolution trickled down slowly to post-communist societies through the opening of borders. In the case of Russia, the trickle had not managed to reform society significantly before resurgent old elites managed to close down the shutters and isolate society again behind a barricade made of exported commodities.

Russian restoration, Chinese convergence

One classical interpretation of nineteenth-century European history holds that England and France were moving in the same democratic liberal direction and, indeed, ended the century with similar political orientations. The difference, so goes the argument, was that Britain arrived at the franchise and democracy via gradual reforms, while France went through a tumultuous century of revolution and restoration, only to reach the same destiny. Looking at Russia and China today, one can develop a similar 'counter-Whig' theory. The political and social structures of China and Russia towards the end of the first decade of the twenty-first century display an increasing similarity, indeed a convergence, although China reached its current state gradually (with the single exception of the 1989 upheaval), while Russia went through a cycle of revolution and restoration. Both Russia and China display the *adaptation of the social and economic rights of the late totalitarian political elite to its interests*. In China this was achieved gradually and with explicit approval of the highest totalitarian echelon that assured the *nomenklatura* and the cadres that privatising and becoming private entrepreneurs would be free of political risk. In Russia, there was no such instruction or guarantee from the top. Consequently, factions of the Russian elite resorted to using fronts, while other factions abstained from taking advantage of the changing circumstances altogether. By the new century, when the absence of risk became obvious and new assets to appropriate became scarce, the Russian *nomenklatura* set to make a final readjustment of their rights to their interests by appropriating the most lucrative properties. To do that, as well as to control the extraction of new wealth from the soil, the KGB sought political power. The Putin Restoration can then be called equally the Putin readjustment of the KGB economic rights to its interests and political status. This Russian restoration was facilitated by developments in the world economy and by the rise in the price of commodities since 2001.

Rather than a transition to democracy, Russia and China display regime convergence. Both countries display greater continuity with late-totalitarianism in terms of social stratification and political regime type than hitherto acknowledged. Both transitions resulted in the adaptation of the economic and political rights of the late-totalitarian elite to its interests, albeit in different geographic and economic environments.

The Russian restoration

Russia is interesting because, unlike other post-totalitarian societies, the immediate post-totalitarian elite of the so-called oligarchs did not appear to be continuous with the late-totalitarian Soviet elite of the 1980s. While the adaptation of the late-communist elite's rights to its interests was quite smooth in the Eastern European satellites of the Soviet empire, in Russia itself, this adaptation was far less smooth, progressing and retreating spasmodically until settling under Putin's Restoration.

The decline and fall of late-totalitarianism started in Russia in the second half of the 1980s. Unlike the later, abrupt revolutions in East Central Europe, the process in Russia was gradual and appeared open-ended to the agents who participated in it. The actors who made the proverbial Russian 'transition' did not know it anymore than the people who made the Renaissance or the Industrial Revolution were conscious of the epochal changes they participated in (Clark 2000).

Once it became clear in 1989 that the governing elite of the Soviet Union would not protect its vassals in East Central Europe, the local elites moved quickly to adapt their rights to their interests, and trans-mute political into economic capital. When communism fell in Eastern Europe, it was obvious that changes were irreversible. Therefore, the adaptation of the rights of the elite to its interests was risk-free. In a

climate of 'new thinking', the 'Sinatra Doctrine' and the Polish roundtable negotiations in the summer of 1989, it became obvious that the
Soviet Union would not intervene to protect its satellites. By contrast,
when the Russian elite adapted its rights to its interests, it was far from
clear how risky this would be. During the Kosygin era in the Soviet
Union, similar economic measures to Gorbachev's were introduced.
However, these were subsequently reversed to the extent that participants had their careers blocked, or, on occasion, were jailed. Indeed,
the Russian *nomenklatura* of the 1980s would have perceived a trend
in Russian history towards failure of reform or mitigation of autocracy.
This historical experience would have led them to predict not just the
failure of Gorbachev's reforms, but also an ensuing autocratic backlash
against reformers (Shevtsova 2007: 7).

The late totalitarian elite were almost by definition risk averse, and
so wished to separate risk-taking from profiting. They achieved this
separation of risk from gain by using fronts that were not so risk averse,
partly for reason of character and temperament, and partly because
they existed on the margins of the elite and so had less to lose. The
fronts assumed the risk in return for some of the profits. Hoffman
(2003: 112) explains that Mikhail Khodorkovsky's early customers
felt they could trust the young *Komsomol* official because they knew
who he was fronting for and that he was being backed by elements of
the elite. Indeed, in the late Soviet environment, businesspeople could
not operate without some protection from the Party and the KGB.
Additionally, there is plenty of evidence for collusion between the oligarchs and elements within the KGB: KGB personnel acted as spies,
obtaining insider knowledge about competitors and firms, sometimes
from the files of the KGB, or acted as commanders of private militias
in the service of the interests of the oligarchs (Hoffman 2003: 159,
160, 165, 272–3).

By and large, wealth in goods and cash was controlled by *nomenklatura* managers. Without access to this wealth, no oligarch would have
had anything to buy or anything to sell. The *nomenklatura*, especially
the managers, made deals with the fronts, who already had protection
from elements in the hierarchy, to assume the risk of selling nominally
state property for a profit in exchange for sharing the spoils. Banking
fronts like Khodorkovsky's could also serve as conduits between the
Communist Party and KGB bosses who embezzled liquid assets and
foreign bank accounts. The last two treasurers of the Soviet Communist
Party were defenestrated or committed suicide. With them disappeared the liquid wealth of the Soviet Communist Party (Hoffman
2003: 125).

After the collapse of the Soviet Union, many within the *nomenklatura*, especially the managers, government bureaucrats and KGB officers who collaborated with them, were able to take the necessary steps to adapt their rights to their interests. They spontaneously privatised the properties they managed for the state. They diverted the cash flow of income, especially from exports, to themselves, took over natural resources by selling them to themselves or their representatives for low prices, stripped the assets of the companies they managed, and took loans from the state bank without intending to repay them, thus fuelling hyperinflation. The Russian voucher scheme, as elsewhere, was a political tool to win popularity for privatization. But voucher holders never challenged, or could have challenged, the control of the managers who used de facto property rights to trump those of the legal holders of the rights in the absence of the rule of law. Some managers used company funds to buy the vouchers. New investment funds managed and subsequently stole the vouchers of ordinary citizens. The same happened in all post-totalitarian societies, democratic or not, for a simple reason – because it was rational if not moral for the elite to behave in this way under the post-totalitarian conjuncture of a weak state and an absent rule of law. Even the cultural legacies of the Habsburg monarchy were no match for such an admixture.

It was in no one's interest to obtain outright ownership rights that came with the assumption of debts, liabilities and risks. As Boris Berezovsky put it, 'in Russia, the first treasure to be privatized would be profit, then property, and finally debt' (Hoffman 2003: 285). Berezovsky was clear – the first thing he wanted was a company's cash flow, followed only later, if at all, by the demands of ownership. The liberated *nomenklatura* was able to forsake the weaker sectors of the Russian population, bail out of the late-communist social contract that guaranteed minimal welfare rights to all (at least those who did not resist the political order), and cut social provision to pensioners, children, education and health services. The banks received money from the government to pay salaries to nurses, miners, teachers and pensioners, but stole the money or delayed its delivery. Even during the later part of the Putin Restoration, when Russia received huge incomes from selling commodities and the state finally began to pay pensions regularly, as well as increased the budget for welfare, health and education, the weakest elements in Russian society had still not recovered from the deprivations of 1991–2004. They were simply too far down the 'pyramid of patronage' (Shevtsova 2007: 149–59).

Yet, this spontaneous redistribution of economic rights was not commensurable with the political class structure of the late-totalitarian

Soviet party-state-society. Some branches of the KGB and the *nomen-klatura* failed to adapt their rights to their interests, failed to see where their opportunities were and, therefore, failed to take advantage of them (Aron 2007: 294). Before the Putin Restoration, some parts of the *nomenklatura*, especially those in the security services who were particularly risk averse, or rigid, or not very bright and entrepreneurial, did not join in the fun. As such, they were left behind while less well-connected and less powerful Russians became wealthy. It may have appeared to some of the oligarchs that they had become 'real' rather than mere fronts, that they could depose the old communist *nomenklatura*, even the KGB, elite. However, they failed to find an alternative power base within Russia. They managed to temporarily neutralise some of the old *nomenklatura* and certainly enriched themselves immensely. However, there was entrenched elite continuity in all branches of government. When the opportunity came, following the financial meltdown of 1998, the old elite staged a restoration. Arguably, following the restoration, the entire Russian bureaucracy has privatised itself. Bureaucrats used their positions to enrich themselves through collecting bribes for decisions and used their control of budgets to purchase goods from their family and friends at inflated prices. Bureaucrats bought their positions according to their expected income from corruption. The situation, therefore, is one of systemic corruption, the kind of corruption that keeps the system of government churning because corrupt bureaucrats support and indeed make up the existing political order. No ruler of Russia under the present regime can clean up the corruption, or undermine their own power base and introduce separation of powers, independent judiciary and press (Shevtsova 2007: 59–61, 70).

Once the oligarchic risk-takers became the big winners of the post-totalitarian era, especially after 1996, they sought to separate their growing fortunes from their backers within the *nomenklatura*. The Putin Restoration corrected this situation by abolishing the fronts and 'returning' the best assets in terms of cash flow to the *nomenklatura*, in particular the KGB elite. The post-2000 restoration can be seen, therefore, as a belated, but final, adaptation of the rights of the KGB elite to their interests, requiring a recovery of some of the property rights that had been redistributed after 1991. Russian economic stratification since 2000 is increasingly isomorphic to the social-political stratification of late-totalitarian Soviet Russia. To rule Russia, Putin needed to control communications and natural resources. Both were in the hands of the oligarchs of the Yeltsin era who grew over-confident, ceased to front for powers behind the scenes and did not share their wealth, trusting the state to protect them. They did not realise that the state was about to come under new management with a solid power base in the security services. Putin's first move was to take over television from Vladimir Gusinsky. He then exiled Berezovsky, jailed Khodorkovsky and expropriated virtually all oil and gas companies. For Russians, it became obvious that the old elite was back (Hoffman 2003: 480–1). In a sense, the 1990s were an exception in Russian history in generating a short period of differentiation between economic and political status. The Putin Restoration restored this strong correlation between political power and economic wealth. If wealth is patrimony granted by the state, it can be taken away just as easily as it can be given (Aron 2007: 219–35; Shevtsova 2007: 3).

Post-totalitarian elite adaptations of rights to interests, spontaneous privatisation, and the transfer of private assets to the state resulted in macroeconomic crises in practically all post-communist economies. After a severe economic crisis and a devaluation of the local currency, governments have been forced to reform their market regulations, often distancing themselves from banks and insurance companies, and imposing some measure of the rule of law. In Russia, however, the 1998 crisis did not lead to much restructuring and rationalising of the market because the rise in oil price and other commodities followed shortly after the crisis. The resulting cash flow filled the pockets of the *nomenklatura*. The cash flow from commodities exports allowed the *nomenklatura* to adapt its rights to its interests without having to compromise and reform. As much as Putin and his clan had to control communications to have political control over Russia, they needed to control oil and gas (Russia's cash flow) in order to achieve economic control. Therefore, the Russian government proceeded to expropriate the natural resources that had been privatised before. This is not a 're-nationalisation' in the sense of a return of state ownership that can then use the cash flow as it would use income tax to pay for its functioning, services and infrastructure development, as one can talk of the national oil company of Norway. Rather this is a re-privatisation in which a different clan comes to control the natural resources and the cash flow that they generate, first for its own benefits, next as a source of political patronage, and finally for strategic interests. Virtually all the bureaucrats around President Putin double as managers of large state-controlled (directly or indirectly) corporations (Shevtsova 2007: 107–8).

The age of the front oligarchs under Yeltsin, particularly during his second term, gave way under Putin to the era of bureaucratic oligarchs, a group which controlled the main monopolies while running the country in the interests of their faction. The cash flow from commodities allowed the government to continue subsidising inefficient parts of the economy, while also financing corruption and embezzlement without recourse to either printing much money or borrowing it from abroad. Indeed, there was so much money in Russia that the elite did not even mind paying pensioners and nurses, in effect restoring the revoked late-communist social contract whereby the elite guaranteed minimal welfare in return for political acquiescence. This system of patronage can continue to thrive as long as the petro-dollars continue to flow in. If – and when – income from commodities falls significantly and durably, the restoration regime will come under severe strain.

The global economic crisis and the sharp fall in the prices of commodities in late 2008 have begun to put pressure on the Putin Restoration. Although the lakes of cash that have been accumulated during the flood years can still feed the trickle-down ravines of the patronage economy, it is unclear how long this can last given the depth of the global recession and the ensuing collapse in demand for commodities. Perhaps even more significant is the *perception* of the Russian elite of the scale of the recession. If it expects cash flows to resume before reserves are depleted, it will attempt to maintain the present regime, perhaps economising with patronage and increasing the oppression of political opponents to project strength against opponents who may think they have a better chance against a weakened elite. If, on the other hand, the elite expect the reduction in cash flows from commodity exports to last into the foreseeable future, it will act to protect its interests. The first victims would be the politically weakest parts of Russian society, pensioners, teachers etc. – the trickle-down effect of state patronage will be blocked. At the same time, the state would have to economise on expenses, most notably those which do not affect directly the elite, such as foreign aggression. It would have to devote more resources for domestic oppression as increasing sections of the population become disaffected (Foroohar 2009). If, despite these measures, cash reserves continue to deplete, different clans within the elite will attempt to appropriate what is left before it is all gone. In such a case, a collapse of the Russian state will be quick, much like the end of the Soviet Union or the collapse of the Yeltsin regime following the 1998 financial meltdown. A more optimistic scenario would suggest that, in response to economic constraints, the Russian state will be reformed, the financial haemorrhage of elite corruption will be blocked and the various inefficiencies within Russia's economy that result from corruption will be eliminated through the introduction of the rule of law, an end to corrupt subsidies and a restructuring and diversification of production. However, this is unlikely. There is no significant group within Russian society with both the interest and power to effect such reforms – no civil society and no elite beyond those with short-term unenlightened self-interest.

The Putin Restoration is instructive because it presents as an ideal type the utopia of the *nomenklatura*, the kind of regime that the late-totalitarian elite would have liked to bring about everywhere. In the atypical case of Russia, the late-totalitarian elite, Putin's *siloviki*, did not suffer from any of the constraints that beset other late-totalitarian elites as they passed into the post-totalitarian era. Unlike Northern European post-communist countries, there has been hardly any civil society and no alternative elites to consider. The commodity boom released the elite from economic constraints that could have forced them to reform the economy or introduce some rule of law.

Leon Aron (2007: 236–51), perhaps the originator of the phrase 'the Putin Restoration', characterises the defining properties of the Putin regime as: establishment of 'a vertical of power'; the re-subjugation of the legislature and the judiciary; and the centralisation of power from the regions to the executive centre in the Kremlin. Politically, Putin reduced the number of senators, raised the threshold for entry into parliament to 7 per cent, prohibited the creation of party blocs to pass this threshold, eliminated single mandate seats in favour of party lists, eliminated regional elections, rigged elections in general, and used the mass media to manipulate the electorate. Opposition candidates could be excluded from elections for reasons as frivolous as spelling mistakes on official forms or expressing opinions that could be branded 'extremist'. Opposition demonstrations were suppressed by force and no expression of opposition either inside or outside the Duma was permitted. Putin's regime also abolished referenda, the election protest box for 'none of the above', and the minimum turnout that was required to validate elections. The Russian president gained control over the body that appoints and may dismiss judges, and judges have been pressured by the state to rule in its interest. Through the United Russia Party, Putin and his elite managed to achieve a practical monopoly over politics. The result is 'nonpolitics', where there is no real opposition, but imitation opposition that is designed by the regime itself (Shevtsova 2007: 47–51).

Aron also notes the non-totalitarian aspects of the Putin Restoration: religious freedom, including freedom of worship and freedom to practise religious education, free emigration and travel abroad, the emergence of some non-political independent civil organisations and, on a local level, private property and private enterprise. By 2007, some of these liberal achievements had been reversed. The Kremlin cracked down on independent political protests and genuine political opposition groups such as the Other Russia organisation. Protesters and party leaders were arrested in demonstrations, perhaps because the Kremlin was sufficiently insecure to be afraid of a Russian-style Orange Revolution, or perhaps because the Kremlin clan wanted to send a message of toughness to competing clans by attacking the opposition (Shevtsova 2007: 276–7). NGOs have become the target of bureaucratic dirty tricks designed to shut them down, especially NGOs with foreign connections. Journalists who oppose the government and expose official corruption have been murdered, though there is still some freedom for the printed press in Russia.

It is possible to unite these diverse late-totalitarian, authoritarian and liberal characteristics of the Putin Restoration by distinguishing popular rights and liberties that are of no interest to the *siloviki* security forces elite (freedom of religion and the printed press, and the right to emigrate) from rights and liberties that could conflict with their interests, power and wealth (fair elections, the independence of the judiciary and a free electronic media). In the post-totalitarian utopia of the *nomenklatura*, the first kinds of freedoms are granted, while the second are withheld.

Chinese adaptation

A comparison with China is particularly instructive. It is possible to observe a kind of convergence between the current political and social structure of Russia and China. In both countries the late-totalitarian elite has successfully adapted its rights to its interests, transmuting its political capital into economic and social capital. However, unlike in Russia, the transmutation of the Chinese political elite into economic elite has been smooth. The Chinese *nomenklatura* has not given up political power even temporarily or partially, nor has it had to create oligarchic fronts. Apart from the Tiananmen Square episode, late-totalitarian China has not passed through political discontinuities, crises or radical liberalisation. Still, in both countries, the late-totalitarian elite controls politics and the economy for its own benefit, political pluralism is very limited, though there is some free print media and freedom to emigrate.

The Chinese and Russian economies are different of course. The first is based on manufacturing and cheap labour, while the second is based on cash flows from exporting commodities. Accordingly, the Chinese elite must 'work', or at least rent out, its workers to foreign investors. Russia has already gone through modernisation, industrialisation and urbanisation, while China still has large rural pre-modern populations. Fears of masses of downtrodden rural poor overwhelming the cities and starting a communist, or at least egalitarian, revolution have led the Chinese elite to be less tolerant than the Russian elite of emerging civil society, including religious groups. Having missed a liberal phase, the Chinese state has not attempted to create a Russian-like Potemkin democracy founded on controlled artificial negativity. But otherwise, politically and socially, the two regimes resemble each other more than they resemble other regimes.

The reason for the different historical trajectories of Russia and China prior to their current convergence lies in the different risk assessments of the Chinese and Russian elites when the opportunities to adapt their rights to their interests emerged. In Russia, the process seemed open-ended and risky. Partial reforms were attempted in the 1920s, 1950s, 1960s and 1980s, only to fail and be reversed. Åslund (2007: 38–40) suggests that the failure of Gorbachev's economic reforms in the first couple of years of his reign forced him to attempt political reforms. In such a risky environment, part of the Russian elite did not act on its interests because it wrongly assessed the risks involved and was risk averse. Another part of the elite sought risk-taking fronts, which led to the rise of the oligarchs. Later, when the actual absence of risk became evident, a further adjustment of economic rights to political muscle became necessary. Securing the newly acquired economic rights of the old-new elite required, at least from their perspective, late-totalitarian political control, and hence the return of late-totalitarian politics to Russia.

By contrast, in China, after the Cultural Revolution and the establishment of Deng Xiaoping's regime, it was made clear by the highest echelons of the Communist Party that 'wealth is glorious'. As such, its pursuit was risk free. Further, in the aftermath of the Cultural Revolution and the demise of the 'Gang of Four', the Communist Party and especially its conservative elements were demoralised and weak; they offered little resistance to Deng's policies. Åslund suggests that, following the Cultural Revolution, the Chinese bureaucracy was also more disciplined than the late-totalitarian Soviet bureaucracy. The Chinese *nomenklatura* could adjust its rights to its interests without fear, smoothly and gradually, without the kind of radical shifts that Russia experienced. Deng made it clear that political reform would not be tolerated, but that economic reform was safe. He and his clique allowed the *nomenklatura* to corrupt, thereby winning its support. As Solnik (1996) argues, the key difference between the Chinese and Russian bureaucracies is that the Chinese corrupt official has been a kind of shareholder of, and tax collector for, the central bureaucracy and so has had an interest in preserving the centralised hierarchy, whereas the

Russian corrupt official needs to break down hierarchical links in order to become rich. The rise in official Chinese corruption has also generated popular resentment of the party and demands for the rule of law, culminating in the upheavals of 1989, the Tiananmen Square massacre, and further unrest in the countryside since (Sun 2004).

One of the legacies of totalitarianism in China, as in Russia, is the lack of differentiation between political and economic elites. China's 'red capitalists' were either high- or middle-ranking Communist Party officials who became entrepreneurs, or relatives of such officials who turned political capital into economic capital by privatising the state, turning its assets into family businesses and using public property as if it was private. As Dickson (2003: 15) writes, 'In addition to blatant corruption, local officials earn income by being partners or board members of local enterprises, by opening their own enterprises, by extorting taxes and fees from farmers and firms, or requiring matchmaker fees to facilitate joint ventures and trade.' The Chinese word for this transformation of political into economic capital is *xiahai*, literally 'plunging into the sea'. Since 2001, the opposite movement, from success in the private economy into membership and co-option in the Communist Party, assures the same merger of economic and political elites, only from a less traditional direction. On a local level, a kind of corporatist order has emerged in which private and public, Communist Party and private entrepreneur appear to have merged (Dickson 2003).

The Russian and Chinese models of post-totalitarianism converge and are socially and politically continuous with late-totalitarianism. In both cases, and unlike post-authoritarian societies, the late-totalitarian elite sought to adjust the rights it had inherited from the revolutionary elite to its interests. In Russia, this process emerged spontaneously. It was unclear how risky it was, and therefore it took a decade for the economic stratification of society to clearly reflect its political stratification. In China, the adjustment was not spontaneous, but directed from above, and therefore smooth and continuous. Irrespective, therefore, of the spontaneity of the adjustment and the different geographical, cultural and historical contexts in which restoration occurred, the process of adjustment of the rights of the late-totalitarian elite to its interests concluded successfully in both cases with economic status reflecting political status.

Conclusions

The revisionist interpretation of the emergence of British democracy advocated by the likes of Jonathan Clark (2000) suggests that democracy emerged as an unintended consequence of confessional struggles about Catholicism and dissent in the eighteenth century. Likewise, arguably the collapse of communist late-totalitarianism and the successful entrenchment of democracy in East Central Europe emerged as the unintended consequences of the spontaneous adaptation of the rights of the late-totalitarian elite to its interests, a process that started slowly well before the end of totalitarianism, but commenced in earnest in Russia under Gorbachev.

The collapse of totalitarianism was elite-driven. From the perspective of the late-totalitarian elite, democracy was an unintended consequence of their quest to adapt their rights to their interests, to be able to transmute their control over state property into private property, accumulate it, and be able to pass it on to their families. The vital interests of the elite did not extend to choice of a particular form of government and direct control of the state, except in cases where the principal sources of cash flow came from exporting commodities, as in Russia and central Asia. Even after forsaking high politics and the media, the Central-East European late-totalitarian elite maintained control over most social institutions, using that control to become wealthy and insure itself against retributive justice. There was no need for it to become involved directly in politics or to draw attention to itself.

1989 was actually more global but less revolutionary than has hitherto been acknowledged. The process of adjustment of rights to interests of the late-totalitarian elite was global, from China through Russia to Central Europe. However, it was gradual rather than disruptive or revolutionary. The spontaneity of the process in the Soviet Union, and the indifference of the *nomenklatura* to political and social changes that did not clash with its interests, created the appearance of radical change. However, below the political upheavals, deeper social and economic processes have been taking place at a more even pace. Eventually, they led to the same goal, the self-liberation of the *nomenklatura*, the adjustment of its rights to its interests, the conversion of its political capital to economic capital and its establishment as a ruling class.

8   One world, many cold wars: 1989 in the Middle East

Richard Saull

Introduction

1989 is, rightly, regarded as a momentous year in the history of modern world politics. By its end the twin logics of the Cold War – superpower geopolitical rivalry and ideological antagonism – no longer dominated international relations as they had done since the collapse of the wartime grand alliance. The geopolitical and ideological reordering of Europe signalled by the overthrow of communist power in East-Central Europe was quickly globalised, as the effects of the changes unleashed within Europe rippled across the world. Whilst this assisted the resolution of a number of regional conflicts involving the superpowers, it also exposed a number of states in the South – formerly allied to the USSR – to an international context where they could no longer count on the Soviet military, diplomatic and economic support that had helped them maintain a significant degree of political and economic autonomy, and without which most could no longer do. Without these sources of external support, most of the states opted for reform programmes that were to lead them towards a much greater involvement in the international capitalist system as economic spaces formerly removed from the socio-economic relations of capitalist development were brought into a global logic of accumulation.[1]

Whilst not seeking to question the historical and global significance of 1989, something which would be intellectually and politically unfeasible, this chapter will problematise the *determining* impact of the events of 1989 in shaping the character of contemporary world politics and those prevailing theoretical arguments upon which such a reading is based. In particular, the chapter focuses on how an alternative reading of the *ends* of the Cold War in parts of the South, most of which

Thanks to George Lawson for comments on an earlier draft of this chapter. The usual disclaimers apply.

[1] For an extended discussion of these developments see Chapters 2 and 5 in this volume.

pre-dated the events of 1989 in Europe, have conditioned the character of post-Cold War world politics in parallel to, and in contradiction with, the events of 1989 in Europe. Involving distinct forms of social and political agency and, consequently, distinct logics of politics, these developments are suggestive of a novel way of contextualising '1989' and post-Cold War world politics.

As with John Hobson's chapter in this volume (Chapter 1), my argument is that '1989' rests on viewing world politics through a distinctly Eurocentric prism based on the assumption that dominant currents of world politics – at least until the last two decades of the twentieth century – are driven or inspired by the outcome of events and conflicts geographically focused on Europe and its immediate periphery. Consequently, developments elsewhere – and in the global South in particular – tend to be subordinated within changes initiating from the developments emerging from, or through the resolution of, conflict within the core states of the world.[2] Further, and relatedly, such a view rests on a conceptual explanatory hierarchy framed on the determining role of the major powers in shaping the character of world politics and, more generally, in theorising world politics as the outcomes of inter-state relationships.

The problem with such a view is that there was no equivalent of the 'European 1989' in the South. This is not to suggest that the political (liberal democracy) and economic (capitalist markets) consequences associated with 1989 did not spread to the South, but that their temporal dynamic and political logic has been distinct and uneven, driven for the most part by specifically *local* dynamics. Thus, the economic element associated with 1989 – the geographical expansion of a particularly liberalised form of political economy in place of statist-developmental economic strategies – originated in the early 1980s from the debt crisis that engulfed the global financial system after 1982. Politically, the spread of liberal democracy in place of authoritarian dictatorship – of both left and right – was accelerated by the collapse of communist power through popular protest from below. Where democracy has been solidified over the last couple of decades, it has been in those locales that had a pre-1989 democratic tradition such as Latin America and parts of Central and Eastern Europe. And overall, the spread of substantive democratic structures throughout the South – especially in the Middle East and the wider Islamic world – has been both mixed and, in

---

[2] John Hobson's chapter (Chapter 1) focusing on the (Eurocentric) intellectual 'framing' and justifications for Western policy after 1989 leaves open the question of the agency associated with local actors, i.e. how ideas and policies were both realised and resisted 'on the ground'.

combination with the vicissitudes of neoliberalism, has produced populist anti-neoliberal forms of politics.

As such, by assigning global significance to 1989 as a temporal moment, we end up *de*-historicising the complexities, particularities and messiness of *asynchronous* historical change around the world, change which takes place at different times and places, driven by different socio-economic and political dynamics, and with more varied, even paradoxical outcomes. These moments and processes of change – many of which occurred prior to 1989 – are either ignored, swept aside or subsumed within a grand narrative of change which focuses on a particular moment (1989) in a particular locale (Europe). This may allow us to develop both parsimonious theories and neat storylines, but it will not help us build explanations which reflect the reality of developments on the ground, not least those which operated at different speeds and via alternative logics. Instead of privileging a sanitised, Eurocentric reading of 1989, this chapter outlines an alternative narrative which challenges the centrality of 1989 as the historical demarcation of contemporary world politics and makes central the differentiated character of the global South.

My argument proceeds in two main parts. First, I provide an alternative theoretical and historical framework for understanding the changing character of world politics in general and the Cold War and its closing stages in particular. This is followed by a historical survey of political developments within the South – focusing on the Middle East and the Islamic world – as indicative of a region in which contemporary world politics has been less influenced by 1989 than by alternative moments and processes. In this way, I seek to substantiate the claim that 1989 is not the historical root of contemporary world politics *tout court*, at least not when viewed from the vantage point of the global South.

The shifting currents of world politics

The dominant interpretation of the global significance of 1989 tends to rest on a particular reading of the Cold War and, indeed, of world politics more generally. In turn, this interpretation is founded on a particular view of history and historical change. Thus, the Cold War is understood as a historical chapter within world politics based on the distinct geopolitical order of bipolarity conferred by the outcome of the Second World War. In this account, the political agents of 1989 – social movements based in revitalised 'civil societies' – are less important than the redrawing of geopolitical boundaries and geopolitical relations ushered in after the wall came tumbling down.

Although there has been a wealth of important analysis and argument about this development, most notably the debate between social
constructivists emphasising the explanatory power of ideas, subjectiv-
ity and the ideational construction (and deconstruction) of diplomatic
relations between the superpowers, and realists emphasising the continuing logic of strategic-military competition,[3] the often unstated
ontological assumption behind this debate is that an understanding
of the Cold War qua international relations is concerned with the
relations between states and, in particular, those between dominant
powers. Further, world history and historical change is collapsed into
macro-structural change at a systemic level involving the arrangements
between the major powers demonstrated by the way in which wars –
and their outcomes – between the Great Powers have been regarded
as the key moments of historical transformation in the international
system. Consequently, what was distinct about the Cold War as an episode in the history of the modern international system was the specific
geopolitical arrangements between the Great Powers – one of bipolarity rather than multipolarity or unipolarity (as has been the case since
the end of the Cold War) – and the particular ideological justifications
deployed by each superpower in its respective rivalry with the other. In
short, the Cold War (i.e. the historical period concluded by 1989) is, to
varying degrees, subsumed within the broader history of (recurrent)
Great Power rivalry.

In spite of its analytical parsimony and theoretical rigour, such an
ontology of the international sphere abstracts to such a degree that it
has to subsume the uneven, complex and contradictory developments
of world politics – identifiable in the relations between and within states
in different locales involving a multiplicity of political actors – such
that, theoretically and historically, the politics emanating from such
relations are given secondary, even cursory, significance. It is not, then,
just about the absence of how (capitalist) socio-economic development
figures in these accounts of the character of international system and
the Cold War,[4] nor how socio-economic development is related to and,
in part, conditions geopolitical relationships (note the varied geopolitical consequences of the way in which the geographical space of Europe

---

[3] Thus the debate on the end of the Cold War – in spite of the surprising and distinct
manner of its ending – did not fundamentally question the prevailing understanding
of what the Cold War was, instead concerning itself with explaining why the superpowers – and the USSR in particular – behaved the way they did. See Koslowski and
Kratochwil (1994); Risse-Kappen (1994); Wohlforth (1994); Brooks and Wohlforth
(2000 and 2008).

[4] Interestingly with regard to the relationship between geopolitical order and socio-
economic reproduction, the origins and spread of neoliberal globalisation – one, if not

was organised socio-economically after 1945),[5] but also the tendency to overlook the international significance of wider forms of agency other than those institutionalised within states. Thus, the analytical and political hierarchy that follows from state-centrism screens out alternative currents of politics, while the assumption that the social and political space within states is hermetically sealed renders international politics co-terminous with inter-state diplomacy. Although it may be the case that Egypt's formal diplomatic relations with the United States and Israel have major, perhaps even prior, material consequences on regional politics, this does not mean that we should occlude other political currents that do not result in the redrawing of geopolitical boundaries but which do affect the fabric of international relations in the region.

In this sense, the heart of the problem in determining the influence of 1989 on *global* politics is that by subordinating and/or erasing distinct logics of politics grounded in different conceptions of political agency and socio-economic organisation, a state-centric ontology is unable to identify patterns of change – and their consequences – below the level of macro-structural/geopolitical transformation. Indeed, by focusing on 1989 as a moment of fundamental transformation, we overlook not only the fact that superpower geopolitical rivalry and ideological competition had effectively ceased by that time in other parts of the world, thus effectively *foreshadowing* the consequences of the events in East-Central Europe later on, but also that these relations concluded in a variety of fashions quite different in character and outcome from the mobilisations from below that overthrew communist rule in East-Central Europe and which laid the basis for the establishment of liberal-democratic capitalist states. Further, the ending of these other 'cold wars' not only had an impact on geopolitical conflict between the superpowers (contributing to the political logic finally revealed in 1989 within the Soviet bloc),[6] it also laid the foundations for novel political dynamics of conflict and resistance that have, with the passage of time, had a greater impact

the, defining aspect of the post-Cold War international order – emerged within the Cold War context. Thus, globalisation was a factor in the latter part of the Cold War and, during the 1980s, was a defining issue in the political economy of much of the South during an era of continued geopolitical competition and rivalry. Consequently, the impact of 1989 on much of the South was mediated by the ongoing changes and impact of the earlier transformation in the international political economy from the early 1980s, which was itself a consequence of the collapse of the post-war Bretton Woods system in the early 1970s.

[5] For an alternative attempt to conceptualise world politics at a systemic level but which incorporates the 'unevenness' of historical development alongside understanding of the socio-economic and political composition of states, see Rosenberg (2006).

[6] Notably with regard to the post-Mao turn in China towards a gradual opening and integration into the operation of the capitalist world market, complemented by the

on international political developments within those regions than the events of 1989 themselves.

What this suggests, contra the prevailing theoretical and historical rendition of 1989, is that world politics during and after the Cold War was – and is – far more complex and varied temporally than is often considered to be the case. Such a conceptualisation recognises the importance of 1989, but also raises the significance of other political processes, such that the impact of regionally derived events – changes of government/state leadership, revolutions, armed conflicts and peace treaties – have a greater impact than developments in the macro geopolitical order, at least in these locales. Thus, whilst the impact of 1989 was clear in East-Central Europe with the sweeping away of state-socialist authoritarian communist regimes and their replacement by new forms of statehood based on liberal-democratic political structures and capitalist-market economies, formations which were at least in part emulated in other parts of the world (note, for example the spread and consolidation of market democracies in parts of sub-Saharan Africa and Latin America), such changes were limited and, in some cases relatively insignificant.

Given this, how is one to make sense of the Cold War – of which the events of 1989 provide the final episode – without succumbing to mere description of the varieties of world politics? What binds the complexity of the Cold War as a period in world history is not just the global character of superpower competition, but the fact that the socio-economic, political and ideological properties of the states (and other political actors that participated in it) shared common features such that, although the United States and the USSR were the dominant actors in the international system, the tendencies revealed in their own socioeconomic and political reproduction were also revealed in the behaviour and orientation of these other political actors, including non-state actors.[7] Simply put, the political constitution and international relations of the superpowers were *symptomatic* of more generalised forms of politics that expanded and contracted over the course of the Cold War (Saull 2007: 1–15).[8] This is not to side with the propagandists in Moscow and Washington who claimed that 'oppositional' developments – be it the

---

termination of geopolitical and ideological confrontation with the United States by the late 1970s.

[7] See Halliday (1986) and Saull (2001).

[8] Such a conceptualisation of the international system over the course of the Cold War is equally applicable to other historical periods. For example, the politics of imperialism during the late nineteenth century saw the domestic socio-economic reproduction of a distinct constellation of class rule within the major capitalist states directly associated with international strategies of international competition and imperial rivalry.

Hungarian uprising of 1956 or the Cuban Revolution of 1959 – were authored or controlled by one or other superpower, but instead to recognise the complementarities in terms of the historical contexts out of which Cold War conflicts emerged, the similarities in the agents involved (such as revolutionary movements), the political objectives sought by both sides, and the wider character of the international relations that each bloc tried to promote. What made world history dominated by the Cold War after 1945, if not after 1917, was not just superpower policies of competition, rivalry and confrontation, but the role of other actors – social forces, political movements and so on – in sustaining this competition. As such the Cold War genuinely did contain a *global* logic.

Whilst the collapse of the wartime alliance after 1945 and the emergence of diplomatic hostility between Moscow and Washington are generally regarded as the historical setting for the origins of the Cold War, the politics and ideological outlook(s) associated with this hostility and conflict pre-date the post-war conjuncture. Most important to this was the emergence of the USSR as a distinct (revolutionary) state after 1917 and the suspicions this aroused in the capitalist world. As I have argued elsewhere (Saull 2007: 16–48), the interwar period was dominated by two logics of international conflict:

(1) inter-imperial rivalry based on the frictions and conflicts between the major capitalist states; and
(2) social-systemic competition between capitalist states and the USSR (and the wider, expanding international revolutionary movement).

Even after 1945, world politics continued to be more complex, shifting and uneven than bipolarity suggests and the term Cold War indicates.[9] Thus, the geopolitical confrontation identified as triggering the Cold War occurred within Europe and then *spread* to other parts of the world – initially East Asia – through the outbreaks of communist revolution.

Significantly, the agents and dynamics involved in the spread of the Cold War concerned *other* communist states (China and North Korea) and *non-state* communist-revolutionary movements (active throughout Asia), highlighting the fact that political and ideological currents

Likewise, these trends are notable in the 'decade of globalisation' in the 1990s, particularly with regard to the prescription of neoliberal structural adjustment policies in many parts of the South combined with the move away from social democracy within metropolitan capitalist states.

[9] Chapter 5, by Fred Halliday, hints at this but, ultimately, emphasises the centrality of the European 'theatre' of the Cold War and the determining significance of changes emanating from Europe on other parts of the world both in the period 1945–89 and subsequently.

associated with the superpowers were actively promoted by other political actors. What determined the persistence of a logic of Cold War and its spread to new geographical areas was, in part, conditioned by the activities and policies of the superpowers. Most importantly, however, it was determined by the shifting balance of social forces within these distinct state locales. Thus, the Cold War 'emerged' or spread to different parts of the world, the result of which was the expansion and contraction of one or other socio-economic and political systems associated with, or allied to, each superpower.[10] And what *determined* the dynamic and evolution of the Cold War, therefore, were developments *within* states, most notably the moments of revolutionary crises that provided openings for revolutionary seizures of power. This resulted in the geographical expansion of the politics of Cold War, as these revolutionary states – to varying degrees – implemented socio-economic and political changes ensuing in major anti-capitalist transformations, placing them into an antagonistic relationship with the major capitalist powers as well as re-orientating them towards the Soviet bloc.

Whilst this dynamic was effectively responsible for the making of the Cold War as a global phenomenon, this logic was also maintained via the preservation of the particular domestic political and economic constitution of existing Cold War states, notably those states that had established communist rule. Further, whilst the 'conflict logic' of the Cold War spread from Europe to East Asia by 1949–50, it also co-existed in parallel with – and sometimes subsumed – other logics of politics, notably decolonisation and Third World nationalism (Westad 2005). Indeed, even whilst the Cold War was spreading to East Asia, other parts of the world were becoming *less conditioned* by the geopolitical-ideological logic of superpower confrontation and the dynamic of revolutionary change. Thus, by the late 1940s, the Cold War – understood as the spread of communist power and the threat of revolutionary crisis and seizure of state power – had effectively passed in Western Europe, such that politics within West European states was concerned with something very different to that of the inter-war period when the spectre of revolution had been a major political factor. And even as

---

[10] Whilst this may read as the political development of the post-colonial South becoming subject to the policies and ideologies of the superpowers – and the USSR in particular (as argued in Arne Westad's (2005) masterly survey of the Cold War in the Third World) – the point that needs emphasising is that there was no singular or pristine logic of Cold War. Rather, its historical evolution and geographical spread after 1917 witnessed not only the inflection of global struggle with particular instantiation, but also the development of relatively autonomous Cold War logics in various revolutionary states, all of which were linked to – but in some ways distinct from – the political, economic and ideological direction of Moscow.

the logic of Cold War was effectively over in Western Europe, Latin America, Africa and the Middle East had not yet been fully absorbed into its orbit.

In this sense, the Cold War was never global – at least not in the sense of capturing world historical time in the singular. Despite the global reach of the superpowers, it was never the case that all, indeed most, parts of the world were subject to a homogeneous logic of geopolitical-ideological rivalry. Further, the Cold War conflict co-existed with alternative logics of politics emergent from local moments, processes and conflicts. It also began and ended in different places, in different ways and at different times.

In sum, therefore, although the Cold War emerged within a distinctly European geographical milieu, its spread to other parts of the world saw the political logic of Cold War conflict inflected with the particular-ities of each new non-European geographical encounter. In doing so, a paradox was revealed. Whilst the geographical spread of Cold War conflict – witnessed in the involvement of the superpowers in new areas of the world – globalised the Cold War, it also ended up fragmenting the *singularity* of the Cold War by multiplying the revolutionary actors involved and introducing distinct political and ideological dimensions derived from each geographical locale and revolutionary experience. Consequently, we can talk of many cold wars – multiplicities of conflict in time and space – situated within a broader political and geopolit-ical logic of Cold War. The primary driver of these multiple cold wars was revolutions, particularly those led by communist movements, and it was the outcomes of each revolutionary process – linked to, but dis-tinct from, that of 1917 – where we should trace Cold War endings and the international consequences thereof. Whilst the spread of revolution served to augment Soviet geopolitical power after 1945 and to globalise the Cold War, their contradictions weakened Soviet power and brought the conflicts to an end. Therefore, whilst the collapse of revolutionary states between 1989–91 in Europe served to transform the *European* regional political context, this was much less the case in other regions where the experience of post-revolutionary states was (and has been) rather different. Whilst the European Cold War ended in 1989, the his-tory of other cold wars needs narrating from a different vantage point. It is to such experiences in the Middle East that I now turn.

Cold War endings in the Middle East

As the broad theoretical-historical framework I have outlined above suggests, world politics is much more complex, uneven and dynamic than the conventional narratives and conceptualisations of 1989 would recognise. Indeed, the logic of 1989 in terms of its relationship with the South has been mediated by particular social, economic and political dynamics contained within these locales. As such, the consequences of 1989 have run in parallel with and, at times, been absorbed or sub-ordinated into, locally driven logics that pre-date 1989. This section illustrates this point via dynamics contained within the Islamic World and the Middle East. My aim is to build a framework beyond *sui generis* historical description, but which retains sensitivity to the politics, peoples and states of the South.

The significance of focusing on the Islamic world and the Middle East is not to concur with Samuel Huntington's (1996) reading of post-Cold War world politics, nor his understanding of the Islamic world, but rather because it is here that the political logic of the last two-to-three decades appears markedly out of sync with the predominant narrative of 1989. Indeed, it is in the Middle East and the wider Islamic world that the political and ideological logic emergent from 1989 – the foreclosure of the revolutionary-insurrectionary mode of politics and the vindica-tion and promotion of liberal democracy and capitalist markets – has been most absent or at least contested. In addition, it is in the Middle East and the wider Islamic world where a pre-or-alternative political logic to that of 1989 is most visible, especially in the way that religiously inspired movements have become the principal sources of opposition to existing regimes and their sources of international support.

Across the Islamic world and the Middle East, the Cold War did not end in 1989. Indeed, rather than viewing 1989 as marking the triumph of market democracy (Fukuyama 1992), we could follow Gilles Kepel (2004: 9) in regarding it as the high-water mark of Islamist resurgence, indicated by the Islamist takeover of Sudan, the rise of Hamas in the Palestinian occupied territories, and the electoral victory of the FIS in Algeria, all of which reflected prior terminations of political struggles and conflict informed by a Cold War logic. These trends combined with the Soviet withdrawal from Afghanistan and the potential for fur-ther Islamist expansion in the Muslim republics of the disintegrating USSR. Some time before 1989, therefore, Soviet influence – and that of its local allies – had been effectively eclipsed in much of the Middle East and the wider Islamic world, thus inaugurating a rather different geopolitical, social and ideological dispensation to these regions than had been the case since the early 1950s.

It was not just the different historical timing of Cold War endings within the Islamic world and Middle East which helps us account for the character of post-Cold War *global* politics, but also the *manner* of these endings. Thus, whilst in East-Central Europe the Cold War ended with minimal violence largely through the popular mobilisations of a revitalised liberal civil society, in the Islamic world the Cold War ended in quite different fashion. In these locales, Soviet influence and the mobilising power of revolutionary and leftist movements were defeated not through the triumph of liberal democracy but rather through the crumbling of the post-colonial developmentalist state combined with, and in part caused by, the smashing of the wider political and secular left by violently illiberal political movements backed by regional states and, at a distance, by the United States.

The illiberal endings of cold wars in these zones bequeathed social and political movements openly hostile to liberal modernisation and incorp-oration into the US-led 'zone of peace' – the *sine qua non* of 1989. On the contrary, the main opposition movements able to mobilise masses 'on the street' tended to be concerned with articulating an alternative political vision, and which – for at least some of the currents within this Islamist tide[11] – were premised on forms of revolutionary organisa-tion and insurrectionary violence (Retort 2005) not too dissimilar from the pre-1989 revolutionary movements that 1989 was supposed to have buried. It was this ideological-political current that grabbed the world's attention in September 2001, a moment which marked the end of the post-Cold War interregnum (Cox *et al.* 1999).

The end of the Cold War in the Middle East

Although disputes as to the territorial integrity of both Turkey and Iran were early sources of Cold War tension between Washington and Moscow soon after the end of the Second World War, it was to take revolutionary change – as was the case elsewhere – to bring the Cold War to the region. In this case, the key development was the overthrow of the pro-Western Egyptian monarchy by the 'free officers' movement in 1952 which, combined with other cases of revolutionary change in the region (in Iraq and Syria in particular), laid the domestic political foundation for the regionalisation of the Cold War.

[11] An important caveat here is that, although one is able to distinguish a broad Islamist anti-imperialist current across much of the Middle East and the wider Islamic world, the jihadi or terrorist elements – particularly those associated with al-Qaeda – remain a small minority within this broader current. It is also important to note that the Islamic character of these movements is not only an understandable response to the failings of, and the corruption and violence perpetrated by a number of authoritarian pro-Western states in the Middle East, but also the only possible response due to the absence of alternative political spaces that could be filled by other, particularly leftist, political currents. See Ayoob (2008).

With the spread of revolutionary nationalism, a social and ideological rupture was established within the Middle East. This pitted the newly emerged radical nationalist states of the region and the revolutionary movements that they supported – committed to programmes of radical political and economic transformation – against the area's dominant classes, as well as the socially and politically conservative regimes of the region led by Saudi Arabia (and Iran). This regional divide conformed to a local antagonism akin to Cold War, though it was imbricated with local cultural, ideological and political dimensions (Heikal 1978). Thus, although the Arab nationalist regimes had volatile, fluctuating and – at some moments – highly conflicting relationships with indigenous pro-Soviet communist movements, they embarked on domestic political and economic transformations of an authoritarian and statist character which had much in common with the Soviet model, particularly in terms of attacking capitalist property relations. Furthermore, their collective endorsement of anti-imperialism centred on expelling Western influence from the region, while their wider sponsorship of revolutionary and anti-imperialist movements provided openings for the expansion of Soviet interests in the region.

Until the early 1970s, these secular-inclined radical nationalist forces were politically ascendant in much of the Middle East, most evidently in Nasser's Egypt and the Ba'athist regimes of Iraq and Syria. Where they had not captured state power, they tended to be the principal oppositional force to more conservative-inclined regimes. This nationalist and anti-imperialist coalition was opposed by pro-US regimes, particularly the oil rich monarchies in the Gulf led by Saudi Arabia. Consequently, an intra-Arab Cold War was played out from the early 1950s until the mid-1970s with each side seeking to undermine the domestic stability and the regional policies of the other. Under the military protection of the United States, conservative regimes were organised and supported by the same social forces that had been overthrown in Egypt and elsewhere.[12] They staked their political legitimacy on upholding traditional patterns of social reproduction anchored in the Islamic faith, buttressed – in the case of Saudi Arabia – by its role as custodian of the two Islamic holy sites, Mecca and Medina (Hiro 2002: 144) and, economically, from the flow of petro-dollars.

---

[12] The other notable examples of radical and revolutionary change in the region in the post-war period that overthrew the power of traditional social and political forces were: Iraq (1958); Algeria (1954–62); Syria (1954 and 1966); Yemen (1962); Libya (1968); and Iran (1979). Many other countries within the region went through periods of political instability involving radical social and political forces such as Lebanon and Jordan in 1958.

The significance of the intra-Arab Cold War was not only that a common political and military front against Israel was difficult to establish amongst the Arab states, but that the social and ideological basis of the Saudi regime and its allies rested on a major social and political contradiction in which illiberal domestic political and cultural regimes had to be incubated from their international entanglements with Western liberal powers.[13] While during the Cold War this suited US political purposes in containing and attacking leftist political forces allied to the USSR, it also meant that the nature of the ideological conflict of the Cold War in the Middle East was of a quite different character to that experienced elsewhere, tinged with distinct religious and cultural currents reflecting the region and some of its leading states.

The Cold War in the Middle East – at least between the leading 'revolutionary' state (Egypt) and the leading conservative state (Saudi Arabia) – was not, therefore, a conflict over capitalism versus communism or 'freedom versus totalitarianism' but rather one between modernisation in a statist-socialist direction[14] and a path of modernisation that rested on the preservation of existing configurations of social power anchored in a mix of pre-capitalist and capitalist social property relations, itself integrated into the international capitalist system through oil exports and deeply hostile to democratic impulses from below. Thus, whilst Nasser's Egypt sought leadership of the Arab world and sponsored radical anti-conservative forces in the region, most notably through its (unsuccessful) intervention in the civil war in Yemen between royalist and republican forces during the mid-1960s (Halliday 1979), the Saudis – with US endorsement – supported anti-Nasserite forces throughout the region, including Yemen.[15] In effect, therefore, throughout the Cold War, with the support of the United States, the financial bounty provided by the oil price hikes in the 1970s and the political opportunities presented by the Soviet intervention in Afghanistan in 1979, Saudi Arabia became a key player – in terms of funding, organisation and ideology – in cultivating distinctly *illiberal*

[13] Thus, while the Saudis embraced US geopolitical cooperation and protection, and exported oil to the West, they also allowed, indeed promoted, the upholding of the austere strictures of Wahhabism and, further, welcomed radical Islamist preachers and activists such as Sayyid Qutb's brother and others, who attacked not only the infidel regimes in Cairo and elsewhere, but, more broadly, what they saw as Western-secular influences throughout the region.

[14] During the mid-1960s this was also pursued in a more systematic fashion in Syria by the radical wing of the Ba'ath party. See Hinnebusch (1993: 181).

[15] There were a number of Saudi initiatives throughout the 1960s to counter the pervasive influence of Nasser's pan-Arab socialism. In 1969, a Saudi initiative established the first official pan-Islamic organisation of intergovernmental cooperation amongst

and anti-universalist forms of anti-communism that would, in time, provide the foundations for contemporary reactionary Islamist movements and their terrorist offshoots.

This Cold War division provided a defining schism within the region from the mid-1950s to the mid-1970s, thus contributing to the global logic of Cold War and the pattern of political developments both within the domestic politics of states and the wider character of regional politics. However, the Cold War also contributed to the other major antagonism within the region – the Arab–Israeli conflict. These two conflicts were intimately inter-connected, most notably during those moments of Arab–Israeli military conflict in 1956, 1967 and 1973. Although the political and ideological pull of Saudi-sponsored conservative Islam was a significant force in the region, it was wider developments in the Middle East, particularly the Arab–Israeli conflict, that would ultimately determine the political outcome of the Cold War in the region. In this respect, the turning point for the fate of radical nationalist forces in the Middle East – a move which opened the door for a revival of political Islam in the region – came via the military humiliation inflicted on Arab nationalist armies in the Six Day War of June 1967. The defeat exposed not only the failings of Nasser's strategy to defeat Israel – one of the central factors in regional politics – but also the ineffectiveness of Egypt's alliance with the USSR.

Whilst the Egyptian/Arab defeat was primarily a regional political issue, it also had an impact on the Cold War as, with Nasser's death in 1970 and his replacement by Anwar Sadat, Egypt began to move away both from its alliance with Moscow and from its support for radical nationalist forces in the region. Under Sadat, Egypt moved to cooperate with Saudi Arabia in its planning for the Yom Kippur War. The diplomatic success of the war for Sadat meant that Egypt could terminate the alliance with Moscow, which duly took place in 1974.[16] In this way Sadat not only transformed the geopolitical and ideological context of the Middle East, but also severely undermined the forces of revolutionary nationalism in the region. And these 'external' developments were complemented by domestic political change within Egypt.[17]

Muslim states, the Organisation of Islamic Conference. See Hiro (1988: 145) and Esposito (2002: 106–7).

[16] Sadat had expelled Soviet military advisers in 1972. However, this did not stop Cairo turning to Moscow for arms prior to the war and only finally ending the alliance in 1974 after having secured its diplomatic goals vis-à-vis the United States. See Al-Sayyid Marsot (1985: 133–4).

[17] The Arab humiliation of June 1967 was also felt in Damascus which was to see the overturning of the radical Ba'athists by a more 'realist' faction led by Hafiz al-Asad, which sought to focus on national unity through rolling back the policies of the radical

Whereas Nasserism had been based on an international relations of anti-imperialism alongside a commitment to the destruction of Israel, buttressed by a domestic policy that attacked traditional land-holding classes and the comprador bourgeoisie through a model of authoritarian statist-developmentalism, Sadat's domestic policies focused on reconstituting the social and political basis of the regime which could break the power of leftist forces (Tucker 1978; Hamad 1981; Niblock and Murphy 1993; Esposito 2002: 83–4; Ates 2005).

Sadat began his domestic programme soon after coming to power with an internal coup against the socialist-leaning Al Sabri section of the ruling party – the Arab Socialist Union. At the same time that he attacked the left, Sadat also cultivated the Islamic clerical establishment located in al-Azhar University through providing state support for mosque construction and permitting the establishment of Islamic student associations (and harassing leftist student groups) (Hiro 1988). The result was a rise in Islamism during the 1970s[18] as the state clamped down on the organised political left and 'used' Islamic militants as its foot soldiers, particularly in the universities (Heikal 1983: 140–7, 220). Overall, Sadat encouraged a much greater public profile and legitimacy for Islamic cultural *and* political currents even associating it with the 'success' of the Yom Kippur War. The irony was that Sadat's policies of moving into diplomatic embrace with the United States and making peace with Israel at Camp David in 1979, alongside his attempts at dismantling the statist economic framework established under Nasser, put him increasingly at odds with the Islamic militants, culminating in his assassination by Islamists in 1981.

The consequences of the changes initiated by Sadat after 1970 indicate that, by the early 1970s, the Cold War had effectively ended in the Middle East. Egypt, the most important Arab state, once the primary font of anti-imperialism within the region and the USSR's principal ally, had shifted its foreign policy towards accommodation with the West. The weakening of Soviet influence in the region and of Egypt's support for leftist-nationalist political struggle combined with the transformation in the balance of social and political forces within Egypt and, correspondingly, the wider region. With the encouragement of the Egyptian state, Islamist social and political forces emerged and grew in organisational and political strength. Further, as John Cooley (2002) and others (Heikal 1983; Talhami 2003; Mamdani 2004) have

left leading to a revival in the fortunes of the Syrian bourgeoisie and, externally, a rapprochement with the conservative Gulf monarchies (Hinnebusch 1993: 182–3).

[18] Article two of the new 1971 constitution stated that Shar'ia was to be the primary source of all new legislation (Sivan 1985: 121).

documented, after the beginning of the Afghan jihad these forces grew even stronger as the Egyptian state served as a 'transmission belt' – with US endorsement – for Islamic militants, many of whom (including bin Laden's aide-de-camp, Ayman al-Zawahiri) had been convicted of offences in Egypt.

With the political failure of the pro-Soviet radical Arab nationalist project both internally (in terms of the construction of a stable basis of socio-economic support for the regime) and externally (with respect to the failure to effectively 'deal' with the problem of Israel), the Middle Eastern regional front of the Cold War came to be replaced, in the 1970s, with new forms of resistance initially cultivated locally as an alternative social basis for Sadat's Egypt. The upshot was that the defining polit-ical conflict with the region had become – by the mid-1970s – heteron-omous of the Cold War; a conflict no longer waged between traditional ruling classes aided by the forces of Western capital against radical nationalist/communist forms of modernity, but a new one between pro-Western authoritarian states committed to capitalist development and integration into the 'civilised' West and Islamist forces committed to expelling Western influence (Dodge and Higgott 2002). It is this con-flict which, to a significant degree, continues to define the region.

While the regional context played a vital role in opening up a space for Islamism, economic changes unleashed by the *intifah* were also sig-nificant. Here, the socio-economic and cultural dislocations created by rapid urbanisation and the failure of the state to meet rising economic expectations from the 1970s onwards (Ayubi 1993: 158–77) were cru-cial in laying the foundations for a social milieu within which Islamist social, cultural and political currents could thrive. Seizing upon what was regarded as the cultural and moral degeneration of cities such as Cairo, unmet economic expectations and a regime appearing ever-closer to the external enemies – Israel and the United States – served as useful calls-to-arms for aspiring Islamists. Although Islamist currents appealed to disparate social constituencies united by a common sense of alienation, it has been the upwardly mobile (in aspiration at least), formally educated and recently urbanised who have been most attracted to the politics of Islamism. As such, it is important to see Islamism as a response to a rapidly moving modernisation, which goes neither suf-ficiently fast nor sufficiently far enough. Indeed, 'they [the alienated] hate modernity because they cannot get it' (Ayubi 1993: 177).

What is important about these developments is that they were largely locally driven. Whilst the United States supported Sadat and other sources of anti-communism in the region, particularly Saudi Arabia, the *Islamic* character rather than the liberal or bourgeois character of opposition and resistance to Soviet/leftist influence was of local origin and locally promoted. Consequently, it was not liberal universalism that won the Cold War in the Middle East, but a combination of a shift in the strategic and economic orientations of states such as Egypt which, in turn, was facilitated by the promotion of illiberal and Islamist forms of anti-leftism. Further, US Cold War strategy was mediated by local political and ideological structures that Washington promoted in Cairo, Riyadh and elsewhere in the region. By encouraging Saudi autonomy and supporting Sadat's reforms the United States promoted political spaces that it did not control, in spite of its geopolitical ascendancy in the region, effectively allowing Saudi Arabia (or elements within it) to cultivate an agenda and network that would come to challenge Western interests after the defeat of the radical-nationalist project. In Egypt, the United States did nothing to prevent the strengthening of social and political forces antagonistic to its ideological vision. And it was out of such forces that the contemporary menace of Islamist terrorism emerged.

Changes in the Middle East centred on developments within Egypt and the Saudi–Egyptian relationship – suggestive of an alternative conjunctural moment through which to make sense of the origins of contemporary political developments in the region – were echoed in developments in the Persian Gulf during 1978–9. Whilst the domestic and international changes associated with the post-Nasser turn in Egypt had effectively redrawn the geopolitical map of the Middle East and, correspondingly, a weakening of the broader forces of the radical left, developments in Iran saw a major political and geopolitical setback for the United States with the overthrow of the pro-American monarchy by a broad coalition of revolutionary forces. On one level, therefore, the Iranian Revolution could be seen as a counter-balance to US advances with regard to Egypt and the Camp David agreement, contributing to the dynamic of Cold War competition and rivalry (Roy 2004: 59). However, as developments within Iran would reveal, the character of politics within the wider Middle East were to be conditioned by a further political current; that of revolutionary Islam with an Iranian and Shi'ite bent.[19]

The Iranian Revolution produced a new form of post-Cold War anti-imperialist politics hostile both to the USSR and its local allies, as well as the United States and its local surrogates – Saudi Arabia in particular. US influence in the region contributed to a new dynamic of

[19] For an excellent survey of the evolution of the international dimensions of the Iranian Revolution, see Panah (2007).

political conflict most notably through the role of Iranian-backed guerrilla movements in Lebanon and political currents in the Gulf. Thus,
whilst the Egyptian turn and the growing influence of Saudi Arabia,
assisted by petro-dollars and the opening ushered by the 1979 Soviet
intervention in Afghanistan, helped produce a new 'revolutionary' form
of Sunni Islamist politics, the Iranian Revolution produced another
'revolutionary front' to the regional political cocktail. While, on the
one hand the United States was assisting and funding (at least indirectly) one branch of the Islamist revival via the Afghan jihad, it also
confronted those Islamist forces – in the Persian Gulf and Lebanon –
supported by Iran and associated with its distinctly Shi'ite brand of
revolutionary Islam.

The key issue here – at least for any understanding of the contemporary politics of the Middle East – is that it was developments pre-
dating 1989 that provide the central causal context for the emergence of
these political vectors, logics which have come to dominate the region
ahead of any liberal-democratic *Geist* emergent from the 'spirit of '89'.
Although 1989 did have an impact on the region – not least via a revived
attempt at peace-making between Arab states and Israel – the contemporary politics of the region and its principal sources of resistance and
anti-imperialism should primarily be seen as products of developments
in the 1970s.

Conclusions

I have made two main arguments in this chapter. First, that world politics is made up of complex and overlapping political currents. As such,
the logic that fuels processes of stability and/or change across different
geographical locales is bound to be varied and uneven. Consequently,
although we can talk of global moments or conjunctures of transformation such as '1989', we need to be sensitive to the heterogeneous quality of world politics. Further, in spite of the hierarchical distribution of
political, economic and military power that characterises world politics,
what ultimately determines the *global* character of a moment or process of change is the degree to which such currents of change perme-
ate domestic state–society relations and come to be reproduced within
these complexes.

The second argument contests the global significance of 1989. Rather
than subsuming the end of the Cold War in the collapse of Soviet-
communist power in 1989, I have argued that the Cold War had multiple and uneven origins, processes and endings. While particularly
evident in the Middle East – where an alternative temporal and political

conjuncture determined the character of Cold War and post-Cold War politics – one could also apply the idea of multiple and distinct endings (and effects) to other parts of the South. These locally driven pre-1989 endings, and the political identities and conflicts associated with them, have been interwoven with the logic of 1989 in conditioning the character of regional *and* global politics. Even as the spirit and momentum of 1989 has contributed to defining the political complexion of the Middle East, more definitive in laying down the foundations of contemporary regional politics have been local social forces, ideological currents and political movements and states.

With reference to the themes identified in George Lawson's introductory chapter, this chapter has offered an alternative way of thinking about the treatment of, and the relationship between, time and space in world politics, particularly as regards the place of 1989 in conceptualisations of international relations and in historical accounts of the end of the Cold War. This chapter has demonstrated how world politics (during and after the Cold War) operates on multiple – sometimes contradictory – temporal logics. This suggests that IR theory, in turn, needs to be more sensitive to the *varied* character of world historical time. Relatedly, contesting the global character of 1989 shows us how the interiors of states – and the balance and dynamic between social forces and political currents within them – continue to be highly uneven and diverse, despite two decades of globalisation. Thus, not only do we need to recognise the evolving and dynamic character of world politics, we also need more circumspection regarding theoretical claims about the global and determining reach of great powers and major ideologies. This, in turn, requires sensitivity to the extent to which Eurocentric tendencies continue to exert a stranglehold on the international imagination.

Part III

Continuity and change

9 One bright moment in an age of war, genocide and terror? On the revolutions of 1989

Chris Armbruster

Introduction

Public attention did not stay with the revolutions of 1989 for very long. The peaceful revolutions in Eastern Europe were followed by war in the Gulf and, soon after, the Balkans. While participants and observers alike experienced 1989 as an 'annus mirabilis', the return of genocide and ethnic cleansing in Europe, and then the wider world, prompted a re-examination of the *darker aspects* of twentieth-century European and world history. Scholarly interpreters spoke of an age of extremes, and identified Europe as a dark continent marred by war, terror and genocide. Even democracy itself was not immune from critique, coming under fire for its 'dark side' and, most notably, the fusion of *demos* and *ethnos* that was seen to generate bouts of ethnic cleansing (Hobsbawm 1994; Mazower 1998; Mann 2005).

After 1989, it seemed as if the legacy of the Cold War and the age of extremes was yet *more* war, terror and genocide. There is palpable uneasiness about the current and future shape of world politics, not least in how the 'war on terror' can lead to a suspension of democracy and human rights, and the return of militarised economies and imperialist politics. As antidotes to these dark visions, scholars have begun to reappraise twentieth-century history, focusing on its brighter moments (Winter 2006; Judt 2008). In these more optimistic narratives, achievements like the declaration and extension of human rights around the world, the redistributive successes of welfare states and the emancipation of women take centre stage. Narratives oscillate, therefore, between 'dark' and 'light'. Recognition of projects centring on human rights, peace and prosperity sits uneasily alongside histories of imperialism, war and terror. Only rarely do these two narratives speak directly to each other. Few attempts are made to *connect* war and peace, terror and liberty, imperialism and independence.

This chapter looks at how 'dark' and 'light' serve as *interrelated* features of the twentieth century, most notably of 1989, and what inspiration might be drawn from this for world politics in the twenty-first century. Three processes are examined: how the legacy of Stalinist terror resulted in an internal structural stasis which, in turn, enabled the break-up of the Soviet empire; how the Soviet empire was integrated into global warfare but this dependency inhibited the rationalisation of the project, thus pushing actors into a second economy and parallel society; and how war, terror and ethnic cleansing ravished Eastern Europe, but ultimately resulted in independent states and societies able to purposefully organise revolutionary change in 1989. In the course of this examination, some conventional narratives of *continuity and change* will be challenged. At the macro-level, rather than affirming that the Gorbachevian reforms brought down the Soviet empire, it will be suggested that the Stalinist legacy was more consequential. At the global level, rather than highlighting how the Soviets gradually lost the Cold War, the internal consequences of dependence on war will be discussed. At the meso-level, rather than evoking ethnic nationalism as the force that broke up the Soviet empire, the continuity of state building will be emphasised. At the micro-level, revolutionary actors built on the Soviet legacy by rejecting it, but also by imposing limitations upon themselves, thus opening the way for a negotiated outcome that, despite the travails of political transition and economic hardship, led to synchronised, largely successful transformation. Unfortunately, those celebrating 1989 as 'peaceful' revolution are so overwhelmed by the desire to contrast the events of 1989 favourably with the perceived darkness of the twentieth century that they fail to comprehend the wider significance of this outcome. *Peaceful revolution* is an oxymoron, a concept that unwittingly reveals just how much the dark legacy of fascism and communism still colours broader perceptions. By contrast, the notion of a *self-limiting* or *negotiated* revolution recognises the continuing hold of violence and the prevalence of conflict (Staniszkis 1984; Lawson 2005). The bequest of the self-limiting revolutionaries to world politics is a blueprint for organising large-scale, rapid transformations in the twenty-first century.

The legacy of Stalinist terror and the breakdown of the Soviet empire

During 1989, the loss of control over the borders of the Soviet empire, in contrast to China, was first palpable and then fatal. Since the collapse occurred simultaneously in both the outer and inner parts of the

Soviet empire (the Baltic, Caucasus and Central Europe), it is perhaps unsurprising that scholars look to *endogenous* rather than exogenous reasons for its breakdown. However, any search for the 'root causes' of Soviet collapse is not straightforward. After all, the Soviet military did not collapse, the state budget was not out of control and absolute economic decline set in only as a consequence of Soviet breakdown. This favours a search for causes in the political realm.[1] Analysts frequently prefer either top–down or bottom-up explanations, attributing the collapse either to Gorbachev or to civil society respectively. Such explanations, however, are implausible – the Soviet order boasted both a considerable administrative (infrastructural) capacity and notable coercive (despotic) power. As such, it did not disappear either voluntarily or without a fight. Rather, the Soviet Union collapsed because of long-term systemic problems resulting from Stalinist terror. This is not to deny the agency of Soviet leadership after Stalin or to suggest that political and economic reform did not happen, but, so the argument goes, it was Stalin's legacy that undid the Soviet empire.

The Soviet order was characterised by relations of command and obedience in which the party and its *nomenklatura* controlled every social sphere. While the Bolsheviks considered terror against enemies and outsiders a legitimate form of political violence, the meaning and consequence of terror changed fundamentally during Stalin's rule. For the first time, terror became a tool to be used *internally*. Some of the mechanisms of terror, as well as the number of its victims, have been disputed (for discussion and further details, see: Getty and Manning 1993; Nove 1994; Conquest 1997; Courtois *et al.* 1997). But it is beyond dispute that Stalinist terror was waged against insiders for twenty years on a vast scale. Terror was directed at the Central Committee and its apparatus in Moscow alongside those of Prague, Budapest and other satellite states. Officials of Gosplan were affected, as were the ministries in Moscow, directors of enterprises in Siberia and the collectivised nomads of Kazakhstan. Terror spread throughout the system: the Red Army lost its leading officers in 1937; during and after the winter campaign against Finland in 1939/40, more officers were executed and soldiers sent to forced labour camps; as the German Wehrmacht attacked in 1941 and the Red Army retreated in defeat, yet more officers were

---

[1] This focus on internal weaknesses does not deny the importance of international pressures on the Soviet Union, particularly the systemic rivalry with the West and the global Cold War, processes discussed later in the chapter. However, the crucial point is that, while international factors were important in establishing the *context* for Soviet decline, internal (particularly political) factors were crucial in terms of understanding the manner and timing of its demise.

executed. Even after taking Berlin in May 1945, returning officers and soldiers were screened by the People's Commissariat for Internal Affairs (Narodnyy Komissariat Vnutrennikh Del, NKVD) and sent to forced labour camps.

Terror was particularly intense at the apex of communist power. Stalinist repression between 1936 and 1938 included five members of the Politburo, 98 of the 139 members of the central committee, 1,108 of the 1,966 delegates to the seventeenth party congress in 1934, and 90 per cent of the party cadres in Leningrad. Only three of the 200 members of Ukraine's central committee survived. In Komsomol, 72 of the 93 members of the central committee were arrested, as were 319 of the 385 regional secretaries, and 2,210 of the 2,759 district secretaries. Several hundred cadres of Comintern were executed. European communist parties were twice hit by terror, first during their exile in Moscow in 1936 and 1937, and then for seven years after 1948. Scripted in Moscow, and organised by the secret police and judiciary organs, prosecutions and proceedings were publicised across Europe, keeping communist parties and their members under threat and in fear of accusations of 'Titoism', 'bourgeois nationalism', 'deviationism' and more. Terror was limited only by logics of territorial control. Many Soviet officials serving abroad were lured to Moscow as a pretext for their arrest. Soviet terror even crept into organisations not subject to Soviet territorial control, such as the Communist Party of the USA (Wright 1950). Members were forced to comply with orders from above, or else were branded as traitors, given a show trial and expelled from the party. The Communist Party of the USA (CP USA) sought to prevent expelled members from securing a means of livelihood, but for *lack* of territorial control and administrative powers could not execute its members or have them sent to forced labour camps.

Much ink has been spilled in analysing Soviet totalitarianism as well as its post-Soviet legacy. In contrast, *the internal and systemic consequences* of Stalinist terror are not well understood. In *Terror and Progress USSR*, the American sociologist Barrington Moore (1954) looked in detail at the consequences of Stalinist terror. Written immediately after Stalin's death, it still is an excellent, theoretically informed guide to Soviet history. Moore presented three alternative scenarios: a perpetuation of totalitarian power politics; a rationalisation of power; or its traditionalisation. At the time, he excluded a possible perpetuation of terror not only with reference to the security needs of the ruling elite, but also because he thought this would threaten Soviet rule altogether. The question was then, how much *rationalisation* would occur, i.e. authority derived from legality and bureaucracy, and how much *traditionalisation*, i.e. authority derived from older traditions. While Moore argued that totalitarian power had acted as a corrosive on traditional forms of legitimate authority, he saw the establishment of a rational-legal order as amounting to a withering of the system itself. As such, Moore stressed indicators of a re-traditionalisation of the Soviet order. More specifically, Moore expected there to be either a push towards rationalisation with an emphasis on responsibility and competence in organisations, or that more traditional ties would reassert themselves with an emphasis on kinship ties and personal loyalty. In the latter case, while formally perpetuating totalitarian rule, local centres would seek both to limit the directional powers of the central apex and evade its control, thus paralysing the system from within.

If we survey the history of the Soviet Union and its allies from the 1950s to the 1980s, it becomes evident that rationalisation of the Soviet order was not achieved, even in the most advanced state – East Germany. Moreover, the repeated *de-mobilisation* of agents of rationalisation such as industrial managers, workers' councils and writers' guilds, reinforced trends towards re-traditionalisation. However, informal patron–client relationships deepened economic shortages by diverting resources from one place to another in return for a private, personal profit. The rise of parallel patronage networks outside formal state control engendered a system in which personal loyalty was more important than function and capability. Although the Soviet empire did not drift inexorably towards paralysis, the sum of its internal military interventions, de-mobilisations and purges pre-empted rationalisation and fostered structural stasis. Structural stasis – the inability of an organisation to mobilise effectively due to blockages in its procedures (Archer 1988; Sztompka 1991) – did not inhibit agency per se, but it did make it virtually impossible for the Soviet bureaucracy to run effectively.

Under the Gorbachev regime, the Soviet leadership attempted to unpick structural stasis via the development of new policies, the reorganisation of party bodies and the replacement of state personnel (Gill 1994; Onikov 1996; Brown 1997). In March 1985, Gorbachev expressly called upon the party to follow his economic reforms in order to accelerate economic development and establish the self-management of enterprises. In April 1986, Gorbachev spoke of the need for *perestroika* (i.e. structural reform) and warned his party that its leading role was not a right to be taken-for-granted, but a privilege to be earned. Elections by secret ballot were introduced for cadres and secretaries from primary party organisations at the workplace to high levels of political office. Gorbachev also advocated a 'socialist pluralism' of opinion alongside legal reform intended to limit the party's functions and redefine its role as a political vanguard. Gorbachev's reforms had far-reaching effects. By March 1987, Gorbachev had retained less than one out of six secretaries and replaced nine out of ten heads of departments in the Central Committee apparatus. Already by 1986 the Central Committee had co-opted 125 new members, a renewal rate of 40 per cent. In 1989, a further 110 members were debarred at a plenary session. At the provincial level, more than 100 of the 159 party secretaries were dismissed. In the autumn of 1988, Gorbachev ordered another reorganisation of the Central Committee apparatus, which nominally freed Soviet ministries and their administration from party directives, thereby separating party from government.

While the staff of the Central Committee could not prevent the loss of its economic, military, cultural and educational departments, or a large reduction in numbers, most members refused to confine themselves to the new bureaucratic environment. The Central Committee was supposed to analyse Soviet affairs and devise strategic proposals for further political and economic restructuring, but it was to leave decision-making to the Politburo and administration to the government. Instead, Central Committee departments continued to issue directives and interfere in the day-to-day management of Soviet affairs. Moreover, Soviet ministries counteracted economic decentralisation by insisting on the highest possible quotas of delivery for centralised collection and distribution, backing up this measure with monthly reviews of plan fulfilment for each enterprise. The ministerial staff likewise resisted reorganisation by creating new administrative bodies for those they had been ordered to abolish and increasing staff while formally reducing the number of administrative sub-units. In short, central staff was *obstructing reform* wherever and whenever it could – until it was too late to save the Soviet project.

Despite the zeal of the reformers, the Soviet control and command systems appeared resistant to fundamental change. In retrospect it is easy to blame Gorbachev and his fellow travellers for the Soviet breakdown. But given the decision to undertake fundamental reforms, Gorbachev did the *right things*, and most of these in the *right order*. The calculation of the Soviet leadership was that their empire had lost ground. To halt or reverse this trend, it was considered essential to roll back Soviet commitments abroad in order to free resources for internal reform. In this way, it was hoped, the Soviets would relax control of the periphery but retain control of the metropolitan centre. Ultimately, of course, this strategy failed. The rationalisation of the Soviet order required a relaxation of tight controls: bosses had to rely on their subordinates and trust that they would carry out orders in the interests of the grand project. As those lower down the hierarchical chain obstructed reforms, the central apex could have restored full authority only via direct coercion. In principle, this was possible as long as imperial borders remained sealed and the coercive apparatus dominated the imperial space. However, mobilisation by direct coercion would have led not only to the dismantling of reform policies, but also would have robbed the leadership of its legitimacy, both at home and abroad. As such, it is unlikely that Gorbachev could have attained his goals by direct coercion, especially as his policies presupposed legality and were to be implemented by persuasion. In short, Gorbachev and his staff were effective only in the things they could personally direct – foreign policy, reorganisation of the Central Committee and a shake-up of key personnel. However, systemic pressures – structural stasis – weighed heavily against them: when called upon to rejuvenate, the party found itself immobile. Immobile, it could no longer hold together the empire.

These processes were neither the fault of Gorbachev nor his close associates – they took place because the Stalinist legacy promoted re-traditionalisation outside the communist order, in parallel networks. As rationalisation failed, Soviet relations of command and obedience gestated into a structural stasis, implying that the Soviet apex would not be able to rely on its staff, i.e. the *nomenklatura*, to perpetuate its rule. Structural stasis did not mean that the agency of most people was blocked or that society had become static, but it did mean that the Soviet leadership could neither mobilise the party effectively nor achieve its intended objectives. Although there was more than one course of action open to Gorbachev, Soviet breakdown became highly probable following the order to remobilise the party and its *nomenklatura* for *perestroika* and *glasnost*. After all, if one seeks to mobilise an organisation, but those within the organisation refuse to follow orders, disintegration eventually becomes inescapable. It may be argued that if the Soviet leadership had refrained from permitting *glasnost* and not embarked on *perestroika*, Soviet rule could have been perpetuated beyond the year 2000, as Gorbachev (1996) came to believe. But in this counterfactual scenario, structural stasis would have pushed the Soviet project from relative into absolute decline, making collapse inevitable. Structural stasis was the legacy of Stalinist terror which rendered attempts at establishing a legal-rational order virtually impossible, leading, in turn, to the breakdown of the system in the Baltic, Caucasus and Central Europe in 1989.

Soviet dependence on the Cold War and inhibited rationalisation

If instability was a core feature of the Soviet system from Stalin to Gorbachev, why did the Soviet order not break down *before* 1989? In this section, it is argued that neither politics nor ideology, but the integration of the Soviet Union into a global system of warfare, real *and* imagined, explains the system's longevity as well as its eventual exhaustion. As long as the USSR was integrated into cold and hot wars around the world, the central command and control apparatus could impose coercive order on Soviet and allied networks. A military logic of perception sustained the Soviets: military projects were launched, technologies stolen, goods bartered, and energy resources traded in return for grain and basic foodstuffs; all to project world power status. Subjected to calls for greater vigilance, the party engaged in a search not just for hostile 'bourgeois' and 'nationalist' wreckers and saboteurs, but also for deserters, traitors and enemies within.

The Cold War has, of course, been extensively researched. It is clear now, if it was not before, that the Cold War was not a symmetrical contest and that the USSR paid a high price for its overseas engagements (e.g. Crockatt 1995; Cox 1998; Saull 2001; Westad 2005). Yet, how and why the Soviet project was dependent on integration into a global regime of warfare, and what the internal consequences were of this integration, is not well understood. Thus the argument here is not so much whether the Soviets 'lost' the Cold War, but rather that, in order to sustain world power status after Stalin, the Soviets had to organise international networks of rule very tightly. And this was no straightforward task. While the party could certainly coerce its allies around the world, from military occupation to the banning of basic cultural freedoms, it could do so only at substantial cost to the Soviet project itself. By relying so extensively on coercion, the *illegality and inferiority* of the Soviet model were laid bare, making it ever more difficult to base legitimate authority on rationalisation.

To understand this point, it helps to distinguish between *social integration* and *system differentiation* (Lockwood 1964; Luhmann 1984; Archer 1996; Mouzelis 1997). In terms of social integration, the Soviet system was premised on a political hierarchy. Given its Stalinist legacy, the Soviet empire relied on warfare and militarisation to impose imperial and domestic integration. At the same time, the Soviet project exhibited a modern level of differentiation between political, economic, military, legal, scientific and artistic systems. Typically, these systems had their own codes, e.g. for science 'true-false' and 'original-unoriginal'. Since the Soviet project was integrated into the global order, these systemic codes could not be insulated and manipulated at will.

At the same time, the Soviet political apex persisted with the *politicised mono-organisational social integration* (Rigby 1990) that the Stalinist regime had instituted. But this type of integration was fundamentally incompatible with modern system differentiation. Partly unwilling, partly unable to proceed via a rationalisation of the order *tout de suite*, modern codes of differentiation contributed to a hollowing out of Soviet organisations from within. Many social relations were re-traditionalised as people increasingly lived in parallel spheres distinct and increasingly autonomous from central control. In short, the perception and rhetoric of the Cold War as a global systemic conflict meant that the Soviet central apex kept its economic networks fully mobilised, its organisations heteronomous (i.e. no organisation or association was autonomous in its order) and heterocephalous (i.e. leaders were appointed from outside and above), insisting on taut planning (Sapir 1990; Kornai 1992). However, although central control via a military logic generated short-term stability, it had detrimental long-term consequences. The system became distorted, focusing only on the availability or non-availability of goods and labour-power. Shortages reigned. And as soon as coercion was reduced, and some decentralisation in decision-making allowed, this led to a well-rehearsed drive towards self-sufficiency by economic units which bartered goods and labour-power among themselves and illegally privatised resources to be subsequently sold on black markets. Conversely, economic organisations would not meet contractual obligations, nor were they reliable partners; rather, they focused on manipulating, firstly, plan figures and, afterwards, indicators of plan fulfilment. Furthermore, while the Soviets nominally adhered to general, formal, legal rules, the empire increasingly governed itself through informal power and exchange relations. Formal institutions were a façade, so much so that the establishment of legitimate authority was achievable only by traditionalisation. Locally, in well-defined spaces such as an office, a film production site or on the shop floor, recognised hierarchies could emerge, but they could not express themselves in autonomous organisation. Judiciary organs served as instruments of the de-mobilisation of society, sanctioning disturbances of a faux internal peace.

The Soviet project was beset by debilitating internal weakness because its mono-organisational structuring may have been compatible with the 'global Cold War', but was incompatible with advanced systemic differentiation required by modern orders. The central apex was able to temporarily and partially impose its practices, particularly via coercive methods, but at the same time, economic, legal and educational codes continued to reproduce autonomously, exposing Soviet practices as inefficient at best, and inhumane at worst. Warfare dependence meant not only that military commitments drained important resources (without producing coercive superiority) but also, and more consequentially, that any meaningful rationalisation of Soviet order was impossible. The party and the coercive apparatus continued to maintain an extra-legal status even as this was eroded in alternative circuits of power. Official networks became spaces of vice, disdain and shame, reinforcing a sense of structural stasis, while retreat from official space into privatised modes of existence was identified with virtue, dignity and pride (Sztompka 1993). The second economy and parallel society became sites from which the leaders of spontaneous privatisation and political revolution emerged.

State building in the Soviet empire and the national revolutions of 1989

To date, this chapter has argued that the legacy of Stalinist terror and the internal consequences of the 'global Cold War' help us to understand how structural stasis emerged in the Soviet system, obstructing belated attempts at *glasnost* and *perestroika*, and, in turn, leading to the collapse of the Soviet empire. Yet the revolutions of 1989 were *distinctly national in form*. Even when people joined hands over 600 kilometres from Tallinn to Vilnius on 23 August 1989, or East Germans fled from Hungary to Austria to reach West Germany, this did not signal the international coordination of revolutionary action. To understand how and why the Soviet project was dismantled country-by-country, it is necessary to examine another chapter of the dark history of the twentieth century.

It is estimated that between 1939 and 1948, more than forty million people died and more than forty million others were deported and displaced in Europe, mainly in Eastern Europe (Ther and Siljak 2001; Naimark 2002; Judt 2005). As a consequence of the Nazi policy of genocide, the deportation and expulsion of people by Soviet forces, extensive boundary shifts, and the treks of refugees across Eastern Europe, territories with titular nations emerged as administrative units either as Soviet republics or as people's republics. The Yalta Agreement is understood as symbolising Western compliance in the Stalinist reordering of Eastern Europe. Undoing Yalta, and the *return to Europe*, was consequently one of the most powerful motivations of nationalist opposition to Soviet rule and of dissidence in the communist system (Rupnik 1989).

It is widely argued that the events of 1989 represented a rush for national independence. The secessionist wars of the late 1980s and 1990s in the Caucasus, the Balkans and around the Black Sea were taken as confirmation of the overriding importance of nation and ethnicity in the new European order. For the period after the Second World War, the prevalence of Soviet nationality policy and the pursuit of national communism is affirmed. Against Sovietisation and Russification, so the narrative goes, local governments were able to limit the reach of the Soviet centre by adopting a defensive nationalist stance, promoting indigenous history and culture while seeking to reduce Russian presence in the administration (Carrère d'Encausse 1979; Simon 1986; Gellner 1997; Smith 1998). Yet, the consequences of collective violence were not just the ethnic and social homogeneity of most post-conflict territories, but also the existence of a Soviet imperial cage (Suny 1997; Martin 2002). This legacy proved important in shaping the revolutions of 1989 as *national state-building projects*.

Soviet imperial rule relied on closed borders and tight control over space. However, this also secured the boundaries of the newly consolidated territorial units. Modernisation enforced a further build-up of state capacity. Socialist states developed a full spectrum of state functions and were activist in terms of both industrial policy and wealth redistribution. Although in important respects socialist states failed to provide public goods such as property rights and clean air, the Soviet project nevertheless entailed an expansion in state capacity and, over four decades, the increasingly native practice and exercise of state power. This route to establishing and consolidating nation-states may have been different than in Western Europe not least because it was, in important respects, involuntary, but it did secure the emergence of relatively strong states.

To understand this, it is important to distinguish between the scope of state functions and the strength of state power (Goodwin 2001; Fukuyama 2006b). *State functions* include basic defence of the realm and the maintenance of order, regulation of education and health systems, and the provision of welfare. *Strong states* are effective in maintaining their functions, while weak states are not. States in Central Europe were generally strong in those functions they fulfilled, whether this means their hold over economic development or the coercion of their people. Indeed, although Soviet Socialist Republics had fewer state functions than their counterparts in the West, state capacity was still higher than is often imagined, particularly in large states such as

Ukraine (Simon 1986; Kuzio and D'Anieri 2002). On the one hand, the Ukrainian elite had been decimated by Stalinist terror, the Second World War and a campaign against 'Ukrainian bourgeois nationalism' after 1945. On the other hand, the Ukrainian SSR united Ukrainians. After the Second World War, most Ukrainians favoured a nativisation of the administrative elite. During the 1960s, ethnic Ukrainians gradually wrested leading political posts from ethnic Russians who had been posted there during Stalin's reign. At the end of the decade, only 10 per cent of the Ukrainian Politburo was Russian. Moves towards Ukrainian 'stateness' did not go unnoticed in Moscow. Thus, for example, in 1973 there was a purge of around 1,000 leading Ukrainian party functionaries, scientists and publishers under charges of 'nationalist deviation'. Nevertheless, the Ukrainian communist party raised the standard of educational qualifications among ethnic Ukrainians while seeking to prevent their participation in programmes of exchange in an attempt to render Russian specialists superfluous. Simultaneously, the Russian language was increasingly dropped in favour of Ukrainian as the main language of instruction in higher education. Ukrainian was also introduced as the primary administrative language of the country.

The experience of Ukraine is symptomatic of the ways in which newly educated, indigenous (and barely stratified) elites emerged during the 1970s. In Central Asian republics, Slav predominance among the leadership gave way to proportional representation; Russian representation sunk to just 25%. Likewise, in the Baltic republics, Russian representation in political leadership positions sunk from roughly 50% to below 20%. By contrast, inside the CPSU, around 70% of the members and candidates of the Central Committee and 80% of Politburo members were Russian. By 1980, a conjuncture emerged of increased indigenous participation in higher education, rising national consciousness and local administrative control: non-Russian students in higher education rose significantly and national elites gained administrative control over many of the resources needed for mobilisation including local party organisations, the local press, and even the local security apparatus. Under the protection of party leaders, a nationally conscious rewriting of history began (Simon 1986). Historical revisionism argued that the USSR existed not as a voluntary union among free and equal nations, but as a result of military conquest, annexation and violent subjugation. Across Central Europe this was not only part of living memory, but also reconfirmed in the most overt manner through military interventions (1956 in Hungary, 1968 in the Czechoslovak Socialist Republic (CSSR), martial law (1981 in Poland) and the ubiquitous presence of the Soviet military, secret service and their local vassals.

Given the emergence of strong local states during the post-war period throughout the Soviet empire, the important point to understand about the revolutions of 1989 is that they were *not* popular uprisings against far-off political elites or military occupation, but orchestrated campaigns of self-limited revolution in which the reaffirmation and consolidation of the nation-state facilitated a negotiated outcome (the Romanian exception notwithstanding). The behaviour of the revolutionaries was strategic, yet tempered. It focused on achieving incremental steps towards democracy and self-rule, but without questioning Soviet hegemony and, thereby, seeking to avoid a clash with the police, secret service and military. Of course, for the revolutionaries, the public espousal of non-violence was compatible with the storming of secret police offices, but this typically happened relatively late in the day. The principal strategy of the insurgents was to wrest the state away from the communist party and its auxiliary forces in order to reconstitute it as national and democratic – as was indicated country-by-country through the deletion of the leading role of the communist party in the new constitutions after 1989.

In this sense, 1989 was not, as many argue, a case of pitching the (socialist) state against (civil) society (e.g. Feher and Heller 1979; Ekiert 1996; Wolle 1998), assuming that the state subdued society, and society reasserted itself against the state. The rise of civic movements in Central Europe and popular fronts in the USSR may have given credence to the sense that self-limiting revolutions were born of the desire to establish civil society as a sphere distinct from the state (Cohen and Arato 1992). However, this narrative misses an important point – *allegiance to the nation-state*. Although communism established a party-state run by the *nomenklatura*, neither dissident intellectuals nor opposition movements had any intention of renouncing or abolishing states per se. Quite to the contrary, the revolutionaries of 1989 constitutionalised the state as democratic, achieving the legal-rational order and legitimation of authority that communists, after Stalin, could not achieve.

The idea and appeal of the self-limiting revolution

The above analysis yields two major insights about the global 1989. First, the military logic of the Cold War enabled the perpetuation of the Soviet project after Stalin, even as alternative circuits of authority exposed Soviet practices as illegal and inefficient. At the same time, national projects of state-building prefigured the way in which the Soviet empire would break up. Second, international and domestic relations were intertwined. The Soviet project was dependent on warfare

and militarisation, both real and imagined. Yet the Stalinist legacy pro-
gressively immobilised the Soviet empire so that a belated attempt at
structural reform led to its disintegration. Thus, the final issue to be
examined is how people *forged* a new and legitimate order out of the
structural stasis and illegitimacy of the old order. Here, the argument is
that a novel form of revolutionary change emerged – the *self-limiting* or
negotiated revolution (Staniszkis 1984; Lawson 2005) – to fit these 'new
times'. In this new form of revolutionary change, process and outcome
are organised in a manner that enables reflexive democratisation and
large-scale socio-economic change. Potentially, this form of transformation has modular appeal – it could stand as an important means for
conducting large-scale, rapid change in the twenty-first century.

The events of 1989 have been contrasted favourably with those of
1917, and even those of 1848, for their lack of violence. Yet this very lack
of violence led many observers to see them not as a revolution but as
something else – a 'refolution' (Garton Ash 1990) perhaps, or a means
for Eastern Europeans to rectify their deviation from a standard path
of development and 'catch up' with the West (Habermas 1991; Gellner
1993). Other observers focused on the lack of new revolutionary ideas
in 1989, leading the transformations to be seen as a 'turnabout' (e.g.
wielkich zmian, rendszerváltás, sametová revoluce, die Wende). Such views
are misguided, revealing more about the paternalistic attitudes of the
commentators than reflecting useful insights. While 1989 certainly did
signify Soviet collapse, the significance of the events lies in how local
actors responded to the situation, in the process forging a new form of
revolutionary change. Indeed, the theory and practice of the self-limiting revolution was developed locally, over time, in a series of encounters with Soviet totalitarianism. The rise of Solidarność (Solidarity) in
Poland in 1980 was the most important of these encounters, leading to
a fully fledged articulation of a novel form of revolutionary change. The
original theorist of the self-limiting revolution is Jadwiga Staniszkis,
the Polish sociologist and Solidarity adviser who became known for
her book on 'Poland's self-limiting revolution' (1984). Her analysis of
the rise of Solidarity shows the theory and practice of negotiated revolutions in the making. Although the revolt led by Solidarity in 1981
was unsuccessful, it served as a trial run for the uprisings later in the
decade. Indeed, the lessons drawn from the experiences of Solidarity
spread around social movements throughout Central Europe in the
mid-to-late 1980s (Kenney 2002; Falk 2003).

A self-limiting strategy contends with the powers that be, that is the
infrastructural capacity and coercive power of the state. In this sense,
a parallel society and second economy are important for autonomous

self-organisation outside the 'official' sphere, but a parallel existence cannot be an end in itself if workers' self-governance, democracy, the rule of law and other aims are to be pursued. Self-limitation is thus best understood not as a description of the aims of the revolution, but as its means. Against the backdrop of Stalinist terror, communist coercion and the wider history of the twentieth century, a self-limiting strategy is not only wise in seeking to prevent loss of life (which, previously, was both easy, given Soviet coercive powers, and also easily meaningless, given this capacity) but also in assuring the rulers of the day of a low risk to life and limb. Of course, the communists were pushed from power and the party vanquished, only it looked very much like a democratic handover of power. However, opposition movements largely proceeded in a disciplined manner – even as Gorbachev promoted *glasnost* and communist organisations were beset by structural stasis, insurgents continued to favour a gradualist approach. Of course, the outcome was unexpected, and had not been imagined in advance even by the revolutionaries themselves. In this way, revolutionary change in 1989 can be said to have been unexpected (particularly in terms of its rapidity), but not unintended.

That the outcome was unexpected and not unintended becomes clearer if one examines this process as a negotiated revolution. Negotiating the revolution was consistent with the self-limiting approach, and negotiation ensured that aims were achieved – free elections, constitutional reform and the 'return to Europe'. While it should be acknowledged that only in Poland (February to April 1989) and Hungary (June to September 1989) roundtable negotiations were decisive in fostering radical change, they *accompanied* revolutions in many more states, leading to power-sharing and free elections in Czechoslovakia, Bulgaria and the German Democratic Republic (Bozóki 2002). Moreover, while the roundtable is a symbol of negotiated revolutions, it is not the only means to achieving this outcome. For example, in the Baltic states, popular fronts were founded by members of the Communist *nomenklatura*, a process that led to declarations of independence in 1990. For the states that emerged from the Soviet breakdown, there is evidence of a correlation of self-limiting revolutions, strong states and democratic constitutions. The negotiated outcome of the revolutions, in turn, established the legitimacy of the new order.

However, most knowledgeable international observers anticipated that transformations would be painful and likely to fail on both logical and historical grounds (Dahrendorf 1990; Elster 1990; Przeworski 1991). It was noted that a synchronised transition of politics, economics and culture was required – something extremely difficult to pull off.

While political transitions would be completed in a shorter time span, observers saw economic and cultural transformations as likely to take decades, particularly the latter, variously analysed as a 'civilisational gap', 'unwanted modernity', 'homo sovieticus', or as the return of the repressed via ethnic nationalism and internecine warfare. The political transition, as such, was also questioned, not least because of seemingly unresolved claims over territory (Offe 1991). Western Europe had needed centuries to consolidate nation-state democracies, it was argued, so Eastern Europe seemed hardly likely to achieve this in just a few years. Indeed, the possible backsliding of democracies in Eastern Europe has been a consistent focus of scholarly attention since 1989. Despite the accession to the European Union of several states in the region, these are often described as fragile democracies that are in constant danger of becoming undone (Armbruster 2008).

As large-scale change continued throughout the 1990s, observers reformulated their reservations by speaking of a path-dependent transformation (Elster *et al.* 1998; Stark and Bruszt 1998). In this variant of the argument, change is not denied outright, but the past is attributed an overwhelming influence – be it via economic planning, the party state or the socialist habitus. Yet, contra the argument made by Aviezer Tucker in Chapter 7 (this volume), large-scale and rapid change was not precluded by Soviet legacies. Whatever quantitative or qualitative indicators one consults, there can be little doubt that those Eastern European countries that underwent a negotiated revolution have achieved their intended outcomes (Merkel 2008): consolidated constitutional democracy, reasonably high growth rates and integration into European and global flows of capital, labour, goods and services.

The interpretation advanced here recognises that intended revolutionary outcomes were achieved only in some countries. It also recognises the high costs of change such as the emergence of economic cycles of boom-and-bust, rising social inequalities and sinking life expectancies. Indeed, my argument is that negotiated revolutions were the *precondition* for securing intended outcomes, making it (more) likely that these costs would be accepted. As such, my interpretation is a long way from conventional narratives. Triumphalist observers, whether neoliberal or neo-conservative, tended to ignore local conditions and advocated a quick transition to the Western model. Counsel from these quarters often only increased the costs of change. For example, privatisation bolstered the market economy in those countries that had undergone a negotiated revolution, but undermined market economies elsewhere. Likewise, constitutional reform bolstered democracy in those same countries, but not in others. For their part, critical observers often continue to invoke the importance of communist and socialist legacies, ignoring the ways in which the revolutions of 1989 have served to neutralise many of these legacies. Negotiated revolutions helped to establish an order that was not susceptible to any simple implementation of the neoliberal blueprint. Countries undergoing a negotiated revolution may have (re-)emerged at relatively low levels of development and income, but it is not plausible to see them as somehow outside the European social model – all of the states that went through a negotiated revolution have welfare institutions and levels of inequality that resemble Western European standards. Indeed, it could be argued that the revolutionary agency enshrined in 1989 enabled the comprehensive redesign of key institutions, including some path-breaking reforms in welfare and education, which could, over time, revitalise the European social model.

Conclusion

The above analyses overturn much conventional wisdom. While many Sovietologists and historians of the twentieth century were transfixed by the Bolshevik revolution and the actions of the Soviet high command, this chapter suggests that the institutional legacy of the terror inside Soviet networks ultimately shaped the destiny of the Soviet empire. Moreover, while some Cold War historians have tended to emphasise the centrality of conflict and war, especially in the Third World, it is here suggested that the Soviet project was critically dependent on the Cold War for its internal cohesion, but that this simultaneously led to a hollowing out of its organisation from within. Most notably, the dysfunctions of Soviet integration techniques, largely reliant on coercion, had the unintended consequence of generating a process of nation-state building which, as the Soviet order disintegrated, enabled a series of national revolutions to take place. This new type of revolution facilitated the simultaneous, synchronous and rapid pursuit of political, economic and cultural transformation. Nation-states purposefully and effectively achieved self-transformation.

It has been argued that a negotiated revolution has been the outcome not only in Eastern Europe, but also South Africa (Lawson 2005). And connections have also been made to the so-called colour revolutions (e.g. Croatia, Serbia, Georgia, Ukraine) which have occurred since 1989 (Forbrig and Demes 2007). In this sense, the revolutions of 1989 stand as a landmark within the dark twentieth century in which a new form of revolution has emerged. That said, the notion of a self-limiting or negotiated revolution requires further exploration. Rather than treating it as a category for the classification of events (and perhaps inadvertently upgrading events of dubious quality to the status of revolutions), it would best be explored as an *ideal type* of revolution. Ideal types are constructed from logical argument and historical evidence, and would include a description of typical aims, means and outcomes. One advantage of employing ideal types is that they serve as tools of comparison for historical cases. Another advantage is that ideal types are intended to travel, potentially informing practice internationally. This is particularly important if world politics in the twenty-first century is geared to inhibiting war, terror and genocide, while fostering negotiated outcomes in situations of conflict and violence.

10 A dangerous utopia: the military revolution from the Cold War to the war on terror

Marc DeVore

Introduction

For four decades, the Cold War was characterised by military competition. The race for dominance on land, at sea, in the sky, in space and in the strategic nuclear arena punctuated this competition, which found public expression in Soviet May Day parades and NATO's REFORGER exercises. After a stand-off of unprecedented length, the Soviet Union abruptly abandoned the competition (1987), watched its client states shift allegiances (1989), and finally disintegrated (1991). With the Soviet Union's demise, the United States intervened with increasing confidence in foreign conflicts and entertained the belief that military power could reshape the international order.

Given the centrality of military competition to the Cold War and the change in the balance of power that characterised its end, it is natural to question the role military developments played in the Cold War's denouement and the shaping of the post-Cold War world. In this context, a theory has emerged, which can be termed the military revolution hypothesis, that links developments in weaponry with the demise of the Soviet Union and the rise of US primacy.

According to military professionals and defence intellectuals, a military revolution has been underway since the 1970s. The core of the military revolution is a set of new technologies that permit armed forces to locate a large number of targets and destroy them precisely at long ranges. Key to the revolution are developments in precision guided munitions (PGMs), digital networks, long-range sensors, reconnaissance systems, unmanned aerial vehicles (UAVs) and stealth technologies. For experts, the proper exploitation of these technologies requires thoroughgoing organisational reform, including flattening hierarchical pyramids, restructuring combat units into smaller and more flexible components and blurring inter-service distinctions.

Besides its status as a technical postulate, the military revolution has become a historic theory with a four-part narrative. According to this narrative:

(1) President Ronald Reagan's administration deliberately engaged the Soviet Union in a high technology arms race with the aim of achieving military superiority and ruining the Soviet economy;

(2) recognising that their armed forces would soon be obsolete, the Soviet leadership abandoned their offensive doctrine and withdrew from Eastern Europe;

(3) after the Soviet Union's demise, the technologies developed under the Reagan administration formed the basis of a 'revolution in military affairs' permitting US forces to vanquish regional adversaries at little cost; and

(4) the further exploitation of these technologies demands 'military transformation', which should provide the United States with an indelible edge against opponents as diverse as al-Qaeda and China (Schweizer 1994; Friedman 2000; Owens 2000[B]; Barnett 2004; Arquilla 2006).

Compared to past military innovations, American proponents of the military revolution claim that it will empower globalised capitalist democracies and enfeeble totalitarian states (Cebrowski and Barnett 2003).

This study examines the history of the military revolution from the last decade of the Cold War to the present day and asks whether the military revolution narrative stands up to scrutiny. Are emerging technologies changing the nature of war? Did fear of these technologies pave the way for a graceful end to the Cold War? Does the military revolution explain the United States' military victories in the former Yugoslavia (1995 and 1999), Iraq (1991 and 2003) and Afghanistan (2001)? And has the military revolution served as a template for drastically reorganising the US armed forces? My argument is that each part of the formulation of the revolutionary military narrative is, for the most part, wrong. Although US military technology advanced dramatically towards the end of the Cold War, these developments contributed little to the decrepitude of the Soviet Union's already faltering economy and failed to convince the Soviet leadership to abandon their superpower ambitions. While the Cold War's finale indeed left the United States in a position of unprecedented military dominance, this was more the artefact of the Soviet Union's collapse rather than, admittedly, impressive developments in US military technology. Arguably, the military revolution's greatest impact has been its post-Cold War impact on US perceptions about the 'fungibility' of military force. Following the Vietnam War, the US armed forces argued that military force should not be employed if stringent criteria were not met. Overwhelming force, clear objectives, an exit strategy and the mobilisation of reserves combined to set a very high bar for when political leaders could use force. After the end of the Cold War, these criteria became an obstacle to the United States' using its impressive military capabilities in support of foreign policy objectives. Within this context, the notion of a high-tech 'revolution in military affairs' was instrumentalised in support of the new era of assertive 'gunboat diplomacy' called for by the Clinton Doctrine and George W. Bush's pursuit of US geopolitical primacy. However, contrary to expectations, the United States' revolutionary new military capabilities have proven largely irrelevant to the new security challenges that have emerged, including peacekeeping, counterinsurgency and re-establishing government in failed states.

The military-technical revolution, 1980–1989

According to the standard 'revolution in military affairs' (RMA) narrative, President Ronald Reagan won the Cold War by challenging the Soviet Union to a high-tech arms race. When the Soviet Union bankrupted itself attempting to keep up, the Soviet armed forces abandoned their traditional offensive doctrine and withdrew from their foreign commitments. For RMA enthusiasts, the Soviet Union's shift to a defensive doctrine in 1985 was a critical event. After the Soviet Union's defeat, the new technologies of the Reagan era became a valuable legacy bequeathed to Reagan's successors.

While a triumphalist narrative of the end of the Cold War is superficially attractive, it obscures the ambiguous legacy of the Reagan build-up. Many of the weapons systems that Reagan promoted exceeded the bounds of 1980s technology. Space-based missile defences, laser weapons and 'assault breaker' systems either never came into service or only entered production after the Cold War ended. Worse, the Reagan build-up undermined crisis stability by accentuating the fundamental asymmetry of the Cold War, wherein Soviet land power in Europe confronted superior US air and sea power overseas. While the Reagan build-up detracted from deterrence stability, there is little proof that it 'forced' the Soviet Union to abandon the Cold War, which owed much more to the 'new thinking' of the Soviet leadership.

When Reagan was elected president in 1980, the East–West balance-of-power was superficially more disadvantageous than ever. Because of its weaker industrial base and navy, the Soviet Union planned to unleash an armoured blitzkrieg, in the event of war, to overrun Western Europe and seize the entrances to the North Sea. From the late 1960s, the Soviet armed forces entertained hopes that they could conduct their offensive conventionally or at least not employ nuclear weapons until NATO did. To prepare for this type of warfare, the Brezhnev administration expanded the Soviet armed forces from 90 motor rifle divisions to 150, and increased the armoured power of each division by 30% and its artillery firepower by 50 to 100% (Friedman 2000). To fund this gigantic arms build-up and improvements to the navy, the Soviet Union dedicated between 15 and 40% of its GDP to defence (Odom 1998; Strayer 1998).

While the Soviet Union expanded its armed forces, NATO defence budgets declined. By the late 1970s, the Soviet Union's 1977 deployment of SS-20 missiles, the 1978 Soviet-Cuban intervention in the Ogaden, and the 1979 invasion of Afghanistan created an atmosphere bordering on crisis. Assumptions about exotic new Soviet anti-submarine warfare technology, the effectiveness of the missile defences and the accuracy of Soviet ICBMs even led Washington 'hawks' to imagine a world where Machiavellian leaders could selectively eliminate US nuclear forces and provoke NATO's collapse (Gray 1979).

Paradoxically, the Soviet General Staff began to worry about the future of Soviet military power at precisely the moment when the Soviet armed forces attained their greatest capabilities. Fundamentally, the basis of military power was shifting from the products of heavy industry, which the Soviets produced efficiently, to new technologically sophisticated weaponry that incorporated micro-electronics. Beginning in the latter phases of the Vietnam War and the 1973 Arab–Israeli War, guided weapons played a more significant role in warfare. Meanwhile, the micro-electronics revolution sweeping civilian economies in the non-communist world promised dramatic improvements in circuit miniaturisation and calculation speeds, and it would only be a matter of time before improvements in data processing found military applications. As Soviet military planners grasped these realities, they became alarmed that the Soviet Union's civilian economy was weak in precisely those dual-use technologies upon which the West's new weaponry was based.

By the late 1970s, Soviet officers began to argue that a military-technical revolution was underway. Tied together, the emerging technologies of informatics and precision guided weaponry would change the art of war, permitting a small number of high quality systems to incapacitate larger enemy forces by surgically destroying enemy weapons and command-and-control nodes directing them. Taken to their logical conclusion, these developments would nullify the Soviet Union's numeric advantage (Gareev 1998). Conscious that their own country lacked the civilian economic base to master the new technologies, Soviet officers feared rather than welcomed the military-technical revolution.

Thus, on the eve of the Cold War's last decade, the military balance was perceived as increasingly unfavourable by the West, but technological trends threatened the Soviet Union in the long term. Elected in 1980, the incoming Reagan administration was deeply committed to a military build-up. However, what type of build-up remained a matter of debate. Because the United States' main weakness lay in quantitative inferiority, many argued that the simplest solution was to build large numbers of moderately sophisticated weapons and base more US forces in Western Europe (Kaldor 1986; Canby 1987; Stevenson 1993). Overall, US weapons were already more sophisticated and costly than their Soviet equivalents, and it made economic sense to compromise on quality in order to field larger forces.

Counter-intuitively, the Reagan administration chose the opposite approach and decided to increase the United States' lead in high-tech weaponry. Monitoring Soviet writings on the military-technical revolution, the Pentagon's Office of Net Assessment alerted US decision-makers about Soviet fears of technological obsolescence. As the Office's director, Andrew Marshall (2002: i), remembers, 'At that time, it was the United States that was laying the groundwork for the revolution, but it was the Soviet military theorists, that were intellectualizing about it ... We concluded that it would be useful to intensify those concerns by further investment in the "reconnaissance-strike-complexes" that were central to their vision.'

Marshall's argument dovetailed with other intellectual currents in the Reagan administration. CIA Director William Casey believed that a reinvigorated arms race would overtax the faltering Soviet economy. By giving this arms race a high-tech dimension, Marshall contributed to Casey's vision. Meanwhile, Reagan himself believed that US technology and the capitalist system could accomplish miracles, destroying missiles and obliterating waves of tanks (Friedman 2000). Influenced by Marshall and Casey, Reagan deliberately chose to conduct a high-tech arms race. Although the arms build-up began late in President Jimmy Carter's administration, which raised the defence budget to 5.3% of GDP in 1980, it assumed massive proportions under Reagan. By 1983, the United States spent 7.1% of its GDP on defence, but because the economy grew as a whole, defence expenditures continued to rise until the United States was spending 49% more annually on defence in 1986 than a decade previously (Stockholm International Peace Research Institute [SIPRI] 1979, 1987). For the most part, the Reagan build-up focused on developing and procuring advanced weaponry. While the defence budget grew by nearly 50%, force structures remained virtually unchanged, increasing by less than 5% (The International Institute for Strategic Studies [IISS] 1978, 1988). With far more money being expended on forces no larger than before, the Reagan build-up massively re-capitalised the armed forces.

The years preceding the Reagan build-up witnessed rapid progress in semi-conductors, lasers and stealth technologies. The Air Force's Wide Area Antiarmor Munitions (WAAM) Project of 1975 aimed to develop a family of 'smart' munitions permitting small numbers of aircraft to destroy large numbers of enemy tanks (GAO/C-MASAD-83-12 1983). Meanwhile, the Navy's work on automated air defence systems focused on defeating saturation attacks (Smith 1981). Finally, the Defense Advanced Projects Research Agency's (DARPA) 'assault breaker' project of 1978 strived to network surveillance systems and long-range precision anti-tank weapons to destroy enemy armored forces. By the late 1970s, Secretary of Defense Harold Brown and Under Secretary of Defense William Perry viewed these projects as forming the basis of an 'Offset Strategy' whereby US technology would offset Soviet numerical superiority. In short, the Reagan administration invested heavily in the programmes inaugurated by the Carter administration and introduced other advanced technology programmes as well. Table 10.1 provides a list of high technology programmes that benefitted from Reagan's build-up.

Since the Soviet Union abandoned its offensive military doctrine seven years after the Carter–Reagan build-up began and two years before the end of the Cold War, the question should be posed whether US investments in high-tech weaponry precipitated either event. Based on the evidence available, the answer appears to be no. If anything, the Reagan build-up prompted the Soviet armed forces to adopt increasingly offensive war plans and provided 'hard liners' with arguments for postponing reforms. Indeed, having forecast the potential of the new technology, the Soviet high command became alarmed at its appearance. However, for the most part, the military-technical revolution did not become a reality overnight and the Soviets thought there was still time to counter US developments (Salmanov 1995). In the short term, the best counter to US high-tech military power was to accelerate the already rapid offensive operations envisaged in war plans. Because US 'maritime strategy' risked depriving the Soviet Union of its secure nuclear second strike within twenty days and NATO's

Table 10.1 *Reagan's 'revolutionary' technologies*

Surveillance and reconnaissance systems	'Smart' weapons	Other high technology programmes
E-8 JSTARS recon. sys.	Tomahawk Cruise Missile	* Strategic Defense Initiative
LANTIRN recon. pod	AGM-129 Cruise Missile	F-117 Stealth Fighter
Aegis AAW System	* AGM/MGM-137 Stealth Missile	B-2 Stealth Bomber
* Aquila UAV	BAT Missile	* A-12 Stealth Aircraft
* Tactic Blue stealth recon. sys.	AGM-114 Hellfire Anti-Tank Missile	MX Missile
* PLSS	* FOG-M Anti-Tank Missile	
* Precision Location Strike Sys.	AGM-159 Joint Stand-Off Weapon	
* All-Source Analysis Sys.	* Counter-Air Missile	
* Advanced Synthetic Aperture Radar System	* Axe Anti-Airfield Missile	
	* AGM/BGM-136 Anti-Radar Missile	
	* MRASM Anti-Runway Cruise Missile	
	* CQM/CGM-121 Air Defense Suppression Drone	
	M712 Copperhead Artillery Projectile	
	ATACM Missile Launcher	

Note
* indicates cancellation.

'follow-on forces attack' doctrine threatened to destroy second-echelon Soviet forces before they could reach the front line, US policies created a situation whereby Soviet ground forces had to conventionally overrun West Europe before US attacks shifted the balance of power (Salmanov 1995; Hattendorf 2004). Because the Reagan administration had not contributed any additional ground forces to NATO's front line in West Germany, Soviet theorists thought they had a three-week window to conquer Europe before US air and sea offensives could exercise a decisive influence. By pushing armoured forces forward before hostilities began, attacking deep (150–300 kilometres) into the NATO rear with armoured operational manoeuvre groups, and conducting operations at a rapid tempo, Soviet forces could disrupt allied defences, neutralise US high technology and reach Europe's Atlantic coast within two to three weeks, twice as fast as previously planned (Odom 1998).

Along with Soviet efforts to accelerate military operations, the US development of long-range PGMs drove the Soviets to value pre-emption. Because PGMs could be used without observable military preparations, the Soviets became increasingly concerned that the United States was developing a surprise attack capability (Salmanov 1995; Gareev 1998). Meanwhile, Soviet analysts deduced that the most effective counter to US technology was to wage non-linear battle which would deny the United States the concentrated targets that its weapons could destroy. However, waging a non-linear battle involved attacking before NATO could mobilise (Glantz 1995).

From the point of view of deterrence, the interaction of US new technology and Soviet doctrinal responses was destabilising. Fearing an American surprise attack and believing that it was in their interest to attack before NATO mobilised, the Soviet armed forces could be tempted to strike pre-emptively during an international crisis. Also worried about US counter-force missiles, missile defences and anti-submarine warfare, Soviet leaders had an incentive to use their nuclear arsenal before it could be attrited to the point of irrelevance (Posen 1982). Although the Soviet General Staff developed doctrinal counters to the military revolution in the short term, the long-term aim of Soviet reformers was to re-shape the military industrial base. The Chief of the Soviet General Staff, Field Marshal Nikolai Ogarkov, hoped that reducing spending on civil defence, tanks, aircraft carriers and nuclear weapons would release resources to reinvest in micro-electronics (Kokoshin 1999). However, entrenched interests stymied efforts to reallocate resources and the Soviet industrial complex failed to articulate a long-term response to advanced US weaponry (Gareev 1998). This effort was further hamstrung by effective Western restrictions on technology transfers, which benefitted from a Soviet informant providing unparalleled data on Soviet technology acquisition efforts (Faure 2004).

Unwilling to internally reallocate economic resources and unable to buy and steal the new technologies, the Soviet technology gap with the United States widened. Whereas Soviet armaments were generally considered to be world-class in the late 1970s, by the end of the Cold War the Soviet Union lagged behind in numerous important areas. When, a decade after the end of the Cold War, the Russian deputy minister of defence evaluated Russian capabilities in fifteen technological areas critical to the military revolution, he rated Russia as world-class in only two technologies and poor in seven (Battilega *et al.* 2001). Thus, despite the efforts of reforms on the Soviet General Staff, the Soviet Union failed to develop technological counters to US revolutionary weaponry. However, in the eyes of Soviet military professionals, military obsolescence was still only a distant prospect at the end of the Cold War. While Soviet officers were less sanguine about their long-term competitiveness, few thought that their state should abandon its superpower aspirations.

Although the Reagan administration invested in revolutionary military technology and the Soviet leadership attempted, but failed, to develop a long-term military counter to this process, this penultimate phase of the arms race was incidental to the end of the Cold War. Ideologically and economically, new generations of Soviet leaders were willing to break with the policies of their predecessors. As early as 1981, the Soviet Politburo secretly renounced the use of force to compel Eastern European governments to obey Soviet dictates (Mastny and Byrne 2006). By the time Mikhail Gorbachev became First Secretary of the Communist Party in 1985, Soviet reformers already considered it necessary to terminate bipolar rivalry and reduce defence budgets. In pursuing these objectives, political reformers disregarded the military-technical revolution. In his effort to obtain a more pliant military leadership, Gorbachev retired Ogarkov. In seeking greater cooperation with the West, Gorbachev then imposed a defensive doctrine on the Warsaw Pact in 1987 (Kokoshin 1999). Finally, also in 1987, the Gorbachev administration agreed to scrap one of its only successes in developing conventional deep-strike weapons – the Oka missile system – as one of the trade-offs for signing the Intermediate-Range Nuclear Forces (INF) Treaty (Zaloga 2006). Thus, from the moment Gorbachev took power, the military revolution and Reagan's high technology military build-up were minor concerns for a group of reformers preoccupied with transforming Soviet society. In this context, forces unleashed by political reforms proved far more lethal to the Soviet state than Reagan's investment in a military-technical revolution.

The new gunboat diplomacy (1990–2000)

With the end of the Cold War, the nature of the debate on military revolution changed. Whereas the Offset Strategy of the Carter administration and Reagan's build-up were driven by the need to compensate for Soviet numeric advantages and to play on Soviet weakness in high-tech methods of warfare, no such focus existed for US military innovation in the 1990s. Prior to the end of the Cold War, the military revolution debate centred on the unlikely contingency of a conventional war in Europe, while largely ignoring the potential impact of the new technologies on the many conflicts and crises that constituted real (as opposed to potential) security challenges. In this context, the military leadership's calls for 'overwhelming force' and 'clear exit strategies' constrained the United States' enormous military force in support of foreign policy objectives. After the 1991 Gulf War, defence policy-makers began arguing that the military revolution would permit the United States to employ force more flexibly and at less cost. Despite the armed forces' own recognition that military technology was changing dramatically, they took few proactive steps to embrace the military revolution of the 1990s and, with the notable exception of the Air Force, resisted the new gunboat diplomacy implicit in the so-called Clinton Doctrine.

Until the 1990s, American military beliefs about the use of force were shaped by the Vietnam War and embarrassing incidents such as Mayaguez (1975) and Desert One (1980). After failing in Southeast Asia, the armed forces rebuilt their professional identity on their ability to fight a short, high intensity, conventional war in defence of a vital national interest. Conversely, military leaders resisted efforts to commit them to other missions or theatres. As part of the military effort to limit political options to use force, General Creighton Abrams imposed the 'total force' concept (1973) whereby it became virtually impossible for a president to deploy ground combat forces without taking the politically charged decision to mobilise reserves (Lock-Pullan 2003). Later, General Colin Powell wrote and publicised the so-called Powell Doctrine as a means of further limiting the likelihood that US military forces would ever face 'another Vietnam'. To this end, Powell insisted that the United States should only use force: as a last resort; in overwhelming quantities; to achieve clear objectives; and when a predetermined exit strategy had been formulated (Cohen 1995).

Until the end of the Cold War, US political leaders tacitly accepted the limitations the military imposed on their ability to use force. The Nixon and Reagan doctrines aimed to accomplish foreign policy objectives by shifting the onus for achieving desirable outcomes from US armed forces to allies and 'freedom fighters'. Likewise, when the United States used its own military forces, it did so timorously. Grenada (1982) and Panama (1989) witnessed the use of overabundant military power to subdue feeble opponents, while clashes with the Iranian Navy and Libyan Air Force occurred in mediums where US forces faced little danger. Only the ill-fated US intervention in Lebanon (1982–4) constitutes an exception to the rule that the US armed forces confined political leaders to all-or-nothing options.

The 1991 Gulf War fundamentally challenged post-Vietnam beliefs about the fungibility of force and inaugurated the post-Cold War debate on the military revolution. Possessing a 500,000 strong army and a plethora of military equipment, Iraq appeared to be a formidable opponent. Believing that the United States could not muster overwhelming force or achieve decisive results, the Chairman of the Joint Chiefs of Staff, Powell, opposed forcibly liberating Kuwait (Cohen 1995). Insistent on the need to expel Iraq from Kuwait, President George H. W. Bush overruled Powell's objections, but met military demands for large forces. Compared with the preceding debates, the actual war proved anti-climactic. After amassing 400,000 personnel in Saudi Arabia, the United States vanquished Iraq after only one month of bombing and four days of ground combat; only 293 Americans died in the pursuit of victory. Given the speed and decisiveness of the campaign, many concluded that the overwhelming force demanded by the armed forces had proven superfluous and that the military revolution predicted in the 1980s had become a reality. Stealth aircraft and cruise missiles struck heavily defended targets with impunity, Patriot missiles reportedly shot down Iraqi missiles and US PGMs destroyed enemy tanks. Because the war showcased so many 'revolutionary' weapons developed since the 1970s, the United States' extraordinary victory was perceived to be a product of the new technologies. During subsequent debates, experts and policy-makers argued that technical changes made it imperative for the armed forces to radically transform themselves and lowered the costs of the United States using force.

In 1992, Lieutenant-Colonel Andrew Krepinevich wrote a confidential report for the Pentagon's Office of Net Assessment arguing that the nature of warfare was changing and that the favoured platforms of the Army, Air Force and Navy were destined for obsolescence (Krepinevich 1992). To frame the emerging policy debate, the Office's director, Marshall, changed the name of the revolution. Rather than referring to a 'military-technical revolution' (MTR), as analysts had done throughout the Reagan era, Marshall began to speak of a 'revolution in military affairs' (RMA). This lexical shift reflected Marshall's desire to steer the military revolution debate away from the technological determinism implied in the Soviet MTR concept and instead emphasise the necessity for US armed forces to proactively change to take advantage of the revolutionary possibilities opened up by new technology (Lomov 1973). Following Krepinevich's study, the Center for Strategic and International Studies (CSIS) concluded that a 'military-technical revolution' was underway (1993), while a popular book by Alvin and Heidi Toffler (1995) argued that an epochal change in warfare was underway.

Influenced by the Office of the Net Assessment and scholarship emanating from think-tanks, the concept of the RMA gradually won over decision-makers in Washington, especially after Perry, one of the architects of America's Offset Strategy, was named Secretary of Defense in 1994. As early as 1995, Perry dedicated part of his annual report to the RMA. Shortly thereafter (1996), he prodded the Joint Chiefs of Staff to evoke information superiority and precision engagement in the armed forces' futuristic Joint Vision 2010 and embedded the notion of an RMA in the 1997 Quadrennial Defense Review (Conley 1998).

Regardless of the growing ubiquity of the RMA in official documents, the services resisted changing procurement priorities. During the Reagan administration, the armed forces supported investments in exotic capabilities because defence budgets were large enough to also fund procurement of their favourite platforms. With the post-Cold War drop in procurement expenditures by 70 per cent, it was no longer a question of buying revolutionary technology and routine modernisation, but a trade-off between the two. When forced to choose, the armed forces preferred guarding their traditional programmes to modernise or replace existing fighters, tanks, artillery, destroyers and aircraft carriers.

For domestic political reasons, the Clinton administration proved unwilling to expend political capital on promoting the RMA. Political difficulties related to Clinton's evasion of the draft during the Vietnam War and efforts to revise military policies towards homosexuals and women left the government leery of another political battle with the military. The result was military evolution rather than revolution. The budget cuts after the end of the Cold War were spread evenly between the armed services and each service retained its existing organisational structures in a reduced form (eighteen Army divisions were reduced to ten and sixteen naval carrier battlegroups were reduced to twelve). This retention of existing structures and continued commitment to long-standing procurement objectives left few resources for investment in revolutionary capabilities. The Clinton administration's most successful RMA initiatives involved reducing the costs and increasing the volumes of PGMs in US arsenals. Whereas laser-guided bombs cost $75,000 apiece, the Clinton administration supported the development of GPS (satellite) guided Joint Direct Attack Munition (JDAM) bombs that cost less than half as much (Weiner n.d.). Similarly, using a higher volume of commercial components, the administration succeeded in lowering the cost of Tomahawk cruise missiles from $1.2 million to $800,000 apiece. US aviation, in general, embraced PGMs more than ever before. Whereas only 10% of US combat aircraft could use PGMs in 1991, 69% were so outfitted in 1995 and 90% by 1999.

Besides these modest RMA projects, the armed services opposed efforts to substitute new concepts for their favoured platforms. When DARPA proposed, in 1996, to develop an inexpensive ($500 million) stealth cruise missile ship, the Navy opposed the so-called 'arsenal ship' because it preferred to acquire destroyers at $2 billion apiece (Friedman n.d.). Similarly, while the Army conducted experiments such as digitising an infantry division and engaging in a long-range reflection on the 'Army After Next', the Army's primary programmes and structures, such as the Crusader artillery systems and armoured divisions, remained decidedly traditional. Meanwhile, the Air Force neglected UAVs and persisted with acquiring new fighter aircraft, even though these were superfluous without the Soviet threat. Thus, while the armed services willingly co-opted the *rhetoric* of military revolution, their spending and organizational patterns remained locked in more traditional paradigms.

Although the Clinton administration failed to induce the armed forces to embrace revolutionary change, perceptions of an RMA shaped US decisions to use force. Whereas the Powell Doctrine's calls for overwhelming force and a clear exit strategy rendered the use of force politically complex, the military revolution appeared to enable US military forces to achieve victory without risking the lives of large numbers of soldiers or committing the United States to lengthy foreign deployments. Air Force claims and civilian perceptions of the utility of air power were central to this development. Since the Air Force's publication of Colonel John Warden's *The Air Campaign* in 1988, the Air Force argued that PGMs and air power would permit the United States to achieve its objectives. After the dramatic victory of 1991, Air Force advocates argued that new technology now made it possible for air power to win wars on its own and without losses to US troops (Hallion 1992). When compared with the encumbering strictures of the Powell Doctrine and the Army's 'total force' concept, the Air Force's vision offered political leaders a military instrument that could be used flexibly in support of diplomatic initiatives and at little domestic political cost. Such a fungible and economic form of military force proved extremely attractive to President Clinton, who was personally convinced that the United States had an obligation to stop genocide and mass-casualty wars.

Powell and other advocates of restraint unsuccessfully attempted to halt the United States' drift to a form of 'gunboat diplomacy' based on air power and long-range attacks. Contesting the Air Force's narrative of the Gulf War, they argued that the air offensive destroyed much less Iraqi military material than reported, contributed negligibly to the Republican Guard's defeat and wholly failed to destroy Iraq's mobile

Scud missiles (Cohen and Keaney 1993; Biddle 1996; Newell 1998). In their eyes, the Gulf War confirmed, rather than refuted, the need for overwhelming force. The clash between advocates of the Powell Doctrine and partisans of the flexible and economic use of force was brought about by the collapse of Yugoslavia. When George H. W. Bush and Clinton both appeared to favour the use of force in 1992, Powell rendered it politically impossible to do so by publicising his opposition to any such intervention (Weigley 1993). Unwilling to overrule Powell during an election campaign, Bush and Clinton shelved their plans to intervene, until the continuing war prompted the Clinton administration to revisit its decision not to use force in 1995. However, when it finally chose to use force, the Clinton administration employed air power, rather than run the political risks inherent in deploying ground forces. Between 28 August and 14 September 1995, US aircraft bombed Bosnian Serb targets on twelve days. Compared with the 1991 Gulf War, when only 8 per cent of US air-delivered munitions were PGMs, 70 per cent were PGMs in 1995 (Owen 2000).

Success in Bosnia reinforced the perception that the United States could employ force at little cost or risk and contributed to US decisions to use force on three further occasions during Clinton's presidency. The United States conducted long-range air and missile campaigns against Iraq, Afghanistan and the Sudan in 1998, and Serbia in 1999. Throughout these three campaigns, the United States did not suffer a single combat death and successfully brought military power to bear on distant objectives. In referring to Kosovo, the penultimate Clinton intervention, one White House official noted that the administration had adopted the 'anti-Powell Doctrine', while another gibed that, 'you won't see Colin Powell on TV today talking about the Powell Doctrine' (Daalder and O'Hanlon 1999). However, the question must be asked about how revolutionary and effective these campaigns were.

While air power advocates point to the 1995 Bosnia campaign as vindication for their arguments, there were at least four other factors weighing on the Bosnian Serb leadership. Besides NATO bombing, the Bosnian Serb situation was becoming increasingly perilous as a result of:

(1) the renaissance of Croatian military power demonstrated in their August blitzkrieg against the Krajina;
(2) the increasing capabilities of the Bosnian Muslim and Croat armies;
(3) Serbia's economic pressure on its allies to come to terms; and
(4) the deployment of an Anglo-Franco-Dutch combat force to Sarajevo to suppress Serbian artillery fire.

In 1998, the United States conducted two brief campaigns combining PGMs, air power and long-range strikes. After terrorist attacks against US embassies in Kenya and Tanzania, US armed forces bombed a supposed chemical weapons factory in Sudan and struck al-Qaeda affiliated training camps in Afghanistan. Later, in December 1998, the United States and United Kingdom conducted four days of intensive bombing against Iraq. Throughout these offensives, the United States manifested its military power with astonishing speed and at long ranges with cruise missiles. The United States expended 415 cruise missiles in four days against Iraq and seventy-five in one volley against Afghanistan. But despite the technological acumen of the US attacks, the attack on the chemical weapons facility in Sudan was unsuccessful – it turned out to be a pharmaceutical factory. Al-Qaeda's leadership survived the strikes in Afghanistan and the chemical and biological weapons facilities in Iraq were figments in intelligence analysts' imaginations. As it turned out, the ability to strike locations anywhere on the globe is only useful if intelligence locates valid targets.

The last military intervention of the Clinton administration was the aerial campaign to coerce Serbia to evacuate Kosovo. A volley of cruise missiles opened the way on 24 March 1999 for attacks by aircraft carrying a high percentage (29 per cent) of PGMs. For the first time, stealth bombers participated in combat operations, UAVs operated continuously over enemy territory and cheap satellite-guided weapons constituted a high proportion of the US arsenal. When Serbia capitulated after seventy-eight days of bombardment, the result was seen as a vindication of air power. However, the Kosovo campaign was not a dramatic military success. Precision attacks inflicted negligible damage on Serbian units engaged in ethnic cleansing and the air campaign failed to decapitate Serbia's leadership or convince its population to revolt. Strategic success was achieved because of Serbia's failure to divide the international coalition and enlist Russian support (Posen 2000).

Overall, the military revolution's record in the first post-Cold War decade is a study of contrasts. On the one hand, faced with declining defence budgets, the US armed forces preserved existing force structures and procurement programmes. To the chagrin of would-be reformers in the Office of the Secretary of Defense, this resulted in the services adopting RMA rhetoric to justify traditional policies. While the armed services resisted radical change, they pursued incremental improvements, such as the growing use of PGMs, illustrated in Table 10.2.

From the point of view of the cost of using force, RMA technology widened options available to US policy-makers. In part because

Table 10.2 *PGMs and military campaigns*

Campaign	PGM capable aircraft (%)	PGMs used (%)
Desert Storm (Iraq, 1991)	10	8
Deliberate Force (Bosnia, 1995)	69	70
Allied Force (Kosovo, 1999)	90	29

of precision strikes, stealth and high-tech surveillance capabilities, the United States vanquished Iraq at little human cost. During the later interventions of 1995 to 1999, the United States proved capable of manifesting force at substantial distances and without suffering combat deaths. In a real sense, the military revolution encouraged the international activism of the Clinton administration and the Tomahawk cruise missile, of which over 1,000 were fired, became the penultimate weapon of Clinton's gunboat diplomacy.

Despite the beguiling results of these military escapades, the true utility of high-tech military force remains questionable. Some interventions (the attacks of 1998) appear not to have achieved any strategic objectives, while others (Bosnia and Kosovo) did so because of the combined effects of bombing and other international developments. Even in the case of the apparent successes in the Balkans, rapid military campaigns have been succeeded by interminable constabulary actions, which still occupy 24,000 NATO soldiers (IISS 2008).

The false promise of transformation, 2001–2008

For true believers of the RMA, the 1990s were a frustrating decade. While conflicts during the decade highlighted the importance of revolutionary technology, the armed forces failed to revise organisational or procurement policies to take advantage of advances in the field. When George W. Bush assumed power in January 2001, he did so with a team of policy-makers who saw transformation of the armed forces as a prerequisite for sustaining US hegemony. Unfortunately for these reformers, the wars waged by the Bush administration bear little resemblance to those they imagined. While both transformation advocates and the armed services focused on waging firepower-intensive conventional war, the United States became mired in lengthy counterinsurgencies.

Despite the armed forces' increasing fondness for the RMA, many within the defence policy-making community considered progress to be inadequate. In 1997, the National Defense Panel (NDP) reported that, 'we are on the cusp of a military revolution stimulated by rapid advances in information and information-related technologies ... If we do not lead the technological revolution, we will be vulnerable to it.' To catalyse transformation – a term first employed in the report – the NDP identified a need for $5–10 billion annually to fund advanced technologies (out of a procurement budget of $60 billion) and recommended creating a Joint Forces Command to implement the RMA (Conley 1998).

Although the NDP report's influence was limited, its message appealed to Republican defence intellectuals. As early as 1992, Secretary of Defense Richard Cheney and his Deputy, Paul Wolfowitz, linked exploiting the 'military-technical revolution' to sustaining US primacy in international relations (Slides for USDP 1991). During their eight years out of power, experience hardened them to the view that the armed forces' attachment to traditional modernisation posed the greatest obstacle to revolutionary reform. If the United States did not embrace radical new technologies and structures, then a future enemy (China) certainly would. When Wolfowitz and Cheney oversaw the drafting of a report entitled 'Rebuild America's Defense' (2000) for the neo-conservative Project for a New American Century (PNAC), they argued that transformation could be obtained with modest ($20 billion per year) increases to defence budgets and the cancellation of three major procurement programmes (the CVX aircraft carrier, Crusader artillery system and F-35 fighter) dear to the armed services. Presidential candidate George W. Bush echoed these sentiments in his first speech on defence policy (1999), when he stated that his objective was to foster 'a revolution in the technology of war' that he would finance by replacing 'existing programs with new technologies and strategies'.

At the same time as they determined how to produce military transformation, Republican intellectuals articulated an ambitious project for linking the RMA to the achievement of broad foreign policy objectives. Whereas the Clinton administration instrumentalised the military revolution to support limited and humanitarian objectives, the Bush administration came to view it as the key to deterring the emergence of a rival great power, eradicating terrorism, spreading democracy and ending the menace posed by 'rogue states'. Putting this view succinctly, PNAC (2000) stated that 'transforming [the Armed Forces] to exploit the revolution in military affairs' was 'the key to prolonging the *Pax Americana*'. After the terrorist attacks of 9/11, military transformation became central to the government's ambitious aim of waging a 'global war on terror' that would embrace much of the planet's surface and end in the reordering of distant societies. Pentagon consultant Thomas Barnett enlarged this vision, arguing that the US military could win a final victory over terrorism and international crime by forcibly integrating large and instable parts of the world into its prosperous and globalised core (Barnett 2004).

Once in power, the Bush administration aggressively pursued their aim of ensuring continued international primacy through military transformation. Only two weeks into the administration, Secretary of Defense Donald Rumsfeld announced that he would conduct a review of the armed forces. To lead this process, Marshall and the Office of Net Assessment were broadly empowered to commission studies, organise workshops and hold seminars (Roxborough 2002). In the preceding years, significant progress had been made in deciding what a transformed military should look like. Capitalising on advances in digital technologies, all future war would be 'network centric'. Connected to the totality of available sensors, including satellites, UAVs and manned reconnaissance platforms, all combat units in an area should share a common operational picture (COP). This would permit them to optimally coordinate ('self-synchronisation') fast-moving swarming attacks with little hierarchical control (Arquilla and Ronfeldt 2000). Because warfare of this sort would leverage speed and connectivity, many traditional military platforms were assumed to be virtually obsolete. Instead of armoured divisions equipped with tanks, land forces would be organised into small agile formations equipped with modular, wheeled vehicles firing a variety of munitions. Rather than being dominated by carrier battle groups, future naval warfare would feature numerous small combatants and large inexpensive arsenal ships. In the sky, satellites and UAVs would supplant manned aircraft.

Initially, Rumsfeld and Marshall planned to fund military transformation by cancelling three military platforms and disbanding two Army divisions. However, the armed services sought to pre-emptively discredit the administration's strategy. Working with supporters in Congress, the military high command insulted Rumsfeld's transformation policy by likening it to Hillary Clinton's 1993 healthcare initiative and leaked news of a tumultuous meeting between Rumsfeld and the Joint Chiefs (Roxborough 2002). Ultimately, a confrontation between the Secretary of Defense and the military was averted because of the terrorist attacks on 9/11. With the nation willing to spend more on defence, it was temporarily possible to pursue both routine modernisation and revolutionary transformation. As a consequence, the Secretary of Defense and the armed services log-rolled their favoured programmes. For example, the Navy exchanged its support for the 'transformational' Littoral Combat Ship for the Secretary's endorsement of the Navy's new destroyer.

The first military operation after 9/11, the Afghanistan campaign, appeared to validate the arguments made by Rumsfeld and his supporters. Operating autonomously from one another, but networked together via a tactical Webpage, US special forces teams developed a detailed operational picture of Taliban movements. Based on this information and data collected by UAVs and satellites, aircraft accurately bombarded Taliban forces. At the key battle of Mazar-i-Sharif, two teams of special forces used these technologies to ensure a victory of 3,000 Northern Alliance fighters against a 10,000-strong Taliban army (Knarr et al. n.d.).

The next campaign, against Iraq, in March 2003, was more equivocal in the use of revolutionary technology. The invasion of Iraq was a conventional operation, featuring 300,000 troops. However, these forces were supported by a range of reconnaissance sensors, including satellites, UAVs and aircraft, and information could be shared via a communications network featuring forty-two times the bandwidth available in 1991. Large numbers of combat aircraft were available to employ PGMs, which constituted 70 per cent of the munitions expended (Desportes 2007). In theory, situational awareness and long-range precision strikes should have permitted US forces to vanquish their adversaries without recourse to close combat. In fact, the Iraq War was filled with examples where remote sensors and digital networks failed to alert US forces of Iraqi movements. Below divisional level, front line commanders suffered from poor situational awareness and most battles began with the two sides blundering into each other. There were even occasions when the Iraqis achieved surprise. At a bridge on the road to Baghdad, three Iraqi brigades possessing 110 armoured vehicles launched a surprise attack against a US battalion (Talbot 2004). In many other engagements urban terrain enabled lightly armed Iraqi paramilitaries to attack at close range (Biddle 2004). Despite the ubiquity of close-combat and the failure of RMA technology, US forces triumphed in twenty-one days because of superior training and firepower.

At the same time as the United States waged its first campaigns of the twenty-first century, the Bush administration persevered with military transformation. Intellectually, this process continued to benefit from Rumsfeld's patronage and Marshall's advice. However, it was increasingly guided by retired Admiral Arthur Cebrowski, who directed a newly created Office for Force Transformation from October 2001. Prodded by the administration, the Army announced its plan for a Future Combat System, consisting of eighteen lightweight platforms,

which would achieve military superiority through battlespace awareness. According to recent estimates, this programme will cost $234 bil-
lion (Jackson n.d.). Meanwhile, the Navy unveiled its plans for fifty-five
modular Littoral Combat Ships, costing $400 million apiece. Finally,
the Air Force revealed plans to acquire sophisticated Unmanned Aerial
Combat Vehicles (UCAVs). All of these ambitious new procurement
programmes were pursued in addition to the armed forces' pre-existing
modernisation projects. As a consequence, the defence budget nearly
doubled. Not counting the wars in Iraq and Afghanistan, which have
been funded through supplemental budgets, US defence spending grew
from $269 billion in 1998 to $509 billion in 2008 (IISS 2008).

While the policy of simultaneously pursuing military revolution and
routine modernisation was proving costly, the later phases of the wars
in Iraq and Afghanistan revealed shortcomings with the military revolution itself. Since its inception, the military revolution concept was tied to
high intensity wars. Faced with prolonged counterinsurgencies, the utility of the military revolution has become uncertain. 'Information dominance' is hard to achieve in an environment where human intelligence
and linguistic skills are more important than the ability to permanently
observe an area with UAVs and satellites. Likewise, long-range PGMs
are worthless against guerrillas concealed amongst civilians. Meanwhile,
improvised explosive devices (IEDs), suicide attacks, rocket and mortar
strikes and rocket propelled grenades (RPGs) permit insurgents to stead-
ily inflict casualties (Henrotin 2006; La Grange and Balencie 2008).

This form of warfare has provoked a series of countermeasures from
US forces that run contrary to the principles of military transformation.
Rather than 'substituting battlespace awareness for passive armor', the
United States augmented the armoured protection of its forces. Humvees
and Stryker armoured vehicles have received additional armour and the
Department of Defense has ordered 12,000 Mine Resistant Ambush
Protected (MRAP) vehicles for $10 billion (IISS 2008; La Grange and
Balencie 2008). Instead of substituting technology for large numbers
of soldiers, the United States decided to increase its ground forces
by 92,000 personnel (IISS 2008). To counter the threat of IEDs, the
United States has also invested over $6 billion in a Joint IED Defeat
Organisation (La Grange and Balencie 2008). Paid for through supplemental budgets, US counterinsurgency procurement programmes
absorbed $47 billion in 2007 – a sum larger than the Russian defence
budget in its entirety (IISS 2008).

The counterinsurgencies in Iraq and Afghanistan are strategically
disturbing considering the Bush administration's ambition to capitalise
on 'military transformation' to reinforce US primacy. While US military forces may defeat other conventional armed forces at little cost to

themselves, disarming an opponent does not equate with achieving political objectives. In Iraq and Afghanistan, 'victory' depended on constituting friendly governments and re-establishing economic and social normalcy. However, sectarianism in Iraq and the Taliban's continuing popularity in Afghanistan have hindered the creation of popular governments.

Rumsfeld's early decision to fund revolutionary transformation and routine modernisation simultaneously and the United States' entanglement in Iraq and Afghanistan have arguably brought US defence policy-making to an existential choice. Today, including the supplemental budgets for Iraq and Afghanistan, the United States spends $622 billion a year on defence – far more than the rest of the world combined (IISS 2008). This budget embraces three distinct procurement paradigms. As illustrated by Table 10.3, there are transformational programmes, routine modernisation programmes, and programmes necessitated by ongoing counterinsurgencies. According to the United States' General Accounting Office, the future total official cost of these programmes exceeds $1.5 trillion (GAO-07–600CG 2007). Considering that the United States has been running annual budget deficits between $150 and 400 billion, many see current US procurement programmes as unsustainable (IISS 2008). For example, the United States' Comptroller General (GAO-07–600CG 2007) argues, 'The Pentagon buys what some want rather than what we need. And as budgets grow tighter, the military is going to have to distinguish unlimited wants from true needs.'

When the time comes to prioritise between different procurement priorities, it is unlikely that the Bush administration's 'transformational' programmes will survive. Lacking the political backing of the armed services and irrelevant to ongoing counterinsurgencies, transformation is the most politically vulnerable part of the United States' procurement agenda. And in some respects, the counter-revolution against military transformation has already begun. Discredited by the war in Iraq, Rumsfeld and Wolfowitz were ousted from government even before the end of the Bush administration. Without their patronage, the Office for Force Transformation was dissolved after its director, Arthur Cebrowski, passed away in 2005. Having lost these supporters, the principal locus for thought on transformation has become the Pentagon's Office of Net Assessment, whose director, Marshall, now approaches nonagenarian status.

Conclusion

After three decades of reflection on military revolution it is worth examining the current state of affairs. Facilitated by developments

Table 10.3 *Conflicting procurement priorities*

'Transformational' systems	'Routine modernization' programmes	Counterinsurgency programmes
Littoral Combat Ship	DDG-1000 Destroyer	MRAP Vehicles
Future Combat System (Army)	CV-21 (CVX) Aircraft Carrier	Armoured HUMVEE
Joint-Unmanned Combat Air Sys.	CGX Cruiser	Up-armouring Stryker vehicles
MQ-9 Reaper UCAV	Virginia Submarines	Vehicle re-sets
Lockheed Minion UCAV	F-22 Fighter	Joint IED Defeat Organization
* Darkstar Drone	F-35 Fighter	Unattended Ground Sensor
Space-Based Radar	F-18E Fighter	ground force increases (92,000 troops)
	V-22 Tilt-Rotor Aircraft	
	* Crusader Artillery System	
	* Comanche Helicopter	

Note
* indicates cancellation.

in micro-electronics, information technologies and material sciences, revolutionary military capabilities have been developed. Rather than being a pure byproduct of exogenous technological change, these developments occurred because US civilian defence policy-makers promoted them. From a technological point-of-view, progress has been spectacular. Whereas only 10 per cent of US aircraft used PGMs in 1991, the proportion of PGM capable aircraft rose to 90 per cent by 1999. While the ubiquity and effectiveness of PGM missiles has increased, their costs have decreased. In parallel, the digital communications bandwidth available to field commanders increased forty-two times between 1991 and 2003. Finally, while only a minuscule proportion of US aircraft featured stealth technology in 1991, many actual and future aircraft, UAVs and ships will be stealthy. As an ensemble, those developments permit previously unachievable military exploits. For example, whereas prolonged bombing campaigns against urban command-and-control targets formerly killed thousands of civilians, seventy-two days of NATO air attacks reportedly killed only 500 Serbian civilians. In terms of reach, US power has also benefitted from cruise missiles and JDAMs that can strike targets globally.

However, military innovation cannot be measured merely in terms of new technology. In terms of the military revolution, true innovation is only possible once existing military structures are superseded by ones capable of fully exploiting new technologies. The leading theorists of the military revolution, from Ogarkov to Marshall, have argued that today's emblematic military structures and platforms are destined for obsolescence. Judged by this standard, innovation has not occurred. According to John Arquilla (2008), US armed forces are 'profoundly in thrall to the past' and its 'military leaders will consistently favor stasis over change'. The main reason for the failure to realise deep organisational change is the domination of armed services by platform communities attached to existing hardware and the structures that accompany them (Builder 1989). As a result, the armed services only supported revolutionary developments when financed in parallel with traditional modernisation. Unfortunately, it has proven problematic financing both 'traditional' and 'revolutionary' agendas, even with the pharaonic defence budgets of Ronald Reagan and George W. Bush.

At present, it is too early to judge the impact that the failure to transform will have. War games at the Office of Net Assessment suggested that a 'transformed' China could defeat a 'traditional' US force in 2020. Arquilla (2008) likewise argues, 'We could find ourselves in the ironic position of outspending everyone else but still going into the next major war with outmoded weapons.' However, such prophecies of doom presuppose that 'transformation' provides the optimal means of organising a military force and that other Great Powers are pursuing this avenue. The first point is contested by traditionalists, who argue that the transformation agenda is misguided, and the second point is far from certain as other Great Powers also face bureaucratic challenges in transforming their armed forces.

Ultimately, the conflicts since the end of the Cold War are indeterminate as to the full impact of the military revolution. New technology has proven its value and increased the speed and distance at which conventional enemies can be defeated. However, in each of these cases, asymmetries in national means played a greater role than purely technical factors. Compared to Serbia, the United States' most capable conventional opponent since 1991, the United States' defence budget was nearly 200 times greater at the time of the Kosovo War (IISS 1998). It is unlikely that we will be able to appreciate the true impact of the military revolution until a Great Power with a transformed military fights one possessing traditional forces. Beyond questioning the value of the military revolution it is also necessary to examine its political impact. Although Reagan embraced the military revolution as a means of achieving military superiority over the Soviet Union, while also precipitating its financial decline, these policies were incidental to the end of the Cold War. The main impact of Reagan's policies was to propel the Soviets to adopt ever-more offensive military doctrines, which rendered the bilateral balance of power in Europe increasingly unstable. Only Gorbachev's political decision to impose a defensive doctrine in 1987 halted this dynamic.

Since the end of the Cold War, belief in a military revolution has comforted US political leaders about their supposed ability to shape international affairs. For the Democrats of the Clinton administration, cheap and effective military force became an argument for military responses to humanitarian catastrophes. For the Republicans of the Bush administration, this same force was vaunted for its ability to preserve and extend the reach of US primacy. As Cebrowski and Barnett (2003) observe, the political agenda behind US transformation was 'to reverse significant acts of aggression within a security system we seek to administer like an empire'. In short, while the RMA has reduced the price of defeating states equipped with ageing conventional forces, it has not facilitated the task of achieving an acceptable political solution to conflicts. Because war is waged to create a post-war order that is more beneficial than its pre-war equivalent, no military action can be judged independently of its political results. To the extent that the military revolution has given political leaders the ability to defeat states, without concomitantly enhancing their ability to shape post-war political outcomes, the revolution in military affairs can be said to serve as a dangerous and beguiling utopia.

11   From Berlin to Baghdad: learning the
      'wrong' lessons from the collapse of
      communism

Barbara J. Falk

Introduction

Closing in on the second decade of the post-communist era and reflect-
ing back on the revolutionary events of 1989 in Central and Eastern
Europe, it is fitting to examine whether and how differing discursive
understandings of the fall of communism have subsequently affected
domestic and foreign policy outcomes, particularly in the United
States. As the sole superpower left standing after the bipolar conflict,
US political elites and policy-makers were easily tempted by 'Cold
War triumphalism' – the claim that the disintegration of the Soviet
Empire in Central and Eastern Europe was a decisive victory for the
United States (Schrecker 2004: 2). Underneath this dizzying hubris,
especially expressed by US neo-conservative hard-liners, existed a set
of assumptions and policy prescriptions for the reorganisation of global order that, allied to the momentum gained by the tragedy of 9/11,
generated a sweeping vision for democratisation in the Middle East
and beyond.

Politicians and foreign policy-makers have long used history to frame
options and make decisions. However, history is usually not taken neu-
trally, but interpreted for what it teaches or portends (May 1973). Thus
US leaders actively took part in constructing the post-Second World
War internationalist order with a view to the isolationist 'mistakes'
made after the First World War. In the making of Cold War grand
strategy, the 'lesson' of Munich loomed large, that is, appeasement was

The author would like to thank Brad Abrams, David Last and Padraic Kenney for providing comments on earlier versions of this chapter, as well as Liam Stockdale and Geoff
Burt for their superb research and editorial assistance. An earlier version of this chapter appeared as Barbara Falk (2009), '1989 and Post-Cold War Policymaking: Were
the "Wrong" Lessons Learned from the Fall of Communism?' *International Journal of
Politics, Culture, and Society* 22(3). Used with the permission of Springer Science and
Business Media.

both dangerous and ineffective.[1] This chapter argues that, among the 'root causes' of Cold War triumphalism were a series of perceived 'lessons learned' from the *annus mirabilis* of 1989 and the collapse of the Soviet Union in 1991. However, in each case, either the 'wrong lesson' was learned, or mistaken conclusions were drawn and/or underestimated from the 'right lesson'. The first five 'lessons' deal primarily with the role of the United States. In all five 'lessons', the key story is misperception both in terms of Cold War history and in terms of how these misperceptions determined mistakes in US policy-making. Iraq emerges as the most obvious example of how these misperceptions played into a larger chain of foreign policy-making assumptions, particularly because shared assumptions about how the Cold War was fought and won remained powerfully present and unifying for decision-makers. The remaining five lessons are drawn primarily from Cold War revisionist historiography, as well as area studies and comparative politics. A reading of these 'lessons' invokes a clearer understanding of what did and did not happen in the latter part of the Cold War, particularly during its endgame.

Lesson 1: 'regime change' from above and outside

The first lesson learned by Cold War triumphalists was a belief in the ability to generate 'regime change' from above and from the outside. This lesson is based on two faulty assumptions: first, that the United States was primarily responsible for the decline and collapse of the Soviet empire and, second, that the arms race was symbolic of the contest as a whole (e.g. Weinberger 1990; Pipes 1995; Gates 1996; Schweizer 2002).

The belief that the United States single-handedly 'won' the Cold War is not a view held solely by the political right, but rather represents a reigning consensus within the US political elite. In a typical speech made during his first presidential campaign at Georgetown University, then-Governor Bill Clinton stressed: 'Thanks to the unstinting courage and sacrifice of the American people, we were able to win [the] Cold War' (Clinton 1991). More than a decade later, then-Senator Barack

---

[1] Ernest May discusses the pitfalls of planning for the future based on the perceived lessons of the past in a variety of critical case examples, including how the post-Second World War scenario was based on preparing for the 'Last Peace' (after the First World War) and how the construction of Cold War foreign and defence policy was based largely on the lessons drawn from the non-prevention of the Second World War. For a similar argument, see Margaret Macmillan's *The Uses and Abuses of History* (2008).

Obama, also on the campaign trail for the presidency, discussed how the Cold War national security architecture constructed by Truman 'helped secure the peace and well-being of the nations of the world' (Obama 2007: 2).

However, it is certainly the case that the US narrative of 'victory', if hegemonic in the North American continent, is hardly universal. European perspectives on the Cold War – when they are not overdetermined by US accounts – differ markedly on key points. First, there is less emphasis on Western victory and more on communist failure, particularly with respect to the structural weaknesses of state socialism and the relative success of global capitalism (Chapter 5, this volume; Kornai 1992). Second, the role of intra-European dissident communities and social movements within Central and East European satellite states is accorded greater status (Garton Ash 1990, 1999). Nonetheless, the US intellectual consensus prevails, and continues to privilege US engagement internationally and in Europe, US military spending (along with 300,000 troops on European soil), US grand strategy (containment), and US leadership (from Truman to Reagan).[2]

No doubt the ability of the United States to 'outspend' the Soviet Union in the Cold War – not only in terms of absolute dollars but more critically as a much lower percentage of GDP – affected the economic health and deterioration of the Eastern bloc. However, the multiple economic failures of 'actually existing socialism', such as the privileging of heavy industry over consumer products, the chronic mismatch between supply and demand (not to mention bottlenecks in production and distribution), the long-term costs of the heavy subsidisation of basic goods such as foodstuffs, and the systemic inability to reward innovation, all collectively sounded the death knell for the command economy (Kornai 1992; Kotkin 2001).[3] Maintaining arsenals of nuclear deterrence was expensive for both sides, but could be more easily absorbed by the US economy via the dynamism of its military-industrial complex.

Nevertheless, it would be incorrect to suggest that the Russians were outspent into submission, or to assume that the arms race played a disproportionate role in the supposed US 'victory' –something made abundantly clear in Chapter 10 by Marc DeVore (this volume).

---

[2] For a convincing analysis of the US scholarly and ideological consensus over competing European narratives, see Cox (2007).

[3] Kotkin (2001: 10–28) notes how the 1970s oil boom masked and delayed the economic decline of the USSR. From the 1970s onward, the Soviet economy entered recession (even by official statistics) and other trends (from rising infant mortality and decreased life expectancy, to increases in the incidence of alcoholism, absenteeism and cancers related to toxic industrialised zones) were early and endemic indicators of decline, unrelated to the struggle with capitalism or the arms race.

Reagan's Strategic Defense Initiative may or may not have been the
'final straw for the Evil Empire', as Margaret Thatcher claimed, but
it was certainly not the only straw.[4] Unfortunately, the idea of militarily induced success twinned with an arrogance regarding US military
superiority contributed to the notion that regime change could be militarily driven and would be successful (Kinzer 2006). Moreover, this
narrative of successful 'regime change' built upon previous experience
of US-led efforts to drive the godless communists from power or stop
them attaining power, often in Cold War proxy conflicts in Africa, the
Middle East and Latin America. Although the televised experience of
eighteen dead US Army rangers being dragged through the streets of
Mogadishu, Somalia in 1993 temporarily dampened the public appetite
for humanitarian adventures abroad, the shock of 9/11 provided neo-
conservative visionaries and unilateralist realists already drunk on Cold
War triumphalism with the energy and political support necessary to
prevail over real and perceived enemies. Belief in the ability of US military might to generate cascading political change in the Middle East
was reinforced by strongly held views regarding what had been accom-
plished in 1989–91.[5] Historians will continue to debate for decades to
come the exact causal nature of the relationship between US actions
in the post-Cold War world and its view of itself as the unquestioned
victor in the superpower struggle, but preliminary conclusions suggest
that this view continues to be a decisive factor.

Lesson 2: the myth of the 'unipolar moment'

In 1990, flush with Cold War triumphalism, right-wing pundit and columnist for the *Washington Post* Charles Krauthammer penned a polemic
for *Foreign Affairs* entitled 'The Unipolar Moment'. Krauthammer
argued that the United States should seize its advantage as the world's

---

[4] The idea that US military expenditures was a major factor that led to the demise of
authoritarian communism in Central and Eastern Europe and the USSR is challenged
by some Russian scholars and by IR scholars operating outside the realist paradigm.
See for example, Arbatov (1992) and Kratochwil (1993). How military efforts co-existed with a larger and integrated Reaganite strategy that included economic warfare
and other 'carrot and stick' polices is discussed by Dobson (2005).

[5] For various complementary and contrasting explanations of the evolution of foreign
policy under the Bush administration, see Ivo H. Daalder and James M. Lindsay,
America Unbound: The Bush Revolution in Foreign Policy (2003); Bob Woodward's trio
of accounts, *Plan of Attack* (2004), *Bush at War* (2002), and *State of Denial* (2006);
Richard Clarke, *Against All Enemies: Inside America's War on Terror* (2004); Ron
Suskind, *The One Percent Doctrine: Deep Inside America's Pursuit of Its Enemies Since 9/11*
(2007); and Peter W. Galbraith, *The End of Iraq: How American Incompetence Created a
War Without End* (2006).

remaining superpower and engage in 'robust and difficult interventionism' (1990/1991: 32). The Cold Warriors had lost their traditional enemy, communism, and rather than argue for US-led multilateral engagement to ensure global governance of a 'new international order', Krauthammer warned of a new kind of security threat: 'small aggressive states armed with weapons of mass destruction and possessing the means to deliver them' (1990/91: 23). Moreover, the showpiece of this new US policy was an aggressive form of democracy promotion, backed up by the means of hard power. After all, since Krauthammer believed the United States won the Cold War, it followed logically that the United States was ultimately responsible for the unleashing of the democratisation impulse among the former satellite states of the Soviet bloc.

Cold War triumphalism and a belief in the opportunity presented by unipolarity infused the February 1992 Defense Planning Guidance (DPG) (an (in)famous document in that it was rejected by George H. W. Bush during his presidency as too militaristic and then resuscitated as the ideological inspiration behind the 2002 National Security Strategy). The DPG, leaked in advance to the *New York Times*, argued for a robust US response to potential strategic competitors – Russia, China and even Germany and Japan – so that they would be deterred from increasing or acquiring nuclear weapons. Again, the underlying assumption was that the United States had defeated the Soviet Union militarily, whitewashing decades of conservative restraint, containment, engagement and détente. The United Nations was understood as little more than the 'chatterbox on the Hudson' and, as the 1990s progressed and the international community failed to respond in a timely manner to the horrors of the nested conflicts in the former Yugoslavia and the genocide in Rwanda, more scorn was heaped on the much-beleaguered organ of inadequate global governance. Unipolarity as a fact began to be translated into unilateralism as a policy.

Moreover, infused with a sense of US exceptionalism, and influenced by Krauthammer and other neo-conservatives, unipolarity was viewed by the Bush White House through a lens of motivational purity (Daalder and Lindsay 2003: 45). The United States was not an empire; the spread of liberty and free markets benefitted everyone. It was a twist on the old saying that what was good for General Motors was good for the United States: what was good for the United States, what the United States wanted, was necessarily good for the world. After all, had not the newly liberated post-communist states of Central and Eastern Europe opted for political and economic models that looked peculiarly American? Krauthammer was joined in accepting and promoting these interlinking assumptions by neo-conservative ideologues involved in the Project for a New American Century (PNAC) and the American Enterprise Institute.[6] Although many in the Bush administration such as Donald Rumsfeld, Dick Cheney and Condoleezza Rice might be categorised as assertive nationalists and realists rather than neo-conservatives, they were certainly united in their assumptions that the United States won the Cold War, that global stability was backed up by US hard power assets, and that, by acting robustly in a unipolar world, the conditions would be set for extending freedom, democracy, liberalised markets, and, thereby, a more prosperous and stable world.

Of course, US ability to act both unilaterally *and* effectively was dramatically misunderstood by Charles Krauthammer, Richard Perle, Paul Wolfowitz, Douglas Feith and their neo-conservative comrades. Indeed, in reviewing their policy prescriptions – from the fall of the Wall to the fall of Iraq – one senses a conflation of the two concepts. In particular, this conflation amounts to a convenient amnesia, for the extent to which containment worked in the long run during the Cold War, it was a multilateral, alliance-driven effort, both politically and militarily. In short, soft power mattered. The institutions of global governance that the United States was instrumental in designing and supporting in the aftermath of the Second World War and throughout the Cold War were now being deliberately sidelined. The thick web of internationalism was seen only as a set of constraints, not as a requirement for engagement or as a mainstay of legitimacy. Indeed, as Daalder and Lindsay argue, the Bush revolution in foreign policy rested on two beliefs, both of which followed from Krauthammer's analysis: first, that the best way to ensure security was to shed the constraints imposed by both allies and international institutions; and second, that 'America unbound' should 'use its strength to change the status quo in the world' (2003: 13). However, what Daalder and Lindsay do not explicitly suggest, although it is implicit in their work, is that the twin assumptions of unipolarity as a state of being and unilateralism as a state of action,

---

[6] A case in point is Richard Perle, a veteran of US–Soviet arms negotiations and long-time supporter and admirer of Soviet dissidents. Perle believed strongly in the power of ideas, of good triumphing over evil, democracy over authoritarianism, and in the likely gratitude of peoples who would be 'liberated' by the United States, just as the former citizens of Central and Eastern Europe had the communist shackles removed with US 'victory' in the Cold War. Interviewed for Adam Curtis' three-part BBC documentary *The Power of Nightmares*, Perle stated: 'The struggle against Soviet totalitarianism was a struggle between fundamental values – good and evil is about as effective a shorthand as I can imagine. And there is something rather similar going on in the War on Terror.'

rested upon a particular and triumphalist understanding of the US 'victory' in the Cold War.[7]

Lesson 3: the end of history

Similarly influential to Krauthammer's call-to-arms was Francis Fukuyama's essay in *The National Interest*, 'The End of History'. Published on the cusp of the fall of communism and later reworked into a bestselling book, Fukuyama suggested that much of the conflict of the twentieth century was due to the clash of 'isms'. Indeed, the Second World War was fought to defeat fascism; the Cold War to defeat communism. Fukuyama reckoned that, by the end of the twentieth century, the only successful regime-type left standing was liberal democracy. Because the original article appeared just prior to the actual fall of communism, his particular argument about the end of history and the actual end of the Cold War tended to be conflated.

Although Fukuyama did not equate the end of history with the end of events, he did suggest that future wars were less likely to be fought on an ideological basis. In so doing, he initially underappreciated religious division and ethnic or national identification as sources of human conflict.[8] In this respect, his Hegelian emphasis (heavily mediated by an idiosyncratic reading of the Russian political philosopher Alexandre Kojève) on the clash of ideologies failed to take into account other ideologies based not on political convictions but on ascriptive characteristics such as ethnicity and religion.[9] Moreover, such conflict – whether

[7] Daalder and Lindsay (2003: 10–12) compare the logic of the Truman Doctrine with proponents of 'rollback' such as John Foster Dulles. Such an analysis glosses over the fact that 'rollback' was never implemented, and not even seriously contemplated at the earliest post-war opportunity, that is during the Hungarian Revolution of 1956. Policies of unilateralism steeped in Cold War triumphalism overlook *realpolitik* constraints on US actions, just as bipartisan consensus on Cold War foreign policy papered over differences between Wilsonian internationalists who championed multilateralism and the descendants of Cabot Lodge who took solace in American dominance of international institutions.

[8] Fukuyama did not predict that Europe in particular would be free from nationalist sentiments (indeed he foresaw the dangers of the 'newly liberated nationalisms' in Eastern Europe. For Fukuyama, nationalism, like religion, 'appears to have lost much of its ability to stimulate Europeans to risk their comfortable lives in great acts of imperialism' (2006c: 272).

[9] Indeed, in a new preface to the most recent edition to The End of History, Fukuyama discusses the threat of 'intensely radicalized and alienated Muslims' and situates radical Islamism as a political ideology. However, because much of the radicalism is restricted to the Muslim world and other interpretations of Islam exist, the challenge of Islamism as ideology is 'less severe than that mounted by communism, which was both globally appealing and linked to a powerful modern state' (Fukuyama 2006c165: 349). Moreover, he disagrees with Samuel Huntington's 'clash of civilisations' thesis because

politically and conveniently manipulated or more deeply psychologic-
ally rooted – is more difficult to defuse. Indeed, as the 1990s progressed, three multinational and multicultural states that emerged
after the First World War – Czechoslovakia, Yugoslavia and the Soviet
Union – all broke up. To continue thinking that the advance of freedom
and democracy would overcome such differences, as many of the original backers of the Iraq War believed, was the height of folly, especially
considering that Iraq was the most unsuccessful of the states created
out of the Versailles treaties (Galbraith 2006: 101). Nonetheless, many
neo-conservatives persist in seeing the war in Iraq as an essential step
in the march towards a freer and more democratic world where terrorism will be defeated in much the same way as was Soviet authoritarianism (Woodward 2004: 427). Ironically, this dedication to freedom and
democracy amounted to an inversion of the Fukuyama thesis, at least
insofar as a commitment to universalistic principles might result in
engaging in wars to foster their promotion, in turn signalling a renewal
of ideologically based conflict rather than its rejection. Moreover, the
ways in which Fukuyama's Hegelian approach dismissed the theoretical poverty and moral relativism of classical or structural realism was
powerfully attractive to neo-conservative thinking.[10]

Fukuyama has not been happy about the neo-conservative hijacking of his ideas. He has treated Krauthammer with particular deri-
sion, arguing that the columnist had become 'strangely disconnected
from reality'. In 'The Neoconservative Moment', a purposeful riff on
Krauthammer's earlier essay, Fukuyama argued that neo-conservatives
like Krauthammer had lost touch with new 'empirical facts' that had
emerged in Iraq and which, in turn, demanded a change of course in US
foreign policy. These new facts, according to Fukuyama, included:

the failure to find weapons of mass destruction in Iraq, the virulent and stead-
ily mounting anti-Americanism throughout the Middle East, the growing
insurgency in Iraq, the fact that no strong democratic leadership had emerged
there, the enormous financial and growing human cost of the war, the failure
to leverage the war to make progress on the Israeli–Palestinian front, and the
fact that America's fellow democratic allies had by and large failed to fall in line
and legitimate American actions ex post. (Fukuyama 2004: 58)

---

he believes the principles of liberty and equality inherent in democracy have (at least
potentially) universal significance.

[10] Robert W. Merry (2005: 200–1) argues that the 'wrong' lesson was learned by the
neo-conservatives in their critique of Kissinger. Kissingerian *realpolitik* – basing politics not on morality but on a hard calculus of national interests – was not faulty,
but Kissinger's assumptions were (i.e. that the United States was in decline and the
Soviet Union was more powerful and imperial in its ambition).

Nonetheless, Fukuyama's main contention that the ultimate victor of historical teleology is liberal democracy is easily manipulated to suggest that democracy promotion by force effectively hurries along such a desirable end to history.

Lesson 4: defining the enemy

One comforting certainty during the Cold War was in knowing who the enemy was: communism. Conveniently, the Soviet Empire had, to paraphrase Kissinger, an 'attack address'. Elaborate military plans were drawn up and repeatedly war-gamed in case the United States and NATO ever faced the Soviet hordes rushing through the Fulda gap in the heart of West Germany. Bipolarity was digestible, understandable, and had its own functional rationale of response and potential escalation in the related doctrines of deterrence and mutually assured destruction. One of the most discomforting outcomes of 9/11 was the realisation of the promise of globalisation – all that had made the free and fluid movement of transnational capital possible, along with the internationalisation of the division of labour and technological capability in communications and transportation – also made transnational terrorism possible, and remarkably successful as well.[11]

Those who have studied the Bush revolution in foreign policy post-9/11, such as Richard Clarke, Ivo H. Daalder, James M. Lindsay, Bob Woodward, Robert W. Merry and Ron Suskind, have all noticed the degree to which a state-based response became the fallback position for dealing with the 'new enemy'. The immediate post-9/11 strategy was to attack Afghanistan in order to unseat the Taliban regime that had knowingly harboured and supported al-Qaeda. This policy reflected a familiar response, consistent with a realist interpretation of international relations. Both Donald Rumsfeld and Dick Cheney agreed early on that transnational terrorists could not survive long without state sponsors. They would literally wither and die if cut off from the vine of state support. Moreover, this conviction was undergirded by two interrelated assumptions: first, that transnational terrorists would team up with rogue states; and second, that this marriage of convenience would be driven by both sides via the desire to acquire weapons of mass

---

[11] On this point, journalist Thomas L. Friedman (1999, 2000: 398–405) was remarkably prescient. Of note is his characterisation of Osama bin Laden as one of a group of 'Super-Empowered Angry Men' whose power was both enhanced by globalisation and by their reaction to it.

destruction (WMD).[12] In essence, the response of the Bush administration did not effectively address the underlying messages of Osama
bin Laden and al-Qaeda: first, that states matter less than they used
to; second, that globalisation has eroded not only sovereignty but also
state capacity; and finally, that non-state actors can be far more bold
in launching damaging attacks on the continental United States than
any state would have dared. By focusing on states rather than networks,
the United States missed the ability to target the enemy accurately and
tailor its response appropriately.

The Cold War was not only state-based, it also represented a clash of
competing ideologies. At the same time, communism and market democracy were ideals associated with the superpowers and their spheres
of influence, and could be criticised both internally and externally for
failure to meet expectations associated with those ideals. Whether or
not one accepts the controversial 'clash of civilisations' thesis advocated
by Samuel Huntington, the current conflict represents an entirely different kind of threat (Merry 2005: 199). Jihadi terrorism is asymmetric,
unconventional and non-linear. The motivational structure of recruitment is complex, including distorted religious interpretation, financial incentives, poor education and a dearth of opportunities mixed
with a pervasive sense of injustice in societies with legacies of violence
and imperialism (Juergensmayer 2003; Stern 2003; Cohen 2007).
Such adversaries cannot be understood within the boundaries of a
Westphalian order.

Moreover, privileging the state tipped the balance in favour of a
military rather than law enforcement response, and focused on hard
rather than soft power. In this calculus, military capability counts, as it
is the only power that is concrete and obviously deployable. Militaries
are the instrument of a Clausewitzian politics by other means when it
comes to states dealing with states, whereas law enforcement agencies
have traditionally been tasked with pursuing transnational criminals.
Needless to say, the militarily muscular state-based option generated
a thorny chain of consequences, from the challenges of the application of law to armed conflict and international humanitarian law
to 'unlawful combatants' on the battlefield through to questions of
detention and what could and should be done to gain 'actionable
intelligence'.

---

[12] For Suskind, these assumptions are the basis of the Cheney 'One Percent' Doctrine,
whereby the United States had to act on the basis of the unimaginable actually occurring, that is, terrorists and/or rogue states acquiring WMD.

Lesson 5: not understanding 'blowback'

'Blowback' is a term used in intelligence tradecraft to describe the law of unintended consequences. First used widely by the CIA and then entering the public lexicon in the aftermath of the Iran–Contra affair, the concept can be extended to an understanding of how Cold War conflicts, particularly proxy wars and covert operations, circumscribed policy options or affected their success in the post-Cold War US foreign policy-making universe. The examples of blowback in the Middle East and Central Asia are legion and overlapping. Cited most often is the case of Osama bin Laden. Bin Laden's transition from the Westernised son of a Saudi construction entrepreneur to a transnational jihadist mastermind occurred with the encouragement and financial assistance of the CIA during their decade-long support for the various mujahideen groups fighting in Afghanistan (Coll 2004). Steve Coll details the lack of expertise within the CIA regarding Afghanistan – from a basic lack of linguistic abilities and cultural knowledge through to a fairly minimal presence on the ground. Moreover, the CIA *encouraged* the recruitment of the more radical Islamists because they were seen as more devoted to defeating the Soviets than other groups. US disengagement from Afghanistan following the withdrawal of the Soviets aided and abetted the jihadist interpretation that the mujahideen had prevailed over a mighty superpower. In turn, this version of events fed the al-Qaeda hubris that defeating the United States would be of the same magnitude as defeating the Soviet Union.

Former US support for Saddam Hussein during the 1980–8 Iran–Iraq war and CIA involvement in the overthrow of Mohammad Mossadegh in Iran in 1953, as well as decades-long support for authoritarian rule in the region, have all contributed to a popular conception that the United States is both disingenuous and hypocritical in its support for freedom and democracy. All the more reason why it was unlikely that the United States would be perceived as a 'liberator' or even as a champion of 'freedom loving-peoples', as had been the case during and after the Cold War.

Within Iraq, one of the most ironic examples of blowback occurred with the political resurgence of Shia communities. Many mistakes were made in the early days of the occupation that, as a whole, fuelled Iraqi anger – from the inability of coalition forces to prevent widescale looting and provide infrastructure support through to the widely reported prison abuses at Abu Ghraib. Nonetheless, the United States seemed unprepared in realising the extent to which the removal of Saddam

Hussein would spell success for Shia clerics and militias. Iranian religious figures had deep connections with their Iraqi Shia counterparts – such as Ali al-Sistani – and had been working for decades to build their influence (Kinzer 2006: 313). In an astonishing reversal of the dictum that the enemy of my enemy is my friend, the friend (Iranian Shia clerics) of my friend (Iraq) was set to become my enemy (foreshadowing the civil war). Galbraith notes with irony that when Bush delivered his famous 'axis of evil' State of the Union address in 2002, there were no greater enemies than Iraq and Iran, but today Iran has no closer ally than an Iraq backed by Iran-friendly ayatollahs (2006: 6).[13]

Finally, blowback occurred in one of the most surprising quarters: elections. Not only did democratic elections not fulfil their promise in Iraq (as ethnic and sectoral divisions were reinforced), but the 'democratic' fallout from the ongoing Iraqi civil war has had dramatic and destabilising consequences for the Middle East more broadly. Indeed, the victory of hard-liners in Palestine and Iran all attest to the ability of local politicians to translate anti-Americanism into electoral success.

Unfortunately, blowback is an ongoing challenge. As Peter Bergen and Alec Reynolds argue, 'The current war in Iraq will generate a ferocious blowback of its own, which ... could be longer and more powerful than from Afghanistan' (2005: 2). The argument that it is better to fight the terrorists abroad than at home – repeatedly used as a justification for continuing the war in Iraq – is not only flawed but may be a further source of blowback.[14] Not only will terrorists not necessarily conveniently flock to Iraq where they can be stopped by sophisticated counterinsurgency campaigns but the war itself has added fuel to the phenomenon of 'homegrown terrorism'. This has certainly been evident in the case of the Madrid bombings as well as the 7/7 attacks in London – in both instances the perpetrators were not al-Qaeda operatives but radicalised locals alienated by what they perceived as their own government's actions as well as righteously inspired by events abroad. Finally, the foreign fighters who have been active in Iraq are unlikely to stand down or return to civilian life, and will represent an ongoing security threat and challenge to both deployed militaries and domestic law-enforcement agencies.

---

[13] Moreover, with Iraq now effectively the region's first Arab Shi'ite state, there are renewed fears, to borrow the words of Jordanian King Abdullah, of a 'Shiite crescent' stretching from Beirut to Tehran.

[14] Bergen and Reynolds (2005: 4) also suggest that as with the Afghan experience, where 'holy warriors' had the opportunity to rub shoulders with and learn from one another, so too will Iraq provide a myriad of networking and 'educational' opportunities.

Not fully comprehending the consequences of blowback and the remarkable level of historical amnesia predicated on it are partially related to the ideas that the end of the Cold War represented not only a victory but a rupture with the past, a new beginning for US primacy and an opportunity for unipolar action. Understanding the myriad possibilities of blowback is difficult, perhaps akin to a political version of Heisenberg's uncertainty principle, with the bottom line being that a certain level of unintended reaction is unavoidable and unpredictable. As Marx said in *The Eighteenth Brumaire*, 'Men make their own history, but they do not make it just as they please; they do not make it under circumstances chosen by themselves, but under circumstances directly encountered, given, and transmitted from the past' (Marx, in McLellan 1977: 300). Thus the choices made by past US administrations and leaders do indeed weigh upon the consciences of the living, and often severely circumscribe what policy choices are available for implementation.

Nevertheless, chains of consequences ought to be clarified and history more fully understood. In Afghanistan, even leaving the question of bin Laden aside, some reflexivity ought to have generated a debate on the potential requirements, costs and success of nation-building. After all, Larry Goodson of the US Army War College has argued that understanding the past and present of Afghanistan, as well as the multiple roles played by empires and neighbours alike, would have resulted in the conclusion that an 'ounce of nation-building prevention' would have been worth 'a pound of military-operation cure' (2003: 97).[15] In Iraq, understanding the complex make-up of the Ba'athist state might have caused a few to question whether or not forcible regime change could result in strengthening Iran's hand in the region and bringing to the world stage the Islamic Republic of Iraq, courtesy of the US government.

Lesson 6: the elixir of speed

Observers of 1989 marvelled at the *speed* of the domino-like collapse of the communist governments of the USSR's satellite states. Indeed, if measured only in the six-month time frame from the events from the

---

[15] Minimally, initial 'nation-building' efforts should have included constant rather than shifting political direction; effective and coherent administration under Iraqi control; the rapid restoration of essential services such as water and electricity; transparent governance with respect to Iraqi and US funds; an injection of capital and aid to prevent sharp and immediate economic decline; and plans to revitalise the Iraqi military and police.

4 June Polish elections through to the success of roundtable talks in Hungary, the German exodus, the fall of the Berlin Wall on 9 November, Czechoslovakia's 'Velvet Revolution' later the same month, through to the execution of Romania's notorious dictator Nicolae Ceauşescu and his wife Elena on Christmas Day, the events seemed nothing short of miraculous. The dramatic results proved that authoritarian leaderships of the region were more than stale and elderly – the emperors of the party-states were naked; their kingdoms fell like houses of cards. It was tempting to think that with a pre-emptive push, the same results could be achieved elsewhere. Moreover, glorious scenes of statue-toppling, crowds delirious with freedom expressing their support for capitalism by rapidly exercising their consumer preference for Western goods, former beleaguered dissidents claiming senior government positions filled with praise for US support – all reinforced this view and could be drawn upon from collective (and selective) memory later.

In reality, the fall of communism – both in the satellite states of Central and Eastern Europe and in the USSR itself – happened neither quickly nor easily. Historians will continue to debate for decades the proximate versus the longer-term causes of the collapse of the Soviet bloc, the relative importance of individual actors or structural flaws within the bedrock of Soviet-style societies. Both the communist 'ideal' and its actual practice have many contenders jockeying for place in this narrative: the rebellion at Kronstadt in 1921, Stalin's ruthless dictatorship, the political purges of the 1930s, the oppression of the Gulag system, or the long, slow economic decline that began during the Brezhnev years.[16] In Central and Eastern Europe, revolts occurred early and reasonably often: in the cities of Berlin and Pilsen in 1953, more broadly in Poland and Hungary in 1956. Efforts to reform communism from above failed with the crushing of the Prague Spring by the invasion of Czechoslovakia in 1968. Reforming the system from below seemed to fail with the imposition of martial law in Poland in 1981 after the initial success of Solidarity's struggle for independent trade unions the previous year. During the Cold War, greater media and political attention was paid to the 'peaks' of tension, such as the Berlin airlift, the Cuban Missile Crisis, or the proxy wars in Korea and Afghanistan, leading to a general ignorance of the relative constancy of dissident activity during the conflict. More scholarly attention was paid to the study of Soviet elites and their impact; thus self-styled

---

[16] Kotkin (2001: 1–9) argues that the death agony of the Soviet system in general and the Soviet Union in particular begins in the 1970s, when it became abundantly clear (at least in hindsight) that the USSR had been eclipsed by the West both economically and militarily.

'Kremlinologists' examined the placement of Politburo members in relationship to the leader and to each other during May Day parades and other minutiae for clues as to the behind-the-scenes intrigue and jockeying for power (e.g. Cox 1998). As the micro-histories of resistance to communist rule are being written by a new generation of post-Cold War scholars whose expertise spans the old East–West divide, it has become increasingly clear that, without the decades-long movements of dissent, communism would not have ended in such an organised, peaceful manner, with opposition elites prepared to step into the breach (Bozóki 1993; Tőkés 1996; McRae 1997; Ekiert and Kubik 1999; Falk 2003; McDermott and Stibbe 2006). Indeed, their activism not only coloured the scope and shape of regime change when the combined confluence of fortuitous circumstances occurred, but made possible the consolidation of democracy.

No doubt many factors contributed to the illusion of speed in 1989 – certainly the role of Mikhail Gorbachev and his now famous 'Sinatra Doctrine' played no small part (Brown 1997). Ironically, the only place in Cold War history where the 'domino theory' was effective was in the fall of communist regimes not, as security-conscious policy-makers once feared, in their original installation.[17] Regardless, drinking the elixir of speed and succumbing to the notion that authoritarian regimes could be toppled not only effectively but quickly and with minimal cost was misleading. The speed with which events occurred in 1989 contributed to the illusion that authoritarian regimes with decades of governing experience and the hard power to crack down on challengers could crumble and wither away. The 'mobilisational moment' that 1989 represented must be situated within the history of the Cold War, and understood as the end of a long process entailing numerous bouts of dissent and regime crackdown. Even in its last cycle, mass mobilisation against the regimes was *internal*, restricted to national contexts. Moscow's puppet leaders in the region proved unwilling to crackdown on their own people and the coercive apparatus appeared equally reluctant to fire on their own citizens without *external* support, that is, from the Soviet Union itself.

---

[17] Indeed it is far easier to tear regimes down than to build them up, and planning for the 'post-war' of any conflict – hot or cold – is crucial to the consolidation of change and lasting peace. The Korean economic miracle of the 1980s and 1990s was preceded by a long and arduous process of state-directed and US-funded reconstruction, complete with thoroughgoing land and economic reform. The post-Second World War destruction in Europe was followed by the ambitious Marshall Plan and although such a programme did not exist following the collapse of communism, arguably the carrot-and-stick approach to elite-driven reform required for accession to NATO and the European Union served broadly the same purposes.

Reviewing policy-making decisions prior to the invasion of Iraq in 2003, one can see how the doctrine of pre-emption provided a substitute for the supposed speed of 1989. Even accepting that pre-emption might, with better planning and execution, have served this role, the next lesson militates against such success: that the populace of any authoritarian state desires to be liberated, rather than choosing the means and methods of their own liberation.

Lesson 7: the role of civil society

Those in the democracy promotion industry in the United States were quick to pick up on a key lesson from 1989: critical to the creation and consolidation of democracy is the development of civil society. Applying 1989 to the Middle East in this respect meant adopting a number of highly contestable assumptions:

(1) external support for civil society necessarily helps to end tyranny;
(2) as during the Cold War, containment alone is not the answer;
(3) peoples of the world innately desire freedom; and
(4) that freedom translates into a US-friendly version of democratic citizenship.[18]

Moreover, all of these assumptions seemed to hold true for the fall of communism and its immediate aftermath. Indeed, the unifying idea that freedom-loving peoples – or at least the risk-takers among them – will organise themselves into movements of dissent in order to advocate democratic values and governance held true for many of the opposition movements of Central and Eastern Europe.

The relationship of a rich associational life independent of both state and market to democratic development has been noted in the US context since Alexis de Tocqueville's famous travels to the country two centuries ago, continuing to reverberate in US perceptions of nation-building.[19] In Central and Eastern Europe, those who searched for a more nuanced understanding than the triumphalist explanation of victory seized upon dissident-led efforts to create and nurture alternative spaces for independent action – what Jacek Kuroń in Poland called

[18] I am grateful here to conversations with Jeff Kopstein, Greg Narbey and David Ost – all of whom are as fascinated as I am with the relevance of the fall of communism to post-9/11 US foreign policy, especially vis-à-vis Iraq.

[19] See in particular Chapters 5, 6 and 7 of Book 2 of Volume II of Alexis de Tocqueville's *Democracy in America* (1969108), in which he discusses the role of associations in US civic life, the necessary connections between such associations and a free and independent media, and the relationship between civil and political associations. As well, see Putnam (1993 and 2000) and Seligman (1992).

'social self-organisation' or Václav Benda in Czechoslovakia called the 'parallel *polis*' – where freedom of expression and association could be extended by practice. Václav Havel formulated this most eloquently with the concept of 'living in truth' in his landmark work *The Power of the Powerless*.[20] In essence, dissidents in the region followed Havel's clarion call to open action and organisation, rejecting the ritualised obedience and quiescence required by the party-state. Their efforts to create islands of freedom rested upon an ethic of responsibility, a belief in the power of the powerless, of seizing hope in a context of hopelessness. Although it would be an exaggeration to state that the existence of the various opposition movements *made* 1989 possible, the existence of such groups and the skill sets developed in order to survive were indispensable: organisational savvy, negotiation skills, legal expertise, ready-made communications networks well versed in interaction with the Western media, and most of all enormous legitimacy at home and abroad.

Jeffrey Kopstein (2006: 86–7) has argued that Europeans and Americans read 1989 differently with respect to the possibilities of democratisation elsewhere. The US narrative privileges a bottom-up approach, whereby sub-state social mobilisation – 'people power' – can collectively, with the right tactics, operational planning and overall strategy, force authoritarian regimes to step aside. The European narrative privileges not 1989 but the aftermath – the elite-driven consolidation process that included the rule of law and the creation of the institutions of the market economy and democratic governance. In short, 1989 was prologue to 2004 – the year in which eight Central and East European states entered the European Union after a carefully driven accession process.[21] Furthermore, Kopstein (2006: 88) argues, 'the script from which the United States was working in Iraq during the spring of 2003 was based on its reading of 1989 in Eastern Europe: topple the leader, pull down his statue, and let civil society take over'.

However, the 'error' of the US narrative is not simply one of over-emphasising the grassroots nature of civil society and its promise, but

---

[20] Havel's influence across the region was far-reaching; *The Power of the Powerless*, published and distributed via *samizdat* and *tamizdat*, was the theoretical handbook of opposition from the date of its publication in 1979 through to 1989. Today it still reads as a compelling and personal call for action and responsibility to those living in authoritarian regimes.

[21] On 1 January 2004, the Czech Republic, Estonia, Hungary, Latvia, Lithuania, Poland, Slovakia and Slovenia all joined the European Union, along with Malta and Cyprus, as a result of lengthy and detailed accession negotiations between the new member states and the EU, coordinated through the Office of the Enlargement Commissioner.

again the assumption of speed. Civil society cannot be instantly created with money and training from the West. To be truly 'grassroots', civil society must be carefully nurtured and embedded in the culture and history of a particular society. Much of the 'success' of civil society is the fact that it is a process, an interactive web of possibility, not a product. In the 1970s and 1980s, procedural norms and models of democratic governance were much discussed and 'tested out' in the fledgling independent civil societies of the region, such as legalism, diversity and tolerance, respect for minority rights, openness and contestation. This took time and the building of coalitions among distrustful groups and partners, overcoming the injustices and suspicions of the past, as well as the working out of various disagreements before common aims and objectives could be agreed.

The idea that hurrying civil society development with money and training could be successful was evident in the partial transformations that occurred in Serbia in 2000, Georgia in 2003, and Ukraine in 2004. The word 'partial' here is critical as in all three cases civil society-driven efforts were not fully embedded in society, did not result in a complete changeover of elites, and could hardly be expected to generate key reforms in institutional governance or to build state capacity. The domestic publics of these states had had enough of corruption, conflict and their international 'pariah' status, and understood these as byproducts of poor and illegitimate governance. Equally, these endemic challenges are beyond the power of civil society to fix. Moreover, opposition 'leaders' did not cut their teeth in opposition movements, but were disaffected elites stymied in their own ambitions by corruption, incompetence and former apparatchiks.[22] Finally, the dark underside of 'civil society' is 'uncivil society' Keane (1996: 107–28). Creating the conditions for a rich associational life also allows for the freedom of expression and association of extreme nationalists, xenophobes, and naive believers in communist-nostalgia to destabilise fragile bodies politic. This is not to suggest that money and expert assistance cannot play a role in building and buttressing civil society, but rather that the recipe is neither easy nor automatically unidirectional.

Lesson 8: free and fair elections

In the West, and particularly in the Anglo-American world, the word 'democracy' is commonly associated with 'free and fair elections'. For this reason, a yardstick by which we measure transitions from

---

[22] On the Ukrainian case, see Karatnycky (2005) and Garton Ash and Snyder (2005).

authoritarian rule is successful electoral conduct and respect for the results. Democratic consolidation tends to be marked by successful changeover of governments or parties following subsequent elections. The experiences of the early 1990s reinforced these beliefs, as elections were usually held within months of the collapse of communism. In most cases, credible (and loyal) oppositions-in-waiting were able to mount candidacies, and parties (initially, at least) grew out of movements of dissent (such as Solidarity in Poland, and Civic Forum/Charta 77 in Czechoslovakia). Moreover, this view of free and fair elections is consistent with a bottom–up view of democracy where parties are outgrowths of healthy and vibrant civil society networks (Kopstein 2006: 89).

However, without some previous experience of democracy (as had been the case during the interwar period in Central Europe), creating electoral processes from scratch may be much more challenging as there is no collective memory or institutional capacity on which to draw. In these situations, as was arguably the case in many of the post-Soviet republics or Russia itself, there were no sizeable independent or pluralist opposition movements out of which parties could be built. Post-Soviet democratisation came to be associated with the electoral legitimisation of corruption, the retail of public assets at firesale prices, and the widespread use of public office for private gain. Moreover, there were no external levers that could be pushed and pulled to reward healthy electoral conduct, accountable and stable governance, or the 'right' policy and legislative mix to generate foreign direct investment, appropriate market regulation to ensure rather than compromise competitiveness, fair and progressive taxation, and the provision of public services consummate with state capacity and the ability to pay. Arguably, the European Union, through the operationalisation of the Copenhagen criteria, the Office of the Enlargement Commissioner, the legislative and policy standardisation required by the national enactment of the *aquis communautaire*, and the negotiation process leading up to membership, played this role brilliantly, pulling and pushing various levers in a classic 'carrot and stick' approach.[23]

In societies where ethnic, cultural and religious division is compounded by relatively recent and violent histories, with radically differing historiographies associated with various groups, holding elections too early may result in at least two negative outcomes. First, the successful party does not see itself as representative of the *demos* as a whole,

---

[23] This is the argument that Kopstein (2006: 90–3) makes as indicative of the 'European' approach to democracy promotion, contrasted with the 'American' approach.

but rather sees the electoral process as a form of state capture in order to serve narrow partisan interests constructed along ethnic, cultural or religious lines. Such a result does not enhance the prospects for a legitimate national government. Second, given a violent or divisive past and a pervasive sense of competitive victimhood, voters will align themselves electorally along ethnic, cultural or religious lines as a form of perceived identity and community protection. Exactly this series of outcomes occurred in Bosnia-Herzegovina following the 1995 Dayton Accord as well as in Kosovo following the NATO campaign of 1999. The 'hurrying' of free and fair elections as a hallmark of democratic progress did not yield the desired results; rather, voters cast their ballots along ethnic, cultural and religious lines – the same divisions the democratic process is ostensibly aimed at overcoming. Indeed, in Iraq in the December 2005 national elections (the third election that year), fewer than one in ten Iraqis voted for parties that crossed either ethnic or religious lines (Galbraith 2006: 3).[24] Nonetheless, the United States was caught between trying to accommodate the aspirations of the then-moderate Shi'ite leadership in their demands for elections, a dangerous compromise given that they tended to elide the distinction between democracy as a system which has built-in checks to prevent the tyranny of the majority, and democracy as majority (50 per cent plus one) rule. As James Dobbins (2005: 18) noted at the time: 'Elections are always polarizing events, and in a fragile, deeply conflicted society such as Iraq's, they could deepen the gulf between Sunnis on the one hand and Shiites and Kurds on the other.' Unfortunately, this pessimistic prediction proved correct. If any lesson might have been learned in advance, it was this one, as exactly the same result had occurred in post-Dayton Bosnia-Herzegovina.

Nevertheless, elections remain as enticing benchmarks and metrics of progress: organising for them and ensuring procedural fairness and respect for results provides the international community or particular interveners with both a reason for involvement and a reason to disengage.[25] Elections also represent seductive opportunities for academic

[24] And, as Galbraith reports (2006: 3), it took four more months of negotiation among Shi'ites, Sunni Arabs and Kurds to agree upon who would occupy the key posts of president, the two vice-presidents, speaker of the Iraqi parliament, and prime minister.

[25] Again, Iraq is hardly the only example – merely the most recent one. The experience of intervention in the 1990s in imposing democratisation via elections under the supervision of the international community has hardly yielded unequivocal success, as the cases of Cambodia, East Timor, Bosnia-Herzegovina and Kosovo all attest. The Bosnian case remains the most studied 'failure' in this regard: see Woodward (1999); Cohen (1997); and Chandler (2000).

engagement and hubris: the involvement of such esteemed democracy scholars as Larry Diamond or constitutional scholars such as Noah Feldman in assisting in the processes of democratic and constitutional reconstruction of Iraq hardly guaranteed success, and could not replace other critical factors, such as the lack of legitimate local leaders that could overcome societal division and reduce legacies of centralisation, violence and civic anomie (Feldman 2003; Smith and Diamond 2004: 130–3).

The lesson to be learned here is not the unimportance of free and fair elections, nor that they should be avoided. Rather, the maturation of a culture of liberalism and tolerance must precede elections, particularly when there is no previous experience of democracy. Where elections were hurried, as in Bosnia-Herzegovina, Kosovo, and now Iraq, the results were the predictable hardening of pre-existing or politically manipulated societal divisions and various ethnic, cultural and religious cleavages into partisan camps. Moreover, assuming that democracy will yield victors that are pro-Western is clearly mistaken. Recent evidence supports this observation, as we have seen in Algeria, where the electoral process was essentially cancelled, in Palestine, where relatively free and fair elections resulted in the victory of Hamas, and in Iran, where limited democracy has not favoured reformers. Finally, contemporary research suggests that although mature democracies generally do not go to war with one another, this is not the case with emerging democracies or those engaged with communal civil wars or challenged by insurgencies, as has been the case in Iraq (Mansfield and Snyder 2005, 2009; Biddle 2006: 8).

Lesson 9: the role of 'outsiders': émigré and diaspora communities

Émigré and diaspora communities were crucial sources of linguistic, cultural and historical expertise to Western governments during the Cold War. Moreover, in these communities, old political divisions were overcome – with time, and in the interest of supporting dissident and opposition movements in their homelands, in much the same way that ideological differences and tactical disagreements were overcome within those movements themselves (Falk 2003, 2008). Such communities in the West began to establish important linkages with their compatriots in their homelands – initially through friendships but later through broader networks of trust and a sense of shared risk-taking – making cross-border communication and collaboration possible. Such networks facilitated the dissemination of *samizdat* abroad, as well as published *tamizdat* to be smuggled back into the various states involved. Key to the success of these networks, however, were these strong interpersonal connections, without which neither internal nor external actors would see one another as credible partners.

Taking such a 'lesson' to heart, Iraq hawks such as Richard Perle, Douglas Feith and David Frum initially saw the potential for a similar kind of arrangement with the main Iraqi opposition group located in the United States, the Iraqi National Congress (INC). Led by Ahmad Chalabi, who was seen by his US supporters (including Cheney, Rumsfeld, Perle and Wolfowitz) as democratic, market-oriented and pro-Western, Chalabi had constructed a London-based 'government in exile' and managed to garner approximately $36 million in US funding. Furthermore, he advocated bold action – ground forces backed by US airpower to defeat Saddam Hussein – in the aftermath of the Gulf War. However, Chalabi was unable to stifle the quarrelling among Iraqi exile groups jockeying for US support and the same divisions that plagued the Iraqi government since the coalition invasion in 2003 were evident in the lead-up to the war. Chalabi was not well liked by the CIA or the State Department, but had strong supporters in the Pentagon and among congressional Republicans.[26] In 2002 and early 2003, Foggy Bottom was initially supportive of the then 'Group of Four' which included the two main Kurdish parties, Iranian-backed Shi'ites and a new group of Sunni leaders. Perhaps the squabbling among factions should have been seen as a harbinger of post-invasion Iraq, with the greater share of the argument focused on how much power might be accorded to each group rather than to the greater good of a post-Saddam Iraq.[27] Worse still, the INC recruited and handed over to senior US officials various sources who produced much of the 'dodgy' intelligence regarding weapons development, such as the supposed mobile bioweapons labs.[28] Moreover, it was unclear the extent to which there was credible support for any of the Washington-based exiles within Iraq, except for the Kurds. Indeed, the Kurds alone

---

[26] Unlike Central and East European dissidents, Chalabi had no 'legs' in his state of origin. Indeed, he turned out to be so lacking in local legitimacy that his party, based on the INC, failed to win a single seat in Iraqi parliamentary elections.

[27] Unfortunately, US expectations were both opposite and optimistic: experts believed that squabbling would cease once the invasion began and the United States assumed its rightful place as regional kingmaker. For an early assessment of the fractious history of the relationship of Iraqi opposition groups to each other and various Washington agencies and departments, see George Packer (2003).

[28] Much of this intelligence was discussed as unreliable in the mainstream press well before the invasion. Indeed, even the CIA was well known to be distrustful of INC assessments regarding WMD.

seemed to have 'learned' the lesson from 1989 regarding strategies of cooperation, collaboration and the building of networks of trust among émigrés and Kurdish diasporas outside of Iraq, and with the minority Kurdish populations in northern Iraq. That such communication was possible given the successful imposition of the no-fly zone should not have been overlooked. Clearly, the ruthlessness of the Saddam Hussein regime in brokering no opposition made it difficult, if not impossible, for such networks to exist.

However, even leaving Chalabi and the INC aside, the Bush administration was encouraged by the counsel they sought from Iraqi dissidents, believing that, as in Central and Eastern Europe, they would be perceived as playing a role in unseating an unpopular and ruthless dictator. A notable example of this groupthink is found in Bob Woodward's account, *Plan of Attack*, detailing how President Bush and Vice-President Cheney met privately in January 2003 with leading Iraqi dissidents. Bush was heartened by the fact that average Iraqis did not hate Israel, which for him was clearly shorthand for pragmatism and reasonableness. Moreover, the dissidents were eager to paint a picture whereby US troops would be met with 'flowers and sweets', downplaying the split between minority Sunnis and majority Shi'ites for their captive audience (Woodward 2004: 258–60).

One could argue that US policy-makers ought to have been forgiven for misreading the capacity and legitimacy of expatriate Iraqis, for they were encouraged by many of the former dissidents of Central and Eastern Europe in their support for intervention in Iraq. Thus Adam Michnik in Poland, Miklós Haraszti in Hungary and Václav Havel in the Czech Republic all supported the US-led invasion.[29] There were a number of reasons for their support, ranging from gratitude for US Cold War engagement with – and support for – dissident movements through to belief in the 'Munich metaphor' in which Saddam Hussein was cast as the modern-day Hitler. Nonetheless, the distinction between the support of former dissidents and the similarity between dissidents past and present was not distinguished. Thus, someone like Richard Perle who had worked tirelessly on behalf of Soviet dissidents while working for Scoop Jackson in the 1970s and 1980s kept looking at the Iraqis hoping to find the next Andrei Sakharov or Natan Sharansky.

---

[29] The complicated reasons for this support are analysed by Padraic Kenney (2006). Of note is his conversation with former Hungarian dissident Miklós Haraszti in Budapest in 2003 just prior to the US-led invasion. I was the 'third person' at the café table that morning and vividly recall Haraszti detailing the many reasons why the intervention ought to be supported, in particular by the former dissidents of Central and Eastern Europe. For recent self-reflections, see Michnik and Kis (2008).

Moreover, there was no Helsinki-type process to assist opposition groups and prominent dissidents were either killed or lucky enough to escape into exile. The efforts of the international community, particularly through the UN and its agencies such as the International Atomic Energy Association (IAEA), focused largely on issues such as 'oil for food' or the potential development capability for weapons of mass destruction. Looking back, strategies of engagement that allowed some form of *apertura* in the medium-to-long term within Iraq might have yielded better opportunities for the development of a fledgling opposition than any sanctions regime, however robust.

Lesson 10: drawing a 'thick line with the past'

One of the most important lessons of 1989 was one of the earliest outcomes, dating back to the 'negotiated' approaches to regime-change and originating in the roundtable talks in Poland and Hungary: drawing a 'thick line with the past'. The idea was to be forward-thinking, to generously acknowledge that many hard choices were made regarding respect to membership in the party, acceptance of *nomenklatura* privileges, or even with respect to collaboration with the secret police. This commitment dates back to the overcoming of political differences among members of the various opposition movements, many of whom were at one time 'true believers'. Yet dissidents also recognised that no one in the *ancien régime* – dissident or party member – was entirely 'clean'. After all, even Václav Havel, while advocating that all should strive insofar as possible to 'live in truth' openly recognised that in one way or another, the 'lie' ran through each and every person. During the decades-long game of regime-versus-dissent cat and mouse, and particularly during the roundtable talks, begrudging respect moved to common cause and even friendship.[30] Although the first decade of post-communism heralded many varieties of lustration and there was certainly a well-documented appetite for revenge and recrimination, most former party members and even leaders were left in peace (Stan 2009). Some were prohibited from holding public office, a few were put on trial.[31] Indeed, 'punishments' were seen as far too mild, and there

[30] The most legendary example was the unlikely friendship that developed between Wojciech Jaruzelski and Adam Michnik – the former jailer and the jailed, the one who authorised martial law and the one who opposed it. For an elaboration, see Rosenberg (1996).

[31] Two notable exceptions were the trials of Wojciech Jaruzelski in Poland and Egon Krenz, the last party leader of East Germany before the fall of the wall. In neither case was their party membership or previous privileged status at issue, but rather their criminal responsibility for specific acts, in Jaruzelski's case the imposition of martial

was much public anxiety and conspiracy theory regarding the extent to which the former *nomenklatura* were able to essentially 'trade' political power for economic power.

As unfair as it might seem to engage in grand societal bargaining to allow the past to remain past, or even have carefully constructed lustration laws that guarantee due process and appeal, in the end the 'let bygones be bygones' approach allowed for transition to proceed smoothly. Most importantly, it allowed those who had a clear stake in the old system to find themselves a place in the new. Functionaries and bureaucrats in the 'grey zone' did not, by and large, lose their positions, and even in the armed forces one could continue to be promoted through the ranks in a professional manner if not too negatively associated with the communist era. The dismantling of the old command economy, involving massive privatisation, currency stabilisation and liberalisation measures certainly generated many economic 'losers' – but this process was not politically motivated. Indeed, the economic success of the former *nomenklatura* should, on this logic, be taken as a sign of overall success rather than failure.

This lesson should have been heeded by the original Coalition Provisional Authority (CPA) in Iraq. Disbanding the Iraqi armed forces and the process of de-Ba'athification were colossal errors that succeeded only in feeding the ensuing insurgency. Only six weeks after the collapse of Hussein's Iraq and the 'victory' of coalition forces, the CPA dissolved not only the secret police and the elite Republican Guard, but also the entire Iraqi army.[32] In effect, this decision created an instant 300,000-plus class of military, political and economic 'losers' who had no opportunity for success in post-Saddam Iraq who in turn tended to be defined by their religious status (as Sunnis were disproportionately more loyal to Saddam Hussein given his pattern of distributing rewards and punishments on a religious and tribal basis). The results were both profoundly destabilising and dangerous.[33] Iraq was already riven by

law in December 1981, and in Krenz's case the 'shoot to kill' policy that governed security forces posted along the Berlin Wall to prevent escape from the East to the West.

[32] Bob Woodward discusses how the 19 May CPA decision to disband the Iraqi army was met with immediate Iraqi protest; on 26 May, as many as 5,000 protestors gathered outside the CPA headquarters. Al Jazeera translated the following remark from Sahib al-Musawi, a former Iraqi major general whose speech was carried live: 'If our demands are not met, next Monday will mark the start of estrangement between the Iraqi army and people on the one hand and the occupiers on the other' (quoted in Woodward 2006: 206).

[33] For a recent analysis, see Gordon (2008). The CPA decision was made without thorough consultation either with the Secretary of State or senior US commanders on the ground.

conflict and, because the very nature of regime change was violent and externally imposed, it may never have been possible to draw a thick line with the past. However, even in post-apartheid South Africa, also a society struggling with a violent past and cleavages based on race and tribal identity, the new government opted for truth and reconciliation over recrimination and prosecution.[34]

Conclusions

It would be a mistake to conclude that the current debacle in Iraq and, to a lesser extent in Afghanistan, is entirely derived from faulty lessons learned from the fall of communism. Indeed, as James Dobbins (2007) has pointed out, there is more than enough blame to go around: leaders in the Bush administration who emphasised compliance and loyalty over open debate; deep structural flaws in inter-agency information-sharing and decision-making; and strategies and force structures that overemphasised military deployments over the police, intelligence and diplomatic efforts. Nonetheless, the policies of pre-emption, democracy promotion and nation-building that have been sullied by the experience in Iraq have roots in particular interpretations regarding the fall of authoritarian communism and the success (and failure) of post-communist democratic consolidation in the region. Assumptions of Cold War triumphalism went hand-in-hand with post-Cold War assertions of unipolarity and unilateralism. An assumed 'end of ideology' downplayed either the persistence or emergence of ethnic or religious sources of conflict, even as the experiences in the former Yugoslavia and in Rwanda proved otherwise. Following the realist assessment of Cold War superpower engagement based on national power and national interests, post-9/11 foreign policy-making continued to privilege states when the obvious threats remained transnational in character.[35] Historical amnesia was coupled with a failure to learn that past policies condition and constrain current options, particularly where blowback was likely and visible.

[34] These reasons also hold for the decision to hold trials for Saddam Hussein and his henchmen, regardless of procedural improprieties, threats and acts of violence that hung over the courtroom. Indeed, the 'Truth and Reconciliation' approach was probably more suited to Iraq than either trials or lustration, if only because much of the violence associated with the Saddam Hussein regime and much of the current counterinsurgency (and the ensuing division of perpetrators and victims) has been along religious and tribal lines.

[35] And here the threats are not simply human in character or design, as is the case with terrorism. Among the greatest threats to human security come from entirely different sources: from global pandemics such as HIV/AIDS, SARS, or a future form of avian influenza, or from natural disasters that have their root causes in the environmental instability caused by global climate change.

However, it is critical to move beyond, in Dobbins' words (2007: 61), 'bumper sticker conclusions' such as 'no more preemption, no more democracy promotion, no more nation-building'. Rather, what is needed is a nuanced re-examination of the conclusions that buttressed such policy recommendations in the first place, in essence, to relearn the lessons and legacies of the *annus mirabilis*. Moreover, understanding the full policy impact – both positive and negative – of the fall of communism also requires considerable modesty, for not all can be learned from the entrails of examining revolutions, even peaceful and successful ones. Democratisation in whatever guise it is promoted – elite-driven or bottom–up – may not be the panacea that should guide anti-terrorism efforts or the modernisation of societies. Yet one conclusion is sure: democratisation is certainly not a shortcut. Establishing the rule of law, a culture of tolerance, respect for diversity, civic engagement, a free and independent media – these institutions so necessary for civil society and democracy – cannot be nourished overnight nor can they topple regimes alone. Rich associational life can bring with it elements inimical to democratic values, which can and do foster ethnic and religious strife. Free and fair elections should be viewed as the end of the process, not the beginning, particularly as they may harden societal divisions rather than lessen them. The role played by émigré and diaspora communities can be either positive or negative depending on the circumstances, the specific case history of the communities involved and the connectedness of those communities to their homelands and – critically – to each other. Finally, drawing a 'thick line with the past', which in the short term might smack of political expediency and a lack of moral fortitude, may be the better option if peace is purchased in the short term, heightening chances for longer-term settlements of historic grievances.

Ironically, the overarching lesson from the experience of the Cold War and its demise by current policy-makers is its overall utility as a paradigm. The Cold War allowed for a remarkable level of bipartisan consensus in Congress, something the Bush administration was partially able to generate after 9/11 under the guise of a 'global war on terror'. Nevertheless, congressional support has been waning given the lack of success in Iraq, however measured. The Cold War made possible – for good and for ill – the creation of a military-industrial complex that worked together with shared operating assumptions regarding the identity and adversarial intent of the enemy. The overarching nature of the conflict simultaneously provided stability and predictability – so much so that John Lewis Gaddis called it 'The Long Peace' and John Mearsheimer suggested that, once it was over, we would soon miss it

(Gaddis 1986, 1987; Mearsheimer 1990a). Indeed, by the end of the 1990s, legions of conservative commentators not only pined for the past when defining national interest was an easier and more heroic task, they also moaned over the docility, inward focus, lust for material possessions and dwindling respect for the state that seemed to define the essence of the Clintonian United States.[36]

To some extent, the bipolar divide over-ideologised other conflicts – thus the national-liberationist war in Vietnam or various battles against authoritarian rule in Africa and Latin America could only be viewed through the lens of a potential communist crusade. Understanding the true nature of these conflicts might have made possible more and better policy options to address the challenges presented. A 'global war on terror' threatens to do the same – various insurgencies and campaigns against national tyrants are now seen as part and parcel of efforts to destabilise local and global orders by means of transnational terrorist networks, populated by extremists viewed as unwilling or not susceptible to co-option into frameworks of governance. The risks of tunnel vision are high, resulting in a continual process of simplification, rather than stimulating public and academic debate that could, at least potentially, foster more sophisticated policy options.

---

[36] See in particular Corey Robin's overview of this topic, in which he cites his personal interviews with William F. Buckley and Irving Kristol, and reviews the plaintive writings of Robert Kaplan, Robert Kagan, David Brooks and their many contemporaries (Robin 2004).

Conclusion: was there a global 1989?

Arne Westad

Introduction

Symbolic dates in history are a bit like world records in sports; they come out of years of preparation and are in most cases superceded quite quickly. Will 1989, in the view of future historians, be one of those spectacular but quickly superceded *anni mirabiles*? While few are in doubt that something important changed in 1989 (or thereabouts), the big question is whether the events of that year changed enough things on a global scale to become a dividing line between two eras? The answer, of course, depends on where you see the world from. If priority is given to Europe and to Great Power politics, then 1989 is a true watershed because of the Soviet decision not to prevent democratic change in countries Moscow had controlled since 1945. Outside Europe, and outside great power politics, the picture is less clear. In China, 1989 symbolised the defeat of the student movement for democracy. In Africa and Latin America, 1989 saw the beginning of the end of some odious dictatorships (South Africa and Chile, for example), but also an increase in US interventionism, the growth of murderous and extremist religious movements, and the spread of ethnic strife. In the overall US approach to the world very little changed, it could be argued, even if the Soviet Union ceased to be its main enemy. And in terms of the way the world's economy worked, 1989 comes right in the middle of a reasonably cohesive though ever-changing period, rather than at its end, something made abundantly clear by Saskia Sassen's chapter in this volume (Chapter 2).

It seems to me, therefore, that we need to disentangle three different aspects of historical periodisation if we are to assess the impact of 1989 within a longer-term perspective. The first of these is the Cold War, the global conflict between capitalism and communism, which became systemic in international relations terms after 1945. The Cold War as a system influenced a lot of things, but it did not determine everything. The second is ideological change in the 1970s and 1980s, away from planning and state intervention towards international and domestic markets, and from closed to relatively open societies. Ideological change underpinned a lot of the events of 1989 but it did not predetermine them. And the third is structural economic change from the 1970s, in which floating currencies, massive changes in productivity and output, and technological transformation combined to create new globalised financial markets and produced big shifts in wealth and power from the West to the East. Economic change helps explain some of the events of 1989, but it does not give priority to that particular year as a changeover from one system to another.

The Cold War

The end of the Cold War did not have one trajectory, but many. In East Asia, the beginning of the end came when China defected wholesale from the Stalinist system of central planning in the late 1970s. In Europe, the Cold War system started to fade when the combined effects of Ostpolitik, Eurocommunism and successful democratic transitions in Southern Europe in the 1970s overcame division lines created in the 1930s and 1940s. The Soviet Union began turning away from interventionism in the late 1970s after beginning to question the cost – both to itself and others – of so-called 'socialist victories' in Africa and Asia that the regime of Leonid Brezhnev had helped bring about. And the Cold War moved towards its end when the United States regained much of its self-confidence and launched an offensive against radical regimes worldwide in the 1980s. All of these developments, and more, created the kind of ending to the Cold War that we saw in 1989–91. And all of them are crucial to understand if we want to make the case for 1989 as a symbol of broader global processes. Are they part of the same phenomenon, or are they separate and different trends that together helped produce 1989 as an end-point of the Cold War? My answer is more with the latter than the former as an examination of each of these developments in turn makes clear.

While most scholars seem to agree that China played a crucial role in how the Cold War ended, there is very little agreement on what *exactly* that role was (Westad 2000). The traditional view sees China's willingness to join a US-led global alliance against the Soviet Union turn the cards on the Soviets. There is, as far as I can see, not much evidence for this view. Much of the Soviet expansion in the Third World came *after* China and the United States started to work together in 1972. The US international position was probably weaker in 1979 than it had been ten years earlier, at least in terms of public perception. What makes

China's role important is not so much its diplomatic and later military alliance with the United States as much as its gradual abandonment of a strictly centralised economic planning system in the late 1970s and 1980s. It was Beijing's defection from the belief that socialism in some Marxist–Leninist form was the future for all societies that upset the Cold War balance by effectively pulling the rug from under Moscow's pretensions of representing the most advanced form of human development. China, in other words, mattered much more because of its societal and developmental changes than because of its often confused and ill-informed diplomacy and military posturing. And the initiative for these changes came from within, as desperate measures to overcome the disastrous results of Mao Zedong's years of terror and social dislocation (Westad 2010).

The policies that overcame the Cold War in Europe were propelled by European integration and the common security process, which provided the degree of West European unity and the measure of penetrability of the East necessary for constructing a new and all-inclusive European order. The new initiatives were almost entirely West European in origin, with West Germany, France, and to some degree Italy the main protagonists. By the early 1980s it was clear that a new European system was coming into being. Ostpolitik had reduced the fear of a revanchist and expansionist Germany in Eastern Europe (and to some degree in the West). Eurocommunism in Italy and France had removed the last remaining chance of parties subservient to Moscow coming into power in the West. And, first and foremost, the successful and rapid absorption of Greece, Portugal and Spain into a West European framework showed that the main European countries were both willing and capable of living up to the promise, first expressed by France's Charles de Gaulle, of creating one integrated continent. Through its own development, Western Europe both helped inspire demands for change in the East and prepared for the day when these demands for change would break into the political process. In Cold War terms it amounted, in effect, to a kind of separate détente, in which European agendas came to run parallel with the superpower tensions of the early Reagan era (Villaume and Westad 2009).

Changes in Soviet policy also came about because of failures in extending 'actual existing socialism' around the world. By the late 1970s, much of the glitter of the successful Soviet–Cuban interventions in Angola and Ethiopia had worn off, and some leaders, especially in the International Department of the CPSU Central Committee, had begun developing principled anti-interventionist views. Third World socialism had to succeed on its own, they argued, and the Soviet Union could neither afford nor benefit from interventions abroad. Many of these critics became key advisers for Mikhail Gorbachev after 1985 and helped him turn the Soviet Union towards a new policy of cooperation with the West and with international capitalism. By 1989, the Cold War confrontation between the Soviet Union and the United States was over (and in these terms it is quite possible to see the development of a non-Cold War international system with the Soviet Union still in existence; the end of the Cold War and the collapse of the Soviet state are not identical phenomena).[1]

Finally, the United States, and especially the American right, regained momentum in the 1980s, helped by the economic and social changes that came out of the 1970s and by Ronald Reagan's appeal to voters through a programme that mixed the further build-up of the US military with lower taxes. While unsustainable in the long run, Reagan's form of military Keynesianism provided the self-confidence that was needed for the United States to engage Gorbachev's team after it was clear that the Soviets wanted to give up the Cold War model of confrontation. It was Reagan's willingness to negotiate and seek rapid solutions to regional conflicts (albeit mostly on US terms) that made it possible for the United States to draw on Soviet weakness in order to produce remarkable examples of bilateral cooperation.

The Cold War as an international system came to an end around 1989 for many reasons, some of which were connected only tangentially. While it is probably right to point to 1989 as the symbolic year in which the Cold War system collapsed, it is essential not to focus on short-term changes in the superpower relationship or politics in Europe in order to understand its broader significance. Some of the developments within the Cold War that produced 1989 had started much earlier and in very different locales, a point which George Lawson is right to raise in his introduction to this volume. That they came together in the late 1980s to produce the sudden collapse of the system was to some extent accidental and certainly not determined by some kind of primal logic contained within the system itself. As such, contra Chris Armbruster's argument in Chapter 9, I see 1989 less in the sense of necessary endogenous crisis than as a process brought about to a great extent by major historical developments which took place *outside* the Cold War context.

---

[1] President George H. W. Bush cautioned the Ukrainian leaders in August 1991 when they were planning to break away from the Soviet Union: 'We understand that you cannot reform your [Soviet] system overnight. America's first system of government – the Continental Congress – failed because the States were too suspicious of one another and the central government too weak to protect commerce and individual rights.'

Ideological change

These arguments about structural change should not be confused with arguments about how the Cold War came to an end, although of course there are overlaps between them. My point is that, if we are to look at 1989 as a watershed in history, we need to know which stream it was a watershed in. And the principal processes of the twentieth century do not have 1989 as a dividing line. If we look at ideological transformation, there seem to be two very broad trends: a swing towards beliefs in state control and planning in the early part of the century, and a swing away from these beliefs in the latter part – what George Lawson describes as 'the triumph of Hayek over Keynes', a triumph probed extensively and expertly by Saskia Sassen in Chapter 2 in this volume. 1989 is perhaps symbolic of the latter shift in the way that 1917 marked the former. But the trends towards markets, individual rights and consumerism were manifest much earlier than the breakdown of the communist regimes in Eastern Europe. Indeed, that breakdown may as well be linked to events all over the region, from the Baltic to the Adriatic and the Black Sea during the 'long 1970s' – the period, roughly, between the collapse of the Czechoslovak communist party in 1968 to the introduction of martial law in Poland in 1981. The ideological change in Eastern Europe was in itself, however, just a part of a much broader, global transformation.

The high point for all kinds of ideas about solving the problems of humanity through rearranging forms of human organisation was the generation after the Second World War. In the socialist countries this goes without saying. But more important in a structural sense was the hegemony of such ideas in a large number of places outside the socialist sphere of influence. In Western Europe, Christian democrats, social democrats, Gaullists and caudillistas shared the view that only through a substantial strengthening of the role of the state in people's daily lives and in the running of the economy could their countries succeed. In the European outposts – Latin America, South Africa, Oceania – the same trends were dominant, although in very different political wrappings. In Africa and Asia, the newly de-colonised states and the states that were breaking away from European domination – such as Iran, Egypt or Thailand – all adopted planning and a development-oriented centralist state formation as their ideal. Even in the United States the period from Roosevelt to Johnson (including eight years of Republican rule) was dominated by a state-centred agenda. By the late 1960s, the ideological trend seemed very much set – even major companies, it has been observed, started adopting concepts and methods borrowed from states in their management techniques (Harvey 2005; Tilly 2005).[2]

During the 1970s this perspective changed. The ascendance of market ideologies of various kinds in Western Europe and in the United States have been covered in detail recently and can therefore be passed over quickly here (e.g. Müller 2009). In the Third World, however, we see similar developments, well before the communist regimes started getting into trouble. While there is no doubt that some of this change happened under strong political and economic pressure from the centres of the world capitalist economy, it is far too simple to write it off as an enforced attribute. In some countries the change towards the market was due to a learning process in which adjustments had to be made after a period of severe disappointment over growth rates and lack of social transformation. Changes in East Asia, especially in China, played a significant role for other countries. However, it is increasingly clear that many of these transformations came from within: after two decades of slow state-led growth, the embrace of the market was a natural reaction, especially in places where state control of the economy had led to high levels of corruption and unaccountability.[3]

Eastern Europe and the USSR were not impervious to these ideological changes. By the late 1970s, much of the faith in the future of state ownership of the economy and of economic planning as engines of high economic growth had vanished, even in those research centres that were charged with the further development of these models. Curiously, the belief in planning died well before the death of socialist ideals – contrary to what was sometimes written at the time, those who were in charge of these polities (a small percentage of the population, no doubt) kept a significant part of their faith in the legitimacy of their project until the collapse actually happened. But without the ability to offer a model that could create prosperity and progress, their political project was hopelessly lost. Poland is, of course, the most obvious instance here: those who implemented martial law had no idea how the economy should be improved, and admitted so more or less openly. Even in East Germany – in many ways the best functioning socialist

---

[2] It is illustrative to note how these very different books from very different angles converge around this point. In addition, Harvey's argument that the years 1978–80 constitute the principal global turning point is very close to my own and, indeed to George Lawson's assessment in the introduction to this volume.

[3] It is worth noting, of course, that ideas about the need for a strong state role in economic development remained strong in East Asia, albeit with a certain marketised-twist. See, for instance Johnson (1982); Chung (2007); Naughton (2008); and, for an overview, Wade (2003).

economy on offer – the collapse of any belief in a future for a planned economy was palpable during the 1980s, as Charles Maier (1997) has shown.

These broad ideological changes were not only linked to ideas about social and economic organisation, they were also connected to new appraisals of individual and human rights coming from groups across the social and political spectrum. Instead of the assumption that rights were less important than material progress and that rights issues were linked mainly to bourgeois or middle-class values, the 1970s and 1980s saw an explosion in working-class and peasant movements such as Poland's Solidarność or Colombia's Asociación Nacional de Usuarios Campesinos that put rights at the top of their ideological agenda (on the former, see Kurczewski 1993 and Cirtautas 1997; on the latter, see Zamosc 1986). More often than not rights demands were followed up by economic demands. But what mattered was that, quite differently from how these claims were made in the early part of the twentieth century, there was now a clear realisation that economic concessions would not be lasting, or in many cases even imaginable, without a fundamental change in the way the state behaved towards its own citizens.

For a very large number of people during the 1980s, the United States came to be seen as an ideal they would like to emulate. While the acceptance, at least within some groups, of the United States as a model had been visible in many parts of the world throughout the Cold War, it was only during the final decade of the conflict that it achieved a kind of hegemony in developmental terms. It was a passing role, and one that was based on creative misunderstandings in many and diverse cultural settings, but it was still a very forceful agent for change. What made it so dominant, I think, was the mixture of the sense of US resurgence under Ronald Reagan's presidency, its increasing hegemony in popular and consumer culture, and the view that in the United States strong individual rights protection, markets and economic growth came together as one package. Given the general ideological changes that I have outlined above, it was a kind of perfect storm. The United States had its best opportunity to change the world just as its enemies were at their weakest, which helps explain the extraordinary impact specific US practices and symbols had on the 1989 revolutions. By the mid-1990s it was, paradoxically, mostly Western Europe and Japan that remained sceptical about neoliberal economics, while Eastern Europe, mainland East Asia, South Asia, Eastern Europe and Latin America were happy to embrace this new-found faith.

In ideological terms, therefore, 1989 is a waystation in a much longer sweep of historical development, and although it is an important one, it should not overshadow the more general content of this broad process of change. The trend towards linking rights and markets – and moving away from planning and state control – continued into the late 1990s and 2000s. In Eastern Europe, Russia, and the Soviet successor states, the eagerness to imitate a vision of Reagan's United States in social and economic development led to a number of avoidable disasters not least in terms of impoverishment, exploitation and rampant social disloca-tion. For many, the moment of maximum US moulding turned out to be a bitter disappointment.

Economic change

From the early 1970s on, world capitalism went through a profound restructuring during which the US economy globalised and thereby, quite literally, brought about economic changes elsewhere. In the early part of this process of change, right after the collapse of the Bretton Woods system, the overall US position in the world economy seemed much reduced, since most people viewed the United States as the main proponent (and beneficiary) of the old system, and noted the general decline in its relative position in terms of finance, trade, productivity and overall output. What was not generally seen was that, by exiting first from the most acute phase of the 1970s crisis, the United States was more able to take advantage of renewed growth in the mid-1980s and 1990s. And as the world economy became increasingly globalised, the United States benefited from importing capital to feed its own econ-omy (with 1988 being the last year in which its foreign assets exceeded its liabilities). Having the world's major reserve currency helped, as did the willingness of foreigners to invest in the United States and to handle its debts with care in order not to unbalance the emerging new system (and, of course, also for political reasons). By 1989 it seemed that the United States was, paradoxically, as dominant in the new economic system as it had been in the old, in spite of the relative decline in its economic position.

The 1970s also signalled the end of the post-war recovery phase for both Western Europe and Japan. Neither handled the transition to a new economic status well, and by the 1990s were therefore in a much weaker position to influence the post-Cold War international setting than the United States. Indeed, both turned inward to a quite remark-able degree, a process chronicled adroitly in this volume by Laure Delcour (Chapter 6). Western Europe did so because of the needs and opportunities created by integrating a capitalist Eastern Europe into its economic system, not least through expansion of German capital and of the EU. Japan attempted, and mostly failed, to change its economic model because of the competition from within its own region (and also because of the ideological swings described above). In each case, the pendulum seemed to have swung back from the extraordinary growth both had experienced until the late Cold War period.

What created the 1980s recovery out of which so much of the buoyancy of international capitalism in 1989 grew, was first and foremost a combination of US spending (including massive military spending) with the creation of a global market, not least in financial terms. Some of this development is obviously linked to significant advances in technology. The combination of computing power and telecommunications, first developed in the United States for military and financial purposes, and then spreading as the Internet in its various forms, contributed to the new economic system of massive capital movements, currency fluctuations, and unhindered restructuring. In the crucial years after 1989, many believed that a new form of stability, similar to that which had existed between the early 1950s and the early 1970s, could be based on the globalisation of capital and the new forms of production that information technology gave rise to. For a while this proposition seemed right, and in the end the 1980s system, or the Washington Concensus, collapsed more as a result of excessive corporate greed than its own inbuilt imbalances, after a lifespan that was only marginally shorter than the system it had replaced.[4]

What was crucial for international affairs in the latest turn of the global economic merry-go-round was the shift that very few people had spotted from around 1989, namely that China (and by implication the economic system of its region) would become the main beneficiary of capitalist accumulation from the mid-1980s to the mid-2000s. Significant for the discussion in this volume, it was around 1989 that Asia again became the continent with the highest total productive output, a reversion to the situation that had existed in all of recorded history except the relatively short stretch from the 1880s to the 1980s, during which first Europe and then North America surpassed the continent. Equally important, perhaps, is the fact that it was in 1989 that China's total production became bigger in value than Japan's (if you use purchasing power parities of currencies and average prices of commodities as tools for comparison). While China's massive growth and

---

[4] Clearly parts of this argument – particularly that regarding contingent greed rather than endogenous necessity as the root cause of the financial crisis – runs counter to that provided by George Lawson and Saskia Sassen in earlier chapters (Introduction and Chapter 2). I leave it to readers to determine the whys and wherefores of this debate.

Japan's relative slump were both still in the future in 1989, this change was an important reminder for what was to come. In spite of the central role of the United States in establishing and maintaining the economic system that functioned on both sides of the end of the Cold War, it now seems unlikely that there will be a third US-based international economic system.

The spirit of 1989?

The growth of China is, of course, a storyline that is in ultimate competition with what is generally seen as the spirit of 1989. Although Aviezer Tucker argues convincingly (Chapter 7, this volume) that much of contemporary Russia and China can be understood via examination of their totalitarian legacies, more often than not, contemporary China appears as the antithesis of 1989, most of which is understood via the limitations on state power brought about by the assertion of individual rights. Was the outcome of China's own 1989 – the crackdown on democracy protesters both in Tiananmen Square and elsewhere – perhaps, therefore, more a harbinger of things to come than the Eastern European revolutions and the changes in Southern Africa and in Latin America?

The problem with this interpretation is that, while the growth in China's economy has certainly been the big story after the Cold War ended, there is no indication that China in terms of ideology, not to mention politics, has reached any form of stability, or, as many Chinese critics argue, any sense of purpose. While it is not uncommon that emerging Great Powers show uncertainty as they assume the mantle of leadership – think of the United States in the 1920s and 1930s – it is very rare that they do not have a story of their rise that is assumed to be a model for the world. Contra the arguments made by some in this volume, I do not think that China has such a model. Its polity is dysfunctional in the extreme and most of the issues raised by the 1989 protests remain unsolved. Making oneself the beneficiary of the world capitalist system through a capacity for hard work and through the profligacy of others is hardly a storyline that will set minds on fire in Sulawesi or Montevideo.

It is, therefore, possible that 1989, as a symbolic moment, could be seen both as an end and as a beginning, in spite of the difficulties that exist in placing the year within patterns of broader ideological and economic change. For Europe, 1989 was an end-point in an almost Fukuyaman sense – the revolutions in the East led to the expansion of economic integration and cooperative forms of security.[5] The European Cold War, going back to 1917, ended and the European Union became the continent's future, albeit a future which has developed more slowly than many then believed (as Laure Delcour chronicles most effectively in Chapter 6). Outside Europe, however, the Cold War international system came to an end in much messier ways. I accept that the global effects of the changes in ideologies and economies that I have discussed here would have had somewhat different trajectories if not for the timing and content of the end of the Cold War in Europe. But just like the impact of the late Cold War was felt more acutely in Asia, Africa and Latin America than in Europe, post-Cold War political settlements were harder to arrive at. While Fred Halliday (Chapter 5) is undoubtedly right in observing that the key fact about the peace deals struck in various corners of the world as the Cold War ended is that they worked, the same cannot be said for the political arrangements that accompanied them, or, indeed, other forms of post-Cold War political orders. The need for peace and stability after what for many people had been a real war, in settings as diverse as the Chinese Cultural Revolution, the 'dirty wars' of South America, or the anti-apartheid struggles in Southern Africa, often came to overshadow the need for better functioning and more representative and/or inclusive political systems. The real challenge still remaining from the global agendas created at the end of the Cold War may therefore be more about democratisation than about any other form of change.[6]

---

[5] Often forgotten today, it was not the United States but the *European Community* that Fukuyama (1989) believed would set the model for the (stultified) future of mankind, not least in his depiction of the impending 'common marketisation' of world politics.

[6] Joshua Clover (2009), in his stimulating discussion of the pop music lyrics of the momentous year, sees democracy in the form of 'people power' as the key message of 1989.

Bibliography

Ackerman, Bruce 1992. *The Future of Liberal Revolution*. New Haven: Yale University Press.

Ágh, Attila 1998. *Emerging Democracies in East Central Europe and the Balkans*. Cheltenham: Edward Elgar.

Al-Sayyid Marsot, A. 1985. *A Short History of Modern Egypt*. Cambridge University Press.

Ambrogi, Thomas 1999. 'Jubilee 2000 and the Campaign for Debt Cancellation', *National Catholic Reporter*, July.

Anderson, Perry and Camiller, Patrick (eds.) 1994. *Mapping the West European Left*. London: Verso.

Arbatov, Georgi 1992. *The System: An Insider's Life in Soviet Politics*. New York: Times Books.

Archer, Margaret S. 1988. *Culture and Agency*. Cambridge University Press.
    1996. 'Social Integration and System Integration: Developing the Distinction', *Sociology* 30(4): 679–99.

Arendt, Hannah 1963. *On Revolution*. New York: Viking.
    1973. *The Origins of Totalitarianism*. New York: Harvest.

Armbruster, Chris 2008. *The Quality of Democracy in Europe. Soviet Illegitimacy and the Negotiated Revolutions of 1989*. New York: Social Science Research Network.

Aron, Leon 2007. *Russia's Revolution: Essays 1989–2006*. Washington, DC: AEI Press.

Arquilla, John 2006. *Reagan Imprint: Ideas in American Foreign Policy from the Collapse of Communism to the War on Terror*. Chicago: Ivan R. Dee.
    2008. *Worst Enemy: The Reluctant Transformation of the American Military*. Chicago: Ivan R. Dee.

Arquilla, John and Ronfeldt, David 2000. *Swarming and the Future of Conflict*. Santa Monica: RAND Corporation.

Åslund, Anders 2002. 'The Advantages of Radical Reform', in Larry Diamond and Marc F. Plattner (eds.), *Democracy After Communism*. Baltimore: Johns Hopkins University Press, pp. 216–23.
    2007. *How Capitalism was Built: The Transformation of Central and Eastern Europe, Russia, and Central Asia*. Cambridge University Press.

Ates, D. 2005. 'Economic Liberalization and Changes in Fundamentalism: The Case of Egypt', *Middle East Policy* 12(4): 133–44.

Ayoob, M. 2008. *The Many Faces of Political Islam*. Ann Arbor: University of Michigan Press.

Ayubi, N. 1993. *Political Islam: Religion and Politics in the Arab World*. London: Routledge.

Azmanova, Albena 2008. 'Transition without Emancipation? 1989 and the Fate of the European Social Model', *Research Network* 1989, Working Paper 11. Available at: www.cee-socialscience.net/1989/papers/index.html.

Bain, William 2003. 'The Political Theory of Trusteeship and the Twilight of International Equality', *International Relations* 17(1): 59–77.

Barnett, Thomas 2004. *The Pentagon's New Map: War and Peace in the Twenty-first Century*. New York: Putnam.

Barnett, Thomas and Cebrowski, Arthur 2003. 'The American Way of War', *Proceedings*, January, 43.

Battilega, John, Beachley, David R., Beck, Daniel C., Driver, Robert L. and Jackson, Bruce 2001. *Transformations in Global Defense Markets and Industries: Implications for the Future of Warfare*. Washington, DC: National Intelligence Council. Available at: www.dni.gov/nic/PDF_GIF_research/defensemkts/russia.pdf.

Belloni, Robert 2007. 'The Trouble with Humanitarianism', *Review of International Studies* 33(3): 451–74.

Belot, Céline and Georgakakis, Didier 2004. 'Enseigner l'Europe', *Politique Européenne* special issue, 14(3): 5–163.

Beneria, Lourdes and Feldman, Shelley (eds.) 1992. *Unequal Burden: Economic Crises, Persistent Poverty, and Women's Work*. Boulder: Westview.

Bergen, Peter and Reynolds, Alec 2005. 'Blowback Revisited: Today's Insurgents in Iraq Are Tomorrow's Terrorists', *Foreign Affairs* 84(6): 2–6.

Beyme, Klaus von 1996. *Transition to Democracy in Eastern Europe*. New York: St Martin's Press.

Bhambra, Gurminder and Demir, Ipek (eds.) 2009. *1968 in Retrospect: History, Theory, Alterity*. Basingstoke: Palgrave Macmillan.

Biddle, Stephen 1996. 'Victory Misunderstood: What the Gulf War Tells Us about the Future of Conflict', *International Security* 21(2): 139–79.

   2004. *Toppling Saddam: Iraq and American Military Transformation*. Strategic Studies Institute, U.S. Army War College, April.

   2006. 'Seeing Baghdad, Thinking Saigon', *Foreign Affairs* 85(2): 2–14.

Bisley, Nick 2004. *The End of the Cold War and the Causes of Soviet Collapse*. Basingstoke: Palgrave Macmillan.

Blackburn, Robin (ed.) 1991. *After the Fall. The Failure of Communism and the Future of Socialism*. London: Verso.

Blaney, David 2001. 'Realist Spaces/Liberal Bellicosities: Reading the Democratic Peace as World Democratic Theory', in Tarak Barkawi and Mark Laffey (eds.), *Democracy, Liberalism, and War*. London: Lynne Rienner, pp. 25–44.

Blokker, Paul 2005. 'Post-Communist Modernization, Transition Studies, and Diversity in Europe', *European Journal of Social Theory*, 8: 503–25.

2008. 'Constitutional Politics, Constitutional Texts and Democratic Variety in Central and Eastern Europe', Sussex European Institute Working Paper No. 105.

Bloom, Allan 1987. *The Closing of the American Mind*. New York: Simon & Schuster.

Bose, Christine E. and Acosta-Belen, Edna (eds.) 1995. *Women in the Latin American Development Process*. Philadelphia: Temple University Press.

Bozo, Frederic 2007. 'Mitterrand's France, the End of Cold War, and German Unification: A Reappraisal', *Cold War History* 7(4): 455–78.

Bozóki, András 1993. 'Hungary's Road to Systemic Change: The Opposition Roundtable', *East European Politics and Societies* 7(2): 276–308.

Bozóki, András (ed.) 2002. *The Roundtable Talks of 1989: The Genesis of Hungarian Democracy*. Budapest: Central European University Press.

Bozóki, András 2003. 'Theoretical Interpretations of Elite Change in East Central Europe', *Comparative Sociology* 2(1): 215–47.

Bradshaw, York, Noonan, Rita, Gash, Laura and Buchmann, Claudia 1993. 'Borrowing Against the Future: Children and Third World Indebtness', *Social Forces* 71(3): 629–56.

Brooks, Stephen G. and Wohlforth, William C. 2000. 'Power, Globalization, and the End of the Cold War: Reevaluating a Landmark Case for Ideas', *International Security* 25(3): 5–53.

2008. *World out of Balance*. Princeton University Press.

Brown, Archie 1997. *The Gorbachev Factor*. Oxford University Press.

Buechler, Simone 2007. 'Deciphering the Local in a Global Neoliberal Age: Three Favelas in Sao Paulo, Brazil', in S. Sassen (ed.), *Deciphering the Global: Its Scales, Spaces, and Subjects*. New York and London: Routledge, pp. 95–112.

Builder, Carl 1989. *The Masks of War: American Military Styles in Strategy and Analysis*. Washington, DC: Johns Hopkins University Press.

Bunce, Valerie 1999. *Subversive Institutions: The Design and the Destruction of Socialism and the State*. New York: Cambridge University Press.

Burgess, John W. 1895. 'The Ideal of the American Commonwealth', *Political Science Quarterly* 10(3): 404–25.

Bush, George W. 1999. Address at The Citadel, South Carolina, 23 September 1999. Available at: www.citadel.edu/pao/addresses/pres_bush.html (last accessed 10 June 2008).

Buzan, Barry 2006. 'Will the "Global War on Terrorism" be the New Cold War?', *International Affairs* 82(6): 1011–18.

Canby, Steven 1987. 'Conventional Weapon Technologies', *SIPRI Yearbook 1987: World Armaments and Disarmament*. Oxford University Press, pp. 85–95.

Carrère d'Encausse, Hélène 1979. *L'empire éclaté – La révolte des nations en URSS*. Paris: Flammarion.

Cassen, Robert (ed.) 1985. *Soviet Interests in the Third World*. London: Sage/RIIA.

Cebrowski, Arthur K. and Barnett, Thomas P. M. 2003. 'The American Way of War', *Proceedings, US Naval Institute*, January: 42–3.

Cerny, Phil 2006. 'Restructuring the State in a Globalizing World', *Review of International Political Economy* 13(4): 679–95.

Chandler, David 2000. *Faking Democracy After Dayton*, 2nd edition. London: Pluto Press.

Chang, Ha-Joon 2007. *Bad Samaritans: Rich Nations, Poor Policies and the Threat to the Developing World*. New York: Random House.

Chirot, Daniel 1996. *Modern Tyrants*. Princeton University Press.

   2002. 'Returning to Reality: Culture, Modernization, and Various Eastern Europes: Why Functionalist-Evolutionary Theory Works', *Tr@nsit online*, Nr. 21. Available at: www.iwm.at.

Chung, Young-Iob 2007. *South Korea in the Fast Lane: Economic Development and Capital Formation*. Oxford University Press.

Cirtautas, Arista Maria 1997. *The Polish Solidarity Movement: Revolution, Democracy and Natural Rights*. Cambridge University Press.

Clark, J. C. D. 2000. *English Society 1660–1832: Religion, Ideology and Politics During the Ancien Regime*, 2nd edition. Cambridge University Press.

Clarke, Richard 2004. *Against All Enemies: Inside America's War on Terror*. New York: Free Press.

Clinton, Bill 1991. 'A New Covenant for American Strategy', Remarks to Students at Georgetown University, 12 December.

Clover, Joshua 2009. *1989: Bob Dylan Didn't Have This to Sing About*. Berkeley: University of California Press.

Cohen, Elliot 1995. 'Playing Powell Politics: The General's Zest for Power', *Foreign Affairs* 74(6): 102–10.

Cohen, Elliot and Keaney, Thomas A. 1993. *Gulf War Airpower Survey, Volume 2*. Washington, DC: United States Government Printing Office.

Cohen, Jared 2007. *Children of the Jihad*. New York: Gotham Books.

Cohen, Jean L. and Arato, Andrew 1992. *Civil Society and Political Theory*. Cambridge, MA: The MIT Press.

Cohen, Lenard J. 1997. 'Bosnia Herzegovina: A Case of Failed Democratization', in Karen Dawisha and Bruce Parrott (eds.), *Politics, Power, and the Struggle for Democracy in South-East Europe*. New York and Cambridge: Cambridge University Press.

Coker, Christopher 1994. *War and the Twentieth Century*. London: Brassey's.

Coll, Steve 2004. *Ghost Wars: The Secret History of the CIA, Afghanistan, and bin Laden, From the Soviet Invasion to September 10, 2001*. New York: Penguin.

Conley, Kathleen 1998. 'Campaigning for Change: Organizational Processes, Governmental Politics, and the Revolution in Military Affairs', *Airpower Journal*, Fall. Available at: www.airpower.maxwell.af.mil/airchronicles/apj/apj98.

Conquest, Robert 1997. 'Victims of Stalinism: a Comment', *Europe-Asia Studies* 49(7): 1317–19.

Cooley, J. 2002. *Unholy Wars: Afghanistan, America and International Terrorism*. London: Pluto Press.

Cooper, Robert 2002. 'The New Liberal Imperialism', *Observer*, 7 April. Available at: www.observer.guardian.co.uk/print/0,38584388912–102273,00.htm.

2004. *The Breaking of Nations*. London: Atlantic Books.

Coppieters, Bruno and Deschouwer, Kris 1994. 'A West European Model for Social Democracy in East Central Europe?', in Michael Waller, Bruno Coppieters and Kris Deschouwer (eds.), *Social Democracy in a Post-Communist Europe*. London: Frank Cass, pp. 1–18.

Courtois, Stéphane, Werth, Nicolas, Panné, Jean-Louis, Paczkowski, Andrzej, Bartošek, Karel and Margolin, Jean-Louis 1997. *Le livre noir du communisme. Crimes, terreur, répression*. Paris: Robert Laffont.

Cox, Michael (ed.) 1998. *Rethinking the Soviet Collapse: Sovietology, the Death of Communism and the New Russia*. London: Pinter.

Cox, Michael 1992. 'Western Intelligence, the Soviet Threat, and NSC-68: A Reply to Beatrice Heuser', *Review of International Studies* 18: 75–83.

1995. *US Foreign Policy after the Cold War: Superpower without a Mission?* London: Frances Pinter, Chatham House.

2002. 'American Power before and After 11 September: Dizzy with Success?', *International Affairs* 78(2): 261–76.

2003. 'Martians and Venutians in the New World Order', *International Affairs* 79(3): 521–32.

2007. 'Another Transatlantic Split? American and European Narratives and the End of the Cold War', *Cold War History* 7(1): 121–46.

Cox, Michael and Hurst, Steven 2002. 'His Finest Hour: George Bush and German Unification', *Diplomacy and Statecraft* 13: 123–50.

Cox, Michael and Stokes, Doug (eds.) 2008. *U.S. Foreign Policy*. Oxford University Press.

Cox, Michael, Booth, Ken, Dunne, Tim and Hill, Christopher 1999. *The Interregnum: Controversies in World Politics 1989–1999*. Cambridge University Press.

Cremona, Marise and Hillion, Christophe 2006. 'L'Union fait la force? Potentials and Limitations of the European Neighbourhood Policy as an Integrated EU Foreign and Security Policy', *EUI Working Papers*, Law no. 2006/39.

Crouch, Colin 2004. *Post-democracy*. Cambridge: Polity Press.

Crockatt, Richard 1995. *The Fifty Years War. The United States and the Soviet Union in World Politics, 1941–1991*. London: Routledge.

Curry, Jane Leftwich and Urban, Joan Barth (eds.) 2003. *The Left transformed in Post-Communist Societies. The Cases of East-Central Europe, Russia, and Ukraine*. Lanham: Rowman and Littlefield.

Daalder, Ivo H. and Lindsay, James M. 2003. *America Unbound: The Bush Revolution in Foreign Policy*. Washington, DC: The Brookings Institution.

Daalder, Ivo H. and O'Hanlon, Michael 1999. 'Unlearning the Lessons of Kosovo', *Foreign Policy* 116, Autumn: 128–40.

Dahrendorf, Ralf 1990. *Reflections on the Revolution in Europe*. London: Chatto & Windus.

David, Roman 2006. 'From Prague to Baghdad: Lustration Systems and Their Political Effects', *Government and Opposition* 41(3): 347–72.

Davis, Mike 1982. 'Extended Deterrence', in *New Left Review* (eds.) *Exterminism and Cold War*. London: Verso.

Dawisha, Karen and Parrott, Bruce (eds.) 1997. *The Consolidation of Democracy in East-Central Europe*, vol. I. Cambridge University Press.

De Tocqueville, Alexis 1969. *Democracy in America*. New York: Doubleday.

Delcour, Laure and Tulmets, Elsa (eds.) 2008. *Pioneer Europe? Testing European Foreign Policy in its Neighbourhood*. Baden-Baden: Nomos.

Delhey, Jan 2001. *Osteuropa Zwischen Marx und Markt. Soziale Ugleichheit und soziales Bewusstsein nach dem Kommunismus*. Hamburg: Krämer.

Delors, Jacques 1992. *Le nouveau concert européen*. Paris: Odile Jacob.

Desportes, Vincent 2007. *La guerre probable*. Paris: Economica.

Deudney, Dan and Ikenberry, John 2009. 'The Myth of Authoritarian Revival', *Foreign Affairs* 88(1): 77–93.

Deutscher, Isaac 1954. *The Prophet Armed*. Oxford University Press.

  1960. *The Great Contest: Russia and the West*. Oxford University Press.

Dickson, Bruce J. 2003. *Red Capitalists in China: The Party, Private Entrepreneurs, and Prospects for Political Change*. Cambridge University Press.

Dobbins, James 2005. 'Iraq: Winning the Unwinnable War', *Foreign Affairs* 84(1): 16–25.

  2007. 'Who Lost Iraq? Lessons from the Debacle', *Foreign Affairs* 86(5): 61–74.

Documents on British Policy Overseas. VII German Unification, 1989–90. London: Foreign and Commonwealth Office, 2009.

Dobson, Alan P. 2005. 'The Reagan Administration, Economic Warfare, and Starting to Close Down the Cold War', *Diplomatic History* 29(3): 531–56.

Dodge, Toby 2009. 'Coming Face to Face with Bloody Reality: Liberal Common Sense and the Ideological Failure of the Bush Doctrine in Iraq', *International Politics* 46(2): 253–75.

Dodge, T. and Higgott, R. (eds.) 2002. *Globalization and the Middle East: Islam, Economy, Society and Politics*. London: RIIA.

Dogan, Mattei and Higley, John 1998. 'Elites, Crises, and Regimes in Comparative Analysis', in Mattei Dogan and John Higley (eds.), *Elites, Crises, and Regimes in Comparative Analysis*. Lanham: Rowman & Littlefield, pp. 3–27.

Donnelly, Jack 1998. 'Human Rights: A New Standard of Civilization?', *International Affairs* 74(1): 1–23.

Doyle, Michael 1983. 'Kant, Liberal Legacies, and Foreign Affairs, Part 1 and 2', *Philosophy and Public Affairs* 12(3 and 4): 205–35, 323–53.

Duchêne, François 1973. 'The European Community and the Uncertainties of Interdependence', in M. Kohnstamm and W. Hager (eds.), *A Nation Writ Large? Foreign Policy Problems before the European Community*. London: Macmillan.

Edgar, David 2009. 'In the New Revolution, Progressives Fight Against, Not With, the Poor', *Guardian*, 25 August, p. 27.

Ekiert, Grzegorz 1996. *The State Against Society: Political Crises and Their Aftermath in East Central Europe*. Princeton University Press.

  2003. 'Patterns of Postcommunist Transformation in Central and Eastern Europe', in Grzegorz Ekiert and Stephen E. Hanson (eds.), *Capitalism and Democracy in Central and Eastern Europe. Assessing the Legacy of Communist Rule*. New York: Cambridge University Press, pp. 89–119.

Ekiert, Grzegorz and Kubik, Jan 1999. *Rebellious Civil Society: Popular Protest and Democratic Consolidation in Poland, 1989–1993*. Ann Arbor: University of Michigan Press.

Elliott, Gregory 2008. 'The Sorcerer and the Gravedigger', in G. Elliott, *Ends in Sight*. London: Pluto, pp. 1–33.

Elson, Diane 1995. *Male Bias in Development*, 2nd edition. Manchester University Press.

Elster, Jon 1990. 'The Necessity and Impossibility of Simultaneous Economic and Political Reform', in Piotr Polszajski (ed.), *Philosophy of Social Choice*. Warsaw: IFIS Publishers, pp. 309–16.

Elster, Jon, Offe, Claus and Preuss, Ulrich 1998. *Institutional Design in Post-Communist Societies: Rebuilding the Ship at Sea*. Cambridge University Press.

Esposito, J. 2002. *Unholy War: Terror in the Name of Islam*. Oxford University Press.

European Journal of Social and Political Theory 2009. 'Special Issue: 1989 and Social Theory', 12 (3): 307–424.

Fagen, Richard, Deere, Carmen Diana and Coraggio, José Luis (eds.) 1986. *Transition and Development: Problems of Third World Socialism*. New York: Monthly Review Press.

Falk, Barbara J. 2003. *The Dilemmas of Dissidence in East-Central Europe: Citizen Intellectuals and Philosopher Kings*. Budapest and New York: CEU Press.

  2008. 'The Legacies of Charter 77: The Gift of Democratic Dissent', in Markéta Devátá, Jiří Suk and Oldřich Tůma (eds.), *Charter 77: From the Assertion of Human Rights to a Democratic Revolution, 1977–1989*. Prague: Vydál Ústav pro soudobé dějiny AV ČR.

Faure, Claude 2004. *Aux Services de la Republique: du BCRA à la DGSE*. Paris: Fayard.

Feher, Ferenc and Heller, Agnes 1979. *Diktatur über die Bedürfnisse. Sozialistische Kritik osteuropäischer Gesellschaftsformationen*. Hamburg: VSA.

Feldman, Noah 2003. *After Jihad: America and the Struggle for Islamic Democracy*. New York: Farrar, Straus and Giroux.

Ferguson, Niall 2008. *Colossus: The Price of America's Empire*. London: Penguin.

Ferrett, Grant and Vulliamy, Ed 2008. 'How a Tiny West African Country became the World's First Narco State', *Observer*, 9 March.

Filippov, Alexander 1992. 'Eliten im postimperialen Reichsraum', *Berliner Debatte – Initial* 6: 45–9.

Finnemore, Martha 2003. *The Purpose of Intervention*. Ithaca: Cornell University Press.

Forbrig, Joerg and Demes, Pavol (eds.) 2007. *Reclaiming Democracy. Civil Society and Electoral Change in Central and Eastern Europe*. Washington, DC and Bratislava: German Marshall Fund of the United States.

Foroohar, Rana 2009. 'The Decline of the Petro-Czar', *Newsweek*, 23 February: 12–15.

Fraser, Nancy 2008. *Scales of Justice*. Cambridge: Polity.

Friedman, Benjamin n.d. 'The Navy After The Cold War: Progress Without Revolution', in Harvey Sapolsky, 'Military Innovation Under Jointness and Centralization', unpublished draft report for the National Defense University.

Friedman, Norman 2000. *The Fifty Year War: Conflict and Strategy in the Cold War*. Annapolis: Naval Institute Press.

Friedman, Thomas 2007. *The World is Flat: The Globalized World in the 21st Century*. Harmondsworth: Penguin.

Friedman, Thomas L. 1999. *The Lexus and the Olive Tree: Understanding Globalization*. New York: Farrar, Straus and Giroux.

Fukuyama, Francis 1989. 'The End of History?', *The National Interest* 16: 3–18.

1992. *The End of History and the Last Man*. London: Penguin.

2004. 'The Neoconservative Moment', *National Interest* 76: 57–68.

2005. 'Building Democracy after Conflict: "Stateness First"', *Journal of Democracy* 16(1): 84–8.

2006a. *After the Neocons*. London: Profile Books.

2006b. *State-Building: Governance and World Order in the 21st Century*. Ithaca: Cornell University Press.

2006c. *The End of History and the Last Man*, with a new Afterword. Toronto: Free Press.

Furedi, Frank 1994. *The New Ideology of Imperialism*. London: Pluto.

2007. *Invitation to Terror*. London: Continuum.

Furet, François 1999. *The Passing of an Illusion*. University of Chicago Press.

Furman Center for Real Estate and Urban Policy. 2007. 'New Housing Data continue to show signs of danger for New York City's Homeowners'. 15 October. New York University.

Gaddis, John Lewis 1986. 'The Long Peace: Elements of Stability in the Postwar International System', *International Security* 10(4): 99–142.

1987. *The Long Peace: Inquiries into the History of the Cold War*. Oxford University Press.

2002. 'A Grand Strategy', *Foreign Policy* 113: 50–7.

Galbraith, Peter W. 2006. *The End of Iraq: How American Incompetence Created a War Without End*. New York: Simon & Schuster.

Galtung, Johan 1969. 'Violence, Peace, and Peace Research', *Journal of Peace Research* 6(3): 167–219.

GAO/C-MASAD-83-12 Report by the Comptroller General of the United States 1983. 'Wide Area Antiarmor Munitions', 26 January 1983.

GAO-07-600CG David Walker 2007. 'Fiscal Stewardship and Defense Transformation: Speech before the United States Naval Academy', 8 March.

Gareev, Makhut 1998. *If War Comes Tomorrow? The Contours of Future Armed Conflict*. London: Frank Cass.

Garton Ash, Timothy 1990. *We the People: The Revolution of '89 Witnessed in Warsaw, Budapest, Berlin, and Prague*. Cambridge: Granta.

1999. 'The Puzzle of Central Europe', *The New York Review of Books*, 18 March, pp. 18–23.

2004. *Free World*. London: Penguin.

Garton Ash, Timothy and Snyder, Timothy 2005. 'The Orange Revolution', *The New York Review of Books*, 30 March.

Gat, Azar 2007. 'The Return of Authoritarian Great Powers', *Foreign Affairs* 86: 59–69.

Gates, Robert 1996. *From the Shadows: The Ultimate Inside Story of Five Presidents and How They Won the Cold War*. New York: Simon & Schuster.

Gel'man, Vladimir and Tarusina, Inessa 2003. 'Studies of Political Elites in Russia', in Anton Steen and Vladimir Gel'man (eds.), *Elites and Democratic Development in Russia*. London: Routledge, pp. 187–205.

Gellner, Ernest 1993. 'Homeland of the Unrevolution', *Daedalus* 22(3): 141–54.

1997. *Nationalism*. New York University Press.

Gerges, Fawaz 2005. *The Far Enemy: Why Jihad Went Global*. Cambridge University Press.

Getty, John A. and Manning, Roberta T. (eds.) 1993. *Stalinist Terror. New Perspectives*. Cambridge University Press.

Giddens, Anthony 2002. *The Runaway World*. London: Routledge.

Giddings, Franklin 1898. 'Imperialism?', *Political Science Quarterly* 13(4): 585–605.

Gill, Graeme 1994. *The Collapse of a Single-Party System. The Disintegration of the Communist Party of the Soviet Union*. Cambridge University Press.

Glantz, David 1995. *The Evolution of Soviet Operational Art, 1927–1991: Volume II, Operational Art, 1965–1991*. London: Frank Cass.

Glenny, Misha 2008. *McMafia. Crime Without Frontiers*. London: The Bodley Head.

Gonzáles Enriquez, Carmen 1998. 'Elites and Decommunization in Eastern Europe', in John Higley, Jan Pakulski and Włodzimierz Wesołowski (eds,), *Postcommunist Elites and Democracy in Eastern Europe*. New York: St. Martin's Press, pp. 277–95.

Goodson, Larry 2003. 'Afghanistan's Long Road to Reconstruction', *Journal of Democracy* 14(1): 82–99.

Goodwin, Jeff 2001. *No Other Way Out: States and Revolutionary Movements, 1945–1991*. Cambridge University Press.

Gorbachev, Mikhail 1996. *Memoirs*. New York: Doubleday.

Gordon, Michael R. 2008. 'Key Move in Iraq Still Haunts U.S. Military', *International Herald Tribune*, 17 March.

Gray, Colin 1979. 'Nuclear Strategy: The Case for a Theory of Victory', *International Security* 4(1): 54–87.

Gray, John 2007. *Black Mass: Apocalyptic Religion and the Death of Utopia*. London: Allen Lane.

Grzymała-Busse, Anna 2003. 'Redeeming the Past: Communist Successor Parties after 1989', in Grzegorz Ekert and Stephen E. Hanson (eds.), *Capitalism and Democracy in Central and Eastern Europe: Assessing the Legacy of Communist Rule*. New York: Cambridge University Press, pp. 157–81.

Haass, Richard 2008. 'The Age of Nonpolarity', *Foreign Affairs* 87: 44–56.

Habermas, Jürgen 1990. 'What Does Socialism Mean Today? The Rectifying Revolution and the Need for New Thinking of the Left', *New Left Review* 183: 3–21.

1991. 'What Does Socialism Mean Today? The Revolutions of Recuperation and the Need for New Thinking', in Robin Blackburn (ed.), *After the Fall: The Failure of Communism and the Future of Socialism*. London: Verso.

2001. *The Postnational Constellation*. Cambridge, MA: MIT Press.

2009. 'Life after Bankruptcy: An Interview with Jürgen Habermas', *Constellations* 16(2).

Hall, John A. 1995. 'After the Vacuum: Post-Communism in the Light of Tocqueville', in Beverly Crawford (ed.), *Markets, States and Democracy. The Political Economy of Post-Communist Transformation*. Boulder: Westview Press, pp. 82–100.

Hall, Martin and Hobson, John M. 2010. 'Liberal International Theory: Eurocentric but not always Imperialist?', *International Theory* 2(2): 210–45.

Halliday, Fred 1979. *Arabia Without Sultans*. Harmondsworth: Penguin.

1984. *The Making of the Second Cold War*. London: Verso.

1989. *Cold War, Third World: An Essay on US-Soviet Relations*. London: Radius/ Hutchinson, issued in the United States as *From Kabul to Managua: Soviet-American Relations in the 1980s*. New York: Pantheon Books.

1991. 'The Ends of Cold War', in Robin Blackburn (ed.), *After the Fall. The Failure of Communism and the Future of Socialism*. London: Verso.

1999. *Revolution and World Politics: The Rise and Fall of the Sixth Great Power*. London: Macmillan.

2003. 'Utopian Realism: The Challenge for "Revolution" in Our Times', in John Foran (ed.), *The Future of Revolutions: Rethinking Radical Change in the Age of Globalization*. London: Zed Books, pp. 300–9.

2008. 'International Relations in a Post-Hegemonic Age', LSE Public Lecture, 30 January.

Hallion, Richard 1992. *Storm Over Iraq: Air Power and the Gulf War*. Washington, DC: Smithsonian Institution Press.

Hamad, O. 1981. 'Egypt's Open Door Policy: An Attempt at Economic Integration in the Middle East', *International Journal of Middle East Studies* 13(1): 1–9.

Hardt, Michael and Negri, Antonio 2000. *Empire*. Cambridge, MA: Harvard University Press.

Harvey, David 2005. *A Brief History of Neoliberalism*. Oxford University Press.

Hattendorf, John 2004. *The Evolution of the U.S. Navy's Maritime Strategy, 1977–1986*. Newport, RI: Naval War College.

Hehir, Aidan 2008. 'The Myth of the Failed State and the War on Terror', *Journal of Intervention and State-Building* 1(3): 307–32.

Heikal, M. 1978. *Sphinx and the Commissar: The Rise and Fall of Soviet Influence in the Arab World*. London: Collins.

1983. *Autumn of Fury*. London: Deutsch.

Held, David, McGrew, Anthony, Goldblatt, David and Perraton, Jonathan (eds.) 1999. *Global Transformations: Politics, Economics and Culture*. Cambridge: Polity.

Henderson, Jeffrey 2005. 'Governing Growth and Inequality: The Continuing Relevance of Strategic Economic Planning', in R. Appelbaum and

W. Robinson (eds.), *Critical Globalization Studies*. New York: Routledge, pp. 227–36.

Henrotin, Joseph 2006. 'Une techno-guérilla aurait-elle défait la meillure armée du monde?' *Défense & Sécurité Internationale*, 18, September: 54–7.

Herbst, Jeffrey 2004. 'Let Them Fail: State Failure in Theory and Practice – Implications for Policy', in R. I. Rotberg (ed.), *When States Fail*. Princeton University Press.

Higley, John, Bayulgen, Oksan and George, Julie 2003. 'Political Elite Integration and Differentiation in Russia', in Anton Steen and Vladimir Gel'man (eds.), *Elites and Democratic Development in Russia*. London: Routledge, pp. 11–28.

Higley, John, Kullberg, Judith and Pakulski, Jan 2002. 'The Persistence of Postcommunist Elites', in Larry Diamond and Marc F. Plattner (eds.), *Democracy After Communism*. Baltimore: Johns Hopkins University Press, pp. 33–48.

Hill, Christopher and Smith, Michael (eds.) 2005. *International Relations and the European Union*. Oxford University Press.

Hinnebusch, R. 1993. 'Syria', in T. Niblock and E. Murphy (eds.), *Economic and Political Liberalization in the Middle East*. London: British Academic Press, pp. 177–202.

Hiro, Dilip 1988. *Islamic Fundamentalism*. London: Paladin Books.
  2002. *War Without End*. London: Routledge.

Hobsbawm, Eric 1994. *Age of Extremes: The Short Twentieth Century, 1914–1991*. London: Abacus.

Hobson, John M. 2009. 'The Eurocentric Origins of International Relations' (unpublished book manuscript).

Hoese, Alexander and Oppermann, Kai 2007. 'Transatlantic Conflict and Cooperation: What Role For Public Opinion?', *Journal of Transatlantic Studies* 5(1): 43–61.

Hoffman, David E. 2003. *The Oligarchs: Wealth and Power in the New Russia*. New York: PublicAffairs.

Hoffmann-Lange, Ursula 1998a. 'Elite Transformation and Democratic Consolidation in Germany after 1945 and 1989', in John Higley, Jan Pakulski and Włodzimierz Wesołowski (eds.), *Postcommunist Elites and Democracy in Eastern Europe*. New York: St Martin's Press, pp. 141–62.
  1998b. 'Germany: Twentieth-Century Turning Points', in Mattei Dogan and John Higley (eds.), *Elites, Crises, and Regimes in Comparative Analysis*. Lanham: Rowman & Littlefield, pp. 169–88.

Horn, Gerd-Rainer and Kenney, Padraic 2004. *Transnational Moments of Change: Europe 1945, 1968, 1989*. Lanham: Rowman & Littlefield.

Hough, Dan, Paterson, William E. and Sloan, James (eds.) 2006. *Learning From The West? Policy Transfer and Programmatic Change in the Communist Successor Parties of Eastern and Central Europe*. London: Routledge.

Hough, Jerry 1986. *The Struggle for the Third World: Soviet Debates and American Options*. Washington, DC: Brookings Institution.

Howard, Sir Michael 2002. 'What's in a Name? How to Fight Terrorism', *Foreign Affairs* 81(1): 8–13.

Howe, Irving 1979. *Celebrations and Attacks: Thirty Years of Literary and Cultural Commentary*. London: Andre Deutsch.

Hughes, James and John, Peter 2003. 'Local Elites in Russia's Transition: Generation Effects on Adaptation and Competition', in Anton Steen and Vladimir Gel'man (eds.), *Elites and Democratic Development in Russia*. London: Routledge, pp. 124–47.

Huntington, Samuel P. 1991. *The Third Wave: Democratization in the late Twentieth Century*. Norman: University of Oklahoma Press.

1993. 'The Clash of Civilizations?', *Foreign Affairs* 72(3): 22–49.

1996. *The Clash of Civilizations and the Remaking of World Order*. London: Touchstone.

2004. *Who are We?* New York: Simon & Schuster.

Hutchings, Kim 2008. *Time and World Politics*. Manchester University Press.

Ignatieff, Michael 2003. 'The Burden', *New York Times Magazine*, 5 January.

2005. 'Introduction: American Exceptionalism and Human Rights', in Michael Ignatieff (ed.), *American Exceptionalism and Human Rights*. Princeton University Press, pp. 1–26.

Ikenberry, G. John (ed.) 2002. *America Unrivalled: The Future of the Balance of Power*. Ithaca: Cornell University Press.

Ikenberry, G. John 2001. *After Victory: Institutions, Strategic Restraint and the Rebuilding of Order after Major Wars*. Princeton University Press.

Ikenberry, G. John and Slaughter, Anne-Marie 2006. 'Forging a World of Liberty Under Law: U.S. National Security in the 21st Century', *The Princeton Project on National Security*. Woodrow Wilson School of Public and International Affairs, Princeton University. Available at: www.princeton.edu/~ppns/report/FinalReport.pdf.

International Institute of Strategic Studies 1978. *The Military Balance, 1978–79*. London: International Institute of Strategic Studies.

1988. *The Military Balance, 1988–89*. London: International Institute of Strategic Studies.

1998. *The Military Balance, 1998/99*. Oxford University Press.

2008. *The Military Balance, 2008*. London: Routledge.

International Monetary Fund. 2005. 'Coordinated Compilation Exercises (CCE) for Financial Soundness Indicators (FSIs)'. 31 December. Washington DC: IMF.

2006. 'Household Credit Growth in Emerging Market Countries'. Global Financial Stability Report: Market Developments and Issues. September. Washington DC: IMF.

Iriye, Akira 1997. 'The Second Clash: Huntington, Mahan, and Civilizations', *Harvard International Review* 19(2).

Ismi, Asad 1998. 'Plunder with a Human Face', *Z Magazine*, February. Available at: www.thirdworldtraveler.com/IMF_WB/ PlunderHumanFace.html.

Jackson, Colin n.d. 'From Conservatism to Revolutionary Intoxication: The U.S. Army and the Second Interwar Period', in Harvey Sapolsky *et al.*, 'Military Innovation Under Jointness and Centralization', unpublished draft report for the National Defense University.

Jenkins, Simon 2007. 'They See it Here, They See it There, They See Al-Qaeda Everywhere', *The Sunday Times* (London), 29 April, p. 16.

Jentleson, Bruce and Weber, Steven 2008. 'America's Hard Sell', *Foreign Policy* November–December: 43–9.

Jessop, Bob 2002. *The Future of the Capitalist State*. Cambridge: Polity.
    2007. *State Power*. Cambridge: Polity.

Johnson, Chalmers (ed.) 1970. *Change in Communist Systems*. Palo Alto: Stanford University Press.

Johnson, Chalmers 1982. *MITI and the Japanese Miracle: The Growth of Industrial Policy, 1925–1975*. Palo Alto: Stanford University Press.

Jordan, David Starr 1901. *Imperial Democracy*. New York: D. Appleton & Co.

Jowitt, Ken 1992. *The New World Disorder: The Leninist Extinction*. Berkeley: University of California Press.

Judt, Tony 2005. *Postwar: A History of Europe Since 1945*. New York: Penguin.
    2008. *Reappraisals: Reflections on the Forgotten Twentieth Century*. New York: Penguin.

Juergensmayer, Mark 2003. *Terror in the Mind of God: The Global Rise of Religious Violence*. Berkeley: University of California Press.

Kagan, Robert 2004. *Paradise and Power*. London: Atlantic Books.
    2008. *The Return of History and the End of Dreams*. London: Atlantic Books.

Kaldor, Mary 1986. 'The Weapons Succession Process', *World Politics* 38(4): 577–95.

Kaplan, Robert D. 1994. 'The Coming Anarchy', *Atlantic Monthly*, February. Available at: www.TheAtlantic.com/atlantic/election/connection/foreign/anarcf.htm.
    2005. *Imperial Grunts*. New York: Random House.

Karatnycky, Adrian 2005. 'Ukraine's Orange Revolution', *Foreign Affairs* 84(2): 35–52.

Keane, John 1996. *Reflections on Violence*, London: Verso.

Keck, Margaret E. and Sikkink, Kathryn 1998. *Activists Beyond Borders*. Cambridge University Press.

Kelley, Judith 2006. 'New Wine in Old Wineskins: Policy Adaptation in the European Neighborhood Policy', *Journal of Common Market Studies* 44(1): 29–55.

Kennan, George ('X') 1947. 'The Sources of Soviet Conduct', *Foreign Affairs*, July: 566–82.

Kennedy, Michael 2002. *Cultural Formations of Post-communism*. Minneapolis: University of Minnesota Press.

Kennedy, Paul 1989. *The Rise and Fall of the Great Powers*. New York: Vintage.

Kenney, Padraic 2002. *A Carnival of Revolution: Central Europe 1989*. Princeton University Press.
    2006. *The Burdens of Freedom: Eastern Europe since 1989*. London: Zed Books.

Keohane, Robert and Nye, Joseph 1973. *Power and Interdependence*. Boston: Little, Brown and Co.

Kepel, Gilles 2004. *Jihad: The Trail of Political Islam*. London: Tauris.

Khanna, Parag 2008. *The Second World: Empires and Influence in the New Global Order*. New York: Random House.

Kidd, Benjamin 1898. *The Control of the Tropics*. New York: Macmillan.
Kinzer, Stephen 2006. *Overthrow: America's Century of Regime Change From Hawaii to Iraq*. New York: Times Books, Henry Holt and Company.
Kirby, Peadar 2006. *Vulnerability and Violence: The Impact of Globalisation*. London: Pluto.
Kitschelt, Herbert 2003. 'Accounting for Postcommunist Regime Diversity. What Counts as a Good Cause?', in Grzegorz Ekert and Stephen E. Hanson (eds.), *Capitalism and Democracy in Central and Eastern Europe. Assessing the Legacy of Communist Rule*. New York: Cambridge University Press, pp. 49–83.
Knarr, William *et al.* n.d. 'Learning from the First Victories of the 21st Century: Mazar-e Sharif – A Preview'. Alexandria, VA: Institute for Defense Analysis (unpublished).
Knodt, Michèle and Princen, Sebastian (eds.) 2003. *Understanding the European Union's External Relations*. London: Routledge.
Kokoshin, Andrei 1999. *Soviet Strategic Thought, 1917–91*. Cambridge, MA: MIT Press.
Kopstein, Jeffrey 2006. 'The Transatlantic Divide over Democracy Promotion', *The Washington Quarterly* 29(2): 85–98.
Kornai, János 1992. *The Socialist System: The Political Economy of Communism*. Princeton University Press.
Koslowski, Rey and Kratochwil, Friedrich V. 1994. 'Understanding Change in International Politics: The Soviet Empire's Demise and the International System', *International Organization* 48(2): 215–47.
Kotkin, Stephen 2001. *Armageddon Averted: The Soviet Collapse, 1979–2000*. Oxford University Press.
Krasner, Stephen 2005. 'The Case for Shared Sovereignty', *Journal of Democracy* 16(1): 69–83.
Kratochwil, Friedrich 1993. 'The Embarassment of Changes: Neo-realism as the Science of Realpolitik without Politics', *Review of International Studies* 19: 63–80.
Krauthammer, Charles 1990/1991. 'The Unipolar Moment', *Foreign Affairs* 70(1): 23–33.
  2004. *Democratic Realism: An American Foreign Policy for a Unipolar World*. American Enterprise Institute Short Publications Series.
Krepinevich, Andrew 1992. *The Military-Technical Revolution: A Preliminary Assessment*. Washington, DC: Office of Net Assessment.
Kristol, William and Kagan, Robert 1996. 'Toward a Neo-Reaganite Foreign Policy', *Foreign Affairs* 75(4): 18–32.
Krugman, Paul 2009. 'How Did Economists Get it So Wrong?', *The New York Times Magazine*, 6 September.
Kumar, Krishan 1987. *Utopia and Anti-Utopia in Modern Times*. Oxford: Blackwell.
  2001. *1989: Revolutionary Ideas and Ideals*. Minneapolis and London: University of Minnesota Press.
Kundera, Milan 1980. *The Book of Laughter and Forgetting*. London: Penguin.
Kurczewski, Jacek 1993. *The Resurrection of Rights in Poland*. Oxford University Press.

Kurth, James 1994. 'The Real Clash', *The National Interest*. Available at: http://findarticles.com/p/articles/mi_m2751/is_n37/ai_16315038?tag= artBody;col1.

Kuzio, Taras and D'Anieri, Paul 2002. *Dilemmas of State-Led Nation Building in Ukraine*. New York: Praeger.

Kyle, D. and Koslowski, R. 2001. *Global Human Smuggling*. Baltimore and London: Johns Hopkins University Press.

La Grange, Arnaud de and Balencie, Jean-Marc 2008. *Les guerres bâtardes: comment l'Occident perd les batailles du XXIe siècle*. Paris: Perrin.

la Serre, Françoise de, Lequesne, Christian and Rupnik, Jacques 1994. *L'Union européenne: ouverture à l'Est?* Paris: Presses Universitaires de France.

Lagerspetz, Mikko 1999. 'Postsocialism as a Return: Notes on a Discursive Strategy', *East European Politics and Societies* 13: 377–90.

Lane, David and Ross, Cameron 1999. *The Transition From Communism To Capitalism: Ruling Elites from Gorbachev to Yeltsin*. London: Palgrave Macmillan.

Latour, Bruno 1993. *We Have Never Been Modern*. Cambridge, MA: Harvard University Press.

Lavenex, Sandra 2004. 'EU External Governance in "Wider Europe"', *Journal of European Public Policy* 11(4): 680–700.

Lawson, George 2005. *Negotiated Revolutions: The Czech Republic, South Africa and Chile*. London: Ashgate.

Leffler, Melvyn 2003. '9/11 and the Past and Future of American Foreign Policy', *International Affairs* 79(5): 1045–63.

Lenin, V. I. 1968. *Selected Works*. Moscow: Progress.

Lieven, Anatol 2001. 'Fighting Terrorism: Lessons from the Cold War', *Policy Brief* 7. Washington, DC: Carnegie Endowment for International Peace.

Lieven, Anatol and Hulsman, John C. 2006. 'Neo-Conservatives, Liberal Hawks, and the War on Terror', *World Policy Journal*, Fall: 64–74.

Light, Margot 1989. *The Soviet Theory of International Relations*. Brighton: Harvester.

Lock-Pullan, Richard 2003. '"An Inward Looking Time": The United States Army, 1973–1976', *The Journal of Military History* 67(2): 483–511.

Lockwood, David 1964. 'Social Integration and System Integration', in G. K. Zollschan and H. W. Hirsch (eds.), *Explorations in Social Change*. London: Houghton Mifflin, pp. 245–57.

Lomov, N. A. (ed.) 1973. *Scientific Technical Progress and the Revolution in Military Affairs (A Soviet View)*. Moscow: Military Publishing House.

Łoś, Maria and Zybertowicz, Andrzej 2000. *Privatizing the Police-State: The Case of Poland*. New York: St Martin's Press.

Lucas, Linda (ed.) 2005. *Unpacking Globalisation: Markets, Gender and Work*. Kampala, Uganda: Makerere University Press.

Luhmann, Niklas 1984. *Soziale Systeme. Grundriss einer allgemeinen Theorie*. Frankfurt: Suhrkamp.

Lundestad, Geir (ed.) 2008. *Just another Major Crisis? The United States and Europe Since 2000*. Oxford University Press.

Lynch, Allen 1992. *The Cold War is Over Again*. Boulder: Westview.

Lyotard, Jean-François 1979. *La condition postmoderne: Rapport sur le sav-oir*. Paris: Minuit; trans. Geoff Bennington and Brian Massumi as *The Postmodern Condition: A Report on Knowledge*, Minneapolis: University of Minnesota Press, 1984.

Mackinder, Halford 1904. 'The Geographical Pivot of History', *The Geographical Journal* 23(4): 421–37.

Macmillan, Margaret 2008. *The Uses and Abuses of History*. Toronto: Viking.

Magri, Lucio 2008. 'The Tailor of Ulm', *New Left Review* 51, May–June: 47–62.

Mahan, Alfred Thayer 1890/1897. *The Influence of Seapower upon History*. London: Sampson, Law, Marston.

Mahbubani, Kishore 2004. 'The West and the Rest', in K. Mahbubani, *Can Asians Think?* Singapore: Times Editions, pp. 49–67.

Maier, Charles 1997. *Dissolution: The Crisis of Communism and the End of East Germany*. Princeton University Press.

Mamdani, M. 2004. *Good Muslim, Bad Muslim: America, the Cold War and the Roots of Terror*. New York: Pantheon Books.

Mann, James 2004. *Rise of the Vulcans: The History of Bush's War Cabinet*. New York: Viking.

  2009. *The Rebellion of Ronald Reagan*. New York: Viking.

Mann, Michael 1997. 'Has Globalisation Ended the Rise and Rise of the Nation-State?', *Review of International Political Economy* 4(3): 472–96.

  2005. *The Dark Side of Democracy: Explaining Ethnic Cleansing*. Cambridge University Press.

Manners, Ian 2002. 'Normative Power Europe: A Contradiction in Terms?', *Journal of Common Market Studies* 40(2): 235–58.

Mansfield, Edward D. and Snyder, Jack 2005. *Electing to Fight: Why Emerging Democracies go to War*. Cambridge, MA: MIT Press.

  2009. 'Pathways to War in Democratic Transitions,' *International Organization* 63: 381–90.

Marshall, Andrew 2002. 'Forword', in Andrew Krepinevich, *The Military-Technical Revolution: A Preliminary Assessment*. Washington, DC: Office of Net Assessment.

Martin, Terry 2002. *The Affirmative Action Empire: Nations and Nationalism in the Soviet Union, 1923–1939*. Ithaca: Cornell University Press.

Mastny, Vojtech and Byrne, Malcolm 2006. *A Cardboard Castle? An Inside History of the Warsaw Pact, 1955–1991*. Budapest: Central European University Press.

May, Ernest 1973. *'Lessons' of the Past: The Use and Misuse of History in American Foreign Policy*. New York: Oxford University Press.

Mazower, Mark 1998. *Dark Continent: Europe's Twentieth Century*. London: 1st Vintage Books.

McDermott, Kevin and Stibbe, Matthew (eds.) 2006. *Revolution and Resistance in Eastern Europe: Challenges to Communist Rule*. Oxford and New York: Berg.

McLellan, David 1977. *Karl Marx: Selected Writings*. Oxford University Press.

McRae, Robert 1997. *Resistance and Revolution in Václav Havel's Czechoslovakia*. Ottawa: Carleton University Press.

Mearsheimer, John J. 1990a. 'Why We Will Soon Miss the Cold War', *The Atlantic Monthly* 266: 35–50.
　1990b. 'Back to the Future: Instability in Europe after the Cold War', *International Security* 15(1): 5–56.
Mearsheimer, John 2009. 'From the Fall of the Berlin Wall to the Crisis of Capitalism'. Speech at the General Conference of the European Consortium for Political Research. Potsdam, Germany, 10–12 September.
Merkel, Wolfgang 2008. 'Plausible Theory, Unexpected Results: The Rapid Democratic Consolidation in Central and Eastern Europe', *Internationale Politik und Gesellschaft/International Politics and Society* 2: 11–29.
Merry, Robert W. 2005. *Sands of Empire: Missionary Zeal, American Foreign Policy, and the Hazards of Global Ambition*. New York: Simon & Schuster.
Michels, Robert 1962. *Political Parties: A Sociological Study of the Oligarchical Tendencies of Modern Democracy*, trans. Eden and Cedar Paul. New York: The Free Press.
Michnik, Adam and Kis, János 2008. 'After Five Years', *The New York Review of Books* 55(12), 17 July.
Migrant Remittances 2008. Worldwide Trends in International Remittances, May 5(2), electronic newsletter jointly sponsored by DFID and USAID. Available at: www.the dialogue.org/PublicationFiles/Migrant%20Remittances–May%202008–Final.pdf.
Miles, David and Pillonca, V. C. 2007. 'European Economics: Financial Innovation and European Housing and Mortgage Markets', *Morgan Stanley Research Europe*. 18 July. New York: Morgan Stanley. Available at: www.germany-re.com/files/00034800/MS%20Housing%20Report%20 2007.pdf (last accessed 26 August 2008).
Mill, John Stuart 1836/1977. 'Civilization', in J. M. Robson (ed.), *Collected Works of John Stuart Mill*, xviii. University of Toronto Press, pp. 119–47.
　1859/1984. 'A Few Words on Non-Intervention', in J. M. Robson (ed.), *Collected Works of John Stuart Mill*, xxi. University of Toronto Press, pp. 111–24.
　1859/1998. *On Liberty and Other Essays*. Oxford University Press.
Mishel, L. 2004. 'Unfettered Markets, Income Inequality, and Religious Values', *Viewpoints*, Economic Policy Institute. Available at: www.epi.org/publications/entry/webfeatures_viewpoints_moral_markets_presentation (last accessed 26 July 2008).
　2007. 'Who's Grabbing all the New Pie?', *Economic Snapshots*, 1 August. Washington, DC: Economic Policy Institute. Available at: www.epi.org/content.cfm/webfeatures_snapshots_20070801.
Moore, Barrington 1954. *Terror and Progress USSR: Some Sources of Change and Stability in the Soviet Dictatorship*. Cambridge, MA: Harvard University Press.
Moser, Carolyn 1989. 'The Impact of Recession and Structural Adjustment Policies at the Micro-level: Low Income Women and their Households in Guayaquil, Ecuador', *Invisible Adjustment*, vol. II, 2nd revised edition. Santiago: UNICEF, Americans and Caribbean Office, pp.137–66.
Mouzelis, Nicos 1997. 'Social and System Integration: Lockwood, Habermas, Giddens', *Sociology* 31(1): 111–19.

Müller, Jan-Werner 2009. 'The Cold War and the Intellectual History of the Late Twentieth Century', in Melvyn P. Leffler and Odd Arne Westad (eds.), *The Cambridge History of the Cold War*, vol. III. Cambridge University Press.

Naim, Moises 2006. *Illicit: How Smugglers, Traffickers, and Copycats are Hijacking the Global Economy*. New York: Anchor Books.

Naimark, Norman 1999. 'Ten Years After: Perspectives on 1989', *East European Politics and Societies* 13: 323–9.

Naimark, Norman M. 2002. *Fires of Hatred: Ethnic Cleansing in Twentieth-Century Europe*. Cambridge, MA: Harvard University Press.

NATO Briefing: Afghanistan 2005. Available at: www.nato.int/docu/briefing/afghanistan/afghanistan-e.pdf.

Naughton, Barry 2008. 'A Political Economy of China's Economic Transition', in Loren Brandt and Thomas Rawski (eds.), *China's Great Economic Transformation*. New York: Oxford University Press, pp. 91–135.

New America Foundation 2008. 'As the Economy Screams: Perspectives and Proposals from the Presidential Campaign', 23 January.

Newell, John 1998. *Airpower and the Battle of Khafji: Setting the Record Straight*. Maxwell Air Force Base: School of Advanced Airpower Studies.

Niblock, Tim and Murphy, Emma (eds.) 1993. *Economic and Political Liberalization in the Middle East*. London: British Academic Press.

Nove, Alec 1994. 'Terror Victims – Is the Evidence Complete?', *Europe-Asia Studies* 46(3): 535–7.

Nuland, Victoria 2006. *NATO's Mission in Afghanistan: Putting Theory into Practice*, NATO Review, Winter 2006.

Obama, Barack 2007. 'Renewing American Leadership', *Foreign Affairs* 86(4): 2–16.

Odom, William 1998. *The Collapse of the Soviet Military*. New Haven: Yale University Press.

Offe, Claus 1991. 'Das Dilemma der Gleichzeitigkeit. Demokratisierung und Marktwirtschaft in Osteuropa', *Merkur* 45(4): 279–92.

Okey, Robin 2004. *The Demise of Communist Europe: 1989 in Context*. London: Edward Arnold.

Olds, Krish, Dicken, Peter, Kelly, Philip F., Kong, Lily and Yeung, Henry WaiChung (eds.) 1999. *Globalization and the Asian Pacific: Contested Territories*. London: Routledge.

Onikov, Leon A. 1996. *KPSS: Anatomia raspada. Vzgliad iznutri apparata TsK*. Moscow: Respublika.

Orozco, Manuel, Lowell, B. Lindsay, Bump, Micah, and Fedewa, Rachel 2005. *Transnational Engagement, Remittances and their Relationship to Development in Latin America and the Caribbean: Final Report*, submitted to the Rockefeller Foundation for Grant 2003 GI 050. Washington, DC: Institute for the Study of International Migration, Georgetown University.

Ottaway, David and Ottaway, Marina 1981. *Afrocommunism*. New York: Africana Publishing House.

Outhwaite, William 2008. *European Society*. Cambridge: Polity.

2009. 'How Much Capitalism Can Democracy Stand (and vice versa)?', *Radical Politics Today*, May. Available at: www.spaceofdemocracy.org/resources/publications/magazine.

Outhwaite, William and Ray, Larry 2005. *Social Theory and Postcommunism*. Oxford: Blackwell.

Owen, John 1994. 'How Liberalism Produces Democratic Peace', *International Security* 19(2): 87–125.

Owen, Robert 2000. *Deliberate Force: A Case Study in Effective Air Campaigning*. Maxwell Air Force Base, AL: Air University Press.

Owens, William 2000. *Lifting the Fog of War*. New York: Macmillan, Farrar, Straus, Giroux.

Oxfam 1999. *International Submission to the HIPC Debt Review* (April). Available at: www.caa.org/au/Oxfam/advocacy/debt/hipcreview.html.

Packer, George 2003. 'Dreaming Democracy', *The New York Times Magazine*, 2 March.

Panah, Maryam 2007. *The Islamic Republic and the World: Global Dimensions of the Iranian Revolution*. London: Pluto Press.

Pearson, Karl 1905. *National Life from the Standpoint of Science*. London: Adam & Charles Black.

Pipes, Daniel 1990. 'The Muslims are Coming! The Muslims are Coming!', *National Review* (November). Original version posted at: www.daniel-pipes.org/article.php/198.

Pipes, Richard 1995. 'Misinterpreting the Cold War', *Foreign Affairs* 74(1): 154–61.

Pitts, Jennifer 2005. *A Turn to Empire*. Princeton University Press.

Posen, Barry 1982. 'Inadvertent Nuclear War? Escalation and NATO's Northern Flank', *International Security* 7(2): 28–54.

2000. 'The War for Kosovo: Serbia's Political-Military Strategy', *International Security* 24(4): 39–84.

Project for the New American Century 2000. *Rebuilding America's Defense: Strategy, Forces and Resources for a New Century*. Washington, DC: Project for the New American Century.

Przeworski, Adam 1991. *Democracy and the Market: Political and Economic Reforms in Eastern Europe and Latin America*. Cambridge University Press.

Putnam, Robert 1993. *Making Democracy Work: Civic Traditions in Modern Italy*. Princeton University Press.

2000. *Bowling Alone: The Collapse and Revival of American Community*. New York: Simon & Schuster.

Pyle, Jean L. and Ward, Kathryn 2003. 'Recasting our Understanding of Gender and Work During Global Restructuring', *International Sociology* 18(3): 461–89.

Rahman, Aminur 1999. 'Micro-credit Initiatives for Equitable and Sustainable Development: Who Pays?', *World Development* 27(1): 67–82.

Record, Jeremy 2007. 'The Use and Abuse of History: Munich, Vietnam and Iraq', *Survival* 49(1): 163–80.

Reinhardt, C. M. and Kaminsky, G. 1999. 'The Twin Crisis: The Causes of Banking and Balance of Payments Problems', *American Economic Review* 89(3): 473–500.

Retort (Boal, I., Clark, T. J., Matthews, Joseph and Watts, Michael) 2005. *Afflicted Powers: Capital and Spectacle in a New Age of War.* London: Verso.

Riabchuk, Mykola 2008. 'Pluralism by Default: Ukraine and the Law of Communicating Vessels', *Eurozine,* 17 September.

Rieff, David 1999. 'A New Age of Liberal Imperialism?', *World Policy Journal* 16(2): 1–10.

Rigby, Thomas H. 1990. *The Changing Soviet System: Mono-Organisational Socialism from its Origins to Gorbachev's Restructuring.* Aldershot: Edward Elgar.

Risse, Thomas, Ropp, Steven C. and Sikkink, Kathryn (eds.) 1999. *The Power of Human Rights.* Cambridge University Press.

Risse-Kappen, Thomas 1994. 'Ideas do not Float Freely', *International Organization* 48(2): 185–214.

   1995. *Cooperation among Democracies: The European Influence on U.S. Foreign Policy.* Princeton University Press.

Robin, Corey 2004. 'Endgame: Conservatives After the Cold War', *Boston Review,* February/March. Available at: www.bostonreview.net/BR29.1/robin.html.

Robinson, Scott S. 2004. 'Towards a Neoapartheid System of Governance with IT Tools', SSRC IT and Governance Study Group, New York: SSRC. Available at: www.ssrc.org/programs/itic/publications/knowledge_report/memos/robinsonmemo4.pdf.

Rose, Richard 2006. 'Diverging Paths of Post-communist Countries: New Europe Barometer Trends Since 1991', *Studies in Public Policy* 418. Aberdeen: Centre for the Study of Public Policy.

Rosenberg, Justin 2005. 'Globalization Theory: A Post-Mortem', *International Politics* 42(1): 2–74.

   2006. 'Why is There No International Historical Sociology?', *European Journal of International Relations* 12(3): 307–40.

Rosenberg, Tina 1996. *The Haunted Land: Facing Europe's Ghosts After Communism.* New York: Vintage.

Roxborough, Ian 2002. 'From Revolution to Transformation: The State of the Field – Military Transformation', *Joint Forces Quarterly,* Autumn. Available at: findarticles.com/p/articles/mi_m0KNN/is_32/ai_105853018/print?tag=artBody;col1.

Roy, Olivier 2004. *Globalized Islam: The Search for a New Ummah.* New York: Columbia University Press.

Rupnik, Jacques 1989. *The Other Europe: The Rise and Fall of Communism in East Central Europe.* London: Pantheon.

Russett, Bruce 1990. *Controlling the Sword.* Cambridge, MA: Harvard University Press.

Rustow, Dankwort 1990. 'Democracy: A Global Revolution?', *Foreign Affairs* 69: 75–91.

Ryazanova-Clarke, Lara. 2008. 'Identity and Masculinity at the Extremities of the Russian Mainstream'. Paper given at the AAASS National Convention, Philadelphia.

Sachs, Jeffrey 1994. *Poland's Jump to the Market Economy.* Cambridge, MA: MIT Press.

Safa, Helen 1995. *The Myth of the Male Breadwinner: Women and Industrialization in the Caribbean.* Boulder: Westview Press.

Said, Edward W. 1978. *Orientalism*. London: Penguin.

Sakwa, Richard 1999. *Post-Communism*. Buckingham: Open University.

2008. '"New Cold War" or Twenty Years' Crisis? Russia and International Politics', *International Affairs* 84(2): 241–67.

Salmanov, G. I. 1995. 'Soviet Military Doctrine and Some Views on the Nature of War in Defense of Socialism', in David Glantz, *The Evolution of Soviet Operational Art, 1927–1991: Volume II, Operational Art, 1965–1991*. London: Frank Cass.

Salter, Mark B. 2002. *Barbarians and Civilization*. London: Pluto.

Sapir, Jacques 1990. *L'economie mobilisée. Essai sur les économies de type soviétique*. Paris: La Decouverte.

Sassen, Saskia 2001. *The Global City: New York, London, Tokyo*, 2nd edition. Princeton University Press.

2006b. *Cities in a World Economy*, 3rd edition. Thousand Oaks, CA: Pine Forge Press.

2007. *A Sociology of Globalization*. New York: Norton.

2008. *Territory, Authority, Rights: From Medieval to Global Assemblages*. 2nd edition. Princeton University Press.

Saull, Richard 2001. *Rethinking Theory and History in the Cold War*. London: Frank Cass.

2007. *The Cold War and After*. London: Pluto Press.

Schecter, Darrow 2007. *The History of the Left from Marx to the Present. Theoretical Perspectives*. New York and London: Continuum.

Schrecker, Ellen (ed.) 2004. *Cold War Triumphalism*. New York and London: The New Press.

Schumpeter, Joseph 1942. *Capitalism, Socialism and Democracy*. London: Allen Lane.

Schweizer, Peter 1994. *Victory*. New York: Atlantic Monthly.

2002. *Reagan's War: The Epic Story of His Forty-year Struggle and Final Triumph over Communism*. New York: Doubleday.

Seligman, Adam 1992. *The Idea of Civil Society*. New York: Maxwell Macmillan.

Shapiro, Ian 2007. *Containment: Rebuilding a Strategy Against Global Terror*. Princeton University Press.

Sharansky, Natan and Denmer, Ron 2005. *The Case for Democracy: The Power of Freedom to Overcome Tyranny and Terror*. Green Forest: Balfour Books.

Shepherd, Alastair, Berenskoetter, Felix and Giegerich, Bastian 2006. 'Europe and the War on Terror', *International Politics* 43(1): 71–109.

Shevtsova, Lilia 2002. 'Russia's Hybrid Regime', in Larry Diamond and Marc F. Plattner (eds.), *Democracy After Communism*. Baltimore: Johns Hopkins University Press, pp. 240–5.

2007. *Russia – Lost in Transition: The Yeltsin and Putin Legacies*, trans. Arch Tait. Washington, DC: Carnegie Endowment for World Peace.

Simon, Gerhard 1986. *Nationalismus und Nationalitätenpolitik in der Sowjetunion. Von der totalitären Diktatur zur nachstalinistischen Gesellschaft*. Baden-Baden: Nomos.

SIPRI Yearbook 1979: World Armaments and Disarmament. Oxford University Press.

SIPRI Yearbook 1987: World Armaments and Disarmament. Oxford University Press.

Sivan, E. 1985. *Radical Islam: Medieval Theology and Modern Politics.* New Haven: Yale University Press.

Sjursen, Helen 2006. 'The EU as a "Normative" Power: How Can This Be?', *Journal of European Public Policy* 13(2): 235–51.

Slaughter, Anne-Marie and Feinstein, Lee 2004. 'The Duty to Prevent', *Foreign Affairs* 83(1): 136–50.

'Slides for "USDP [Under Secretary of Defense for Policy] Brief to DPRB [Defense Planning Resources Board]" on June 5, 1991' at *The National Security Archive*. Available at: www.gwu.edu/~nsarchiv/nukevault/ebb245/doc01.pdf.

Smith, Anthony D. 1998. *Nationalism and Modernism.* London: Routledge.

Smith, Karen 2003. *European Union Foreign Policy in a Changing World.* London: Polity.

  2005. 'Still "Civilian Power EU"?' *European Foreign Policy Unit Working Paper* 2005/1.

Smith, Michael 1981. *Antiair Warfare Defense of Ships at Sea.* Alexandria, VA: Center for Naval Analysis, September.

Smith, Tony and Diamond, Larry 2004. 'Was Iraq a Fool's Errand? What Really Went Wrong', *Foreign Affairs* 83(6): 130–3.

Sobjerg, Lene Mosegaard 2007. 'Trusteeship and the Concept of Freedom', *Review of International Studies* 33(3): 457–88.

Solana, Javier 2003. 'A Secure Europe in a Better World', European Strategy of Security, Brussels. 12 December.

Solnik, Steven L. 1996. 'The Breakdown of Hierarchies in the Soviet Union and China: A Noninstitutional Perspective', *World Politics* 48: 209–38.

Spencer, Herbert 1902. *Facts and Comments.* New York: D. Appleton & Co.

Spengler, Oswald 1926. *The Decline of the West.* Oxford University Press.

Stan, Lavinia (ed.) 2009. *Transitional Justice in Eastern Europe and the Former Soviet Union: Reckoning with the Communist Past.* London: Routledge.

Standing, Guy 1999. 'Global Feminization through Flexible Labor: A Theme Revisited', *World Development* 27(3): 583–602.

Staniszkis, Jadwiga 1984. *Poland's Self-Limiting Revolution.* Princeton University Press.

Stark, David and Bruszt, Laszlo 1998. *Postsocialist Pathways: Transforming Politics and Property in East Central Europe.* Cambridge University Press.

Stenning, Alison and Hörschelman, Kathrin 2008. 'History, Geography and Difference in the Post-Socialist World: Or, Do We Still Need Post-Socialism?', *Antipode* 40(2): 312–35.

Stern, Jessica 2003. *Terror in the Name of God: Why Religious Militants Kill.* New York: HarperCollins.

Stevenson, James 1993. *The Pentagon Paradox: The Development of the F-18 Hornet.* Annapolis: Naval Institute.

Stocking, George W. 1982. *Race, Culture and Evolution.* University of Chicago Press.

Stoddard, Lothrop 1920. *The Rising Tide of Color Against White World Supremacy.* New York: Charles Scribner's Sons.

Strange, Susan 1986. *Casino Capitalism*. Manchester University Press.

Strayer, Robert 1998. *Why Did the Soviet Union Collapse? Understanding Historical Change*. Armonk, New York and London: M. E. Sharpe.

Sumner, William Graham 1911. *War and Other Essays*. New Haven: Yale University Press.

Sun, Yan 2004. *Corruption and Market in Contemporary China*. Ithaca: Cornell University Press.

Suny, Ronald G. 1997. *The Soviet Experiment: Russia, The USSR, and the Successor States*. Oxford University Press.

Suskind, Ron 2007. *The One Percent Doctrine: Deep Inside America's Pursuit of Its Enemies Since 9/11*. London: Pocket.

Sztompka, Piotr 1991. *Society in Action: The Theory of Social Becoming*. University of Chicago Press.

   1993. 'Civilizational Incompetence: The Trap of Post-Communist Societies', *Zeitschrift für Soziologie* 22: 85–95.

Talbot, David 2004. 'How Technology Failed in Iraq', *Technology Review*. MIT, November.

Taleb, Nicholas 2007. *The Black Swan*. London: Allen Lane.

Talhami, G. H. 2003. 'Muslims, Islamists, and the Cold War', *Small Wars and Insurgencies* 14(1): 107–26.

Tanji, Miyume and Lawson, Stephanie 1997. '"Democratic Peace" and "Asian Democracy": A Universalist-Particularist Tension', *Alternatives* 22(1): 135–55.

Teitelbaum, Michael S. and Winter, Jay M. 1985. *The Fear of Population Decline*. London: Academic Press.

Ther, Philipp and Siljak, Ana (eds.) 2001. *Redrawing Nations: Ethnic Cleansing In East-Central Europe, 1944–1948*. Lanham: Rowman & Littlefield.

Tilly, Charles 2005. *Trust and Rule*. Cambridge University Press.

Tinker, Irene (ed.) 1990. *Persistent Inequalities: Women and World Development*. New York: Oxford University Press.

Tismaneanu, Vladimir (ed.) 1999. *The Revolutions of 1989*. London: Routledge.

Toffler, Alvin and Toffler, Heidi 1995. *War and Anti-War: Making Sense of Today's Global Chaos*. New York: Grand Central Publishing.

Tőkés, Rudolf 1996. *Hungary's Negotiated Revolution: Economic Reform, Social Change, and Political Succession*. Cambridge University Press.

   1997. 'Party Politics and Participation in Postcommunist Hungary', in Karen Dawisha and Bruce Parrott (eds.), *The Consolidation of Democracy in East-Central Europe*. Cambridge University Press, pp. 109–49.

Toussaint, Eric 1999. 'Poor Countries Pay More Under Debt Reconstruction Scheme?', July. Available at: www.twnside.org.sg/souths/twn/title/1921-cn.htm.

Transatlantic Trends Survey 2006 Principal Investigators: Pierangelo Isernia, Craig Kennedy, German Marshall Fund of the United States, Philip Everts and Richard Eichenberg.

Trotsky, Leon 1984. *Europe and America: Two Speeches on Imperialism*. New York: Pathfinder Press.

Tucker, Judith 1978. 'While Sadat Shuffles: Economic Decay and Political Ferment in Egypt', *MERIP Reports* 65: 3–9.

UNDP (United Nations Development Programme) 2005. 'A Time For Bold Ambition: Together We Can Cut Poverty in Half', UNDP Annual Report 2005.

(United Nations Development Programme) 2008. 'Human Development Report 2007–2008', UNDP Annual Report. New York: UNDP.

Vachudová, Milada Anna 2005. *Europe Undivided. Democracy, Leverage, and Integration After Communism.* Oxford University Press.

Van der Pijl, Kees 1984. *The Making of an Atlantic Ruling Class.* London: Verso.

Verdery, Katherine 1999. 'What was Socialism, and Why Did it Fail', in Vladimir Tismaneanu (ed.), *The Revolutions of 1989.* London: Routledge, pp. 63–86.

Villaume, Poul and Westad, Odd Arne (eds.) 2009. *Perforating the Iron Curtain. European Détente, Transatlantic Relations, and the Cold War, 1965–1985.* Copenhagen: Tusculanum.

Vobruba, Georg 2005. *Die Dynamik Europas.* Wiesbaden: VS Verlag für die Sozialwissenschaften.

Vujačić, Veljko 1996. 'Historical Legacies, Nationalist Motivation, and Political Outcomes in Russia and Serbia: A Weberian View', *Theory and Society* 25(6): 763–801.

Wade, Robert 2003. *Governing the Market: Economic Theory and the Role of Government in East Asian Industrialization.* Princeton University Press.

Wallace, Helen, Wallace, William and Pollack, Mark 2005. *Policy-Making in the European Union.* Oxford University Press.

Waller, Michael 1994. 'Winners and Losers in the Early Post-Communist Elections in East-Central Europe', in Michael Waller, Bruno Coppieters and Kris Deschouwer (eds.), *Social Democracy in a Post-Communist Europe.* Ilford: Frank Cass, pp. 84–102.

Walt, Stephen 1987. *The Origins of Alliances.* Ithaca: Cornell University Press.

Waltz, Kenneth N. 1993. 'The Emerging Structure of International Politics', *International Security* 18(2): 44–79.

Ward, Kathryn 1991. *Women Workers and Global Restructuring,* Ithaca: Cornell University Press.

Ward, Kathryn and Pyle, J. 1995. 'Gender, Industrialization and Development', in Chris E. Bose and Edna Acosta-Belen (eds.), *Women in the Latin American Development Process: From Structural Subordination to Empowerment.* Philadelphia: Temple University Press, pp. 37–64.

Ward, Lester F. 1903/2002. *Pure Sociology.* Honolulu: University Press of the Pacific.

Warnock, Veronica Cacdac and Warnock, Francis E. 2008. 'Markets and Housing Finance'. Available at: http://ssrn.com/abstract=981641 (last accessed 24 August 2008).

Wasilewski, Jacek 1998. 'Hungary, Poland, and Russia: The Fate of *Nomenklatura* Elites', in Mattei Dogan and John Higley (eds.), *Elites, Crises, and Regimes in Comparative Analysis.* Lanham: Rowman & Littlefield, pp. 147–67.

Wedel, Janine 1998. *Collision and Collusion. The Strange Case of Western Aid to Eastern Europe 1989–1998.* New York: St. Martin's Press.

Weigley, Russell 1993. 'The American Military and the Principle of Civilian Control from McClellan to Powell', *The Journal of Military History* 57(5): 27–58.

Weinberger, Caspar W. 1990 *Fighting for Peace: Seven Critical Years Inside the Pentagon.* New York: Warner.

Weiner, Sanford n.d. 'Evolution in the Post-Cold War Air Force: Technology, Doctrine and Bureaucratic Politics', in Harvey Sapolsky, 'Military Innovation Under Jointness and Centralization', unpublished draft report for the National Defense University.

Weiss, Linda 1998. *The Myth of the Powerless State.* Ithaca: Cornell University Press.

Westad, Odd Arne (ed.) 2000. *Reviewing the Cold War: Approaches, Interpretations, Theory.* London: Frank Cass.

Westad, Odd Arne 2005. *The Global Cold War.* Cambridge University Press.

2010. 'The Great Transformation: China in the Long 1970s', in Niall Ferguson, Charles Maier, Erez Manela and Daniel Sargent (eds.), *The Shock of the Global: The International History of the 1970s.* Cambridge, MA: Harvard University Press.

Wheeler, Nicholas J. 2000. *Saving Strangers.* Oxford University Press.

White, Gordon, Murray, Robin and White, Christine (eds.) 1983. *Revolutionary Socialist Development in the Third World.* Brighton: Wheatsheaf.

White, Stephen and Kryshtanovskaya, Olga 1998. 'Russia: Elite Continuity and Change', in Mattei Dogan and John Higley (eds.), *Elites, Crises, and Regimes in Comparative Analysis.* Lanham: Rowman & Littlefield, pp. 125–46.

White, Stephen, Batt, Judy and Lewis, Paul G. 2003. *Developments in Central and Eastern European Politics.* Basingstoke: Palgrave Macmillan.

Wilkinson, Paul 2005. *International Terrorism: The Changing Threat and the EU's Response.* Chaillot Paper 84, Paris: European Union Institute for Security Studies.

Winter, Jay 2006. *Dreams of Peace and Freedom: Utopian Moments in the Twentieth Century.* New Haven: Yale University Press.

Wohlforth, William 1994. 'Realism and the End of the Cold War', *International Security* 19(3): 91–129.

1999. 'The Stability of a Unipolar World', *International Security* 24(1): 5–41.

Wolf, Martin 2005. *Why Globalization Works.* London: Yale Nota Bene.

Wolle, Stefan 1998. *Die heile Welt der Diktatur. Alltag und Herrschaft in der DDR 1971–1989.* Berlin: Ch. Links Verlag.

Woodward, Bob 2002. *Bush at War.* New York: Simon & Schuster.

2004. *Plan of Attack.* New York: Simon & Schuster.

2006. *State of Denial.* New York: Simon & Schuster.

2008. *The War Within: A Secret White House History.* New York: Simon & Schuster.

Woodward, Susan 1999. 'Bosnia and Herzegovina: How Not to End Civil Wars', in Barbara F. Walter and Jack Snyder (eds.), *Civil Wars, Insecurity, and Intervention*. New York: Columbia University Press.

World Bank 2005a. 'Global Economic Prospects 2005: Trade, Regionalism and Development'. Washington, DC: The World Bank.

2005b. 'Increasing Aid and Its Effectiveness', in *Global Monitoring Report: Millennium Development Goals: from Consensus to Momentum*. Washington, DC: The World Bank, pp. 151–87. Available at: http://siter-esources.worldbank.org/INTGLOBALMONITORING/Resources/ch5_GMR2005.pdf.

2006. *Global Economic Prospects: Economic Implications of Remittances and Migration*. Washington, DC: The World Bank.

2008. *Migration and Remittances Fact Book 2008*, March. Washington D.C.: World Bank.

Wright, Lawrence 2006. *The Looming Tower: Al-Qaeda and the Road to 9/11*. New York: Knopf.

Wright, Richard 1950. 'Part I: The Initiates', in Arthur Koestler (ed.), *The God That Failed. Six Studies in Communism*. London: Hamish Hamilton, pp. 121–66.

Wydra, Harald 2007. *Communism and the Emergence of Democracy*. Cambridge University Press.

Young, Robert J. C. 1995. *Colonial Desire*. London: Routledge.

Zahab, Mariam Abou and Roy, Olivier 2004. *Islamic Networks: The Pakistan-Afghan Network*. London: Charles Hurst & Co.

Zakaria, Fareed 2008. *The Post-American World*. New York: Norton.

Zaloga, Steven 2006. *Scud Ballistic Missile and Launch Systems, 1955–2005*. London: Osprey.

Zamosc, Leon 1986. *The Agrarian Question and the Peasant Movement in Colombia: Struggles of the National Peasant Association, 1967–1981*. Cambridge University Press.

Zielonka, Jan 2006. *Europe as Empire: The Nature of the Enlarged European Union*. Oxford University Press.

Index